KERUX COMMENTARIES

EPHESIANS

KERUX COMMENTARIES

EPHESIANS

A Commentary for Biblical Preaching and Teaching

GREGORY S. MAGEE
JEFFREY D. ARTHURS

Herbert W. Bateman IV
EDITOR

KREGEL
MINISTRY

Ephesians: A Commentary for Biblical Preaching and Teaching

Published by Kregel Ministry, an imprint of Kregel Publications, 2450 Oak Industrial Dr. NE, Grand Rapids, MI 49505-6020.

Unless otherwise indicated, the translation of the Scripture portions used throughout the commentary is the authors' own English rendering of the original biblical languages.

Italics in Scripture quotations indicate emphasis added by the authors.

The Hebrew font, NewJerusalemU, and the Greek font, GraecaU, are available from www.linguistsoftware.com/lgku.htm, +1-425-775-1130.

All photos are under Creative Commons licensing, and contributors are indicated in the captions of the photos.

Map on page 38 was designed by Shawn Vander Lugt, Managing Editor for Academic and Ministry Books at Kregel Publications.

ISBN 978-0-8254-5834-7

Printed in the United States of America
21 22 23 24 25 / 5 4 3 2 1

Contents

EDITOR'S PREFACE TO THE SERIES

The Kerux Commentaries series, unlike other commentaries written for preachers, joins experts in biblical exegesis with experienced communicators of biblical truth. Together they bring a heightened refinement in the handling of the Bible. Every volume emphasizes text-based truths that bridge from the context of the original hearers and readers to the twenty-first-century world. The name *kerux* (KAY-rukes) captures the aim of the series. Just as a *kerux* was one who proclaimed the official announcement of the king, so the forty-five volumes in this series will enable the preacher or teacher to accurately and authoritatively communicate the message of our divine King.

Every volume presents preaching units that offer *exegetical, theological,* and *homiletical* material to guide preachers and teachers to accurately interpret the Bible and ultimately engage today's world.

EXEGETICAL ANALYSIS	➡	**THEOLOGICAL FOCUS**	➡	**PREACHING/ TEACHING STRATEGY**

Solid *exegetical analysis* of the biblical text reveals the literary-theological movement of every biblical passage. The exegetical authors (trained experts in interpretation) engage the biblical text by interacting with original languages that shed light on interpretation (e.g., syntax, grammar, structure), hermeneutical issues relevant to a given passage (e.g., genre analysis), and pertinent secondary literature. From the exegetical analysis is derived a theological focus. The gnomic truths of a passage—those truths that transcend time and culture—emphasize the *theological focus* of each preaching unit. Following the careful exegetical analysis and insightful theological synthesis, homiletical authors (trained experts in preaching) offer suggestions for communicating the text. Based on the popular "big idea" preaching model, every preaching unit offers *preaching strategies,* contemporary connections, suggestions for creative presentation, illustrations, and more. These tools help the preacher and teacher effectively proclaim Scripture.

Kerux commentaries are written for trained pastors and teachers who speak regularly, who have some knowledge of Greek and Hebrew, and who spend a significant time preparing to preach and teach God's Word. As a result, each volume offers:

- a detailed introduction and outline.
- a summary of all preaching sections with their primary exegetical, theological, and preaching ideas.
- preaching pointers that join the original historical context with the contemporary one.
- insights from the Hebrew and Greek text.
- a thorough exposition of the text.
- sidebars of pertinent information and historical background.
- appropriate charts and photographs.
- a theological focus to passages.

- a contemporary big idea for every preaching unit.
- present-day meaning, validity, and application of a main idea.
- creative presentations for each primary idea.
- key questions about the text for study groups.
- lists of books and articles for further reading.

Many thanks to Jim Weaver, Kregel's former acquisition editor, who conceived of this commentary series and further developed it with the team of Jeffrey D. Arthurs, Robert B. Chisholm, David M. Howard Jr., Darrell L. Bock, Roy E. Ciampa, and Michael J. Wilkins. Much appreciation is extended to Dennis and Paul Hillman, whose thirteen-year tenacious commitment to the series contributed to Kerux becoming a reality. Finally, gratitude is extended to the two authors for each Kerux volume; the outside reviewers, editors, and proofreaders; and Kregel staff who suggested numerous improvements.

—Herbert W. Bateman IV

PREFACE TO EPHESIANS

As we have worked on this book together we have grown to appreciate how the different sections contribute to understanding and preaching the text. The exegetical idea, theological focus, and preaching/teaching idea at the beginning of each chapter were composed after much study and discussion and are there to direct readers through the content that follows. The preaching pointers were especially fun to write. The first paragraph brings modern readers into the original readers' world, and the second paragraph helps us see how much modern readers' needs are still the same. The expositional work in each chapter aims to help current readers appreciate the meaning of Ephesians in that original setting. The explanation of each verse deals carefully with language, rhetoric, theology, and background issues whenever those elements are relevant for understanding Paul's discourse. While we did not always have space to "show our work" on every exegetical decision, we have tried to show enough to help readers understand the major choices that have been made and how those decisions contribute to our interpretation of Paul's message in the passage. Sidebars and translation analysis sections shed additional light on the meaning and significance of Paul's teachings.

The theological focus and exegetical/theological synthesis sections function as important bridges from interpretation to application. Ephesians is a richly theological book that reflects many themes that were central in Paul's ministry to the churches he served. The preaching and teaching material is designed to offer guidance and strategies for how to think about teaching the passage, identify features and content to focus upon in the passage, and share various creative options for communicating truths in effective, creative, and memorable ways. Ephesians really is a treasure for God's people, and we hope that its profound, inspiring, and practical message takes center stage in this commentary. As commentators we have certainly had great material to work with.

EXEGETICAL AUTHOR'S ACKNOWLEDGMENTS

To Emily,
for her love and support

It has been quite the gift to contribute to a commentary in Ephesians after enjoying reading it and reflecting on it for so many years. I'm grateful to my college Bible study leader Rick Hove for encouraging our group to study and memorize Ephesians. After college, in a different part of the world, I had opportunities to delve into the letter with a team of missionaries and then study it with local believers in our city. In more recent years I spent four summers leading college students through Ephesians in Greek and helped teach it to high school students at our home church. With each group of people and in each season of life, God has used Ephesians to stir in my heart a deep wonder at the love, generosity, and power he blesses us with in Christ.

For this latest chance to engage with Ephesians, I have really enjoyed collaborating with Jeffrey Arthurs. From our first meeting in 2015 and through many phone calls and email exchanges since then, Jeffrey has been an encouraging, flexible, and insightful coauthor. Jeffrey's heart for God's truth and for ministering to God's people shines through in each chapter. I am also grateful for Herb Bateman's work as our editor. He has kept the vision for the Kerux series front and center and has offered feedback that has improved the writing and organization of the book. Other members of the Kregel team have made significant contributions along the way to help prepare this book for publication. This has truly been a team effort. Many thanks to Taylor University as well, for granting me a sabbatical that freed up precious time to make progress on this project. Finally, my wife Emily, my children, and the rest of my family have given encouragement and practical help in many ways. I could not do this without their love and support.

—Gregory S. MaGee

PREACHING AUTHOR'S ACKNOWLEDGMENTS

For Pastor Robert Nitz,
my first pastor,
the first man to preach the gospel to me,
a true herald of the Word

No man is an island, and no book is either. Dozens of colleagues, pastors, mentors, and teachers have stood beside me as I wrote my portion of this book. Aware that I am leaving out nearly all of them, and feeling uncomfortable doing so, I would nevertheless like to acknowledge two colleagues who have been a joy to work with. The first is my writing partner, Greg MaGee. We met through this project, and I have grown as an exegete and thinker because of him. Thank you, Greg. Let's do it again sometime (but maybe with something shorter like a conference paper!). The second is Jim Weaver, who conceived of the massive undertaking called Kerux and oversaw it for years. Jim recruited me to the vision of creating a commentary specifically designed for preaching, a vision I believe in heart and soul. Jim's vision has become reality and will, I pray, bless the church for decades.

—Jeffrey D. Arthurs

OVERVIEW OF ALL PREACHING PASSAGES

Ephesians 1:1–14

EXEGETICAL IDEA
Paul gave accolades to God for having blessed Jews and Gentiles thoroughly in Christ by choosing and adopting them, redeeming them, and giving them his Spirit, as he prepared to restore all things in Christ.

THEOLOGICAL FOCUS
God deserves our applause for his works in Christ and by the Spirit to bless believers and restore the world.

PREACHING IDEA
Let's applaud God for including us in his story.

PREACHING POINTERS
Paul and his readers lived in a diverse and complex world in which various stories—whether supplied by the Roman imperial cult, Greco-Roman gods and goddesses, Greek mythology, or Jewish tradition—vied to become sources of meaning for people's lives. Different rulers or patrons (those with wealth and clout who could help their less influential clients), gods and goddesses (such as Artemis of the Ephesians; Acts 19:23–41), and mythic heroes (such as Castor and Pollux, the twin sons of Zeus; cf. Acts 28:11) competed for people's loyalty in the Gentile world. Jewish people could look to past paragons of faith in the OT or to figures such the courageous Maccabean martyrs (2 Macc) to find deeper meaning in life. The house churches across Asia Minor lived in a Greco-Roman society where people of different cultural and religious backgrounds shared no common story and honored no single benefactor. Paul wanted his readers to know that, whether Jew or Gentile, they possessed a common heritage and fit as diverse individuals into a common "story" as beneficiaries of God's blessings in Christ. As a result, they could with one voice pay tribute to the God who had graciously extended these blessings to them in Christ Jesus.

Similar dynamics exist in many churches today. We live in a pluralistic society. Naturally, congregations are composed of men and women; young and old; Democrat, Republican, and Independent; and so forth, that mirror our pluralistic society. One person's hero is a theologian while another person's is a social activist. One may watch conservative news and another favors a moderate or broad-minded news program. There may be young people who favor gun control, and others who may not. Is there one story that unites them? Yes, the story of God's plan to save his people. Is there one hero we all acknowledge? Yes, our triune God, so let's applaud him for including us in his story.

Ephesians 1:15–23

EXEGETICAL IDEA

Paul prayed that God would help readers know him and appreciate their God-given hope and inheritance, as well as the power that had already been demonstrated in Christ's resurrection and position of all-encompassing authority.

THEOLOGICAL FOCUS

Believers can know God by appreciating the God-given hope, inheritance, and power that overflows to them in Christ.

PREACHING IDEA

God, please help us to know intimately our hope, inheritance, and power.

PREACHING POINTERS

Paul's first-century readers lived in a world marked by awareness of a vast array of spiritual powers. Both Jews and Gentiles witnessed instances of demon possession and sorcery (Mark 1:23–28; 5:1–20; 7:24–30; 9:17–29; Acts 13:6–11; 16:16–18). In Jewish literature, 1 Enoch frequently mentioned angels, identified them by name, and described their activity and responsibilities, and the Qumran War Scroll anticipated good and bad angels fighting on behalf of the "sons of light" and the "sons of darkness." For Gentiles, religious worship encompassed devotion to local deities in addition to the pantheon of Greek and Roman gods and goddesses. Both Jews and Gentiles in Asia Minor dabbled in a variety of religious rites and ceremonies that promised to give practitioners a greater sense of control over life but instead often kept them in bondage to the unpredictability of unseen forces. Paul's readers had broken free of this spiritual slavery (Acts 19:11–20) when they encountered Christ's unparalleled authority and hope. God's Spirit now worked in them to produce spiritual growth and provide spiritual power, in line with the resurrection power and eternal authority experienced by Christ Jesus himself.

Our day parallels Paul's day in that many people are captivated by the world of spiritual powers. This is seen in missionaries' stories of demon possession and in pop culture. William Friedkin's movie *The Exorcist* (1973) was the first of many movies on demon possession. Similarly, Frank E. Peretti's fictional work *This Present Darkness* (1986) launched his long-running series of books on spiritual warfare. People today are fascinated by the unseen world, and Paul's prayer draws on that desire when he depicts God's mighty power that raised Christ from the dead and the hope this brings us for a future inheritance. Our hope is grounded in Christ. His resurrection is ours and we want to experience the power and confidence that this brings; so we pray: God, please help us to know intimately our hope, inheritance, and power.

Ephesians 2:1–10

EXEGETICAL IDEA

Though Paul and his readers were formerly doomed and helpless sinners, God graciously saved them and re-created them by uniting them with Christ's resurrected life and spiritual resources.

THEOLOGICAL FOCUS
God's grace brings salvation and new life in Christ to doomed and helpless sinners.

PREACHING IDEA
We were the walking dead; now we're alive in Christ.

PREACHING POINTERS
Paul and his readers lived as a spiritual minority group within a complex and challenging world. They were followers of a still relatively unknown Messiah in an environment in which people believed in gods and pagan ideas and practiced lifestyles that were starkly different from the beliefs and practices of the small Christian congregations in the province of Asia Minor. Paul's readers needed to be deeply rooted in their identity and purpose in the world in order to grow in Christ and effectively serve his interests over the long haul. To help his readers grapple with their new identity and purpose, Paul painted vivid, contrasting pictures of their lives before and after encountering Christ. He revisited the darkness of his and their former lives, the undeserved grace of God's saving intervention, and the powerfully transformed spiritual condition they now enjoyed as a result of God's gift of new life in Christ. He announced that the spiritually dead had now been made alive.

For congregations in the post-Christian world, our circumstances are quite similar. We are a shrinking minority, and we follow a relatively unknown Messiah, although his name is heard often in film, literature, blogs, and conversation. We too need to grapple with our identity in Christ so that the world does not squeeze us into its mold, a mold that says that identity is comprised of how we dress, what we drive, how we decorate, and where we dine. Just as Paul used vivid language and the logic of contrast (dead/alive, walking in sin/walking in good works), so does the preaching idea as it captures the good news of God's grace: once we were the walking dead, but now we are alive in Christ.

Ephesians 2:11–22

EXEGETICAL IDEA
Through Christ's sacrifice former spiritual outsiders, the Gentiles, along with spiritual insiders, the Jews, had become part of a new, unified, and reconciled people who experienced the Father's presence in the Spirit.

THEOLOGICAL FOCUS
Jesus Christ brings diverse people together into a right relationship with God and one another, in the Spirit.

PREACHING IDEA
God has torn down the walls, so let the walls come down!

PREACHING POINTERS
During Paul's time, religious and cultural barriers separated Jews from Gentiles. The Jews' monotheistic worldview, practice of circumcision, observance of dietary laws, and celebration

of distinct religious festivals set them apart from their Gentile neighbors. A literal wall even kept the Gentiles from entering the inner courts of the Jerusalem temple. The Jews, who were in a covenant relationship with God, were spiritual insiders, while people from all other nations (the Gentiles) were spiritual outsiders. Now, upon the arrival of Jesus, God sorted people into new categories according to their response to Christ Jesus. Many Gentiles had entered into a relationship with God through faith in Jesus, and Paul wrote this passage to help them recognize what a stunning gift God had given them by making them insiders through Christ. Likewise, the Jews needed to realize that God had sent Jesus to restore them to a right relationship with God and secure for them permanent insider status as well. Jews and Gentiles together were now part of something new, and Christ had brought them into this new relationship in the same way—by shedding his blood for them.

Barriers continue to divide people. Some barriers are literal, like the one that once divided East Germany from West Germany, or the Great Wall of China that was originally constructed to divide a newly consolidated empire from northern invaders. Other barriers are ideological, evident during radio and television talk shows, on social media posts, and in speeches. People tend to demonize the "other." Demonization can even occur in the church when we separate from one another over secondary doctrinal issues, but through Jesus, unity exists with diversity. That theological indicative is the basis of the moral imperative in 4:3, "Maintain the unity of the Spirit in the bond of peace." Because God has torn down the walls, let the walls come down!

Ephesians 3:1–13

EXEGETICAL IDEA
Paul's imprisonment was nothing compared to his God-given opportunity to reveal the mystery of God's eternal plans to put his wisdom on display in Christ and through a unified church.

THEOLOGICAL FOCUS
Participating in this groundbreaking era of God's story is well worth the sacrifice.

PREACHING IDEA
God's messenger might be chained, but God's message is unchained.

PREACHING POINTERS
Paul's readers lived during uncertain times. They participated in a fledgling spiritual movement whose ultimate success still seemed in doubt. They had received encouraging reports about the progress of the gospel in various parts of the Roman Empire, but they also continued to hear unsettling news about the hardships of Paul, a respected apostle and visible leader in the early church. Roman authorities had imprisoned Paul for years in Caesarea and Rome, after his initial arrest in Jerusalem (Acts 21:26–28:31). Incarceration was considered shameful in the Roman world, since it marked the prisoner as a criminal in the eyes of society. What should the readers make of this distressing setback? Was Paul's mission worth the sacrifice? If authorities regarded Paul as a shameful criminal, what would become of the readers' own standing in

broader society? Friends and acquaintances of a once-respected prisoner would feel tempted to distance themselves from him. Paul's readers needed a healthy dose of the eternal perspective that inspired Paul's ongoing willingness to endure persecution.

We face setbacks today too. In many parts of the world Christians are persecuted for the faith. The persecution can range from "mere" shaming to outright physical hostility. While no one can predict the future, it seems that the post-Christian West may be moving toward the ill-treatment known in parts of Asia, the Middle East, and Africa. For Western Christians, lesser forms of "persecution" exist even today—the employee is passed over for promotion because she won't play ball with the company's unethical practices, an applicant to graduate school is rejected because he included a statement about his belief in objective truth, or a family member feels the cold shoulder when arriving at the reunion. When mistreated for the gospel, how can we not lose heart (v. 13)? By adopting Paul's attitude. He had an eternal perspective on both the gospel and his sufferings, and that perspective injects hope into all who suffer for the faith. Ultimately, the hope is that even if the messenger is chained, the message is unchained.

Ephesians 3:14–21

EXEGETICAL IDEA
Paul praised God and prayed confidently that the all-powerful Father, by his Spirit, would empower Paul's readers to know and experience the abundant love of Christ in their hearts.

THEOLOGICAL FOCUS
Believers can pray that God's Spirit will empower them and help them to experience the love of Christ in deep and personal ways.

PREACHING IDEA
God, empower us to know your unknowable love.

PREACHING POINTERS
Many of Paul's readers had emerged from a pagan background in which the Greco-Roman gods were distant, demanding, and unpredictable. These new followers of Christ were beginning to understand the idea that a loving God had made a personal relationship with him possible, but deeply experiencing this truth was another matter. Paul's consequential teachings about the good news of Christ could easily remain on the surface of the lives of Paul's readers. These truths needed to sink in deeply at the heart level so that the message of God's love could shape the readers' identity and permeate their attitudes, actions, and affections. The readers could not manufacture this outcome on their own. They needed God's Spirit to knit Christ's personal and ongoing ministry of love within their hearts. Paul assured his readers of his commitment to intercede for them before the Father, who was able and willing to meet their need to experience his love inwardly and genuinely.

Likewise, for some people today God can seem distant, demanding, and unpredictable. He is like a divine watchmaker who creates the universe, winds it up, and lets it go, rarely touching human concerns again. Historically that has been called "deism," and it is alive and well today according to sociologists Christian Smith and Melinda Lunquist Denton. In *Soul Searching: The Religious and Spiritual Lives of American Teenagers* (2005), the authors conclude that many young adults view God in terms of "moral, therapeutic deism." In contrast to the deistic God who makes few demands on us, some world religions and even some branches of Christianity picture the Almighty as a glowering drill sergeant or disapproving governess. Garrison Keillor pokes fun at such a church in the fictitious town of Lake Wobegon, Minnesota, a parish that he names Our Lady of Perpetual Responsibility. This passage from Ephesians proclaims the true God, neither distant nor glowering, but full of love. The prayer Paul made for the Ephesians applies to all of us: God, empower us to know your unknowable love.

Ephesians 4:1–16

EXEGETICAL IDEA
When Paul's readers invested in their relationships with one another, embraced shared beliefs in Christ, and ministered according to the gracious gifts they received from the exalted Christ, they could experience spiritual growth and unity together, with each believer contributing to that growth.

THEOLOGICAL FOCUS
Believers grow and experience unity together in Christ when they invest in their relationships with one another, celebrate shared beliefs, and draw upon Christ's gracious gifts for ministry.

PREACHING IDEA
To live in unity, let's remove our pride, avoid the riptide, and not hide.

PREACHING POINTERS
Paul's Gentile readers were used to unifying around the emperor and Rome, for the glory of Rome. Jewish readers had rallied around God's law and the temple for unity. Now that they were recipients of great blessings in Christ, readers needed to replace the glory of Rome and love for law and temple with an even stronger unifying vision and a more compelling sense of corporate identity and purpose. This new identity and purpose was found in Christ and the church. Paul's readers needed input on pursuing this new identity and purpose as a group because God had made them a united body and had called them to a corporate mission. The prospect of growing together in Christ may have seemed particularly daunting given the complicated relational and religious dynamics between Jewish and Gentile believers in Christ. Added to this, Paul's readers faced the challenges of relating to one another constructively in ordinary interpersonal relationships. But Christ did not leave Paul's readers to fend for themselves. He had supplied the example and the spiritual resources for their success.

Today followers of Jesus are tempted to find identity in culture, politics, and religion. Being a fan of a pop culture idol and finding unity with similar people is sometimes more important than our identity as Christ-followers. Sometimes our national identity overshadows our spiritual identity. Being American (or Canadian, Guatemalan, etc.) overshadows our self-concept more than being

Christian. The same can be true of our political parties and religious or denominational identities. But God has not unified us around earthly parties. Following the dense and awesome theology of chapters 1–3, this passage turns to application, urging us to keep the unity of the Spirit. To do that, humility, good teaching, and transparency would be needed. To live in unity, let's remove our pride, avoid the riptide of false teaching, and not hide from one another.

Ephesians 4:17–5:2

EXEGETICAL IDEA

Paul's readers needed to put off the spiritually resistant old person and its distorted thinking and behavior, be inwardly renewed in Christ, and put on the new person with Christlike treatment of other believers in areas such as constructive speech, conflict resolution, generosity, and forgiveness.

THEOLOGICAL FOCUS

Believers should embrace their new identity in Christ and express this new identity by their loving treatment of fellow believers.

PREACHING IDEA

New life in Christ sparks a new style of living.

PREACHING POINTERS

Many of Paul's Gentile readers lived in the shadow of their past, which was marked by separation from God, flawed perspectives, and self-centered behavior. OT texts such as Psalm 115:4–8 and Isaiah 44:9–20 recognized the absurdity of idolatry and the spiritual blindness that accompanied it. Now, Christ had saved Paul's readers and had incorporated them into his new family. These believers needed to make a clean break from their past. They inhabited two worlds—a broader world of idolatry and self-interest, and the new spiritual community that consisted of devoted but still flawed followers of Christ. Paul's readers needed reminders about how to detach themselves from worldly patterns and identify more strongly with Christ and his diverse people. Paul provided them with many practical examples about how to abandon old, misguided, and destructive habits and implement new, Christlike practices that built up the body of Christ and reflected God's love and forgiveness.

Followers of Christ today still feel pulled into mindsets and practices that are at odds with their new life in Christ. Some of the old practices are heard daily in blogs, talk radio, and political acrimony. A "tribalized" mindset can cause us to find people of like mind, preach our views to the choir, and demonize anyone who holds an opposite conviction. Another of the old practices is deceit, which can take the form of "spin" and propaganda and are common tools of persuasion. This passage is up to date on the issue of immorality too. Movies, television shows, and songs ranging from country to hip-hop make unchecked pursuits of sensual pleasures seem normal. For Christians, this is not how we learned Christ (v. 20). Foul talk, lying, outbursts of anger, and immorality belong to the distorted world of the old person, not the new, and the old ways must be put off (v. 22). Truthfulness, kindness, forgiveness, and love are our new virtues that help us imitate God as we allow new life in Christ to spark a new style of living.

Ephesians 5:3–14

EXEGETICAL IDEA

Paul's readers needed to reject sexual immorality, greed, and other vices that clashed with their kingdom identity and live instead as Christ's light, being ready to shine Christ's powerful, transforming light in a dark world.

THEOLOGICAL FOCUS

Believers should reject conduct that clashes with their identity and live as Christ's light in a dark world.

PREACHING IDEA

Live as Christ's light in the midst of a dark culture.

PREACHING POINTERS

Paul had devoted much space to how his readers should live consistently with their new spiritual status. This suggested that some of Paul's readers were still vulnerable to falling back into the sinful patterns of their past. The Gentile world was known for its sexual immorality, wild parties, violent gladiator contests, and extravagant living. Other entanglements in sin were more subtle. Paul's readers ran the risk of treating sin too lightly and not understanding how out of place sin was in the Christian life. In this section, Paul wanted to draw distinct, unambiguous lines between two opposing cultures. The first was the rotten culture of unchecked sinful desires and disobedience. The second was the life-renewing culture of God's kingdom. For Paul, the choice was clear, and there was no middle ground. His readers needed to reject the sinful vestiges of their past and shine Christ's light into the darkness around them.

The Ephesians' story is a twenty-first-century story too. The sexual revolution of the 1960s has continued unabated, as seen when the popularity of the acronym YOLO, "You Only Live Once," is used to justify many self-indulgent activities. The surrounding culture may say "your body is your own" when it celebrates sexual immorality in movies, but God says something different. Then there is the sin of covetousness. It can saturate the church, not just the culture. The advertising industry tries to create discontent and desire for whatever is new, shiny, fast, and sexy. Credit cards make luxuries possible while they chain people with "easy" payments; and today even credit cards seem quaint as we pay with our phones—a fingerprint, pleasant ding, and the item is ours! This passage also addresses our speech. Imagine the manual laborer who wants to honor Christ yet finds himself slipping into crude speech. When break time comes his coworkers gather for coffee and off-color stories, and he finds it hard to swim against the tide. This passage helps believers live as light, and it gives hope that we can do so because of Christ. Thus, we can live as Christ's light in the midst of a dark culture.

Ephesians 5:15–21

EXEGETICAL IDEA

Paul's readers were called to live wisely and strategically in the broader, evil world, to seek to understand and follow God's will, and to be filled with the Spirit's presence and influence in their corporate worship, outlook, and relationships.

THEOLOGICAL FOCUS

Believers should live strategically in their interactions with those who do not know Christ and keep in tune with the Spirit in corporate worship and relationships.

PREACHING IDEA

To live strategically, sync with the Spirit.

PREACHING POINTERS

As their identity as followers of Christ became more firmly established, Paul's readers needed to grapple with the implications of their identity. First, how should they represent Christ and his kingdom to those people who worshipped idols and glorified power and pleasure? They needed to disengage from their old practices in that environment but remain as a force for light in dark settings. Paul's readers likely saw this as a daunting task and recognized their need for Paul's input and God's wisdom. Second, how should they strengthen themselves internally in their churches to facilitate vibrant worship, spiritual growth, and harmony in relationships? They knew that God had provided his Spirit to dwell among them, but how could they make the most of the Spirit's presence? Paul gave them guidance for living strategically with people outside the church while shoring up their spiritual strength as a community of believers.

We too live in a pluralistic world. Urbanization as well as the ubiquity of social media mean that we live in a global village like never before, so guidance is needed. Today, we increasingly rub shoulders with people of many cultures and religions. A United Nations report indicates that by 2050, two-thirds of humanity will live in cities, up from 55 percent in 2018 (Lardiei, 2018) Most people in Western culture have floated down the stream into post-Christendom as seen in the rising group of "nones" who do not identify with any religion. Perhaps your congregation has a public school teacher who swims in a lake of humanism, or public school students who face a blitzkrieg of relativism. How can they represent Christ in a school where anything goes if it is deemed "authentic" to who you define yourself to be? How can they live missionally and present a striking contrast to the current milieu? We can live strategically by syncing with the Spirit.

Ephesians 5:22–33

EXEGETICAL IDEA

Paul's readers cultivated strong marriages when wives respectfully submitted themselves to their husbands and husbands selflessly loved and tenderly cared for their wives, since marriages reflected the intimate bond and ordered structure of Christ's union with his body, the church, and Christ had sacrificially loved and purposefully led the church.

THEOLOGICAL FOCUS

Wives and husbands are to treat one another in marriage according to the model of the ordered, loving, and united relationship between Christ and the church.

PREACHING IDEA

A good marriage is a great mirror of Christ and the church.

PREACHING POINTERS

Paul's vision of a new humanity in Christ needed to make a meaningful difference in his readers' household relationships. Like other people in Greco-Roman society, Paul's readers lived in households that often included husbands and wives, children, other relatives, and slaves. Paul's readers' new life in Christ gave them an opportunity to experience relationships that were uniquely different from their old way of life. Marriage relationships were fundamental in Paul's time, and they could be undermined through disrespect, abuse, and adultery. The presence of God's Spirit in their midst meant that Paul's readers needed to commit to a better way. How was Paul's readers' new status as adopted children of God in Christ supposed to influence their relationships with their spouses? Paul found a potent answer in the ordered, loving, and intimate bond between Christ and the church.

From domestic abuse, to passive aggressive behavior, to no-fault divorce, the institution of marriage needs a shot in the arm today. The divorce statistics in the United States may seem encouraging because divorce is declining, but take a closer look. The likely reason why divorce is declining is because fewer people are marrying. Living together outside the covenant of marriage is on the rise. Using the magnificent theology of Christ and the church, this passage shows us how wives submit to and respect their husbands and how husbands love and sacrifice for their wives. Christian devotion rises no higher than our home lives. The passive husband who escapes to the TV room can grow in Christlikeness when he hears how the Lord Jesus loved the church and gave himself for her. Christ's love is selfless, tender, and attentive. The frustrated wife who derides her husband can grow in Christlikeness too when she hears how the church submits to Christ. In the same way, she should submit to and respect her husband.

Ephesians 6:1–9

EXEGETICAL IDEA

As the authority and promises of Christ the Lord shaped harmonious relationships between children and parents and then slaves and masters within the structure of Paul's readers' households, children would obey their parents, fathers would patiently train their children spiritually, slaves would obey their masters, and masters would acknowledge slaves' equal dignity through fair treatment.

THEOLOGICAL FOCUS
Believers should remember the authority and promises of Christ the Lord as they live spiritually purposeful and constructive lives within their household and in other important relationships.

PREACHING IDEA
Under the same roof, Christians are under the same Lord.

PREACHING POINTERS
Paul hoped that his readers would buy into his vision that the whole created order would one day be renewed under Christ's leadership (Eph. 1:9–10). They had begun to experience the first effects of that through their shared experiences of Christ's presence. But Greco-Roman society still operated by flawed systems and norms that fell far short of God's perfect kingdom standards. It was not easy for them to consistently put into practice kingdom values in a setting in which those values clashed with societal patterns. Some of Paul's readers were witnessing a breakdown in relationships between children and parents. Paul's readers lived in a broader society that they could not change structurally right away, but with a focus on the Lord and an eternal perspective they could still make changes so that their households might reflect the light of Christ more powerfully through values of equality and relationships of harmony.

We live in a vastly different culture today, but points of relevance are still abundant. Slavery is condemned, but this passage about slaves and masters is still relevant to other relational arrangements. In Christ, all are equal in value and dignity, even if they have differing roles that call for submission and obedience. Our culture today also differs from the first century in terms of parents and children. Children are sometimes pampered, or perhaps children are neglected by absentee fathers. This passage has plenty of relevance for both children and parents. The middle schooler who thinks disobedience is clever can grow in Christlikeness with this passage. Parents who are given to habits that exasperate sons and daughters must put away those habits. Everyone who wields authority or is under authority is addressed, as we learn that Christians under the same roof are under the same Lord.

Ephesians 6:10–24

EXEGETICAL IDEA
Paul's readers could stand strong in their identity and mission in Christ, against the Devil and other hostile spiritual powers, by taking full advantage of God's spiritual armor and praying for all believers and for Paul's ministry as an imprisoned ambassador for Christ.

THEOLOGICAL FOCUS
Believers should stand strong against spiritual opposition by taking advantage of Christ's divine resources and praying for the church's effective mission.

PREACHING IDEA

For protection against spiritual forces, put on the armor of God.

PREACHING POINTERS

Though Paul's readers had experienced the challenges of living as a marginalized group that was out of step with the world around it, they may have wrongly assumed two things. First, they may have identified humans or earthly authorities as their true enemies. Second, they may have felt that they were not up to the task of standing their ground within this hostile spiritual environment. Paul turned his readers' attention to the spiritual forces behind their troubles and encouraged them that God had given them everything they needed to not only survive but also thrive within their adverse settings. Gentiles throughout Asia Minor sought protection from hostile spiritual forces by summoning their own spiritual power through magic and incantations, and the Jewish people of that day also recognized the need for protection against spiritual darkness. Paul identified Christ as his readers' ultimate hope for standing strong against spiritual evil. By reminding his readers of the divine power found in Christ, Paul emboldened them with the hope that echoed Jesus's promise that "I will build my church, and the gates of Hades will not prevail against it" (Matt. 16:18).

Believers today can also be confused about our true enemy, thinking it is the grouchy boss, the government, or Hollywood. But behind people and institutions are the spiritual forces of evil in the heavenly places (Eph. 6:12). Some are interested in spiritism, and palm readers and psychic advisers are common. James Emery White summarizes: "Most Americans mix traditional faith with beliefs in psychics, reincarnation, and spiritual energy that they say can be found in physical objects such as mountains, trees and crystals." This passage helps us see the reality of spiritual forces and how to resist them. God offers all that is necessary. For protection against spiritual forces, we put on the armor of God.

ABBREVIATIONS

GENERAL ABBREVIATIONS

A.D.	in the year of our Lord (*anno Domini*)
B.C.	Before Christ
DSS	Dead Sea Scrolls
ET	English Translation
HB	Hebrew Bible
LXX	Septuagint (the Greek OT)
NT	New Testament
OT	Old Testament

TECHNICAL ABBREVIATIONS

acc.	accusative
adj.	adjective, adjectival
adv.	adverb, adverbial
ap.	apposition
ca.	circa
cf.	compare (*confer*)
ch(s).	chapter(s)
conj.	conjunction
dat.	dative
e.g.	for example
et al.	and others (*et alii*)
etc.	and so forth, and the rest (*et cetera*)
flor.	flourished (*floruit*)
fut.	future
gen.	genitive
i.e.	that is (*id est*)
impv.	imperative
indic.	indicative
inf.	infinitive
instr.	instrumental
mid.	middle
n(n).	note(s)
neut.	neuter
nom.	nominative
p(p).	page(s)
pass.	passive

perf.	perfect
prep.	preposition, prepositional phrase
pron.	pronoun
ptc.	participle
rel.	relative
repr.	reprinted
rev.	revised
sbjv.	subjunctive
subj.	subject
subst.	substantival
s.v.	under the word (*sub verbo*)
temp.	temporal
v(v).	verse(s)

BIBLICAL

Old Testament

Gen.	Genesis
Exod.	Exodus
Lev.	Leviticus
Num.	Numbers
Deut.	Deuteronomy
Josh.	Joshua
Judg.	Judges
Ruth	Ruth
1 Sam.	1 Samuel
2 Sam.	2 Samuel
1 Kgdms.	1 Kingdoms (LXX)
2 Kgdms.	2 Kingdoms (LXX)
1 Kings	1 Kings
2 Kings	2 Kings
3 Kgdms.	3 Kingdoms (LXX)
4 Kgdms.	4 Kingdoms (LXX)
1 Chron.	1 Chronicles
2 Chron.	2 Chronicles
1 Par.	1 Paraliponmenon (LXX)
2 Par.	2 Paraliponmenon (LXX)
Ezra	Ezra
Neh.	Nehemiah
Esther	Esther
Job	Job
Ps./Pss.	Psalm(s)
Prov.	Proverbs
Eccl.	Ecclesiastes
Song	Song of Songs
Isa.	Isaiah
Jer.	Jeremiah
Lam.	Lamentations
Ezek.	Ezekiel
Dan.	Daniel
Hos.	Hosea
Joel	Joel
Amos	Amos
Obad.	Obadiah
Jonah	Jonah
Mic.	Micah
Nah.	Nahum
Hab.	Habakkuk
Zeph.	Zephaniah
Hag.	Haggai
Zech.	Zechariah
Mal.	Malachi

New Testament

Matt.	Matthew
Mark	Mark
Luke	Luke
John	John
Acts	Acts
Rom.	Romans
1 Cor.	1 Corinthians

2 Cor.	2 Corinthians	Philem.	Philemon
Gal.	Galatians	Heb.	Hebrews
Eph.	Ephesians	James	James
Phil.	Philippians	1 Peter	1 Peter
Col.	Colossians	2 Peter	2 Peter
1 Thess.	1 Thessalonians	1 John	1 John
2 Thess.	2 Thessalonians	2 John	2 John
1 Tim.	1 Timothy	3 John	3 John
2 Tim.	2 Timothy	Jude	Jude
Titus	Titus	Rev.	Revelation

EXTRABIBLICAL SOURCES

Old Testament Apocrypha

2 Macc	2 Maccabees
3 Macc	3 Maccabees
4 Macc	4 Maccabees
Sir	Wisdom of Jesus the Son of Sirach (Ecclesiasticus)
Tob	Tobit
Wis	Wisdom of Solomon

Old Testament Pseudepigrapha

1 En.	1 Enoch (Ethiopic Apocalypse)
Jub.	Jubilees
Pss. Sol.	Psalms of Solomon

Classification of the Dead Sea Scrolls

[a], [b], [c], etc.	manuscript identifiers
ar	Aramaic (e.g., 4QApocrDan ar)
1Q	Cave 1, Qumran
4Q	Cave 4, Qumran
Q	Qumran

Dead Sea Scrolls

Number	*Abbreviation*	*Name*
CD	Damascus Document	Cairo Genizah copy of the Damascus Document
1QM	1QWar Scroll	Milḥamah *or* War Scroll
1Q28	1QS	Rule of the Community
1Q28a	1QSa	Rule of the Congregation
4Q174	4QFlor	Florilegium
4Q246	4QapocDan ar	Apocryphon Daniel
4Q252	4QCommGen A	Commentary on Genesis A
4Q266	4QD[a]	Damascus Document[a]

OTHER ANCIENT SOURCES

Church Fathers

Jerome	Church father and translator of the Latin Vulgate; ca. 342–420
Comm. Eph.	*Commentary on Ephesians* (*Commentariorum in Epistulam ad Ephesios libri III*)
John Chrysostom	Church father and archbishop of Constantinople; ca. 347–407
Hom. Eph.	*Homilies on Ephesians*

Classical and Ancient Christian Writings (Greek and Latin Works)

Aristotle	Greek philosopher, scientist; 384–322 B.C.
Pol.	*Politics* (*Politica*)
Cicero (Marcus Tullius)	Roman statesman, orator, and writer; 106–43 B.C.
Leg.	*De legibus*
Off.	*De officiis*
Verr.	*In Verrem*
Cod. Justin.	*Digest of Justinian* (*Codex Justinianus*)
Columella	Roman soldier and farmer; flor. A.D. 50
Rust.	*De re rustica*
Did.	Didache
Dionysius (of Halicarnassus)	Greek historian, teacher of rhetoric; flor. ca. 20 B.C.
Ant. rom	*Antiquitates romanae*
Eusebius (of Caesarea)	Bishop and church historian; ca. A.D. 264–ca. 340
Praep. ev.	*Preparation for the Gospel* (*Praeparatio evangelica*)
Gaius	Roman jurist; flor. A.D. 130–180
Inst.	*Institutiones*
Irenaeus	Bishop of Lyon, Greek theologian; ca. A.D. 130–ca. 200
Haer.	*Against Heresies*
Josephus	Romano-Jewish historian; ca. A.D. 37–ca. 100
A.J.	*Jewish Antiquities* (*Antiquitates judaicae*)
B.J.	*Jewish War* (*Bellum judaicum*)
Ag. Ap.	*Against Apion*
Lucian (of Samosata)	Assyrian satirist and rhetorician who wrote in Greek; ca. 125–180
Tox.	*Toxaris*
P.Oxy.	*The Oxyrhynchus Papyri*
Philo (of Alexandria)	Jewish philosopher; ca. 20 B.C.–A.D. 50
Hypoth.	*Hypothetica*
Spec. Leg.	*On the Special Laws* (*De specialibus legibus*)
Virt.	*On the Virtues* (*De virtutibus*)
Pliny (the Younger)	Roman lawyer, magistrate, and writer; ca. A.D. 61–ca. 113
Ep.	*Epistulae*
Plutarch	Greek biographer and philosopher; ca. A.D. 46–120
Mor.	*Moralia*
Quintilian	Roman rhetorician and teacher; ca. A.D. 35–ca. 100
Inst.	*Institutio oratorio*

Seneca (the Younger)	Roman philosopher, statesman, and playwright; tutor to Nero; ca. 4 B.C.–A.D. 65
Ep.	*Epistulae morales*
Ira	*De ira*
Strabo	Greek historian and geographer; ca. 63 B.C.–ca. A.D. 23
Geogr.	*Geography* (*Geographica*)

PERIODICALS

BBR	*Bulletin for Biblical Research*
Bib	*Biblica*
BSac	*Bibliotheca Sacra*
CBQ	*Catholic Biblical Quarterly*
CTR	*Criswell Theological Review*
EuroJTh	*European Journal of Theology*
ExpTim	*Expository Times*
GNS	*Good News Studies*
JBL	*Journal of Biblical Literature*
JETS	*Journal of the Evangelical Theological Society*
JSNT	*Journal for the Study of the New Testament*
NTS	*New Testament Studies*
ResQ	*Restoration Quarterly*
WTJ	*Westminster Theological Journal*

SERIES

AB	Anchor Bible
ACCS	Ancient Christian Commentary on Scripture
BECNT	Baker Exegetical Commentary on the New Testament
BNTC	Black's New Testament Commentaries
ECC	Eerdmans Critical Commentary
ICC	International Critical Commentary
JSNTSup	Journal for the Study of the New Testament Supplement Series
LCL	Loeb Classical Library
NAC	New American Commentary
NCCS	New Covenant Commentary Series
NICNT	New International Commentary on the New Testament
NSBT	New Studies in Biblical Theology
SBLDS	Society of Biblical Literature Dissertation Series
SBLStBL	Society of Biblical Literature Studies in Biblical Literature
SGBC	Story of God Bible Commentary
TNTC	Tyndale New Testament Commentaries
WBC	Word Biblical Commentary
WUNT	Wissenschaftliche Untersuchungen zum Neuen Testament
ZECNT	Zondervan Exegetical Commentary on the New Testament

REFERENCES

ANF	Roberts, A., and J. Donaldson, eds. *The Ante-Nicene Fathers: The Writings of the Fathers down to A.D. 325.* 1994 (1885–1887). Revised by A. C. Coxe. 10 vols. Repr., Peabody, MA: Hendrickson.
BDAG	Danker, F. W., W. Bauer, W. F. Arndt, and F. W. Gingrich. 2000. *A Greek-English Lexicon of the New Testament and Other Early Christian Literature.* 3rd ed. Chicago: University of Chicago Press.
BDF	Blass F., A. Debrunner, and R. W. Funk. 1961. *A Greek Grammar of the New Testament and Other Early Christian Literature.* Chicago: University of Chicago Press.
CNTUOT	Beale, G. K., and D. A. Carson, eds. 2007. *Commentary on the New Testament Use of the Old Testament.* Grand Rapids: Baker Academic.
DBIm	Ryken, L., J. C. Wilhoit, T. Longman III, eds. 1998. *Dictionary of Biblical Imagery.* Downers Grove, IL: InterVarsity Press.
DLNT	Martin, R. P., and P. H. Davids, eds. *Dictionary of the Later New Testament and Its Developments.* Downers Grove, IL: InterVarsity Press.
DMBI	D. K. McKim, ed. 2007. *Dictionary of Major Biblical Interpreters.* 2nd ed. Downers Grove, IL: InterVarsity Press.
DNTB	Evans, C. A., and S. E. Porter, eds. 2000. *Dictionary of New Testament Background.* Downers Grove, IL: InterVarsity Press.
DPL	Hawthorne, G. F., R. P. Martin, and D. G. Reid, eds. 1993. *Dictionary of Paul and His Letters.* Downers Grove, IL: InterVarsity Press.
EDNT	Balz, H., and G. Schneider, eds. 1990–1993 (1978–1980). *Exegetical Dictionary of the New Testament.* ET. 3 vols. Grand Rapids: Eerdmans.
HALOT	Koehler, L., W. Baumgartner, and J. J. Stamm. 2001. *The Hebrew and Aramaic Lexicon of the Old Testament.* Translated and edited under the supervision of M. E. J. Richardson. Study ed. 2 vols. Leiden: Brill.
NDBT	Alexander, T. D., and B. S. Rosner, eds. *New Dictionary of Biblical Theology.* Downers Grove, IL: InterVarsity Press, 2000.
OCD	Hornblower, S., and A. Spawforth, eds. 2012. *The Oxford Classical Dictionary.* 4th ed. Oxford: Oxford University Press.
TDNT	Kittel, G., and G. Friedrich, eds. 1964–1976. *Theological Dictionary of the New Testament.* Translated by G. W. Bromiley. 10 vols. Grand Rapids: Eerdmans.

TRANSLATIONS

CSB	Christian Standard Bible
ESV	English Standard Version
KJV	King James Version
NASB	New American Standard Bible
NET	New English Translation
NIV	New International Version
NKJV	New King James Version
NLT	New Living Translation
NRSV	New Revised Standard Version
RSV	Revised Standard Version

INTRODUCTION

OVERVIEW OF INTRODUCTORY ISSUES

Author: The apostle Paul

Provenance: Paul wrote while under house arrest during his first Roman imprisonment.

Date: A.D. 60 or 61

Readers: The letter's recipients were believers in house churches located throughout the Roman Province of Asia (Asia Minor).

Genre: Epistle (Letter)

Historical Setting and Occasion: The letter's recipients were living in a multicultural world marked by religious and cultural diversity. Paul's readers needed to understand the blessings and responsibilities of the new life and new identity they shared as both Jews and Gentiles in Christ Jesus.

Theological Themes: The letter describes believers being united with one another in Christ Jesus, adopting a distinct way of living in Christ, and sharing in and displaying the exalted authority of Christ.

Structure and Argument: Paul helped readers recognize the blessings of new life that God had given them in Christ Jesus (Eph. 1–3) and guided them in how their calling should affect their corporate and individual experience in all areas of life (Eph. 4–6).

AUTHORSHIP OF EPHESIANS

At first glance there is not much to say about the authorship of Ephesians: the apostle Paul wrote it! This is the conclusion in this commentary too. Nevertheless, there are debates about whether Paul actually wrote the letter. For more than 1,700 years, Christians affirmed that Paul wrote Ephesians, but in the last few centuries a number of scholars have contested this view. They suppose instead that a later author wanted to use Paul's name to gain a greater hearing for the later author's own work. According to this theory, the author worked carefully to imitate Paul's content and style. The goal was to simultaneously advance ideas important to the imitator but also avoid discovery that someone other than Paul had written the letter. The imitator did not simply use Paul's name but added details about Paul's calling, imprisonment, and prayer needs in order to reinforce the charade that Paul wrote the letter.

Different scholars point to different reasons for their skepticism that Paul wrote Ephesians, but there are five main reasons that stand out. First, some scholars say that Ephesians lacks the personal touch and detail found in Paul's undisputed letters. They say that Paul did not reminisce about his past history with his readers or greet specific people, as he did in some other letters. But from Acts 19–20 we know that Paul had spent nearly three years stationed in Ephesus and had developed deep bonds of affection with the believers there. According to skeptics, the "real Paul" would have communicated with more warmth and familiarity.

In response, this first objection overlooks other possible reasons for the formal tone of Ephesians. Does the tone match a plausible occasion and purpose for the letter within Paul's ministry context? And does the letter consistently reflect that tone from start to finish? Affirmative answers to these two related questions should put to rest any notion that the tone of Ephesians rules out Paul as the author. One such theory about the letter's occasion and purpose will be discussed later in this chapter, in the section on the recipients' identity. Even Bart Ehrman (2013, 183), who dismisses Paul's authorship of Ephesians on other grounds, discounts arguments that appeal to the general and formal tone of Ephesians.

Some scholars raise a second objection to the position that Paul wrote Ephesians. They say that the author failed to create a genuine portrait of Paul in the letter (cf. Mitton, 1951, 15; Barrett, 1973–1974, 239–40; de Boer, 1980, 359–80; Collins, 1988, 167–69; Lincoln, 1990, lxii–lxiii; Dunn, DLNT, 890). They think that the artificial "Paul" too casually appealed to receiving exclusive revelation as a way to exercise authority over his readers' lives, whereas in earlier letters Paul had found it necessary to contend for his apostolic standing within a greater network of Christian leaders. These scholars also say that Paul's suffering in prison was simultaneously flattened and glamorized. An expression of humility (Eph. 3:8), even when resembling an excerpt from an earlier letter (1 Cor. 15:9), supposedly rung hollow in its new formulation.

In response to this second objection, when we look at Ephesians the portrait of Paul aligns comfortably with both Paul's self-presentation from earlier letters and the most likely circumstances behind the letter. First, the image of Paul that emerges from Ephesians resembles Paul's earlier portrayals of his ministry in both content and perspective. Upon careful examination of the relevant passages in Ephesians, we can identify credible reasons for why Paul himself characterized his authority and suffering in the ways he did (MaGee, 2013, 128–69). Second, Paul's first Roman imprisonment, the likely setting from which Paul wrote Ephesians, was a house arrest that restricted his movements but did not place great physical or emotional demands on him (Acts 28). Paul's passing references to his imprisonment (Eph. 3:1; 4:1; 6:19–20) fit well with this setting. Furthermore, Paul introduced rather than argued for his authority as an apostle, which was fitting for a letter written to a broad audience, many of whom had not had personal dealings with Paul (see discussions about the letter's recipients later in this chapter). Paul's discussion of his ministry in his letter to the Romans, another audience that was relatively unfamiliar with him, reflects a similar tone (van Roon, 1974, 87).

A third objection comes from some scholars who raise suspicions that Ephesians borrowed from Colossians without fully understanding what Colossians was saying. They claim that there are striking verbal similarities between the two letters but that the author of Ephesians did not successfully preserve the underlying ideas from Colossians (esp. Mitton, 1951, 64–67; 83–97). Whole sections from the letters correspond to one another, including Paul's prayers for his readers' strength and wisdom (Col. 1:9–12; Eph. 1:15–19), an introduction to Paul's Gentile-focused ministry (Col. 1:24–29; Eph. 3:1–13), and practical ways of putting off the old self and putting on the new self in Christ (Col. 3:5–14; Eph. 4:25–32). Beyond the topical similarities, there are verbal parallels as well. The closest wording is found in Paul's description of Tychicus and the purpose of sending him to the recipients of the letter (Col. 4:7–8; Eph. 6:21–22), and in instructions for ordered relationships in households (Col. 3:18–4:1; Eph. 5:22–6:10).

In response to this third objection, Ephesians and Colossians do resemble one another in a number of passages. But the topical overlap is attributable to the likelihood that Paul wrote the letters at a similar time and for a similar purpose. Most of the verbal correspondences occur in unsurprising sections such as greetings (Col. 1:1–2; Eph. 1:1–2), a recounting of Paul's calling to ministry (Col. 1:25–26; Eph. 3:2, 9), household instructions, and the sending of Tychicus. Examples of supposed inconsistency in the use of terms in the two letters (for words such as "mystery" and "fullness") are explained by Paul's broadened focus from Christ in Colossians to Christ and the church in Ephesians (Bruce, 1977, 426). In short, there is little evidence that one author wrote Colossians and then a different author extracted and reworked excerpts from Colossians and integrated them into Ephesians.

Intriguingly, there are also subtle but undeniable echoes of Paul's letter to the Romans throughout Ephesians as well (cf. Bruce, 1977, 426–27). Verbal parallels include unbelieving Gentiles being "futile" in their thinking, "darkened" in their understanding, and marked by "impurity" (Eph. 4:17–19; Rom. 1:21, 24), Christians being "members of one another" (Eph. 4:25; Rom. 12:5), and Paul's ministry being a gift of God's grace to him (Eph. 3:2; Rom. 15:15). Conceptual affinities are also quite strong. In both letters, Paul exhorted believers to wake up from spiritual slumber and walk in the light (Eph. 5:8–14; Rom. 13:11–14). He put a spotlight on his specific calling to the Gentiles (Eph. 3:1, 8; Rom. 1:13; 11:13). He drew upon Isaiah 52:7 to commend the feet that brought the gospel of peace (Eph. 6:15; Rom. 10:15). He used the "co-" prefix (συν- prefix; "together with") to express the idea of believers sharing in Christ's death or resurrection (Eph. 2:5–6; Rom 6:5, 6, 8; 8:17, 29). In broader strokes, the central themes of sin, grace, faith, the saving work of Christ, the crowning virtue of love, and the ministry of the Holy Spirit took center stage in both letters.

It would have been extremely challenging for an imitator of Paul to incorporate Colossians so overtly but Romans more faintly. Using one letter as a template would be difficult enough. Drawing from two at once, *but in consistently different ways*, would be nearly impossible without disrupting the flow of the discourse. Ephesians includes wording that resembles verses in other letters as well (2 Cor. 1:3 and Eph. 1:3; 2 Cor. 1:22 and Eph. 1:13–14; 1 Cor. 15:9 and Eph. 3:8; Phil. 4:18 and Eph. 5:2; 1 Thess. 5:8 and Eph. 6:14, 17), further diminishing the probability that even a skilled imitator could have created Ephesians in Paul's name. The connections between these earlier letters and Ephesians never seem forced. The familiar wording is integrated seamlessly into the surrounding context.

The most likely scenario for how the writing unfolded is that Paul wrote Ephesians shortly after he wrote Colossians and that he sought to articulate some common ideas to similar audiences in both letters. Paul's letter-writing process may have required, in collaboration with a paid scribe, the following stages: discussing and assembling notes, preparing a rough draft, making additional revisions and edits, and composing the final draft (Richards, 2004, 91–93). If Paul followed this general process with Colossians, the memory of its contents would be especially fresh in Paul's mind when he wrote Ephesians. One can even envision Paul still having some of his notes from Colossians at his disposal when he and his writing assistant were composing Ephesians. Ephesians would reflect Colossians quite noticeably. On the other hand, since it had been some time since Paul wrote his earlier letters, they left more sporadic traces of themselves in Ephesians. In short, the letter is no patchwork of borrowed phrases from Colossians and the earlier letters. On the contrary, Ephesians stands as an impressive and internally consistent work that reflects the complex and familiar thinking of Paul.

A fourth charge sometimes levied against Paul's authorship of Ephesians is that there are theological discrepancies between Ephesians and the undisputed letters (Lincoln, 1990, lxiii–lxv; Ehrman, 2013, 185–87). For instance, some scholars point to a shift in eschatology from a predominantly future manifestation of God's deliverance on his promises to an already-realized reception of those blessings. They note that Ephesians portrays believers as already being seated at Christ's right hand, in the heavenly places (2:6), and as having already received all spiritual blessings (1:3). The author depicted salvation as having already occurred for believers (2:5, 8–9), instead of as something to be fully experienced in the future. Some skeptics of Paul's authorship also see a gravitation away from churches as local congregations to the church as an abstract universal entity (Eph. 1:22; 3:10; 5:23–32). Still others posit that the author's view of the church feels more institutionalized than Paul's original vision for the church. Apostles and prophets take their place alongside Christ Jesus as the cornerstone of the church (Eph. 2:20; compare with 1 Cor. 3:11), and the apostles and prophets can even be deemed "holy" (Eph. 3:5), as if they are esteemed leaders from an earlier era (Mitton, 1951, 19, 38). Many of these supposed theological departures from the true Paul are said to reflect a later stage of Christianity's development.

In response to this fourth objection, some of these seeming discrepancies are resolved when we recognize how flexible and comprehensive Paul's theology had always been. His thinking encompassed both the already and the not yet of salvation and its blessings, allowing him to emphasize one or the other aspect, according to the need. This flexibility was undergirded by a robust theology of believers' union with Christ and reception of the Spirit. Believers became united with Christ Jesus and thus now and later shared in his identity and status. The promised eschatological gift of the Spirit exposed believers to the full range of God's already and not-yet blessings. As a result, in the undisputed letters Paul could highlight the current realities of new life in Christ (in addition to future promises) when he claimed that believers were already saved (Rom. 8:24) and glorified (Rom. 8:30). Believers had entered an existence of new life (Rom. 6:13) and new creation (2 Cor. 5:17), had gained access to Christ's resurrection power (Phil. 3:10; 4:13; 2 Cor. 4:11), and had received all of the blessings promised to the children of Abraham (Gal. 3:7–9, 14). In Ephesians, Paul certainly acknowledged the future dimension of God's blessings (to accompany already-realized blessings), enlisting ideas such as hope, inheritance, a future bliss in God's presence, and a future day of redemption (1:14, 18; 2:7; 4:30; 5:5). He stressed the present realities of salvation for a purpose, though—to give his readers confidence in their current status and identity in Christ, even in the midst of a world filled with sin and hostile spiritual forces (cf. Fuchs, 2015, 34–35).

Paul also had a comprehensive and adaptable view of churches and the church. Paul wrote to multiple churches in Ephesians (as will be argued in the section on the original readers), but he saw them all as part of a larger, universal church under Christ's headship. Paul had already taken for granted this idea of one unified church in his earlier letters (1 Cor. 10:32; 11:22; 12:28; 15:9; Gal. 1:13; Phil. 3:6). In addition, Paul's recognition of the foundational role of apostles and prophets accorded well with 1 Corinthians 12:28. They were "holy" in that they were set apart for God's service, as Paul described himself in other places (Rom. 1:1; Gal. 1:15). In Ephesians, Paul still left room for a vibrant, participatory community of faith alongside these primary leaders. Believers all pitched in to contribute to the church's growth (Eph. 4:12–16), and they ministered to one another with edifying words and songs (Eph. 5:19).

A fifth proposed reason for suspecting that someone else wrote Ephesians is that the language and style is said to depart from Paul's typical practice (Lincoln, 1990, lxv–lxvi; Ehrman, 2013, 184–85). The author of Ephesians used a number of words and phrases that did not appear in Paul's earlier letters. Ephesians also features elaborate sentences that, once they get rolling, keep accumulating more and more modifiers and amplification (Eph. 1:3–14, 15–23; 3:2–7, 14–19; 4:11–16), which is a less common occurrence in Paul's earlier letters.

In response, this fifth objection to Paul's authorship suffers from some shortcomings. First, even sophisticated statistical analyses of word usage are under-determinative for letters as brief as Ephesians. The best statistical studies on Paul's letters are cautious about reading too much into observations that are drawn from such brief letters (cf. Neumann, 1990; Mealand, 1995, 61–92). Second, the number of unique words or phrases in Ephesians does not stand out as unusual when compared to the unique vocabulary in other letters by Paul (Hoehner, 2002, 26–27). Third, we can often identify specific reasons that Paul included an uncommon word or phrase in Ephesians. For instance, "the heavenly places" supports the strong interest in spiritual warfare in Ephesians, and "eternal plan" (3:11) concurs with the emphasis on God's purposeful and wise agenda for the world. Fourth, long sentences, though admittedly more prevalent in Ephesians than in the rest of the Pauline corpus, are not unknown elsewhere. Paul tended to adopt a more flowing and ornate style of writing when he expressed praise to God or lifted up prayers for his readers (cf. Rom. 8:38–39; 11:33–36; 1 Cor. 1:4–8; 2 Cor. 1:3–5; Phil. 1:3–11; 1 Thess. 1:2–5; 3:11–13; 2 Thess. 1:3–10; cf. Hoehner, 2002, 28; Carson and Moo, 2005, 484). There just happens to be a lot of that type of discourse in Ephesians, a letter that focuses on the authority of Christ and the grace and power he makes available to believers. In other words, the style fits the subject matter of Ephesians.

In summary, arguments against Paul's authorship of Ephesians fail to account for Paul's ability to apply complex and insightful theological guidance to different settings according to the specific needs there. As we will soon see, Ephesians was particularly well suited for multiple congregations of believers who resided throughout the province of Asia Minor. Paul himself wrote the letter to address the needs of the churches in that region.

Saint Paul Writing His Epistles by Valentin de Boulogne (1620). Public domain.

Once Paul's authorship of Ephesians has been accepted, we can seek to appreciate his status and circumstances when he wrote. Paul introduced himself as an apostle who was called by God's grace and entrusted with a message and ministry directed especially to the Gentiles (Eph. 1:1; 3:1–9). The original apostles had been chosen by Christ to testify about him (Mark 3:14; Acts 1:2) and guard the integrity of the message of Christ through their authoritative teaching (Acts 2:42; 16:4; Eph. 2:20). Christ unexpectedly chose Paul as well when he had revealed himself to Paul on the road to Damascus (Acts 9:1–9; 22:6–11; Gal. 1:15–17). The resurrected Christ's direct appearance to Paul (1 Cor. 9:1; 15:8), along with the clear instructions that Christ relayed to Paul through Ananias (Acts 9:15–16; 22:14–15), had imprinted Paul's calling as an apostle deeply into his heart. Paul's self-perception as an apostle drove his discourse in Ephesians. He was determined to fulfill the calling that God had given him. Accordingly, Paul communicated as a servant (Eph. 3:7) and ambassador (Eph. 6:20) of the gospel, seeking to faithfully convey God's truth and wisdom to his readers. Paul hoped to help initiate his Gentile readers into life with Christ and integrate them into a unified family made up of both Jews and Gentiles.

PLACE OF WRITING

Paul specified that he was in prison at the time he wrote Ephesians. Paul had been imprisoned because of his allegiance to Christ (3:1; 4:1), but we know little else about his confinement from Ephesians alone. Paul promised that his colleague Tychicus would update his readers on more of the details when he visited them (6:21–22). Governors were supposed to use incarceration for temporary confinement, not as a permanent punishment, so Paul would have faced either eventual release or a sentence drawn from a range of punishments (Cod. justin, 48.19.6–8). Extrabiblical sources described varying degrees of severity in prison conditions. While Paul's imprisonment was certainly on his mind, he did not seem particularly distressed by it, which suggests an environment similar to the house arrest in Rome that was recounted in Acts 28. This leads us to the likely date the letter was written.

DATE OF WRITING

Paul probably wrote Ephesians in the early 60s, while he was under house arrest in Rome for two years (Acts 28:16, 30). Paul had been arrested previously in Jerusalem, transferred to Caesarea, and held there for two years (Acts 24:27). After a harrowing journey by sea to Italy, Paul had reached Rome and had been stationed there at the time when the book of Acts ended. Assuming that Paul wrote Ephesians during this first Roman imprisonment, it was in the wake of more instances of Jewish rejection of the gospel and further outreach to the Gentiles (Acts 28:23–31). The circumstances of Paul's confinement according to both Acts 28 and Ephesians were vague, but reading between the lines, neither account suggested a physically taxing or emotionally exhausting ordeal. The tone was similar in both accounts, resembling also the accounts in Colossians and Philemon, which were also written during Paul's first Roman incarceration. Because of reports of a devastating earthquake in Colossae in A.D. 61, we can infer that Colossians was written no later than that date. If Colossians was written shortly before Ephesians, a date of A.D. 60 or 61 for Ephesians is most likely.

Paul's House-Arrest Letters

Ephesians, Colossians, Philemon, and possibly Philippians were likely written during Paul's first imprisonment in Rome.[5] The letters each addressed a slightly different issue and advanced a distinct theme as a result:

Letter	Issue Addressed	Theme
Ephesians	The place of Jews and Gentiles in God's eternal plans	One new humanity in Christ
Colossians	Syncretism (mixing other religious ideas with Christ)	The supremacy of Christ
Philemon	A strained relationship between a master and slave	Relational reconciliation
Philippians	Concerns over Paul's imprisonment	Joy in the gospel's advance

At this time in early church history, believers had been wrestling with the question about Gentile inclusion in the family of God for several decades. Peter's initial inroads into non-Jewish communities had paved the way for Paul's Gentile-focused ministry. The success of this ministry had brought with it considerable controversy, requiring multiple efforts to find common ground (cf. Gal. 2:1–10; Acts 15:1–21). The predominantly Jewish church was undergoing a massive paradigm shift in those early days. They had been prompted by God to leave behind old notions about clean and unclean and learn to embrace "unclean" Gentile believers in Christ as fully legitimate in the eyes of God. Though the Jerusalem Council (Acts 15:1–30) had marked a major turning point in the official position of the early church, Paul continued to guide churches in the practical implementation of this unity and equal status in God's sight. Paul's letter to the Romans, written just a few years before Ephesians, represented his most comprehensive views to date on God's dealings with Jews and Gentiles. Ephesians mirrors many of Paul's conclusions from Romans on this topic, though without spending so much time arguing about the role of the Law in God's saving plans. Instead, Paul presented the readers of Ephesians with a captivating vision of a unified church within God's grand plans for the world.

ORIGINAL READERS

The identity of Paul's original readers may seem quite straightforward, since the title and first verse of the letter identify the Ephesians as recipients. But there are good reasons to believe that the Ephesians were not the sole recipients of the letter. Believers after the time of Paul likely added titles to all of Paul's letters, so the title itself does not confirm the identity of the recipients. Furthermore, in what is distinct among Paul's letters, a scribe copying the letter may have inserted the reference to Ephesus in Ephesians 1:1. Some of the earliest surviving Greek copies of Ephesians omit the words "in Ephesus" (ἐν Ἐφέσῳ) in Ephesians 1:1. In other words, those manuscripts record that Paul simply wrote to "the saints." This evidence suggests that Paul himself did not address the letter to the Ephesians specifically. It is true that scribes who copied biblical manuscripts did sometimes make copying mistakes, so an early scribe may have accidently omitted a reference to the Ephesians that Paul had originally included. More likely, though, a scribe added the words after the fact, perhaps to make the letter conform more closely to what Paul wrote in other letters, which all included specific names of cities or people in the opening verses. That would mean that Paul had intended to omit a place name when he wrote the letter. But why would he do so?

Ruins of Laodicea. Courtesy of Greg MaGee.

There is a reasonable theory that accounts for both the manuscript evidence and the tone of the letter. If we look at Colossians, which we contend was written around the same time as Ephesians, we can see some indications that

1 There are some indications that Philippians was written during an earlier period of Paul's ministry, perhaps shortly before he wrote 2 Corinthians, while he was imprisoned in in Asia Minor (cf. 2 Cor 1:8–9). The tone of Acts 28, Colossians, Philemon, and Ephesians also diverges somewhat from the circumstances detailed in Philippians.

Paul had been thinking about expanding the distribution of his letters beyond churches in single cities. Paul had instructed the churches of Colossae and Laodicea to exchange letters (Col. 4:16). Paul had also seemed to think of believers from three neighboring cities—Colossae, Laodicea, and Hierapolis—as part of one larger, regional ministry (Col. 4:13–15; cf. 2:1). With Ephesians, Paul may have chosen to write a letter that was suitable for readers from multiple cities, consisting of believers both familiar and unfamiliar to him. Paul refrained from addressing specific churches to keep his letter applicable to as many congregations as possible. He likewise bypassed greeting or otherwise naming specific individuals, which contributed to the relatively impersonal tone throughout the letter. At some point early in the copying process, a scribe, inspired by Paul's convention of including a specific addressee, chose to add "in Ephesus" because of the prominence of the city or the presence of an actual copy of the letter in the church there.

If Ephesians was not written to Ephesus alone, how do we identify the other recipients with any confidence? Acts depicted Paul's initial ministry in Ephesus as extending throughout "the province of Asia" (19:1, 22, 26; 20:18; cf. 21:27; 24:18; 2 Cor. 1:8). Ephesus was the largest city in the area (Strabo, *Geogr.* 14.1.24) and served as Paul's base of operations in the province of Asia. This Roman province was situated in the western part of Asia Minor, or modern-day Turkey.[2] Even early on, Paul mentioned multiple churches in Asia Minor in his greetings to the Corinthians (1 Cor. 16:19). The comparable spiritual backgrounds detected in Ephesians and Colossians, which was addressed to a city also in Asia Minor, suggests that the recipients lived in similar environments. The grouping of seven cities from Asia Minor in Revelation invites us to think of this wider circle of churches in Asia Minor as a unit as well. It seems plausible that Paul would have wanted to write a letter that served the needs of all known churches in that province. Possible recipients included the churches of Ephesus, Pergamum, Smyrna, Sardis, Laodicea, and Hierapolis.

HISTORICAL SETTING AND OCCASION FOR WRITING

Paul wrote to believers from a geographical area that he had invested in deeply. Paul had spent approximately three years in Asia Minor, headquartered in Ephesus (Acts 19:1–41; 20:13–38). The region was known for its diversity of peoples and beliefs, loyalty to Rome and its leaders, and beliefs marked by pervasive spiritual activity and visible manifestation of spiritual power, even among the Jewish community there. In spite of the politically ambitious and spiritually unpredictable environment in Asia Minor, gatherings of believers in Christ had sprouted up and begun to flourish. Even as they had experienced the grace and power of God, they still faced great obstacles both externally and internally. They had to learn to establish roots in the Lord Jesus Christ, resisting the pull back into their spiritual

2 This commentary will typically refer to the Roman province of Asia as "Asia Minor," even though the two designations are not always used equivalently, in order to distinguish it from the full modern continent of Asia.

pasts or the ongoing distractions of a pluralistic world. They also faced the challenge of growing together as a unified church made up of both Jews and Gentiles. There was a lot riding on this grand experiment of diverse peoples finding one common identity in Jesus Christ.

From historical sources we know that cities in Rome's province of Asia Minor such as Ephesus and Hierapolis were eager to build a reputation for loyalty to Rome through their propagation of the imperial cult (for description of specific archaeological evidence for the imperial cult in Ephesus, see Miller, 2010, 326–27). The imperial cult was a complex phenomenon that was influenced by practices in Egypt and then evolved from the time of Alexander the Great to Julius Caesar and the emperors that followed him. The imperial cult consisted of efforts to uphold and cultivate an empire-wide allegiance to Rome. Out of gratitude for the peace, order, and prosperity they experienced, people throughout the empire honored Rome and its leaders with expressions of loyalty and devotion, and they recognized the touch of the divine in Rome's history and leaders. The best architects, artists, and poets built temples, created statues, and composed poems in honor of Rome's leaders, and cities carved out special days in the calendar for festivals (Horsley, 1997, 11–13). Typically, living emperors were coy about welcoming overt worship or reverence for their divinely inspired leadership, but dead emperors were immediately counted among the gods and goddesses in stature. Some cities in Asia Minor promoted the imperial cult and displayed their respect for political power in doing so (Arnold, 1992, 37–38; Ferguson, 2003, 85, 202, 208, 211; Schnabel, 2004, 1207–1209).

Political power was not the only form of power admired and coveted. Asia Minor was known for its fascination with spiritual power and its manifestations. Studies of the region have demonstrated the pervasiveness of spiritual activity in the form of magic, incantations, divination, and more traditional rituals directed to regional deities and the Greek and Roman gods and goddesses (Arnold, 1992, 14–20; Schnabel, 2004, 1221–1222).

Worship of Gods and Goddesses in Asia Minor

The people of Asia Minor worshipped many gods and goddesses, from regional deities to the famous major Greek gods and goddesses. Some of the classical gods and goddesses were more prominent than others in Ephesus the surrounding area (Rives, 2007, 55–56), and the Greek and Roman names and roles of these most popular deities are listed in the table below.

Popular Greco-Roman Gods and Goddesses in Asia Minor

Greek name	Roman name	Role
Zeus	Jupiter	King of the Gods
Hera	Juno	Goddess of Marriage
Poseidon	Neptune	God of the Sea
Apollo	Apollo	God of Archery, Music, and Medicine
Artemis	Diana	Goddess of the Hunt
Athena	Minerva	Goddess of Wisdom
Aphrodite	Venus	Goddess of Love and Desire
Demeter	Ceres	Goddess of the Harvest
Dionysus	Bacchus	God of Wine

The mysterious workings of the supernatural realm both fascinated and intimidated many inhabitants of the area (cf. Acts 19:13–20), and the people harnessed supernatural power for their own benefit (Ferguson, 2003, 173–74, 213). Magical practices and astrological beliefs probably merged with devotion to the goddess Artemis, whose splendid and expansive marble temple adorned Ephesus (Arnold, 1992, 20–24, 28–29; cf. Acts 19:23–41). The stunning temple of Artemis, one of the seven wonders of the ancient world, was the pride of the region. Elaborate worship of Artemis included animal sacrifice, votive offerings, and festivals, and she was honored above the many deities that attracted followings in Ephesus and the surrounding region (Schnabel, 2004, 1211–14). Paul's Gentile readers in particular had grown up within this spiritually active but misguided environment.

Artemis of the Ephesians

Artemis, the goddess of the hunt, daughter of Zeus and Leto, and twin sister of Apollo, functioned as the patron deity of Ephesus and the surrounding region. Her name and reputation was central to the civic and religious identity of the people in the region. Her significance to the region was attested by the massive temple where she was venerated, the appearance of her image on many coins from the area, and the yearly festivals held in her honor (Rives, 2007, 108–10). Artemis had the reputation of goodness to her devotees and being responsive to their entreaties (Trebilco, 2004, 21). Her followers also relied on her unrivaled spiritual power and authority as a safe haven from other supernatural forces that they believed threatened them (Arnold, 1992, 21). She was known by various lofty titles (such as "Savior" and "Queen of the Cosmos") that paid homage to her transcendent power in the spiritual realm (Trebilco, 2004, 22).

Major cities in the Roman province of Asia Minor had significant Jewish populations. The

Statue of Caesar Augustus, in Corinth.
Courtesy of Greg MaGee.

Diaspora, or dispersion, of the Jews that had begun in OT times under Assyrian and Babylonian rule had eventually brought Jews to Asia Minor. There, they had gained allowances to worship Yahweh and follow traditional Jewish practices (cf. Josephus, *Ant.* 12.119–128; 14.223–227). The Jews of the Diaspora maintained and cultivated their distinct identity and loyalty to Yahweh through regular gatherings at synagogues and celebration of Jewish festivals (Barclay, 2011, 118–19). Texts from the OT Scriptures and Jewish literature from the Second Temple period (from the Apocrypha, Pseudepigrapha, or Dead Sea Scrolls) continued to shape their beliefs, practices, and attitudes.

The monotheistic practices of Jewish residents of Asia Minor kept them out of step with the surrounding culture, and this had sometimes

Ruins of the Temple of Artemis.
Courtesy of Greg MaGee.

led to trouble with Roman officials (Barclay, 1996, 269–74). The Jews at least had the benefit of a long history, which gave them some credibility to outsiders and insulation from harassment. The Jews of the Diaspora sought to remain faithful to Yahweh, but they also adopted some Greek customs and mindsets due to their interactions with broader Greek culture. There are also indications that some Jews in Asia Minor had developed syncretistic religious beliefs and practices, conforming to the broader spiritual atmosphere of the region (Arnold, 1992, 31–34; Arnold, 2012, 9–20). Jews from Asia Minor were among those who opposed Stephen early on in the growth of the church (Acts 6:9).

This historical evidence about the political and religious landscape concurs with the data found in Acts 19–20. In Paul's original visit to Ephesus and the rest of Asia, Luke reported that Paul's team initiated contact with both Jews and Greeks (Acts 19:8–10). Paul spread the gospel throughout the region and saw God work wondrous miracles through his team (19:11–12). They also encountered Jewish exorcists who were rebuked and overwhelmed by demons when they had tried to cast out demons in Jesus's name (19:13–16). This event led many to publicly repent and denounce their practice of sorcery by burning valuable incantation scrolls (19:17–19). A progress report at this point summed up the gospel's power in a region in which power (political and spiritual) had great currency: "In this way the word of the Lord spread widely and grew in power" (Acts 19:20 NIV).

God's powerful work in the region also met with strenuous opposition. Some Jews rejected Paul's gospel and plotted against his ministry (Acts 19:9; 20:19). Jews from Asia Minor later led the way in having Paul arrested in Jerusalem and incarcerated for years in Caesarea and Rome (Acts 21:27–28; 24:18–19). Trouble also arose from the non-Jews when people who had been impacted by the gospel stopped buying shrines to the goddess Artemis (19:23–41). This threatened the honor of Artemis and struck a blow to the region's civic pride, and a riot in Ephesus broke out as a result. The riot may have been the most memorable disruption during Paul's ministry in Asia Minor, but his brief but frank comments about severe trials in Asia Minor (2 Cor. 1:8–10) further corroborated the picture of heated opposition to the message and power of Christ in the region of Asia Minor (cf. Rom 16:3–4; Schnabel, 2004, 1222).

When Paul initially planted churches in Ephesus and elsewhere in Asia Minor he viewed

Theater in Ephesus, Site of Riot
Sparked by Paul's Ministry. Courtesy of Greg MaGee.

the area as fertile but contested ground spiritually. He spent an extended length of time in the region because he saw the spiritual door that God had opened there (1 Cor. 16:8–9). But according to the same verses, he also realistically appraised the potency of the opposition there. And as a spiritually attuned believer, Paul discerned that both the open door and the opposition consisted of stronger spiritual forces at work. Paul put this spiritually sensitive worldview on display in the book of Ephesians.

A close reading of Ephesians and its companion letter, Colossians, suggests that the spiritual dynamics witnessed in the region did not change much in the years that followed Paul's ministry there, though the intensity of opposition to the gospel may have subsided some. Paul stressed the authority of Christ Jesus over all powers in both letters. The false teachers who were targeted in Colossians displayed syncretistic tendencies that included the desire to manipulate the spiritual realm and find protection against malevolent spiritual powers (Arnold, 1996, 228–44). Ephesians recognized the reality of spiritual forces in the heavenly realms and gave extensive guidance on being equipped for spiritual battle. Paul also warned against entanglements with pagan values and practices in Ephesians (4:17–19; 5:8–16), which was a particular danger for the large portion of the letter's Gentile recipients, since they had emerged from this context (2:1–3).

Through Paul's ministry, God had raised up house churches in the region of Asia Minor, in spite of the challenges of opposition and the diverse backgrounds among the believers there. Socially and organizationally, the churches Paul addressed in Ephesians were small house churches that were becoming integrated into a wider network of churches in the region and even in the whole Roman world (Meeks, 1983, 190). Many of the readers were Gentiles (Eph. 2:11). They were in the process of loosening old allegiances and becoming connected to other believers in Christ as a new body. They were still learning how to be churches in which Jewish and Gentile believers in Christ Jesus saw each other as equals and family members. They faced the challenge of growing as a unified church against opposition from both Jews and Gentiles (cf. Acts 19). The readers of Ephesians needed clear reminders that God was on the move, carrying out his perfect plans in Christ. Paul encouraged his readers to find safe harbor in Christ as they awaited the day when all spiritual forces would be unmasked as powerless. Paul wanted the readers to rely on God together, as unified churches of Jews and Gentiles that previewed the final gathering of believers from all tribes and nations under Christ's leadership (Eph. 1:9–10; Rev. 7:9–10). This leads us to some of the central themes Paul advances in Ephesians.

THEOLOGICAL THEMES

Being United in Christ

Phrases such as "in Christ," "in him," "in the Lord," or its equivalents are peppered throughout the letter. These phrases are part of the fabric of Ephesians, especially in the first three chapters, and they are central to the logic of the letter. In Christ Jesus, believers experience the full range of God's blessings for his children. God applies his saving love to sinners in need of grace in the person of Jesus Christ. It is because God's people are united with Christ, through faith, that they have relational access to God and enjoy all of the benefits of being his children. Christ's sacrificial and effective work draws believers into deep union with him, and thus deep communion with Father, Son, and Spirit. Believers grow into their refashioned identity, with Christ at the center. That means that Christ is now the determining factor for the believer's new identity and for the church's corporate experience. Believers' identity and destiny are now wrapped up in the identity and destiny of Christ Jesus. The truth of believers' union with Christ is a rich doctrine that undergirds many of Paul's letters but is never so sharply on display as it is in Ephesians.

The reality that all believers are united in Jesus Christ is the key to believers' unity with one another. All believers benefit equally from God's gracious gift of Christ. Through faith believers are received into the body of Christ and become a holy temple where God dwells by his Spirit (2:18–22). They live in loving fellowship with Father, Son, and Spirit, as well as with each other. In addition to the compact "in Christ" language, one other grammatical feature drives these truths home in a succinct way. The versatile "co-" prefix (- prefix) is attached to verbs and nouns to communicate an idea of "together with." Individual believers are thus made alive "together with" Christ, raised "together with" Christ, and seated "together with" Christ (2:5–6), sharing in his exalted glory. Whether Jew or Gentile, believers are citizens (of God's kingdom) "together with" other believers, joined "together with" each other in Christ, and built "together with" one another in Christ (2:19–22; 4:16). As a reiteration of these points, Ephesians highlights that Gentiles (alongside Jewish believers) are heirs "together with" them, have become one body "together with" them, and are sharers "together with" them of God's fulfilled promise in Christ Jesus (3:6). Believers thus share in Christ's divine life through their union with him but also share in one another's experience as well.

Walking in Christ

Ephesians presents believers' new existence of being united with Christ as the gateway to an ongoing life of walking with Christ. The word "walk" (περιπατέω) surfaces on multiple occasions throughout the letter (2:2, 10; 4:1, 17; 5:2, 8, 15). The image connotes a distinct gait by which a person's life is recognized. Sometimes that gait resembles the steps of the world (2:2), or of lost and misguided people who do not know the Lord (4:17), or of the unwise (5:15). Those who have been reconciled to God and made new in Christ, however, are called to conform to a better way. The letter exhorts Christians to walk wisely (5:15) and in a way that is consistent with their new identity as children of light (5:8). They should stride wholeheartedly into the good works God has already placed in their paths (2:10).

A believer's life should be marked by love (5:2) and holiness (4:17; 5:8) in particular. First, in keeping with the teachings of the OT and Jesus, Ephesians commends love as the most crucial Christian virtue. The letter paints a picture of believers receiving and then sharing the abundant love and forgiveness of Christ (4:32; 5:2). They must internalize Christ's love for them in the deepest recesses of their hearts (3:16–19). This love then overflows to others within the church and within families (5:25–33). The exhortation to love one another fits well with the letter's emphasis on the corporate life of the church. Believers are not called to walk with God in isolation but as part of the growing and mutually supporting body of Christ (4:1–16). Love must mark the corporate life of the church (4:15–16).

Second, believers must live in holiness. They embrace their identity in Christ by putting off their old ways and living as a new creation in Christ Jesus. Many of Paul's readers had emerged out of Gentile backgrounds, wandering in darkness and being enslaved to sinful desires (2:1–3; 4:17–19; 5:3–7). God had now chosen them for something better—holiness and blamelessness (1:4; 5:27). These believers, and others who followed after them, comprise a holy temple in which God dwells (2:21–22). God has already made believers new and holy in Christ, so they are ready to grow into their status as God's holy people. This process of growth requires consistent habits of putting off their old selves and embracing their new identity in Christ, which has been designed for righteousness and holiness (4:20–24). This theoretical transformation could then be applied to any number of specific, practical areas of daily living (4:25–5:2). Believers need wisdom for being God's holy people in a distorted world (5:15–17). The letter thus highlights prayer as a crucial tool for living wisely (6:18–20), and Paul even prayed on two occasions for his readers (1:15–23; 3:14–21).

Christ's Authority in Heaven and Earth

Ephesians highlights Jesus Christ's authority and reign. His authority is cosmic, prevailing over all rulers in "the heavenly places" and on earth. The distinction between the heavenly places and the visible world is important in Ephesians. Christ's supremacy is a settled fact in the heavenly places, but the world awaits the full, visible expression of his reign. He occupies a position of supreme authority in the heavenly places, over all rulers and powers (1:20–22). Because believers are united with Jesus, they too are raised and seated in the heavenly places (2:6). Correspondingly, Ephesians affirms that believers have already received every spiritual blessing in the heavenly realms (1:3).

In the future, Christ Jesus will assume his comprehensive rule over the entire visible world as well. The letter makes this end goal clear at the beginning of the letter when it reveals that God's plan is to restore everything in Christ, reordering things both in heaven and on earth under his reign (1:9–10). But until then God puts his reconciled and unified church on display to the rulers and authorities of the heavenly places, as a sneak preview of God's cosmic work of reconciliation (3:10). This church, made up of Jews and Gentiles who have been reconciled together to God and made one in Christ (2:13–18), works to preserve the unity that Christ has secured for them (4:1–6). As Christ's unified body, they grow in maturity (4:11–16) and partake in Christ's power for daily living (1:19) and for their struggle against forces in the heavenly places that oppose them (6:12). In other words, the church is given the resources they need to function as "exhibit A" of what it looks like to be remade and governed by the exalted Christ.

Sit, Walk, Stand

One memorable way to remember how these themes work together is through the images of "sit" (καθίζω) "walk" (περιπατέω) and "stand" (ἵστημι). Believers, through their union with Christ, share in Christ's position at the right hand of God. Followers of Jesus are thus seated in the heavenly places, in Christ (Eph. 2:6). Everything about believers' identity in Christ should shape the way they walk as well. This walk should reflect believers' inspiring calling as God's holy and dearly loved children (Eph. 4:1; 5:1). In the face of estrangement in a world of darkness and inevitable opposition by spiritual forces of evil, believers can stand strong in the divine resources that Christ supplies (Eph. 6:10–12). Christ's saving ministry affects everything about their identity, way of life, and success in mission.

STRUCTURE AND ARGUMENT

In a rough sense, Ephesians begins with three chapters on doctrine and concludes with three chapters on practice. While this is true generally, Paul tended to interweave doctrine and practice throughout the letter, showing the desired outcome of right belief in various places in chapters 1–3, and grounding good praxis in sound theology in chapters 4–6.

Determining Paul's argument in Ephesians requires careful attention to Paul's agenda for each section. Speech-act theory prods us to look beyond the bare meaning of language to inquire about the intended effects of the language. Authors and speakers communicate with various purposes in mind, including to inspire, challenge, rebuke, and inform. Passages such as Isaiah 55:10–11 and 2 Timothy 3:16–17 display the reality of God's purposeful use of communication to shape and transform his people. Paul's carefully crafted discourse in his letters often reinforced believers' identity and trained believers in worship and obedience. Interpreters of Ephesians should show basic sensitivity to speech-act dynamics by always asking the "why" question as a follow-up to the "what" question. In other words, what

Paul said is only part of the story. Why he said it (for what purpose) is often the key to discerning the direction of the discourse.

In the first two chapters of Ephesians, Paul sought to reinforce the reality of his readers' calling by God and their unity and shared identity in Christ. In chapter 1, Paul's lengthy blessing (*berakah*) and prayer marveled at God's gracious, saving work and Christ's authority in the present age and the age to come. In chapter 2, Paul conveyed the doctrinal truths of how sinners became reconciled to God and reconciled to other believers. In chapter 3, Paul's goal was to clarify his God-given platform to instruct them and to affirm his commitment to their best interests. He did this by revisiting his apostolic calling and purpose before offering his second heartfelt prayer for them. Chapters 4–6 were written with the purpose of inspiring believers with a vision for corporate church life that flowed from their new identity in Christ. In these three chapters, Paul consistently supported his instructions with theological reasoning. The instructions covered corporate life, distinctive Christian conduct, responsibilities in household relationships (in the form of a so-called household code), and being equipped for spiritual battle. Paul concluded the letter with an introduction to Tychicus, the letter carrier, and brief greetings.

OUTLINE

APPLAUDING AND APPRECIATING BELIEVERS' RICHES IN CHRIST JESUS (1:1–23)

- Applauding God's Plan to Bless Believers in Christ (1:1–14)
- Knowing God by Appreciating His Hope, Inheritance, and Power (1:15–23)

GOD GIVES NEW LIFE AND RECONCILIATION IN CHRIST JESUS (2:1–22)

- God's Gracious Gift of New Life in Christ for Sinners (2:1–10)
- Christ Reconciles Sinners to God and to Each Other (2:11–22)

SUFFERING FOR THE GOSPEL AND PRAYING FOR GOD'S PEOPLE (3:1–21)

- Suffering for a Great Cause (3:1–13)
- A Prayer to Experience God's Power and Love (3:14–21)

WALK IN UNITY, A NEW IDENTITY, LOVE, AND LIGHT (4:1–5:14)

- United in Christ, Equipped to Grow Together (4:1–16)
- A New Identity Brings New Practices (4:17–5:2)
- Shine Christ's Light in a Dark World (5:3–14)

SPIRIT-FILLED RELATIONSHIPS AND DIVINE RESOURCES FOR SPIRITUAL BATTLE (5:15–6:24)

- Strategic and Spirit-filled Living (5:15–21)
- Marriages That Reflect the Union of Christ and the Church (5:22–33)
- Honoring the Lord in Household Relationships (6:1–9)
- Equipped in Christ for Spiritual Battle (6:10–24)

FOR FURTHER READING

Arnold, Clinton E. 1992. *Power and Magic: The Concept of Power in Ephesians*. Grand Rapids: Eerdmans, 1992.

Ferguson, Everett. 2003. *Backgrounds of Early Christianity*. 3rd ed. Grand Rapids: Eerdmans.

Ridderbos, Herman. 1975. *Paul: An Outline of His Theology*. Translated by John R. De-Witt. Grand Rapids: Eerdmans.

Schreiner, Thomas R. 2001. *Paul, Apostle of God's Glory in Christ*. Downers Grove, IL: InterVarsity.

Wilson, Mark. 2012. *Biblical Turkey: A Guide to the Jewish and Christian Sites of Asia Minor*. Istanbul: Ege Yayinlari.

APPLAUDING AND APPRECIATING BELIEVERS' RICHES IN CHRIST JESUS (1:1–23)

In Paul's first chapter in Ephesians, he turned his readers' gaze to God and his generosity toward his people. After a brief greeting (1:1–2), Paul unfolded God's eternal plans to bless believers through the Son and by the Spirit (1:3–14). In three places in the passage, Paul called for a fitting and wholehearted response to God's grace and majesty. He then proceeded to pray that his readers would grasp the riches of their hope, inheritance, and power in Christ (1:15–23). This chapter reveals Paul's own vibrant life of praise and prayer, and it opens up the potential for readers to experience a similar wonder and appreciation of their heritage in Christ.

This major section, Applauding and Appreciating Believers' Riches in Christ Jesus (1:1–23), contains two preaching units: "Applauding God's Plan to Bless Believers in Christ (1:1–14)" and "Knowing God by Appreciating His Hope, Power, and Inheritance (1:15–23)."[1]

---

1 A "For Further Reading" section is included at the end of each major section of this book. There, readers will find both scholarly and popular works related to the passages covered in that section.

Ephesians 1:1–14

EXEGETICAL IDEA
Paul gave accolades to God for having blessed Jews and Gentiles thoroughly in Christ by choosing and adopting them, redeeming them, and giving them his Spirit, as he prepared to restore all things in Christ.

THEOLOGICAL FOCUS
God deserves our applause for his works in Christ and by the Spirit to bless believers and restore the world.

PREACHING IDEA
Let's applaud God for including us in his story.

PREACHING POINTERS
Paul and his readers lived in a diverse and complex world in which various stories—whether supplied by the Roman imperial cult, Greco-Roman gods and goddesses, Greek mythology, or Jewish tradition—vied to become sources of meaning for people's lives. Different rulers or patrons (those with wealth and clout who could help their less influential clients), gods and goddesses (such as Artemis of the Ephesians; Acts 19:23–41), and mythic heroes (such as Castor and Pollux, the twin sons of Zeus; cf. Acts 28:11) competed for people's loyalty in the Gentile world. Jewish people could look to past paragons of faith in the OT or to figures such the courageous Maccabean martyrs (2 Macc) to find deeper meaning in life. The house churches across Asia Minor lived in a Greco-Roman society where people of different cultural and religious backgrounds shared no common story and honored no single benefactor. Paul wanted his readers to know that, whether Jew or Gentile, they possessed a common heritage and fit as diverse individuals into a common "story" as beneficiaries of God's blessings in Christ. As a result, they could with one voice pay tribute to the God who had graciously extended these blessings to them in Christ Jesus.

Similar dynamics exist in many churches today. We live in a pluralistic society. Naturally, congregations are composed of men and women; young and old; Democrat, Republican, and Independent; and so forth, that mirror our pluralistic society. One person's hero is a theologian while another person's is a social activist. One may watch conservative news and another favors a moderate or broad-minded news program. There may be young people who favor gun control, and others who may not. Is there one story that unites them? Yes, the story of God's plan to save his people. Is there one hero we all acknowledge? Yes, our triune God, so let's applaud him for including us in his story.

APPLAUDING GOD'S PLAN TO BLESS BELIEVERS IN CHRIST (1:1–14)

LITERARY STRUCTURE AND THEMES (1:1–14)

This section consists of typical greetings in 1:1–2 and then a quite atypical extended section of theological reflection in 1:3–14. This extended section of praise has been classified as a eulogy or the Jewish *berakah* (from the Hebrew word for blessing), in which the author extols the greatness and beauty of God. In this case, Paul's focus of praise was God and his saving plans, orchestrated by the Father, experienced in the Son, and unleashed by the Spirit. First, Paul the apostle greeted fellow believers, in Christ Jesus (1:1–2). Then, as an introduction to the rest of the passage, Paul blessed God for blessing believers with wonderful blessings in Christ (1:3). Paul's readers were chosen and adopted into God's family (1:4–6). They were also redeemed and forgiven through Christ's sacrifice and entrusted with knowledge about God's cosmic plans (1:7–10). Finally, they were selected to belong to God's story and family and marked by the Spirit for the present and future privileges that accompanied being incorporated into God's people (1:11–14).

Paul moved seamlessly (both grammatically and conceptually) from topic to topic. The exact logic of the grammatical connections between each verse, and even within some verses, should not be pursued too rigidly. The rhetorical power in the passage is in the overall effect of the collection and repetition of related topics in tight proximity. This is one passage where readers will not want to lose the forest for the trees.

- ***Paul's Greeting to Fellow Believers, in Christ (1:1–2)***
- ***God Deserves Accolades for Blessing Paul's Readers (1:3)***
- ***God Has Blessed Believers by Including Them in His Family (1:4–6)***
- ***God Has Redeemed Believers and Promised to Restore All Things in Christ (1:7–10)***
- ***Both Jews and Gentiles Belong to God and Have Been Given God's Spirit (1:11–14)***

EXPOSITION (1:1–14)

Paul wrote this section of his letter to direct his readers' awe, admiration, and praise to God. In the readers' world, people looked to various divine and human figures as objects of their wonder and praise. In particular, Artemis of the Ephesians, whose magnificent temple and image was thought to have fallen from heaven (Acts 19:35), promised to provide the people of Asia Minor greater meaning and purpose in life (Acts 19:27–28). But while Artemis and other larger-than-life figures inspired great devotion, the only one who deserved the readers' ultimate praise and loyalty was the God who had touched every important aspect of their lives and every significant era of history. In this passage Paul demonstrated that all spiritual blessings—from the personal blessings enjoyed by the believing Jews and Gentiles of that time to the cosmic blessings that would touch the entire created order—flowed from God through the person and work of Jesus Christ and by the action of the Holy Spirit. All of this would bring glory to God and ignite believers' praise to him.

Paul's Greeting to Fellow Believers, in Christ (1:1–2)

As an apostle, Paul addressed his readers while also recalling the grace, peace, and relationship with God that he and his readers shared.

1:1. Paul's opening self-description to his readers was similar to those found in other letters.[1] He identified himself as an "apostle of Christ Jesus" (ἀπόστολος Χριστοῦ Ἰησοῦ) and recognized that this calling came "through the will of God" (διὰ θελήματος θεοῦ). Paul did not write simply as one believer to others. He wrote specifically as an apostle of Christ Jesus. Apostles in early Christianity were the authoritative witnesses to the resurrected Christ (1 Cor. 15:3–11). They proclaimed the good news (gospel) of Christ and guarded the integrity of that message among the early churches. Paul, who had become an apostle in a unique way at a later time, nonetheless took his task of testifying about Christ with single-minded seriousness. When Paul addressed the recipients of this letter, he did so consciously and intentionally as an apostle, or one of Christ's official spokespersons. Paul's conversion and calling story always loomed large in his mind, and this was reflected in his acknowledgment of God's will. He remembered that he didn't choose Jesus (in fact, he had opposed him!) but that Jesus had dramatically chosen him, Paul, on the road to Damascus (Acts 9:1–19; Gal. 1:11–17).

In verse 1, Paul addressed the recipients, most of whom he had never met, as "saints" or "holy ones" (ἅγιοι). This was his preferred way of referring to his readers (or those who would hear the letter being read) throughout the letter. The designation was familiar from many of Paul's other letters and also fit well with the emphasis in Ephesians on both Jewish and Gentile believers being chosen and marked for heavenly blessings in Christ. Paul greeted his Gentile readers in particular as saints, in spite of their past alienation from a holy God (Eph. 2:11–12; 4:17–19) and immersion in idolatry (cf. 1 Thess. 1:9–10). Because of the work of Christ on their behalf, Paul now called them saints.

> *TRANSLATION ANALYSIS:* As mentioned in the introductory section of this book, the textual evidence suggests that "in Ephesus" was not part of the original letter. Paul probably penned this letter for multiple churches, rather than for the Ephesians specifically. Though major English translations include "in Ephesus" or something similar, many versions include a footnote (NIV, ESV, NASB, NRSV, CSB) or place "in Ephesus" in brackets (NET) to indicate that many early manuscripts did not include that phrase.

Paul affirmed these readers as "faithful" (πιστός) as well, which reflected Paul's emphasis on the important role of faith in the Christian life. Similar to "saints," the "faithful" designation reflected how God saw the readers, with a view toward what he called them to be in practice as well. More significantly, the readers were faithful *"in Christ Jesus"* (ἐν Χριστῷ Ἰησοῦ). They were deemed faithful because of their union with Christ Jesus. No theme is more prominent in the letter than the theme of God carrying out his saving plans *in Christ.* Paul's readers were not recipients of God's blessings from a distance. Rather, followers of Christ from both Jewish and Gentile backgrounds had been graciously drawn into God's love and presence in relational connection as Christ shared himself, especially through his sacrificial death, with them. Paul drew upon this idea of being united

1 Though there were different types of letters in antiquity, most followed a similar structure, especially at the beginning and end of the letter (cf. Stowers, 1986, 20; Gray, 2012, 70–78). The author began with an address, greetings, and perhaps a prayer or wish for the recipient's good health. The body of the letter followed, and then the author typically closed with a brief farewell and other well-wishes.

with Christ every time he mentioned believers being in Christ or in him (see Schnelle, 2003, 481–82; Campbell, 2012, 406–14).

1:2. Paul followed with his traditional greeting, as he extended affirmations of "grace" (χάρις) and "peace" (εἰρήνη) to his readers (ὑμῖν, "to you"). Grace and peace were part of the recipients' heritage because they were united with Christ. Paul noted that grace and peace came "from God our Father and the Lord Jesus Christ" (ἀπὸ θεοῦ πατρὸς ἡμῶν καὶ κυρίου Ἰησοῦ Χριστοῦ), thus giving proper credit for these blessings and preparing the way for an extended tribute to the Father and Son in 1:3–14.

God Deserves Accolades for Blessing Paul's Readers (1:3)

The magnitude and scope of God's spiritual blessings for believers, given in Christ, prompted Paul to declare God's blessedness.

1:3. Paul opened this section with the repeated idea of "blessing" (from the εὐλογέω word group). Paul blessed God because God had blessed believers with countless blessings. In a world filled with many gods, idols, and powerful rulers, God alone was worthy of Paul's readers' praise. Paul began by praising God: "Blessed be the God and Father of our Lord, Jesus Christ" (Εὐλογητὸς ὁ θεὸς καὶ πατὴρ τοῦ κυρίου ἡμῶν Ἰησοῦ Χριστοῦ). Paul credited God the Father with showering these blessings on believers, though the inclusion of "our Lord, Jesus Christ" indicated Jesus's centrality in securing these blessings as well. Paul distinguished between God the Father and Jesus the Lord but linked them in relationship (through the "Father" language) and in mission (in the rest of the passage). The title "Lord" previewed a theme in the letter—the exalted Christ possessed authority over the entire universe and all seen and unseen powers.

> **_Berakah:_ A Jewish Prayer Form**
>
> The appearance of "blessed" (εὐλογητός) in verse 3 recalled a number of other Jewish and Christian prayers that began similarly and applauded the greatness of God. These prayers are often classified as *berakoth* (singular, *berakah*), from the Hebrew word for "blessing" (which is typically translated as εὐλογητός in the Septuagint). These prayers surfaced in the OT and other Jewish literature as outbursts of praise, when the author, moved by the excellence of God, felt compelled to proclaim his praises (see examples in Gen. 24:27; Ruth 4:14; 1 Sam. 25:39; 2 Chron. 6:4; Ps. 72:18–19; Dan. 2:20–23). Paul and other Jews expressed the *berakah* as a form of verbal tribute to Yahweh, who had proven himself faithful and worthy of honor through his provisions and interventions for his people. The Jews incorporated these prayers into both personal and communal worship, and their use helped maintain a Godward focus in the people's lives (Kirby, 1968, 84–89; Thielman, 2010, 37–39). Speaking such prayers on a regular basis helped imprint the reality of God's gracious character and mighty acts on his people's hearts.

Paul further identified God as the one who had "blessed" (εὐλογήσας, aor. act. ptc.) Paul and his readers. The blessed God was the giver of blessings to his people. Paul grouped himself with his readers (ἡμᾶς, "us") as recipients of these blessings. Paul's vision of life in Christ was at the same time personally intimate and corporately shared. Paul continued to explore the theme of believers being one in Christ, whether Jew or Gentile, multiple times as the letter progressed.

> **A God Who Blesses**
>
> God's many ways of blessing his people with spiritual blessings fueled Paul's prayer of blessing to God. God's ability to bless flowed from his status as creator of all things and king over all

of his creation, meaning that he had unlimited resources at his disposal. His motivation to bless was rooted in his gracious character—"his pleasure and will" (1:5) or "riches of his grace" (1:7) or "good pleasure" (1:9)—and his determination to carry out his saving plans to a world alienated from him. Genesis 12:2–3 stated God's intention clearly: "I will bless you . . . and all peoples on earth will be blessed through you." God extended blessings to Abraham and his descendants, as part of his covenantal commitment. But he also specified his resolution to unleash blessings on all people through Abraham's family. Paul stated directly in Galatians 3:14 that through Christ Jesus, Abraham's descendant, God had fulfilled this promise to bless the Gentiles. In Ephesians 1:3–14, Paul pondered the full scope of those blessings for those who were united with Christ.

Paul made the audacious claim that God had blessed the readers *"with every"* (ἐν πάσῃ) spiritual blessing in Christ. Paul hinted at the logic of this bold pronouncement in the remainder of verse 3. First, these blessings were *"spiritual blessings"* (εὐλογίᾳ πνευματικῇ), not measurable advantages in worldly status or comfort. They were blessings overflowing from the presence of the Spirit in their lives (see Eph. 1:13–14; 2:18, 22; 3:16; 4:30). Second, the blessings were in some way situated and activated "in the heavenlies" or "in the heavenly places" (ἐν τοῖς ἐπουρανίοις). Later in the letter, Paul described how believers had already been united with Christ in God's heavenly domain (Eph. 2:6; cf. Eph. 1:20; 3:10; 6:12). Since this was the case, in a spiritual sense Paul's readers were already imbibing in the full range of blessings associated with being in perfect communion with God. Paul insisted that this was true even while believers were undergoing hardships (such as Paul's imprisonment) on earth. Believers were simultaneously living in the real world of a fallen existence and the perfection of heavenly intimacy with the Father, Son, and Spirit. Third and most important, it was because believers were *"in Christ"* (ἐν Χριστῷ) that they possessed the entirety of God's blessings. Being "in Christ" referred to the relational incorporation of Paul's readers into the life of Christ. The union with Christ that the readers experienced was their sole venue for partaking in God's blessings.

"In Christ" in Ephesians 1:1–14

Verse	Phrase	Significance
1:1	in Christ Jesus	Readers were faithful in Christ
1:3	in Christ	Readers were spiritually blessed in Christ
1:4	in him	Readers had been chosen in Christ
1:6	in the beloved	Readers had been given grace in Christ
1:7	in whom	Readers enjoyed redemption in Christ
1:9	in him	God's plans had been prearranged in Christ
1:10	in Christ, in him	God would bring all things together in Christ
1:11	in whom	Readers had been selected in Christ to belong to God
1:12	in Christ	Paul and other Jews had placed their hope in Christ
1:13	in whom (2x)	Readers had been sealed with the Spirit in Christ

God Has Blessed Believers by Including Them in His Family (1:4–6)

God's purposeful work of choosing believers to be in a holy relationship with him and adopting them through Christ into his family highlighted the excellence of his grace.

1:4. After announcing the scope of believers' blessings (1:3), Paul supported his announcement. He explained ("for," καθώς) the ways in which believers were blessed with every spiritual blessing in Christ. The main assertion of verse 4, that "[God] chose" (ἐξελέξατο) believers in Christ, was modified by three supporting ideas according to the following structure:

He chose us
  in him
  before the foundation of the world
  for us to be holy and blameless before
    him, in love

The language of God choosing, or of believers being chosen, was not unusual in Paul's letters (Rom. 8:33; 9:11; 11:5, 7, 28; 1 Cor. 1:27–28; Col. 3:12; 1 Thess. 1:4; 2 Tim. 2:10; Titus 1:1). Paul used this language to impress upon his readers the significance of their new identity in Christ.

Paul did not use the language of "choosing" with philosophical goals in mind, hoping to resolve the question of determinism and free will. He aimed instead at the process of identity formation among his believers when he used the language of election. His readers, many of whom were Gentiles who had emerged from a polytheistic worldview of raw idolatry (see 1 Thess. 1:9–10; Acts 19:17–19), in which the gods and spiritual powers seemed unpredictable (Schnabel, 2004, 621), needed to hear that they became inheritors of God's blessings not by accident but according to God's predetermined, perfect plans. Paul was indebted to OT concepts of election when he used this language. God created a special bond with the Jews, as his chosen people. He defined a relationship of faithfulness and love with them, and he appointed them for the holy task of representing his glory to the other nations of the world (Deut. 14:2 LXX; cf. Neh. 9:7; Isa. 14:1; Acts 13:17). Paul extended this idea of being chosen to anyone, Jew or Gentile, who was "in Christ."

Paul used the phrase "in him" (ἐν αὐτῷ) to refer to Christ. Some have surmised that the primary point was that God chose *Christ*, and thus those who were *in Christ* were likewise chosen (see M. Barth, 1974, 107–9). But rather than remove any emphasis on God choosing believers, Paul used the phrase "in him," along with the other modifiers that followed, to qualify what this election looked like. The readers were chosen because they were in Christ, for sure, but they were still chosen. Paul placed the two ideas comfortably beside one another (cf. Ridderbos, 1975, 347). With "in him," Paul specified that God's people were chosen in the context of their union with Christ.

Paul then expressed the time frame of believers' election ("before the foundation of the world"; πρὸ καταβολῆς κόσμου). Five times in the opening section of the letter Paul enlisted "pro-" (προ-) as either a preposition or prefix to describe God's work, portraying the stunning truth that God's plans for Paul's readers were rooted in eternity past. Nothing had happened by accident or as a last-minute response to the world's desperate situation. With the wording "before the foundation of the world" modifying "he chose us," Paul affirmed that on a personal level God had desired and planned for the readers' welfare all along.

Paul continued by indicating God's desired outcome for choosing believers (εἶναι, purpose inf., "to be"). God had resolved "for us to be holy and blameless" (εἶναι ἡμᾶς ἁγίους καὶ ἀμώμους). The word "holy" (ἁγιός), a cognate of "saints" (ἅγιοι), recalled Paul's opening description of his readers in verse 1. In his typical way, Paul envisioned his readers growing (in holiness) into what they had already become (saints). "Holy" (ἁγιός) and "blameless" (ἄμωμος) fit well together as a pair, and Paul used this same pairing again in Ephesians 5:27. God had chosen Paul's readers to be set apart exclusively for him (holy) and unmarred by moral defect (blameless). Paul planned to develop this outworking of faith and holy living later in the letter, but for the time being, he painted the picture of believers being brought into the magnificent presence of God. Together, these "holy and blameless" followers of Christ were presented "before him" (κατενώπιον αὐτοῦ) as a beautiful bride, before the one who had loved them and given himself for them (Eph. 5:25–26). With Ephesians 1:4, Paul anticipated a glorious future day when God's people would see him face-to-face (cf. 1 Cor. 1:8; 1 Thess. 3:13; 5:23). Paul's addition of "in love" (ἐν ἀγάπῃ) at the end of verse 4 completed the idea of a loving gathering between the God of the universe and his chosen people.

> *TRANSLATION ANALYSIS:* The placement of "in love" (ἐν ἀγάπῃ) is ambiguous in the Greek, leaving two main options. First, "in love" could modify "being holy and blameless before him" in verse 4 (NET, NRSV, CSB, NKJV, KJV). Second and less likely, "in love" could attach to material from verse 5, highlighting God's loving motivation for predestining believers (NIV, ESV, NASB). Something that supports linking "in love" to the believer standing before God (verse 4) is Paul's description of God's abundant supply of love in Christ to the believer in Ephesians 2:4–5, as well as the believer's ongoing immersion within the love of Christ in Ephesians 3:16–19.

1:5–6. Paul continued his careful work of identity construction for his readers by supplementing the main verb from verse 4 (ἐξελέξατο) with the further explanation, "for he predestined us" (beginning with the adv. ptc. προορίσας). Looking at verses 5–6 as a whole, Paul presented an initial action of God, accompanied by its motivation and result:

> For he predestined us for adoption to himself, through Jesus Christ (main action)
> according to the good pleasure of his will (motivation)
> to the praise of his glorious grace, which he gifted to us in the beloved (result).

The word for "predestined" (προορίζω) matched well with the other *"pro-"* prefixed terms in the passage. To predestine meant to determine a course of action in advance (BDAG, s.v. "προορίζω," p. 873). As with other words in the passage, Paul used the term for predestination to remind his readers of the forethought and wisdom God had demonstrated in his saving plans, along with his eternal care for them. God intended all along to bring them into a new family, composed of Jews and Gentiles, so that together they could be his special people (see Gen. 12:2–3).

Paul did not leave predestination lingering as an abstract concept. Paul's readers had been predestined *for* something, namely, "for adoption to God" (εἰς υἱοθεσίαν . . . εἰς αὐτόν). In other words, the readers had been adopted into God's family. "Adoption" (υἱοθεσία) powerfully captured what happened especially to Paul's Gentile readers when they had experienced God's saving grace. They were welcomed into a new family and given the privilege of addressing God as *Abba*, or Father (see Rom. 8:15; Gal. 4:6). The Father of "our Lord Jesus Christ" (Eph. 1:2) had become the Father of Paul's readers too. Throughout the Bible, being part of God's family was not considered automatic. It happened only through God's gracious action and a Spirit-enabled transfer of a person into God's family. God had delivered this gift of adoption "through Jesus Christ" (διὰ Ἰησοῦ Χριστοῦ), brief wording that alluded to the ministry of Jesus, especially the sacrificial work on the cross that Paul made explicit elsewhere in the letter (Eph. 1:7; 2:13, 16; 5:2, 25).

Adoption and Its Benefits

In the Roman world, adopted children were completely integrated into their new families, and any connection to a prior family was ended. The law recognized adopted children as fully belonging to the new family and enjoying the financial implications of this new relationship. The father typically paid off the adopted child's existing debts, and the law recognized the child as an heir (Lyall, 1969, 466). When Julius Caesar had adopted Octavian as his son, Octavian (later known as Caesar Augustus) became his primary heir. Paul took this basic Roman idea of adoption and set it within the framework of God's saving plans for the world (cf. Rom. 9:4; Ridderbos, 1975, 197–98). God had first chosen and adopted Israel (cf. Exod. 4:22; Isa. 1:2), had redeemed her from slavery in Egypt so that they could be his treasured possession, had provided for the provision of sins in the sacrificial system, had regularly revealed how he was running the "family business" (Amos 3:7; Heb. 1:1), and had promised them a great inheritance. These were all the things Paul included (Eph. 1:3–14) in his list of benefits that his readers now enjoyed in Christ, since they were now chosen and adopted by God. With the arrival of Christ Jesus, God opened up the possibility of adoption into his family to all people.

Paul then specified that God's motivation for adopting believers into his family was "according to the good pleasure of his will" (κατὰ τὴν εὐδοκίαν τοῦ θελήματος αὐτοῦ), or consistent with his benevolent and perfect will. God had chosen to bestow this gift freely and without being coerced in any way, provoked only by his generous character.

In verse 6, Paul presented the result of praise for God's excellent or glorious grace (εἰς ἔπαινον δόξης τῆς χάριτος αὐτοῦ, "unto the praise of his glorious grace"). "Glory" (δόξα) was a weighty spiritual term that highlighted the unsurpassed excellence of God's being and character. This was the first of three times Paul interrupted his contemplation of God's works to call forth a response of praise from recipients of God's grace (1:12, 14). Paul added that God's "grace" (χάριτος) was "graced," (ἐχαρίτωσεν), or gifted, to Paul's readers "in [God's] beloved" (ἐν τῷ ἠγαπημένῳ), Jesus. Paul used the two terms "grace" (χάριτος) and "love" (ἀγάπη) liberally in the letter. Paul insisted that God's saving plans could not be appreciated apart from them. Grace motivated God in all of his actions, and love overflowed—from God to Christ to believers—in the process. The phrase "in the beloved" (ἐν τῷ ἠγαπημένῳ), followed the familiar "in Christ" pattern that specified that Christ was the one in whom all God's blessings were realized.

God Has Redeemed Believers and Promised to Restore All Things in Christ (1:7–10)

Additional gracious and wise blessings that God gave Paul's readers included redemption and forgiveness of sins, along with the disclosure of his eternal and unfolding plans, aimed toward a final day when all things would be restored under Christ's reign.

1:7. Because Paul's readers were in Christ, the beloved (ἐν ᾧ, "in whom"), or because they were united with Christ through faith, they possessed the interrelated spiritual blessings of redemption and the forgiveness of sins (ἔχομεν τὴν ἀπολύτρωσιν . . . τὴν ἄφεσιν παραπτθμάτων; cf. Col. 1:14). Paul told his readers that they "have" (ἔχω) a claim on God's gracious redemption and forgiveness. Their full redemption, which included the resurrection of their bodies, would follow at the return of Christ (Rom. 8:23; Eph. 1:14; 4:30). With the spiritual blessing of "redemption" (ἀπολύτρωσις), Paul drew upon a word that meant release from slavery and being set free through payment of a ransom (BDAG, s.v. "ἀπολύτρωσις" 2a, p. 117; EDNT, 138, 2).

Redemption in Roman and Jewish Contexts

Paul's readers would have been well familiar with slavery and redemption, since slavery was pervasive in the Roman world. While masters could arrange for the release of their slaves after a period of successful service or upon the death of the master, a third party could also secure the release of a slave through a payment (Ferguson, 2003, 60–61; cf. Philem. 18). Even more than Roman slavery, Paul probably had the Jewish backdrop of redemption in mind when he chose this imagery. The Israelites had been redeemed from their slavery in Egypt when God had intervened on their behalf. This dramatic redemption from slavery in Egypt had required the shedding of the blood of the Passover lambs (Exod. 12:22–27; cf. Wright, 2013, 730). But because of sin and covenantal unfaithfulness, Israel continued to need a Redeemer who would deliver them from sin and its consequences (Isa. 41:14; 44:22–23; 49:7, 26; 52:9; 59:20; 60:16; 63:16; Jer. 31:11; Hos. 13:14; Mic. 4:10). Paul's readers enjoyed ultimate redemption in Christ and through his sacrifice on the cross.

Paul's association of redemption with "the forgiveness of sins" (ἡ ἄφεσις τῶν παραπτωμάτων) in this verse indicated that he was speaking of redemption from slavery to sin and judgment (Eph. 2:1–3). God forgave "sins" (NIV, NKJV, KJV, NLT) or "trespasses" (ESV, NASB, NRSV, CSB) that consisted of any "violation of [God's] moral standards" (BDAG, s.v. "παράπτωμα" b, p. 770). The means of this redemption and forgiveness was through the sacrificial shedding of Christ's blood (διὰ τοῦ αἵματος αὐτοῦ, "through his blood"). Jesus himself previewed the significance of his blood for the forgiveness of sins (Matt. 26:28; cf. Rom. 3:24–25; Heb. 9:22). Christ's death on the cross brought believers release from their slavery to sin and forgiveness in God's sight.

1:8. As was the case with the blessing of adoption, Paul's readers received redemption and forgiveness "according to the riches of his grace" (κατὰ τὸ πλοῦτος τῆς χάριτος αὐτοῦ). God's good gifts proceeded from the riches of his grace. God had showered this grace on Paul and his readers (ἧς ἐπερίσσευσεν εἰς ἡμᾶς, "which he showered on us"), in keeping with God's perfectly wise and insightful plans for this world (ἐν πάσῃ σοφίᾳ καὶ φρονήσει, "in all wisdom and insight"). Paul saw God's grace and wisdom acting in concert. God's actions toward believers were unmistakably generous and benevolent, and these actions fit perfectly within his brilliant plans for the world as a whole.

TRANSLATION ANALYSIS: The phrase "in all wisdom and insight" (ἐν πάσῃ σοφίᾳ καὶ φρονήσει) could be attached to either prior material (CSB, NET, NKJV, KJV) or, less naturally, subsequent (NIV, ESV, NASB, NRSV) material. If it modifies wording from prior verses (Eph. 1:7–8), it could refer to either believers' receipt of wisdom and insight (Lincoln, 1990, 17; Hoehner, 2002, 213) or God's exercise of wisdom and insight in his bestowal of grace to believers (Thielman, 2010, 61–62). The eulogy of Ephesians 1:3–14 shined much light on the wisdom of God's plans, so the wisdom and insight in verse 8 more likely characterized God's own glorious actions.

1:9. Paul moved conceptually from redemption on a personal level (1:7–8) to how this redemption fit into the grander scope of God's plans (1:9–10). God had showered his grace on Paul and his readers in another way "by making known to us the mystery of his will" (γνωρίσας ἡμῖν τὸ μυστήριον τοῦ θελήματος αὐτοῦ). Paul and his readers had been given privileged information about God's eternal purposes. When Paul talked about a "mystery" (μυστήριον), he described divine knowledge that had been previously hidden but had made known through Christ Jesus and his ministry. Christianity was founded upon both events and their significance. Paul's readers had heard about the epoch-shifting events of Christ's incarnation, life, death, and resurrection. God had also disclosed to them how these events brought God's promised work to completion.

A Mystery Now Revealed

Paul used the term "mystery" (μυστήριον) to refer to information about God's eternal plans that only God could reveal, in his perfect timing. The roots of this idea of mystery were found in Daniel 2:17–23, 27–30, 47 (Bockmuehl, 1990, 199–200). God had now revealed the full extent of his plans and had shown how the plans were all coming to fruition because of Christ's ministry (Eph. 1:9; 3:3, 4, 9; 5:32; 6:19). Paul used the term "mystery" in this way in other letters as well (Rom. 11:25; 16:25; 1 Cor. 2:7; 4:1; 15:51; Col. 1:26–27; 2:2; 4:3; 2 Thess. 2:7; 1 Tim. 3:9, 16). Paul expected his readers to share his sense of wonderment that God had chosen to disclose "the rest of the story" in Christ.

God disclosed his will to believers "according to his good pleasure" (κατὰ τὴν εὐδοκίαν αὐτοῦ). As he had done in verse 5, Paul specified the driving force behind God's gracious acts. This "good pleasure" (εὐδοκία) extended beyond a mere feeling to a settled course of action that was thoroughly good. God had predetermined to activate this benevolent plan in Christ (ἣν προέθετο ἐν αὐτῷ, "which he purposed in Christ"), reinforcing the centrality of Jesus Christ to God's saving plans for the world.

1:10. The time horizon God had in mind (signaled by the prep. εἰς, "unto") for carrying out Christ's saving work extended to the culmination of salvation history ("unto the administration of the fullness of time," εἰς οἰκονομίαν τοῦ πληρώματος τῶν καιρῶν). Paul directed his readers' attention to the future day when all of God's plans would come to fruition. This lofty language was appropriate to the sweeping and conclusive nature of God's story that Paul unveiled.

Paul marveled that the final chapter of God's story consisted of bringing all things together in Christ, under his restorative governance (ἀνακεφαλαιώσασθαι τὰ πάντα ἐν τῷ Χριστῷ). The term Paul used to affirm that God would "restore" (ἀνακεφαλαιόω) all things under Christ's governance has various English connotations related to bringing unity (NIV, ESV), summing up things (NASB), gathering (NRSV, CSB, NKJV), or exercising authority (NET). In context, though, this "restoration" can best be understood as God's rearrangement and renewal of his entire creative work under the singular governance or reign of Christ (cf. BDAG, s.v. ἀνακεφαλαιόω 1, p. 85).

Paul's use of the weighty term "restore" (ἀνακεφαλαιόω) to describe the perfect placement of all creation under Christ's rule tapped into an epic story of God's past, present, and future script for this world. In the beginning, God formed a good and ordered world and filled it with life, carrying out each creative purpose with delight and to perfection. All of God's good creation was entrusted to the image-bearing human beings that God had breathed life into. In the wake of humanity's fall from glory, God was not shaken from his commitment to the world and creatures he had created. He had already predetermined to give creation a new beginning "in Christ" (or "in the Messiah," ἐν τῷ Χριστῷ), under the leadership of the one who perfectly represented God as his image. In this light, "all things" (τὰ πάντα) did not support universal salvation (cf. Stott, 1979, 42–44), but rather the comprehensive kingship of Jesus the Messiah over a renewed creation. Paul noted that Jesus's reign would one day extend even over the unseen world, since God was ordering "the things in heaven and on earth" (τὰ ἐπὶ τοῖς οὐρανοῖς καὶ τὰ ἐπὶ τῆς γῆς) in and under Christ Jesus.

TRANSLATION ANALYSIS: In both Ephesians 1:10 and 1:12, Paul included the article ("the") before "Christ" (ἐν τῷ Χριστῷ). This likely indicated that Paul intended to highlight the Messianic office of Jesus with this inclusion of the article (Hoehner, 2002, 221–22; Talbert, 2007, 47; Bock, 2019, 41). This tied into the way Paul in Ephesians developed the theme of Gentiles sharing in the blessings of God's people through Jesus. Though this commentary will follow the convention of most English translations and retain "Christ" as the translation (of Χριστός), it is important to keep in view the origins of this term and its acknowledgment that Jesus had fulfilled the Messianic promises of God from the OT (cf. Bateman et al. 2012, 357–59).

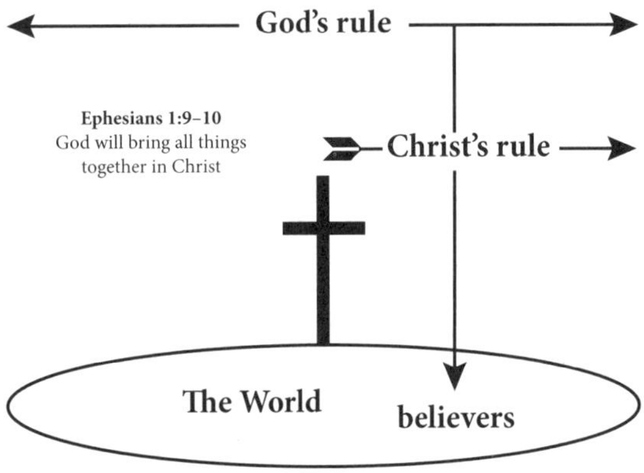

Christ was the key to the whole endeavor, and Paul strove to make this obvious by adding an extra "in him" (ἐν αὐτῷ) to the "in Christ" already in the sentence: "to restore all things together in Christ—things in the heavens and on the earth—in him" (see CSB, NKJV, KJV). It was Christ Jesus, the perfect image of God and second Adam, who would help the created world attain the potential that had been envisioned by God when he told Adam and Eve to carry out his benevolent dominion over the entire created order. God had prepared his redeemed and restored people to shine in the meantime as "exhibit A" of God's cosmic reclamation program (Eph. 3:10).

Both Jews and Gentiles Belong to God and Have Been Given God's Spirit (1:11–14)

In Christ, God displayed his excellence by selecting first Jews and then Gentiles to belong to his story and family, as people from both groups were sealed with God's Spirit as a promise for their inheritance until the day of God's final redemption of his people.

1:11. Once again, Paul made Christ the link between ideas, by using "in whom" (ἐν ᾧ) at the beginning of verse 11 to connect back to "in him" (ἐν αὐτῷ) from the end of verse 10. This relative clause introduced another blessing (καί, "also") God had given to believers. Paul told his readers that in Christ, "we were selected to belong" (ἐκληρώθημεν; lit., "assigned by lot") to God. This association of "in Christ" and being selected to belong connected believers' destiny with Jesus's (see BDAG, s.v. "κληρόω" 1, p. 548). The surrounding context suggested that Paul spoke about believers being selected to belong to God's story and family. Through their union with Christ believers had been incorporated into God's Christ-centered plans for the world (1:9–10, 11b) and had been included in God's family (1:12–14).

Paul and his readers had been selected to belong in God's story and family, "since they were predestined" (προορισθέντες, causal ptc.; NET) by him. Paul returned to the word "predestine" (προορίζω; cf. v. 5), reminding readers that their selection into God's family had been "according to (God's) plan" (κατὰ πρόθεσιν). Paul's readers had been selected to belong because of God's predetermined decision to include them in his greater, foreordained plan for the world. The two προ-prefixed words in close succession drove home the point that God knew what he was doing, having shaped a perfect plan for the world from before time. The God who had crafted a plan for the world was now using his infinite resources to carry out his mission, down to the last detail. He worked "according to the plan of the one who carries out everything according to the counsel of his will" (κατὰ πρόθεσιν τοῦ τὰ πάντα ἐνεργοῦντος κατὰ τὴν βουλὴν τοῦ θελήματος αὐτοῦ). Paul painted the picture of a wise, undisturbed architect of a master plan for the universe who then proceeded to implement his plan with energy and focus. Even with the massive scope of this grand story, God had graciously included believers as treasured recipients of his redeeming work.

1:12. Paul specified the purpose (εἰς τὸ + inf.) for God prearranging to include believers in his story and family. God had resolved that a first wave of believers would be gathered to himself. Paul referred to this group as "us" (ἡμᾶς) and the ones "who had first hoped in the Christ" (τοὺς προηλπικότας ἐν τῷ Χριστῷ), the promised Messiah from the family of David (cf. 2 Sam. 7:12–16; Ps. 110:1; Isa. 9:1–7; 11:1–10). Paul elsewhere talked about believers as those who had hoped in Christ (1 Cor. 15:19; cf. Rom. 15:12; 2 Cor. 1:10). Paul noted that this group's inclusion brought further praise to God's glory (εἰς τὸ εἶναι ἡμᾶς εἰς ἔπαινον δόξης αὐτοῦ, "that we would be for the praise of his glory").

But who was this group, specifically in contrast to a second group that followed it in 1:13? The best possibility is that Paul was viewing things from a salvation-historical perspective, with the Jews (and Jewish Christians) being seen as the first wave of God's saving work. Both Jesus and Paul, and undoubtedly many of the other early Christians, were well aware of the missional order of "to the Jews first, and then to the Gentiles" (Rom. 1:16; cf. Matt. 3:9; 10:5–6; 15:21–28; Acts 13:46; Rom. 2:9–10). Paul talked about "those who first hoped in Christ" as the fulfillment of this first stage of gospel outreach (Barth, 1974, 130–33; Stott, 1979, 45; Witherington, 2007; Cohick, 2010, 52). Others are not as convinced about the implied delineation between Jews and Gentiles (Lincoln, 1990, 36–38; Klein, 2006, 53–54; Hoehner, 2002, 231–232; Arnold, 2010, 91; Thielman, 2010, 75). But in Ephesians 2:11–22, Paul spoke with this very sensitivity to God's work among Jews and then Gentiles, and it is likely that he had this same order in mind in Ephesians 1:12–13.

Paul sprinkled references to "hope" (ἐλπίς, which is at the root of τοὺς προηλπικότας) throughout Ephesians (Eph. 1:18; 2:12; 4:4). The term reflected the future-oriented aspect of the Christian faith. Paul saw Christ as the key to delivering on the promises of God. Jewish believers in Christ in particular appreciated the wealth of promises God had made to his covenantal people throughout the OT. Christ was the current and future fulfillment of all of God's promises, so believers had put their hope in Christ for the realization of those promises.

1:13. Paul resumed (repeating ἐν ᾧ, "in whom," from 1:11) his survey of how the gospel spread from the first wave to the second wave of people. This second wave (καὶ ὑμεῖς, "you also") most likely consisted of the more surprising recipients of God's grace—the Gentiles. They had heard a message from the first wave—the Jewish Christians—and had responded to that message in faith (ἀκούσαντες . . . πιστεύσαντες, "heard . . . believed"). Entering God's family followed the sequence of hearing and believing (Rom. 10:14–17). The message was described as both "the word of truth" (τὸν λόγον τῆς ἀληθείας) and "the gospel of your salvation" (τὸ εὐαγγέλιον τῆς σωτηρίας ὑμῶν). It was a message of the highest kind of truth, truth about God's intervention in this world, through his Son. It was also a message of "good news" (or "gospel," εὐαγγέλιον), since it announced a way of salvation for a world that was lost and alienated from God (cf. Eph. 2:1–3; 11–12). Christ had secured salvation for Paul's readers (Eph. 1:3; 2:5, 8; 5:23), even as they awaited a final deliverance when Christ returned (Eph. 1:14; Rom. 5:9; 10:9; 1 Cor. 3:15; 5:5; 2 Cor. 2:15; Phil. 1:28; 1 Thess. 5:8–9).

When Paul's readers had believed in this saving message, something highly significant had taken place: "you were sealed with the Holy Spirit of promise" (ἐσφραγίσθητε τῷ πνεύματι τῆς ἐπαγγελίας τῷ ἁγίῳ). Here, the third person of the Trinity makes his first overt appearance in the letter, with a focus on his ministry to believers. Paul's readers were sealed "in Christ" (both occurrences of ἐν ᾧ likely modify "you were sealed," as reflected in CSB) and "with the Spirit" (τῷ πνεύματι). The imagery of sealing conveyed the idea of God's ownership and safeguarding of believers, and it fit well with the prior themes of adoption and redemption.

The Sealing of the Spirit

The verb "to seal" (σφραγίζω) meant "to mark with a seal as a means of identification . . . so that the mark denoting ownership also carried with it the protection of the owner" (BDAG, s.v. "σφραγίζω" 3, p. 980). Wax seals were used on official letters and documents (1 Kings 21:8; Neh. 9:38; Esth. 3:12; Jer. 32:10–14), important books (Isa. 29:11; Dan. 12.4; 1 En. 89:71) and even objects such as stones guarding entrances (Dan. 6:17; Matt. 27:66; Rev. 20:3). Wax seals also verified the origins or ownership of containers, and other types of seals were found on livestock or even slaves (Lincoln, 1990, 39; Keener, 2014, 544). When the Holy Spirit sealed believers, this testified that God vouched for believers as his own people (2 Cor. 1:22; Rev. 7:4–8; 9:4) and promised to keep and protect them until Christ returned for them. Later, in Ephesians 4:30, Paul again referred to the Holy Spirit sealing Paul's readers for the day of redemption.

Paul described the Spirit as "the Holy Spirit of promise" (τῷ πνεύματι τῆς ἐπαγγελίας τῷ ἁγίῳ), which connected the concept of promise to the person of the Holy Spirit. Jesus himself had promised that the Father would send the Spirit to the disciples (John 14:16, 26; 15:26; 16:7). But there may have been an even broader understanding of "promise" in this passage. In Galatians 3:14, Paul linked the fulfillment of the blessings promised to Abraham with the bestowing of the gift of the Spirit. Passages such as Ezekiel 36:24–28 and Joel 2:28–32 associated the arrival of the Spirit with the realization of the promises of God. The Spirit was thus not a gift received in isolation; the Spirit was the gateway through which "every spiritual blessing in Christ" (1:3) reached believers' lives.

1:14. For Paul, the Spirit functioned as a down payment or initial installment of the readers' full inheritance to come (ὅ ἐστιν ἀρραβὼν τῆς κληρονομίας ἡμῶν). A "down payment" (ἀρραβών) guaranteed the future delivery of a promised payment in full (2 Cor. 1:21–22; 5:5; BDAG, s.v. "ἀρραβών," p. 134). If the Holy Spirit of promise opened the door to all spiritual blessings, then that included the eschatological blessings connected to Jesus's future return as well. The Spirit's presence in believers' lives provided assurance that God would one day fulfill all of his promises to his people.

Blessings That Are "Already" and "Not Yet"

In Ephesians 1:3–14, Paul moved from a strong affirmation of spiritual blessings already received in Christ (v. 3) to an acknowledgement that the fullness of those blessings was yet to come (v. 14). Paul's readers had been chosen (v. 4), adopted (v. 5), redeemed and forgiven (v. 7), selected to belong to God (v. 11), and sealed with the Spirit (v. 13). The Spirit's presence guaranteed that when Christ returned, Paul's readers would receive their full inheritance from God and enjoy his presence forever as his dearly loved people (v. 14). God would deliver this full inheritance as part of his majestic work of restoring all things under Christ's perfect reign (v. 10). Though Paul described both present and future blessings in this passage, he placed the emphasis on the fact that believers could already embrace and celebrate the spiritual blessings of their guaranteed eschatological inheritance.

Chief among these promises was the relational union God would enjoy with his people.

Paul indicated the end result (εἰς, "for") of the Spirit's work, which was God's final redemption of his people (see Rom. 8:23; Eph. 4:30; Bruce, 1977, 430), so that he could be with them. The phrase "for the redemption of the possession" (εἰς ἀπολύτρωσιν τῆς περιποιήσεως) more likely described God's possession, namely, his people, (NIV, NASB, NRSV, NET, NLT) than it did the readers' possession (ESV). Believers were the ones who were redeemed (Eph. 1:7; 4:30). The Spirit's presence in Paul's readers' lives ensured that God would one day fully and visibly claim the people he had purchased for himself through Christ's sacrifice (Eph. 1:7).

Paul closed this first section of the letter with the already familiar refrain: "to the praise of his glory" (εἰς ἔπαινον τῆς δόξης αὐτοῦ). God's final redemption of his people, his very own treasured possession, would bring to fruition the beautiful vision articulated in many of the covenant arrangements throughout the Bible: "You will be my people, and I will be your God" (Lev. 26:12; Jer. 24:7; 30:22; 31:33; 32:38; Ezek. 11:20; 14:11; 36:28; 37:23, 27; 2 Cor. 6:16; Heb. 8:10; Rev. 21:3). This relational union had always been at the heart of God's intentions for his people. God resolved to redeem a people for his very own, so that they could enjoy eternal fellowship with him in a new heavens and new earth. He gave his very own Spirit as his promise of this eventual communion. All of this reflected the magnificence of God and his plans, calling forth applause from his people.

THEOLOGICAL FOCUS

The exegetical idea (Paul gave accolades to God for having blessed Jews and Gentiles thoroughly in Christ by choosing and adopting them, redeeming them, and giving them his Spirit, as he prepared to restore all things in Christ) leads to this theological focus: God deserves our applause for his works in Christ and by the Spirit to bless believers and restore the world.

God deserves believers' praise, as the passage makes clear near its beginning when it proclaims, "Blessed be God!" (v. 3). Three times the passage insists that God's wonderful character and actions elicit enthusiastic accolades from his people (vv. 6, 10, 12). Praise is the most fitting response to God's generous blessings.

The passages locates God's blessings to believers within the panoramic sweep of his eternal plans for a new beginning for the entire created order (v. 10). Believers' blessings fit within this greater story of God's work in the world. While God has orchestrated this story since before the beginning of time, his blessings for believers are realized now through the believer's union with Christ. Believers are blessed *in Christ* (v. 3), chosen *in him* (v. 4), given grace *in the beloved,* have redemption and forgiveness *in him* (v. 7), and are included in the eternal cosmic plans that are designed and carried out *in him* (vv. 10–11). Through the Holy Spirit believers receive the immediate blessings of belonging to God as well as the guarantee of future blessings on that day when God will reorder all things in heaven and on earth in and under Christ (vv. 13–14).

PREACHING AND TEACHING STRATEGIES

Exegetical and Theological Synthesis

Paul underscored certain truths about those who follow Jesus. When readers were "in Christ," they were chosen, adopted, redeemed, forgiven, informed about God's plan, and sealed by the Spirit. God had crafted a breathtaking "story"—his plan—and he had included believers in it. These blessings from God the Father were mediated through Christ and the Spirit. Because Paul's readers were "in Christ," they were the recipients of grace, carried on the tide of God's love. The apostle Paul modeled the appropriate response: because God had blessed them, they were to bless him: they were to "applaud" him (v. 3). That was their *raison d'être*—to glorify God (vv. 6, 10, 12) and enjoy him forever. Blessing God is done primarily by speaking words of adoration, but Paul also included the point that believers praise God by living holy and blameless lives (Eph. 1:4). Paul developed this idea further in the second half of the letter, and in the meantime he simply invited readers to stand in awe of God's love, mercy, wisdom, and power.

Preaching Idea

Let's applaud God for including us in his story.

> Note: Although verses 1–2 form a separate pericope, it may not be necessary to preach an entire sermon on the letter's salutation.

Contemporary Connections

What does it mean?

What does it mean to applaud God for including us in his story? The first part of the preaching idea captures the idea of blessing God (*berakah*). Applauding someone or something we appreciate happens nearly every day at events such as a retirement banquet or sports event. I (Jeffrey) vividly remember the applause from more than ten thousand people in attendance at an event that honored pastors. The moving tribute was a way of blessing them as the applause rolled on and on for more than two minutes. In the same way, followers of Christ honor or "applaud" him with their words and actions.

The second part of the preaching idea, including us in his *story*, captures the panoramic depiction of salvation, the string of actions God has performed for us (calling, adoption, redemption, etc.). This might be illustrated with everyday examples of being included. For instance, when treats are being handed out at a birthday party, children squirm and say, "Remember me, remember me!" They mean, "Include me, bless me too, in this event"; and of course, the host then includes them in the event with a treat. In the same way, God has opened the door and invited us to his spiritual feast. As 2 Peter 1:3–4 (ESV) says, "His divine power has granted to us all things that pertain to life and godliness . . . so that through them you may become partakers of divine nature." Ephesians 1:1–14 is so dense with theological terms as it describes the "story," that you may want to create a short sermon series just from this passage.

A contrast could be drawn between God's magnificent gift of salvation and the sometimes worthless, sometimes extravagant gifts we give at Christmas. Every year since 1926, Neiman Marcus has published the "Christmas Book," filled with those kinds of gifts. In 2019, you could give a custom designed doghouse for only $75,000, an hour in the chair with famous makeup artist Mario Dedivanovic for only $400,000, or a 007 Aston Martin designed by actor Daniel Craig who played James Bond. Only seven cars were available and—you guessed it—they cost $700,007.[2]

Is it true?

Is it true that we should give God our applause because he's included us in his story? In everyday life when people welcome us into their home, team, small group, or recreation, we naturally thank them. It is a joy to be included. That is also our response to God when he includes us in his plan. The Bible gives many examples of God's people giving him the praise he deserves. Moses and the people sang a song of praise after God delivered them from the Egyptians through the Red Sea (Exod. 15:1–18). When God revealed how David's family would feature in God's story for the world, David offered heartfelt words of praise in response (2 Sam. 7:18–29). Solomon also applauded God after the dedication of the

---

2 https://www.nbcdfw.com/entertainment/the-scene/Neiman-Marcus-Releases-2019-Christmas-Book-563310581.html.

temple (2 Chron. 6:12–42). Some of the Psalms declare God's praises for blessing his people and including them in his story (Ps. 78; 105; 136). Paul paused to applaud God's name after he had recalled God's awe-inspiring plans for Jews and Gentiles in salvation history (Rom. 11:33–36). When God shows his grace and power by including undeserving people in his story, God's people applaud him to express their praise.

A rich passage like this is hard to contain in a single preaching idea, so depending on your listeners, you may want to tackle some of the supporting ideas as well. Check out a way to address one of them: predestination.[3]

Now what?

How might we "applaud" God? This could be done in the church service itself. The congregation could put the preaching idea into immediate action with a time of testimony. A smaller congregation may offer spontaneous testimonies of praise, or in a larger church a planned testimony from one of the leaders could applaud God. Blessing God could also be done by singing. A series of songs could be placed after the sermon. In that case, the sermon might move seamlessly into those songs without a conventional conclusion. In this church service, perhaps all of the prayers could be composed only of praise, with supplication being "off-limits."

Prompts to Help People Share a Testimony

- I have seen God in my life when . . .
- God spoke to me through . . .
- Here is the attribute of God that means most to me right now . . .
- If God had not . . . I would be . . .
- Because God did . . . for me, I want to do . . . for others.

Applauding God can also be done privately. In one of our devotional times, we might discipline ourselves to focus solely on praise. As above, supplication could be off-limits. Singing or listening to praise songs is another way to applaud God in our hearts. Some people spend hours a day in their cars, so why not use that time to applaud God? Perhaps the congregation could be challenged to write a psalm that applauds God. Examples from your own or others' journals could be presented as models.

But applauding is more than saying words. It also includes acts of kindness, charity, and justice. Because humans are the *imago Dei*—the

3 One of the ideas that supports the preaching idea may spark disagreement: predestination. Listeners may respond: "Is it true that God chooses some people to be part of his story? Does that mean that he does *not* choose others? That sounds arbitrary and unfair!" To defend this passage's assertion that God does indeed predestine those he has chosen, here are three suggestions.

First, the purpose of the passage is that we worship, or "applaud," God. As we preach, we can model this. We need not debate about him as though we are apologists. By applauding God even as we preach, we assume a worshipper's stance that should hopefully affect our tone and delivery. In turn we might then influence the listeners to approach the doctrine of predestination with a warm spirit.

Second, while this passage is one of the most comprehensive statements in the Bible of God's initiative and power in salvation, it does not say everything. In particular, this passage does not spend much time on another biblical truth—human responsibility. But the passage implies our need to respond to God, especially in verse 13, which speaks of hearing and believing the gospel. By acknowledging the fact of human responsibility, biblical to the core, listeners may be more likely to concur with this passage's depiction of the doctrine of predestination.

Third, it's difficult to fully harmonize God's sovereignty with human responsibility. This is an "antimony"—an apparent contradiction between two true statements. The Bible teaches both, so we do too, but in this passage, God's sovereignty is on center stage. As the author of the story, God creates the storyline, develops the characters, and moves the plot to a happy ending.

image of God—the way we treat one another is a way of honoring (or dishonoring) God. That is what Jesus taught in Matthew 25:40: helping "the least of these my brothers" is equivalent to helping Jesus himself. A simple act of kindness like picking up your children's board game, strewn across the floor, can be a way of applauding God. Or a more profound act like giving sacrificially to a clean water project in Africa blesses God by blessing others.

Creativity in Presentation

Everyone who has ever performed a musical recital, performed in a play, or delivered a well-crafted speech appreciates applause. Perhaps to accentuate this reality, there may be someone in the congregation gifted in singing or playing a musical instrument. Perhaps he or she might play or sing a moving piece that generates applause from the congregation. That then can become an analogy for how we should applaud God for his "performance," all of the spiritual blessings he has lavished on us.

Perhaps someone can share their story, their spiritual journey. Or perhaps someone has been chosen for a special task or has been adopted. When preaching on the doctrine of adoption, I (Jeffrey) held my own infant son on my lap for a few minutes, explaining how my wife and I had adopted the little stranger. Listeners reported that this was the "high point" of the sermon because it not only explained the doctrine but also moved the heart.

Illustrating the second part of the preaching idea (his story) might be done with a flip chart or presentation slide: write the long list of terms ("chosen," "adopted," "redeemed," etc.), then draw a circle around all of them and above write "his story." Another type of visual aid could serve a similar purpose: to explain the complex stages of the "story," move from one side of the platform to the other: first God *chose* us (stand in a certain place to explain this), then God *predestined* us (move to a new position to explain this), then God *adopted* us. . . .

The metaphors in the text could be used for other low tech visuals. For example, while discussing "sealed with the Holy Spirit," melt wax onto an envelope and then use an imprint to seal it. Or to illustrate the OT allusion to redemption—how Israel was delivered from Egypt by placing blood on the doorframe of their houses—hold up a board stained red.

The following illustration might be used to illustrate how God is worthy of our applause. Every year there is an event in Wales that reaches back to ancient times: the National Eisteddfod. At the height of the summer, eight days of competition mark one of the largest musical and literary festivals anywhere in Europe. Around 150,000 people gather to hear the best poets of the land present their finest work. At the climax of the festival, and after deliberation by a panel of strict judges, one poet is crowned "worthy" of sitting in the Chief Bard's throne. But several times over the years, the judges have intoned before the throng: "Neb yn deilwng" (NEYB-un dzay-oon)—*no one is worthy* of sitting in the throne, so the chair sits empty. A sword is even placed across the seat barring anyone from taking the throne. This idea of worthiness is something we find throughout the Bible as well. Who is worthy to sit on the throne? Only one—Jesus Christ (Rev. 5:2–5).[4]

As mentioned above, following the sermon with testimonies or a set of songs could serve as the conclusion of the sermon. "Come Behold the Wondrous Mystery" by Keith and Kristyn Getty echoes many of the themes of this passage.[5]

The point to stress is this: Paul blessed God for blessing us. So, let's applaud God for including us in his story.

4 For pictures and a fuller explanation of the National Eisteddfod see https://amgueddfa.cymru/erthyglau/2010-07-25/Cenedl-syn-anrhydeddu-beirdd.

5 For an example, search YouTube for music videos about Jesus sitting on the throne.

The preaching idea could be developed in two moves:

- God has included us in his story. (vv. 3–11, 13–14)
- Therefore, let's applaud God. (vv. 3, 6a, 12b, 14b)

DISCUSSION QUESTIONS

1. Name some of the "spiritual blessings" Paul mentioned. What do they mean?
2. As you've examined these terms, did any of the illustrations strike you? Why, or in what way?
3. What difference does being "in Christ" make to your sense of who you are or your understanding of your identity?
4. How can you applaud God with your words for his lavish grace?
5. How can you applaud God with your behavior?
6. What do you think it will look like one day when all things are restored and united under the leadership of Christ? What part of this vision is most appealing to you?

Ephesians 1:15–23

EXEGETICAL IDEA

Paul prayed that God would help readers know him and appreciate their God-given hope and inheritance, as well as the power that had already been demonstrated in Christ's resurrection and position of all-encompassing authority.

THEOLOGICAL FOCUS

Believers can know God by appreciating the God-given hope, inheritance, and power that overflows to them in Christ.

PREACHING IDEA

God, please help us to know intimately our hope, inheritance, and power.

PREACHING POINTERS

Paul's first-century readers lived in a world marked by awareness of a vast array of spiritual powers. Both Jews and Gentiles witnessed instances of demon possession and sorcery (Mark 1:23–28; 5:1–20; 7:24–30; 9:17–29; Acts 13:6–11; 16:16–18). In Jewish literature, 1 Enoch frequently mentioned angels, identified them by name, and described their activity and responsibilities, and the Qumran War Scroll anticipated good and bad angels fighting on behalf of the "sons of light" and the "sons of darkness." For Gentiles, religious worship encompassed devotion to local deities in addition to the pantheon of Greek and Roman gods and goddesses. Both Jews and Gentiles in Asia Minor dabbled in a variety of religious rites and ceremonies that promised to give practitioners a greater sense of control over life but instead often kept them in bondage to the unpredictability of unseen forces. Paul's readers had broken free of this spiritual slavery (Acts 19:11–20) when they encountered Christ's unparalleled authority and hope. God's Spirit now worked in them to produce spiritual growth and provide spiritual power, in line with the resurrection power and eternal authority experienced by Christ Jesus himself.

Our day parallels Paul's day in that many people are captivated by the world of spiritual powers. This is seen in missionaries' stories of demon possession and in pop culture. William Friedkin's movie *The Exorcist* (1973) was the first of many movies on demon possession. Similarly, Frank E. Peretti's fictional work *This Present Darkness* (1986) launched his long-running series of books on spiritual warfare. People today are fascinated by the unseen world, and Paul's prayer draws on that desire when he depicts God's mighty power that raised Christ from the dead and the hope this brings us for a future inheritance. Our hope is grounded in Christ. His resurrection is ours and we want to experience the power and confidence that this brings; so we pray: God, please help us to know intimately our hope, inheritance, and power.

KNOWING GOD BY APPRECIATING HIS HOPE, INHERITANCE, AND POWER (1:15–23)

LITERARY STRUCTURE AND THEMES (1:15–23)

Ephesians 1:15–23 builds upon 1:3–14 and anticipates further exploration of themes later in the book. The lofty tone from 1:3–14 continues as Paul's prayer directs his readers to the great privileges they possessed in Christ, who ruled over all authorities and kingdoms. Structurally, verses 15–19 contain Paul's thanksgiving and prayers for his readers. He prayed specifically that their knowledge of God and his gifts to them would grow, aided by God's gift of spiritual wisdom and revelation. Then, without breaking his stride, Paul turned in verses 20–23 to magnifying the spiritual power of God demonstrated in Christ. The same power Paul's readers could summon for their lives had been put into action in Christ's resurrection and exaltation.

Paul used a number of words related to prayer and spiritual knowledge in 1:15–19, along with first- and second-person pronouns that reflected the relationship between Paul and his readers. Terms emphasizing the comprehensive scope of Christ's authority (cf. the repetition of "all" or "every" and terms from the "fullness" word group) marked the discourse of 1:20–23. As with many of Paul's thanksgiving and prayer sections in his other letters, in Ephesians 1:15–23 Paul previewed topics that he planned to revisit in more detail later. From the centrality of the virtues of faith and love, to growing in the knowledge of God and his work in Christ, to the sweeping authority of Christ, to the extent of divine resources that were at the disposal of believers and the church as a whole, Paul laid the groundwork in this section for developing rich teachings later in the letter.

- ***Paul's Thankful Prayers for His Readers (1:15–16)***
- ***Prayers to Appreciate Divine Hope, Inheritance, and Power (1:17–19)***
- ***God's Power in Christ's Resurrection and Comprehensive Authority (1:20–21)***
- ***Christ's Reign in the Church Previewed His Authority over All Things (1:22–23)***

EXPOSITION (1:15–23)

Paul prayed for his readers in a way that reflected his priority that they know God deeply by fully appreciating the access they had to their divine hope, inheritance, and power. Paul reminded his readers that Jesus Christ reigned at the right hand of God, and any spiritual power that either Jews or Gentiles could encounter had been subjected to Christ's authority (1:21). Paul's readers were used to hearing and thinking about spiritual forces, since Asia Minor was rife with spiritual activity. The book of Acts alone mentioned the work of Jewish exorcists (19:13–14), the widespread use of books of magic (19:18–19), and ardent worship of the goddess Artemis across the province (19:23–41). Extrabiblical sources attested to popular preoccupation with spiritual phenomena in Asia Minor (Arnold, 1992, 15–20). Similar to the first half of chapter 1, Paul located believers' experience and hope within the broader reality of Christ's supremacy. His current subjugation of all spiritual powers (Eph. 1:21) and his reign as head of the church (1:22–23) was just the first step in conclusively expressing his complete authority over the entire *cosmos* (1:10).

Paul's Thankful Prayers for His Readers (1:15–16)

Paul shared that he was inspired by reports of his readers' faith and love, which motivated him to give thanks and pray for them frequently.

1:15. Paul began verse 15 with "on account of this" (διὰ τοῦτο), sparking the question of what "this" was referring to. Most likely, Paul had all of 1:3–14 in mind as the launching point for 1:15–23. Paul began praying for his readers with the full weight of God's blessings still fresh in his mind.[1] With "I" (κἀγώ, a contraction of καί and ἐγώ), Paul shifted the focus from the grand sweep of God's eternal project to Paul's own prayers for the readers' growth in God's blessings.[2]

The reason Paul gave thanks and prayed for his readers was that he had heard (ἀκούσας, causal ptc.) good things about their spiritual progress. Most likely he had not interacted with them in person, but he affirmed them for their reputation of showing "faith" (πίστις) and "love" (ἀγάπη). He had heard that they possessed a faith that was rooted "in the Lord Jesus" (ἐν τῷ κυρίῳ Ἰησοῦ) and a love that was extended to "all of the saints" (τὴν εἰς πάντας τοὺς ἁγίους), or all fellow believers in their network. Paul's prayers were motivated by the good reports he had heard about his readers' faith and love. Paul's readers clung to Christ with unrelenting devotion, and they loved others, especially fellow believers.

Loving Other Believers

When Paul endorsed loving "the saints" (τοὺς ἁγίους), or other believers, he did not promote disregarding showing love to people outside the faith. In Galatians 6:10, Paul exhorted believers to "do good to all people, especially to the family of believers." Paul did not advocate withholding love from nonbelievers but understood that a special bond connected fellow believers. Paul's readers had all been adopted into God's family (Eph. 1:5), so they related to each other as spiritual family members, sharing a permanent kinship that entailed deep mutual commitment and generosity.

1:16. Spurred on by the thought of their faith and love (1:15), Paul assured his readers that "I do not cease giving thanks for you" (οὐ παύομαι εὐχαριστῶν ὑπὲρ ὑμῶν). His thankfulness for them reflected his gratitude for their response to God's work in and through them (Pao, 2002, 20). Paul found joy when believers under his care thrived spiritually (1 Thess. 2:19–20). Paul told his readers that he thanked God for them "when I make mention of you in my prayers" (μνείαν ποιούμενος ἐπὶ τῶν προσευχῶν μου). Paul's unceasing thanksgiving marked his prayers for them. Paul ministered to various churches from a distance through his prayers (1 Thess. 1:2–3; Philem. 4–5). Imprisonment did not curtail Paul's ministry to his readers but steered it in a different direction. These prayers accompanied his ministry of letter writing to the churches during his imprisonments. With great persistence, Paul remembered the strengths and spiritual needs of his readers, bringing them before God in prayer.

Prayers to Appreciate Divine Hope, Inheritance, and Power (1:17–19)

Paul prayed that God would give his readers spiritual knowledge of God, resulting in their appreciation of the hope, inheritance, and power God had given them.

---

1 The NRSV connects "on account of this" (διὰ τοῦτο) to what follows ("I have heard of your faith in the Lord Jesus and your love toward all the saints, and for this reason . . .). But the phrase (διὰ τοῦτο) almost always refers to prior material, and it likely does so here as well, even if in a rather loose way.

2 Some plausible translation options for the term "I also" (κἀγώ) include "I for my part" and "I in particular" (BDAG, s.v. "κἀγώ" 3b, 4, p. 487; cf. Thielman, 2010, 93). The use of "I" in tandem with "you" (ὑμᾶς) also put the spotlight on Paul's relationship with his readers (cf. this idea in reverse in Ephesians 6:21).

1:17. Next, Paul introduced the content of his prayer for his readers (with ἵνα; cf. Moule, 1960, 145). When Paul prayed for the work of God in his readers' lives, he described God as "the God of our Lord, Jesus Christ" and "the Father of glory." The first title, "the God of our Lord, Jesus Christ" (ὁ θεὸς τοῦ κυρίου ἡμῶν Ἰησοῦ Χριστοῦ) associated the God of salvation history with Jesus (cf. Bock, 2019, 49–50; Matt 22:32; Acts 3:13). The wording "of Jesus Christ" (Ἰησοῦ Χριστοῦ) may have also acknowledged Jesus's ministry as the Messiah ("Jesus, the Christ"; cf. John 20:31). The second title (ὁ πατὴρ τῆς δόξης) recalled the ascriptions of praise to God's glory in Ephesians 1:6, 12, and 14. God's glory was associated in the OT with the palpable display of his radiant presence, or more metaphorically with the brilliance and goodness of his character. God's gracious and powerful work for believers reflected his excellent character, previewing his majestic presence that believers would one day experience in full.

Paul interceded for his readers, asking God that "he would give you spiritual wisdom and revelation in the knowledge of him" (δώῃ ὑμῖν πνεῦμα σοφίας καὶ ἀποκαλύψεως ἐν ἐπιγνώσει αὐτοῦ). Paul used the plural form of "you" (ὑμῖν) in his prayer, which signified either all of the individual readers or the believers as a group. Paul wanted his readers to be drawn ever deeper into the knowledge and worship of their incomparable God. God's gift of "spiritual wisdom and revelation" (πνεῦμα σοφίας καὶ ἀποκαλύψεως; cf. Wallace, 1996, 90–91; NET; NLT) assisted Paul's readers in knowing God. Paul did not refer explicitly to the Holy Spirit when he used "spirit" (πνεῦμα) in this prayer, but since God was the one who gave the wisdom and revelation, Paul likely thought of spiritual insight as Spirit-enabled insight. Paul prayed that the Spirit who had sealed his readers when they believed (Eph. 1:13) would guide them in their ongoing spiritual growth.

Paul prayed that believers would receive spiritually revealed insight for a growing, relational knowledge of God. "Wisdom" (σοφία) and "revelation" (ἀποκάλυψις) were related terms that indicated supernatural insight into the work and purposes of God. Throughout the Bible wisdom was a gift that God shared with his people, and revelation was dependent upon God doing the revealing. But this ongoing growth in wisdom and revelation was rooted in the revealed mystery that had now been made known in Christ. God had made known his eternal plans in Christ to believers (Eph. 1:9; 3:3–6), so Paul's readers were able to grow into a fuller awareness of God and his ways as they received wisdom and revelation to do so. This spiritual wisdom and revelation was designed specifically for believers' progress "in the knowledge of him [God]" (ἐν ἐπιγνώσει αὐτοῦ). God had already established a relationship with Paul's readers by adopting them into his family, through Christ. He continued to disclose himself to them through his generous endowment of spiritual wisdom and revelation.

1:18. The reason (from πεφωτισμένους, ptc. of cause, acc. case attracted to the acc. ὑμᾶς later in the verse; ESV; NRSV; Lincoln, 1990, 47; Hoehner, 2002, 262) Paul prayed that God would give ongoing Spirit-enabled knowledge of himself to Paul's readers was because they had been enlightened already (by God) in their spiritual understanding. They possessed the capacity to know God more because he had opened their eyes and unveiled their hearts for this purpose (cf. 2 Cor. 3:14–4:6). The metaphorical idea of God "having enlightened the eyes of the hearts" (πεφωτισμένους τοὺς ὀφθαλμοὺς τῆς καρδίας) confirmed that a divinely enabled recognition of God's true character was the crucial element for growing in a relational knowledge of him. The imagery of being enlightened in the eyes of the hearts denoted that Paul's readers now had a clear vision of God (eyes), arising in the inner place (heart) from which their motivations, beliefs, and values sprouted. Biblically, the heart was the unseen center of life and the core of the person that had to be awakened and responsive to God in order for true faith to grow (cf. Ezek. 36:24–28). The enlightenment of knowing Christ stood in contrast to being "darkened in understanding" before receiving new life in Christ (Eph. 4:18; cf. Eph. 5:8). Paul stressed that this enlightenment was a gift from God that allowed believers to experience the spiritual progress described in the following verses.

Paul's introduction to his prayer led to three parallel prayer requests in Ephesians 1:18b–19. Paul prayed that his readers would know these three truths as a result (εἰς) of receiving spiritual wisdom and revelation. The three outcomes are grammatically parallel (as seen in the repetition of τίς or τί), though Paul elaborated on the third item significantly. In all three cases Paul identified God as the source of the anticipated gift. God had called them, had provided the inheritance, and had supplied his power. The blessings looked to the readers' past (calling), future (inheritance), and present (power).

First, Paul wanted them to know "the hope to which he has called you" (NIV, ESV), or the hope that stemmed from God's calling on their lives (ἡ ἐλπὶς τῆς κλήσεως αὐτοῦ). "Hope" (ἐλπίς) and "calling" (κλῆσις) were linked once again in Ephesians 4:4. Paul invited readers to recall how God had summoned them to himself in the past, and this became their source of hope. This prayer item was fitting as a springboard from how the readers' calling and hope had been described in 1:3–14. They were called to a holy calling, by grace, to participate in God's eternal blessings in Christ (Rom. 8:30; Phil. 3:14; 1 Thess. 2:12; 2 Thess. 2:14; Heb. 3:1; 9:15; 1 Peter 5:10). God had called believers to himself, to claim them as his adopted children and to give them all of the accompanying benefits of being in his family. He had selected them and marked them out for a special purpose and place in his eternal plans. Paul's readers needed spiritual enablement for these truths to really sink in, so that the truths would leave a lasting imprint on their identities and aspirations in life.

Second, Paul prayed that believers would know "the richness of the glory of God's inheritance among his saints" (ὁ πλοῦτος τῆς δόξης τῆς κληρονομίας αὐτοῦ ἐν τοῖς ἁγίοις). With "richness" (πλοῦτος) and "glory" (δόξα), Paul infused words of spiritual weight to highlight the great worth of this inheritance. As with the hope of God's calling, this inheritance came from God, and the inheritance directed readers' gazes toward the ultimate future, when God would deliver his promises to his people. Paul's words pictured a scene of believers dwelling securely and joyfully with God forever in a renewed and perfect world. This glorious inheritance awaited all of God's people at the return of Christ.

TRANSLATION ANALYSIS: There is some debate about whether Paul was describing a God-given inheritance for the apostles' readers (NRSV; Abbott, 1897, 30; Best, 1998, 167) or the readers being God's own inheritance (NLT; Lincoln, 1990, 59; Hoehner, 2002, 267; Thielman, 2010, 99–100, Arnold, 2010, 108; Bock, 2019, 53). In favor of the former, Paul and the rest of the NT typically used language of "inheritance" and "inherit" in reference to what believers would one day receive from God (Eph. 1:14a; 5:5; Matt. 5:10; Acts 20:32; 1 Cor. 15:50; Gal. 5:21; Heb. 9:15; 1 Peter 1:4; cf. Col. 1:12). Also, the parallel concepts of God's calling and God's power that appeared before and after the inheritance in the passage suggested that the emphasis was upon God as the ultimate source of these spiritual blessings for believers. The weight of evidence suggests that the inheritance in Ephesians 1:18 corresponded to the readers' inheritance mentioned in Ephesians 1:14a.

1:19. Third, Paul continued (καί, "and") his prayer with the request to God that readers would appreciate the magnitude of God's power (τὸ ὑπερβάλλον μέγεθος τῆς δυνάμεως αὐτοῦ, "what is the surpassing greatness of his power"). This power abounded to God's people, including Paul and his readers (εἰς ἡμᾶς, "to us"), identified as "those who believe" (τοὺς πιστεύοντας). God's gifts were often targeted specifically to those in a covenant relationship with him. Only those who were united with Christ through faith were able to draw upon the life-giving power that flowed through him. This resource was available to them even now, in their present circumstances.

Paul further expounded on this power in the second half of verse 19. God exercised his power "according to the exertion of his mighty strength" (κατὰ τὴν ἐνέργειαν τοῦ κράτους τῆς ἰσχύος αὐτοῦ). This chain of words (e.g., the genitives) combined similar words to intensify the theme of God's power at work (cf. the similar grouping in Eph. 6:10). The continued addition of descriptors slowed down the discourse, allowing the readers to savor the idea of having access to that great power for their lives.

God's Power in Christ's Resurrection and Comprehensive Authority (1:20–21)

God's active power for believers had also been at work in Christ when God raised Christ from the dead and placed him at the position of highest authority, above all other powers and entities.

1:20. Paul began this section by making the startling claim that the power believers drew upon was the very same strength that God had demonstrated in Christ's experience. A relative clause (beginning with the pronoun ἥν) linked this section to the previous one, though Paul shifted his attention from believers to Christ. The "exertion" (ἐνέργεια) of God's power flowed to Paul's readers because God had first exerted (ἐνήργησεν) his power in Christ. Divine power had been exercised "in the Christ" (ἐν τῷ Χριστῷ), perhaps highlighting the context of Jesus's ministry as the Messiah. Since Paul's readers were united with Christ, they shared in this power.

Paul recalled two events in particular that had displayed the working of God's power in Christ Jesus. The first had been when God raised Jesus from the dead (ἐγείρας αὐτὸν ἐκ νεκρῶν, "when he raised him from the dead"). Paul's readers depended upon the same power that had reanimated Christ when he conquered the grave on the third day! This was power that brought life out of death. The second event Paul highlighted was the exaltation of Christ. Not only did God raise Christ by this power, but "he seated Christ at his right hand" (καθίσας ἐν δεξιᾷ αὐτοῦ). God the Father and Son now dwelt together "in the heavenly places" (ἐν τοῖς ἐπουρανίοις), which was the same location of the readers' spiritual blessings (Eph. 1:3). In fact, later in the letter Paul insisted that believers themselves were raised and seated in the heavenly places with Christ, because of their relational union with Christ (Eph. 2:6).

The Resurrection and Exaltation of Christ

Paul contended that believers shared in the same divine power that had been activated in Jesus Christ's resurrection and exaltation. These two events featured prominently in early Christian preaching and worship. The early Christians moved from timidity and confusion in the Gospels to being bold witnesses for Christ in the book of Acts, largely because they had seen Jesus in all of his glory, risen from the dead. Christ's resurrection was also at the center of Paul's own turnaround from foe to friend of Christ and the church (Acts 9, 22, 26). The image of Christ sitting at the right hand of God was featured frequently in the NT. The early church took its cues from Psalm 110 and its vision of a victorious priest-king seated at the right hand of Yahweh and exercising his rule and judgment over the nations (cf. Mark 12:36; Acts 2:34–35; Heb. 1:13; 1 Pet. 3:22). The early Christians rejoiced in the reality that the risen Christ currently reigned from heaven and would one day return to implement that reign over the earth.

1:21. At this point the prayer faded into the distance, and Paul turned his attention to magnifying Christ. Paul extended the thought of 1:20 by marveling at the fact that Christ's place at God's right hand put him "far above every ruler, authority, power, dominion, and every name that is named" (ὑπεράνω πάσης ἀρχῆς καὶ ἐξουσίας καὶ δυνάμεως καὶ κυριότητος καὶ παντὸς ὀνόματος ὀνομαζομένου). The powers Paul referred to may have included earthly rulers and empires whose actions were influenced by spiritual forces in the unseen world (Wink, 1984, 60; Wright, 2013, 1284–1288; cf. *DPL*, 746–52; Keener, 2014, 544), though as Paul made clear later (Eph. 6:12), believers were to consider the hostile spiritual powers to be the true enemy (cf. 1 En. 67–69; 1QM I, 13–15). Paul proclaimed that Christ's subjugation of rulers was complete, with the repetition of "every" (πάσης and παντός). Paul highlighted Christ's authority over "every name that is named" (παντὸς ὀνόματος ὀνομαζομένου). Some Jews showed an interest in the names of angelic beings (Dan. 8:16; 9:21; 10:13, 21; 12:1; 1 En. 8–9; 20; 40; 69), and some Gentiles even sought to exercise control over the spiritual realm by naming spiritual forces in their prayers and pronouncements of magical formulas (cf. Acts 19:19; Ferguson, 2003, 227–32). Christ's dominion over any named power had both a present and future component, enduring "not only in this age but also in the age to come" (ὀυ μόνον ἐν τῷ αἰῶνι τούτῳ ἀλλὰ καὶ ἐν τῷ μέλλοντι). Paul's language encompassed all varieties of powers during all time periods (*DPL*, 749). Christ ruled over them all, forever.

The Unseen World

Throughout Ephesians, Paul's interest in Christ's rule spanned beyond the visible world to the unseen realms, where an assortment of spiritual forces operated. This aligned with Christ being exalted in the heavenly places (Eph. 1:20), which was an arena of spiritual activity often featured in Ephesians (1:3; 2:6; 3:10; 6:12). The readers in Paul's day were well attuned to the reality of unseen spiritual forces, though the churches in the province of Asia Minor may have focused too much on the powers themselves as opposed to Christ's victory over them (Col. 2:18–19). Paul reassured these readers of Christ's triumph over malevolent spiritual forces, and he later explained how believers could draw upon Christ's victory and the resources he supplied for their own stand against hostile spiritual agents (Eph. 6:10–18).

Christ's Reign in the Church Previewed His Authority over All Things (1:22–23)

God had subjected all things under Christ's feet and had made Christ head over the church (1:22), which as Christ's body experienced the full presence of the one who was designated to fill all things in the future (1:23).

1:22. Paul further expressed (καί, "and") the unsurpassed power of Christ by affirming that "he [God] has put all things under his [Christ's] feet" (πάντα ὑπέταξεν ὑπὸ τοὺς πόδας αὐτοῦ). The main verb (ὑποτάσσω) meant "to subject" or "to subordinate" (BDAG, s.v. "ὑποτάσσω" 1a, p. 1042). As the unspoken subject of the sentence, God did the subordinating, by placing "all things" (πάντα) in submission to Christ. This wording, drawn from Psalm 8:7, continued to paint a picture of what Christ's magnified status looked like in the grand scheme of things. In this passage, Paul enlisted the same pairing of OT passages (Psalm 8 and Psalm 110) that he did in 1 Corinthians 15:24–28, as previews of Christ's final authority and victory.

All Things Are under Christ's Feet

Psalm 8 beautifully recounted that God had put all things under the feet of the "son of man" (Ps. 8:6), which described humanity in this context. In his day, David had been amazed by humanity's God-given calling to rule as God's agents over the works of his creation, recalling the original directive God had given to those made in his image and likeness (Gen. 1:26–28). In the wake of human failure, Jesus had fulfilled humanity's calling in his incarnational ministry and had been the complete embodiment of the image of God. Since Jesus was the son of man *par excellence*, humanity's commission was his commission. Now that he had ascended to the right hand of God, everything had been subjected under Jesus's feet. This reality would become fully evident when Christ returned and carried out that dominion over the cosmos, sharing his rule with the people he came to represent (cf. Heb. 2:5–13; 9:27–28; Wright, 2013, 1050).

Paul made the additional point (καί, "and") that Christ's elevation over all kingdoms found a parallel in his headship over the church. The very one (αὐτόν, "him") who ruled over all powers had been assigned a similar role in the church. God had "designated [Christ] as head" (ἔδωκεν κεφαλήν) "over all things with respect to the church" (ὑπὲρ πάντα τῇ ἐκκλησίᾳ). Paul perceived the correlation between the certain eventual reality of Christ's supremacy over the seen and unseen world and Christ's current governance of the church. The church's present experience of Christ's leadership served as a compelling preview of Christ's eventual, but already secured, reign over the entire cosmos. Christ's leadership in the church was exhaustive, covering "all things" (πάντα, which mirrored the "all things" God had subjected under Christ's feet in 1:22a). In Ephesians, Paul used the term "church" (ἐκκλησία) for the universal church (BDAG, s.v. "ἐκκλησία" 3c, p. 304), consisting of all believers who were in Christ, rather than for any individual congregation. The individual churches receiving Paul's letter were all part of a global community of believers, and this global community enjoyed the blessing of Christ's reign in their midst.

TRANSLATION ANALYSIS: The term "designated" (ἔδωκεν) is also translated as "gave" (ESV, NASB, NET, NKJV, KJV), "made" (NRSV, NLT), and "appointed" (NIV, CSB). The words that followed ("as head over all things for the church") fit most naturally with the sense of "appointed" or "designated" (BDAG, s.v. "ἔδωκεν" 7, p. 242; cf. Eph. 4:11; 1 Cor. 3:5; Num. 14:4; Isa. 42:6). With the wording "for the church," (τῇ ἐκκλησίᾳ), Paul apparently highlighted the correspondence between Christ's creation-wide rule and his reign in the church (cf. Col. 1:15–18). Paul claimed that just as God had given Christ rightful authority to govern the universe, he had also appointed him to be head "over all things" (ὑπὲρ πάντα) pertaining to the church (dat. of respect; cf. BDF §197). Paul's wording reflected the head-body relationship between Christ and the church that was completed in verse 23 and seen in Ephesians 5:23 and Colossians 1:18 as well. Less likely, the clause meant that God had supplied Christ to be "over all things" (in the universe) for the church's benefit (cf. NLT), which would stress the church's connection and access to the one who had authority over all powers (Thielman, 2010, 111–12; Arnold, 2010, 115–16; Bock, 2019, 57–58).

1:23. Paul further characterized the status of the church as Christ's body (ἥτις ἐστιν τὸ σῶμα αὐτοῦ, "which is his body"). Christ's headship over the church resulted in a head-to-body relationship between Christ and his people. The discourse transitioned smoothly from a feet-head pairing (Christ's relationship to the cosmos) to a head-body combination (Christ's relationship to the church). The image of a body attached to a head appreciated Christ's authority over the church within the context of unity and connection (Eph. 5:22–33), in contrast to his domination over worldly and spiritual powers that were placed under his feet. The image of the church as the body of Christ resurfaced again multiple times throughout the letter (Eph. 3:6; 4:4; 4:12–16; 5:23–30).

TRANSLATION ANALYSIS: The use of "head" (κεφαλή) to describe Christ's relation to the church (and in chapter 5, to describe husbands' relation to their wives) brings the interpreter into tricky waters. Though the term typically denoted authority, it also occasionally indicated origin. Certainly, Christ was in some sense the origin of the church's life and ministry. But in this context "head" (κεφαλή) carried the connotation of authority (BDAG, s.v. "κεφαλή" 2a, p. 542; Arnold, 2010, 115; Thielman, 2010, 116–17; Bock, 2019, 57–58). The body of Christ lived under the head's leadership as a foretaste of Christ's promised comprehensive reign over all things.

The church was not only the body of Christ; it was also "the fullness" (τὸ πλήρωμα) of Christ. Paul had previously spoken about the "fullness of times" in 1:10, in reference to the perfect time when God determined to bring his plans to completion. Paul returned to fullness language in 1:23 to present the church as a vibrant entity, filled by Christ and infused with his presence (pass. sense for πλήρωμα, referring to the church, as with John Chrysostom, Hom. Eph. 3.1.20–23, ACCS, 119; Lincoln, 1990, 75–76; Thielman, 2010, 114; Arnold, 2010, 118; Bock, 2019, 59). In Ephesians 4:12–16, Paul proceeded to describe the church as still growing into this fullness, so the fullness language in 1:23 referred more to the church's calling and ultimate potential. Since the church, by design, was the fullness of Christ, it acted as the unique conduit and embodiment of Christ's activity in the world (Ridderbos, 1975, 391–92).

Jesus was currently making his kingdom and presence known in and through his redeemed people. But the church was simply the current "fullness" (τὸ πλήρωμα) "of the one who [eventually] fills everything completely" (cf. NIV, CSB; Moule, 1960, 160; τοῦ τὰ πάντα ἐν πᾶσιν πληρουμένου). In other words, before long Christ would return in kingly authority over all things, and his presence would flood the new creation (active force of filling). What Christ had started with his body, the church, he was assured to complete with the world.

This Age and the Age to Come

Ephesians 1:15–23 reflected the widespread understanding of history seen in the early church (hinted at in Paul's distinction between "this age" and "the coming [age]" in v. 21). Christ had launched his kingdom in his incarnational ministry (as part of this age), but the completion of his work and consummation of his kingdom was yet to come (the coming age). Paul thus prayed that his readers would grow into the "not yet" blessings (1:15–19a) that had already been dispensed in Christ (1:3). Moreover, Christ's own broader authority had already been affirmed (1:19–23), even though believers awaited the future day when all things would be brought together under Christ (1:10).

THEOLOGICAL FOCUS

The exegetical idea (Paul prayed that God would help readers know him and appreciate their God-given hope and inheritance, as well as the power that had already been demonstrated in Christ's resurrection and position of all-encompassing authority) leads to this theological focus: Believers can know God by appreciating the God-given hope, inheritance, and power that overflows to them in Christ.

The passage displays knowing God as the target of Paul's constant prayers for his readers (v. 17). Paul elsewhere identified his own purpose in life as knowing Christ, and he understood this as a lifelong quest (Phil. 3:8–14). The opportunity to know God is a gift of grace, enabled by the spiritual wisdom and revelation he generously provides (v. 17).

Followers of Christ seek to know God not in the abstract, but by letting the stunning hope, inheritance, and power that is theirs in Christ sink in and shape their identity (vv. 18–19). Paul prayed regularly for his readers because he understood that this identity-forming journey takes time. It is part of the lifelong process of "put[ting] off your old self," being "made new in the attitude of your minds," and "put[ting] on the new self" (Eph. 4:22–24). The believers' riches are something to be internalized, not just through knowledge but also through experience. The hope believers cherish in Christ should strengthen them against opposition and clarify what God has called them to do. Recognizing the great worth of their future inheritance should help them resist the pull of lesser things. They can draw upon the power available to them in order to represent Christ in a world of darkness.

Those who know Christ can lean into their hope, inheritance, and power because Christ is risen and enjoys complete authority over all things (vv. 20–21). As head of the church he shares all good gifts with his body (Eph. 4:7–11). His presence fills the church and his power overflows to his people. Christ is triumphant over all spiritual forces, and believers can participate in his victory.

PREACHING AND TEACHING STRATEGIES

Exegetical and Theological Synthesis

In this passage Paul prayed with thanks (vv. 15–16) and intercession (vv. 17–23) by asking that his readers would be enabled to know experientially how God had blessed them in Christ. Specifically, he asked that God would help them know the hope of his calling (v. 18), the riches of his inheritance (v. 19), and the greatness of his power that had raised Christ from the dead (v. 20a). In an extended depiction of the resurrection, Paul pictured Christ as seated at God's right hand far above all authorities in this age and the age to come. God had put all things under Jesus's feet and had made him the head of the church (vv. 20b–23).

Preaching Idea

God, please help us to know intimately our hope, inheritance, and power.

Contemporary Connections

What does it mean?

What does it mean to say, "God, please help us to know intimately our hope, inheritance, and power"? It means that we can take Paul's prayer for the Ephesians and makes it our prayer too. We need help to see the astounding power we have in Jesus Christ. The best evidence of that power is the resurrection, and that is the same power God gives us for eternal life and holy living. Romans 6 makes that case when it says that we were baptized into the death of Jesus (thus dying to sin) and raised from this dead with Jesus so that "we too might walk in newness of life" (Rom. 6:4 ESV). Not only do we need help in comprehending God's power, we also need help in experiencing his hope. Anxiety and depression have become major mental health problems afflicting 18 percent of Americans. Women are twice as likely to experience these debilitating problems. (https://adaa.org/about-adaa/press-room/facts-statistics). In Ephesians 1:18, hope is linked to calling. When God calls, he superintends our salvation to the final day and promises an inheritance in heaven. In addition to knowing God's power and hope, we also ask God to open our eyes to see our inheritance. He has promised that our light and momentary affliction in this world is preparing an eternal weight of glory (2 Cor. 4:17).

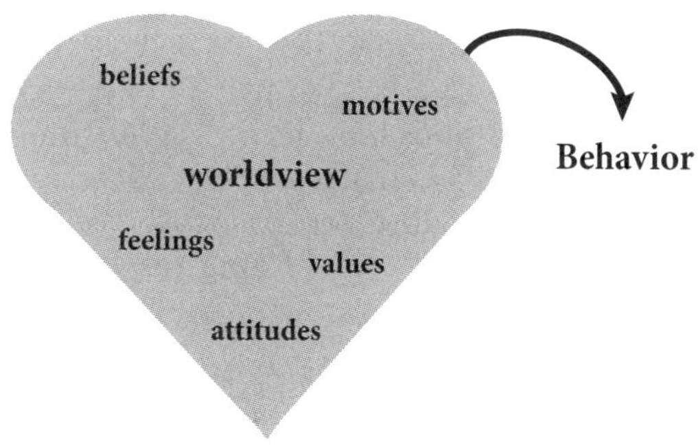

A Biblical View of the Heart

The metaphor of "heart" supports the preaching idea by conveying a crucial theological concept (v. 18). Figure 1 shows a simple drawing that might help clarify its meaning.

Is it true?

Do we really need God to help us know intimately our hope, inheritance, and power? We all desire experiential knowledge of people we love, such as our spouse, children, and friends. Think of the actions we go through to gain this intimate knowledge—taking long walks together, playing games together, and learning the loved one's favorite songs, flavors, and hobbies. We become students of those we love. We need to do that with God also, because that is where our hope, inheritance, and power reside. But we are hindered by our limited capacities. In this world we have never experienced pure love or unalloyed holiness, and thus we have no earthly analog to the hope and power God provides. That is why we ask God to open "the eyes of our hearts" (1:18).

We may need spiritual illumination particularly with God's power. As mentioned under the "Preaching Pointers", belief in demonic powers may seem more real than God's power. The preacher might affirm that evil powers are evident in Scripture, and that they exert their power in remarkable ways. Yet God exerts his power in even more remarkable ways, and not only in visible ways that are "miraculous," but also in mundane or concealed ways. The point is that God's power is real, not just Satan's power, and we should ask God to help us believe that. Testimonies might add a convincing element in affirming the preaching idea. The testimonies could magnify God's power in deliverance from demons and disease, or in overcoming "normal" sins such as smoldering resentment and addictive sins such as pornography.

Now what?

What might it look like in daily experience to pray and ask God to help us to know intimately our hope, inheritance, and power? Prayer is elusive for many followers of Christ. It needs feet to walk on—a concrete plan to engrain as habit—so these suggestions may help cultivate prayer as a way of life:

- Set aside a time every day for prayer. One discipleship program calls this the "Daily Appointment with God." Thinking of our prayer time as an appointment helps participants schedule and maintain a regular devotional time. For some listeners, the time might be first thing in the morning; others pray at lunch time; and others might prefer prayer as the last thing they do at night. The "daily appointment" does not need to be long, but it must be consistent to develop a Christian worldview.
- Journal. Many people find that writing down their prayers helps them to be intentional. Having a journal also provides a record of what we have been praying for and how God has answered.
- Pray the Scriptures. What better way to pray in the will of God than to paraphrase the Bible as our own requests? Ephesians 1:15–23 would be a great place to start, and of course, the Lord's Prayer and the Psalms are tailor-made for devotional use.
- Sing. My wife and I (Jeffrey) sing the Psalms a few times a week. First we read the psalm in the Bible; then we sing it using a metrical Psalter (the poem is put into verse form—see "For Further Reading"), then we use the psalm to make our own requests to God.

How to Spend an Hour with God

Pastor Mark Haines offers the following: "Here's a way to structure an hour in prayer with twelve Bible-based sections. Spend about 5 minutes on each focus point and you will spend an hour in prayer before you know it." (https://pastors.com/how-to-spend-an-hour-in-prayer)

1. Praise God for His Traits. The Psalms are an excellent source for mining a list of the Lord's attributes.
2. Wait in God's Presence as He Loves You. Silently invite Jesus to help you experience his love.
3. Confess. Ask the Holy Spirit to search your life for some attitude or action he wants to change.
4. Read the Bible aloud.
5. Pray the Bible. Paraphrase the verses you just read to make them a prayer.
6. Pray for Others. Jesus is interceding for us in heaven. Join him in this holy work.
7. Pray for Your Needs. Present your requests to your loving Heavenly Father.
8. Thank God. Recount all his blessings and answers to prayer.
9. Sing. Sing your favorite hymn or worship song.
10. Meditate. Mull over a verse that stood out in your reading.
11. Listen. Simply invite the Spirit to speak and listen.
12. Praise God Again. Worship him for who he is.

Creativity in Presentation

Prayer could be employed throughout the sermon. The congregation might pray verses 17–20 together. A young person could pray for an older person (and vice versa) that God would open their eyes. After each section of the sermon, members of the congregation representing various demographic groups could pray about the point just covered. Following the service, a special opportunity for prayer could be offered in a side room or at the altar. Perhaps a layperson could pray for the pastoral staff and a pastor could close the teaching with a prayer for the whole church.

To illustrate the trouble we have seeing spiritual truths, the preacher might try a visual analogy: ask someone in the congregation to read print that is too small to be seen clearly. Perhaps a young person with 20/20 vision and an older person with glasses could volunteer. But even 20/20 vision does not avail because the print is so small. Then magnify the print so that they can read it easily. Just so, we ask God to "magnify" our hope, inheritance, and power so we can see it clearly.

You might introduce the Christian fictional work of Frank Peretti. His novel *This Present Darkness* focuses attention on the power of a believer's prayer over spiritual darkness.[3] Peretti has captivated people over the years with his long running series of books on spiritual warfare. Perhaps the young people of the church could take one of the scenes from the novels and present it as a skit or group reading.

Peretti's Works[4]

This Present Darkness (1986)
Piercing the Darkness (1989)
Prophet (1992)
The Oath (1995)
The Visitation (1999)
Illusion (2012)
Probing (2017)

Perhaps a dialogue about hope could be prepared. The preacher could ask listeners what hinders them from experiencing hope in Christ. Some churches use texting to accomplish the same thing. Listeners text their questions while the sermon is underway, and some of the questions are projected on screen or read aloud by the preacher.

3 A summary of the book can be found at https://en.wikipedia.org/wiki/This_Present_Darkness.
4 https://www.bookseriesinorder.com/frank-e-peretti.

To carry that creative option even further, the preacher could write the listeners' responses to the question above on a large poster board which is set up so that it blocks the congregation's vision. Behind the poster is a second, smaller poster. On the second poster are the words "hope," "inheritance," and "power." After discussing the things that block our vision, remove the first poster to reveal the second.

In short, the point to communicate is this: God, please help us to know intimately our hope, inheritance, and power.

A possible outline for the sermon could be arranged as follows:

- The past: let's pray to understand the hope of our calling.

- The future: let's pray to understand the glory of our inheritance.

- The present: let's pray to understand the immeasurable power we have in Christ.
    - This power raised Christ from the dead.
    - This power enthroned Christ in heaven.
    - This power installed Christ as head of the church.

DISCUSSION QUESTIONS

1. Do you understand the hope of your calling? If you did, what difference might it make in your daily experience?

2. Do you understand the glory of your inheritance? If you did, what difference would it make?

3. Do you understand the power God has exerted for you? If you did, what difference would it make?

4. Do you ever pray for enlightenment about these things? Why or why not?

5. How might you start to pray for enlightenment? When, specifically, will you schedule time for this type of prayer?

6. What difference could Christ's authority over all things make for you when you feel concerned about the many seen and unseen challenges of life?

FOR FURTHER READING

Campbell, Constantine. 2012. *Paul and Union with Christ: An Exegetical and Theological Study*. Grand Rapids: Eerdmans.

Carson, Donald A. 2014. *Praying with Paul: A Call to Spiritual Reformation*. 2nd ed. Grand Rapids, Baker.

Packer, J. I. 1993. *Knowing God*. Downers Grove, IL: InterVarsity.

Reeves, Michael. 2012. *Delighting in the Trinity: An Introduction to the Christian Faith*. Downers Grove, IL: InterVarsity.

Sanders, Fred. 2017. *The Deep Things of God: How the Trinity Changes Everything*. 2nd ed. Wheaton, IL: Crossway.

Tennent, Julie and Timothy. 2017. *A Metrical Psalter: The Book of Psalms Set to Meter for Singing*. Franklin, TN: Seedbed.

GOD GIVES NEW LIFE AND RECONCILIATION IN CHRIST JESUS (2:1–22)

In this second major section, Paul surveyed the stunning contrast of his readers' states before and after knowing Christ. He marveled that God had made formerly dead sinners alive in Christ Jesus (2:1–10) and had made formerly divided Jews and Gentiles into a new, unified, and holy people in Christ (2:11–22). In both passages Paul covered similar ground, moving from his readers' former condition to their new status in Christ. While in the first passage Paul considered the personal implications of how individuals experienced this grace in Christ, in the second passage he reinforced individual reconciliation to God but also captured the reconciliation that believers from very different backgrounds (Jew and Gentile) would enjoy with one another, as one new humanity in Christ Jesus.

This second major section, God Gives New Life and Reconciliation in Christ Jesus (2:1–22), is divided into two preaching units: "God's Gracious Gift of New Life in Christ for Sinners" (2:1–10) and "Christ Reconciles Sinners to God and to Each Other" (2:11–22).

Ephesians 2:1–10

EXEGETICAL IDEA

Though Paul and his readers were formerly doomed and helpless sinners, God graciously saved them and re-created them by uniting them with Christ's resurrected life and spiritual resources.

THEOLOGICAL FOCUS

God's grace brings salvation and new life in Christ to doomed and helpless sinners.

PREACHING IDEA

We were the walking dead; now we're alive in Christ.

PREACHING POINTERS

Paul and his readers lived as a spiritual minority group within a complex and challenging world. They were followers of a still relatively unknown Messiah in an environment in which people believed in gods and pagan ideas and practiced lifestyles that were starkly different from the beliefs and practices of the small Christian congregations in the province of Asia Minor. Paul's readers needed to be deeply rooted in their identity and purpose in the world in order to grow in Christ and effectively serve his interests over the long haul. To help his readers grapple with their new identity and purpose, Paul painted vivid, contrasting pictures of their lives before and after encountering Christ. He revisited the darkness of his and their former lives, the undeserved grace of God's saving intervention, and the powerfully transformed spiritual condition they now enjoyed as a result of God's gift of new life in Christ. He announced that the spiritually dead had now been made alive.

For congregations in the post-Christian world, our circumstances are quite similar. We are a shrinking minority, and we follow a relatively unknown Messiah, although his name is heard often in film, literature, blogs, and conversation. We too need to grapple with our identity in Christ so that the world does not squeeze us into its mold, a mold that says that identity is comprised of how we dress, what we drive, how we decorate, and where we dine. Just as Paul used vivid language and the logic of contrast (dead/alive, walking in sin/walking in good works), so does the preaching idea as it captures the good news of God's grace: once we were the walking dead, but now we are alive in Christ.

GOD'S GRACIOUS GIFT OF NEW LIFE IN CHRIST FOR SINNERS (2:1–10)

LITERARY STRUCTURE AND THEMES (2:1–10)

This passage divides roughly into three sections, the first two of which portray the readers' spiritual status before and after encountering Christ's saving grace, and the last that summarizes the gracious but purposeful nature of the readers' salvation. In 2:1–3 Paul painted a bleak picture of the sin, enslavement, and judgment that characterized life apart from Christ. God's merciful intervention, described in 2:4–7, had allowed the readers to share in Christ's life, resurrection, and exaltation. In the third section, 2:8–10, Paul reinforced the fact that readers had received God's saving grace through faith, but since readers had been re-created by a supernatural work of God, their new lives were now designed to carry out God's good works.

Paul made contrasts between death (2:1) and life (2:5), a sinful world (2:2) and the heavenly places (2:6), and walking in step with sinister and indulgent worldly values (2:2–3) and walking to fulfill God's perfect plans (2:10). Paul twice used the word "formerly" (ποτέ) to specify that the old status no longer applied to believers. On two occasions, Paul repeated almost verbatim material emphasizing human sin (2:1, 5) and God's grace in salvation (2:5, 8), to help frame the central turning point of the passage—that God had made Paul and his readers alive with Christ (2:5). From Ephesians 2:1–10 to 2:11–22 Paul moved from the general to the particular by establishing the universal experience of believers' transformation in Christ before presenting how God had brought Jews and Gentiles into a peaceful relationship with himself, creating one new reconciled family of believers in Christ.

- ***Complicity in Sin and a Corrupt World Brings God's Judgment (2:1–3)***
- ***A Gracious God Gives Sinners Life and Unites Them with Christ (2:4–7)***
- ***God's Grace Brings Salvation and Enables Good Works (2:8–10)***

EXPOSITION (2:1–10)

Throughout this passage Paul explored themes close to his heart—human sinfulness, God's grace, salvation in Christ, and new creation. Paul extended the benefits of Christ's resurrection and exaltation (1:20) to the readers (2:6). By virtue of their union with Christ, Paul's readers had entered into Christ's presence spiritually and shared in his glorious position in the heavenly places. Paul's readers probably observed the quest for spiritual transformation and new life in Jewish and Gentile populations around them. The appetite for dramatic spiritual renewal was present, but the options available, whether in other messiahs who rose up as potential deliverers for Israel or in mystery religions that offered the possibility of profound spiritual awakenings, did not deliver on their promises. Paul gave the definitive answer to Jews' and Gentiles' need for spiritual transformation: a gracious God had powerfully saved sinners through Christ Jesus and made the spiritually dead come to life.

Complicity in Sin and a Corrupt World Brings God's Judgment (2:1–3)

Because Paul and his readers were formerly spiritually dead, sinful, and entangled in a world system governed by the devil, they had been subject to God's judgment.

2:1. Upon the completion of his prayer (Eph. 1:15–23), Paul continued to address his readers (καί ὑμᾶς, "and you") but shifted the focus to their former spiritual condition. Paul recalled the time when his readers were dead in their sins and transgressions. To cover this ground, Paul began a sentence in verse 1 but did not provide the main verb of the sentence until later. Later in verse 5, he completed his thought about God's dramatic intervention in the readers' lives.

With "when you were" (ὄντας, temp. ptc.) Paul set the stage for highlighting God's decisive action in Christ by recalling the readers' entrenched and helpless spiritual condition at the time. The readers had been "dead" (νεκρός) apart from Christ. Their lives were spiritually barren, lacking any spark of the divine life or fruitfulness that comes only through Jesus. Calvin notes that "we never become duly sensible of how much we owe to Christ, nor estimate sufficiently His kindnesses towards us, until the unhappiness of our state outside Him has been set before our eyes" (Calvin, 1965, 121).

The readers' spiritually dead condition had been in the context of the "transgressions" (παραπτώματα) and "sins" (ἁμαρτίαι) that had marked their lives. Paul used these closely related terms to connect readers' past spiritual deadness to their resistance to God and their appetite for sin. Though Paul had already celebrated the readers' forgiveness of "transgressions" (παραπτώματα) in Christ (Eph. 1:7), he still reminded them of how deadly and pervasive these sins had been in their previous experience (cf. Rom. 5:12–17; 6:23; 8:2; Col. 2:13).

TRANSLATION ANALYSIS: Due to the fact that the main verb "he made [us] alive" (συνεζωοποίησεν) does not appear until 2:5b, there are various ways in which verse 1 is translated. While "when we were dead" (ὄντας νεκρούς) is a possible rendering, many other translations (NIV, ESV, NASB, CSB, NRSV) convert the participle (ὄντας) to a main verb ("you *were* dead"), seeking to avoid initiating one cumbersome sentence that would not be resolved until Paul himself reset his bearings in 2:4–5. The NKJV adds the main verb from 2:5 to the beginning of 2:1 ("you He made alive") in order to clarify where Paul was going when he launched into his description of the readers' formerly helpless condition. The NET retains the participial force of ὄντας ("although you were dead") and attempts to mimic the way Paul trailed off at the end of 2:3 (without completing the sentence) before resuming his original thought in 2:4–5.

2:2. Paul had more to say about his readers' transgressions and sins (the rel. clause beginning with ἐν αἷς recalled the transgressions and sins). What Paul said about these transgressions and sins applied only to their former situation (from ποτέ, "formerly"). Paul repeated "formerly" (ποτέ) a verse later in order to set up the overt contrast between their previous condition and their new life in Christ. The readers used to "walk" (περιπατέω) in these transgressions and sins (2:2a). Later in this section (2:10), Paul urged his readers to walk in the path of good works that Christ had now opened up to them.

Walking through Life

Elsewhere in Ephesians (2:10; 4:1, 17; 5:2, 8, 15) and many of Paul's other letters Paul employed the term "walk" (περιπατέω) to depict pursuing distinct patterns of living. Imagery of walking and paths also frequently surfaced in the OT to communicate the idea that living life was a journey that was filled with choices about which direction to proceed in and what moral choices to make (Exod. 18:20; Prov. 4:14; Isa. 65:2; Jer. 7:23–24). In the case of Ephesians 2:2, Paul reminded his readers that they had pursued a path littered with sins and transgressions, before Christ had altered their route.

Paul further characterized the readers' former manner of conduct with the first of two phrases that began with a preposition meaning "according to" or "in step with" (κατά).[1] First, Paul noted that his readers used to keep in step with the world's way of doing things (2:2b). Paul used the phrase "the age of this world" (ὁ αἰών τοῦ κόσμου τούτου) to describe the surrounding culture's prevailing values and practices until the full arrival of the kingdom of God. Elsewhere Paul spoke of a present evil age (Gal. 1:4) and warned against being conformed to this age (Rom. 12:2). The world, in its resistance to God's kingdom, was marked by the types of sins and transgressions in which Paul's readers once indulged.

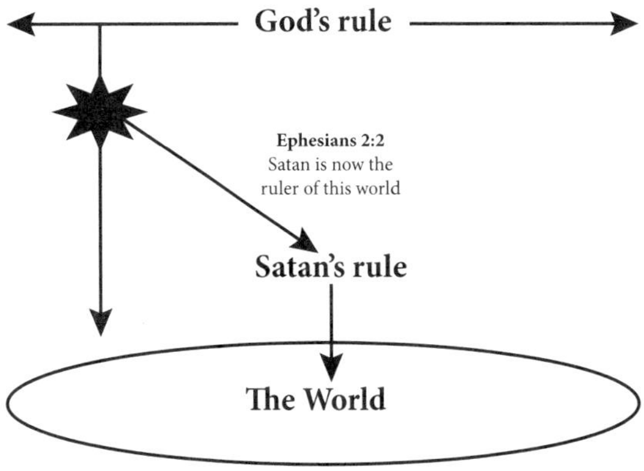

Satan's Temporary Reign over a Fallen World

Second, Paul's readers had formerly kept "in step with" (κατά) the spiritual forces that still governed the lives of the disobedient (Eph. 2:2c). Paul did not attribute the sin and rebellion that was characteristic of this world to simple choices and habits. Paul's readers had not merely acted as independent agents in their past lives, making a series of choices fully on their own power. They had been caught up in spiritual forces much larger than themselves. Paul perceived an evil spiritual authority that governed the spiritual forces influencing all of those who were separated from Christ, as his readers once were. This "ruler" (ἄρχων) likely described the devil (cf. Eph. 4:27; 6:11, 16), or Satan (Matt. 4:10; Acts 26:18; Rev. 12:9; 20:2), whom Jesus had labeled "the ruler of this world" (John 12:31; 14:30; 16:11). In another letter Paul referred to the "god of this age" who held unbelievers in his clutches by blinding them to the saving work of Christ (2 Cor. 4:4). Satan's possession of this temporary rule recalled the serpent's deceptive usurping of humans' rightful dominion (Gen. 3), which God had delegated to them (Gen. 1:26–28).

Satan ruled over "the domain of the air" (ἡ ἐξουσία τοῦ ἀέρος; BDAG, s.v. "ἐξουσία" 6, p. 353). This ambiguous phrase (and its gen. relationship to "ruler") may have indicated an unseen arena over which Satan wielded his authority. This domain was in opposition to God's kingdom, as seen with "the domain of darkness" (ἡ ἐξουσία τοῦ σκότους) in Colossians 1:13 (cf. similar spiritual dualism 1QM, 1Q28, CD, John, 1 John). In the worldview of that time, the "air" (ἀήρ), the nearer atmosphere and domain of spiritual forces, was distinct from heaven, from which God ruled (Arnold, 2010, 131–32; Keener, 2014, 545). Paul's mention of "air" assumed a world in which unseen forces in close proximity to the world but beyond human perception were influencing realities "on the ground." Satan exercised influence over unbelievers indirectly, via intermediate spiritual channels.

Paul followed this language with a parallel idea: that the ruler (the devil) governed "the spirit" (τό πνεῦμα) that "energizes" (ἐνεργέω) the actions of sinful people (with "ruler" governing "spirit"; NET; Wink, 1984, 82–83). The evil one exercised this spiritual influence even "now" (νῦν) in the broader world, as a malevolent imitation of God's spiritual activity (using a verb, ἐνεργέω, that had already been applied to God's righteous enterprises in Ephesians 1:11, 20). Lest this description paint a picture that removes human responsibility, Paul added

1 Paul occasionally used the combination of "walk" (περιπατέω) and "according to" (κατά) elsewhere in his letters (Rom. 8:4; 2 Cor. 10:2). The construction conveyed the influences that governed or characterized a person's way of life.

that the victims of Satan's machinations were rightly called "sons of disobedience" (οἱ υἱοὶ τῆς ἀπειθείας), suggesting their culpability in their entanglement with spiritual activity that opposed God. The term for "disobedience" (ἀπείθεια) denoted a settled resistance to God and his plans (cf. Rom. 11:30–32). One scholar has summarized Paul's view on sin in this way: "Humankind in Adam has both embraced sin and become sin's slaves" (Westerholm, 2013, 35). Both of these components are present in Ephesians 2:1–3.

2:3. Advancing (καί, "and") his train of thought by way of a relative clause (beginning with ἐν οἷς), Paul explained that in keeping with their immersion in a corrupt world, Paul and his readers used to live for their sensual longings (2:3a). Paul shifted smoothly from second-person plural (ὑμᾶς, "you") to first-person plural (ἡμεῖς, "we") in this verse. Paul may have aimed to group himself with his readers in the descriptions of their former (ποτέ, "formerly") resistance to God (Lincoln, 1990, 88; Schnackenburg, 1991, 92; Klein, 2006, 71; Arnold, 2010, 132; Thielman, 2010, 125), though alternatively he may have included Jews' sins more broadly alongside Gentiles' characteristic sins as well (Barth, 1974, 216; Cohick, 2010, 61–62). Either way, Paul rhetorically strengthened this move by adding "all" (πάντες), leaving no one untouched by sin and its consequences. This included both Gentiles and Jews, as Paul strategically contended in Romans 1–3. Paul stressed that within the broader arena of a corrupt and fallen world, all people "conduct themselves" (ἀναστρέφω) in similarly misguided and sinful ways.

Paul and his readers had all wallowed "in the desires of our flesh" (ἐν ταῖς ἐπιθυμίαις τῆς σαρκὸς ἡμῶν). Paul used "flesh" (σάρξ) in its negative sense here, as a metaphor for the seat of fallen humanity's sinful appetites. Paul and his readers had lived for sensual desires by "doing" (adv. ptc. of means, ποιοῦντες) what their sensuality and thinking had directed them to do (2:3b). Instead of carrying out God's will, Paul and his readers used to carry out "the will of the flesh and [self-focused] mindsets" (τό θέλημα τῆς σαρκὸς καὶ τῶν διανοιῶν). With this pairing of "flesh" (σάρξ) and "thoughts" (διάνοια) Paul envisioned a two-pronged command center of unrestrained desires and stubbornly independent thinking that had directed them in their former lives. Paul later returned to his exploration of sinful desires and thinking in Ephesians 4–5.

Paul wrapped up his assessment of his and their former fallen condition with an additional point (καί, "and"). Paul emphasized the bottom line: he and his readers had been (ἤμεθα, "we were") subject to God's judgment, along with the rest of the world (2:3c). Paul specified that this had been true for Paul himself, along with his readers, since they had all been stuck in the same quandary. Paul and his readers had been "children of wrath" (τέκνα ὀργῆς), destined for judgment (gen. of destination; Wallace, 1996, 101). Paul employed an idiom beginning with "children of" to stress an essential feature of their former existence—being doomed to receive God's wrath.

Paul and his readers formerly were "by nature" (dat., φύσει) children of wrath. Paul insinuated that the problem of sin and judgment had accompanied their entrance into the world (cf. Gal. 2:15) and affected people at the core of their being (BDAG, s.v. "φύσις" 1, 2, p. 1069–1070). God's "wrath" (ὀργή), the expression of his righteous judgment against sin (Rom. 2:5; Eph. 5:6), had been their unavoidable lot, apart from some drastic, unexpected change beyond human control. The fate of Paul and his readers had been the same as the fate of the rest of fallen humanity (ὡς καὶ οἱ λοιποί, "as also the rest"). As in Romans 5:12–21, all of humanity was implicated in sin and corruption, and all would die and face judgment apart from a dramatic entrance by God onto the scene.

A Gracious God Gives Sinners Life and Unites Them with Christ (2:4–7)

Despite the bleak situation of Paul and his readers, God's mercy and his desire to demonstrate his grace had motivated him to intervene by saving them, raising them with Christ, and seating them with Christ in the heavenly places.

2:4–5. Paul began a new thought in verse 4 and completed it in verse 5: God had made Paul and his readers alive in Christ, despite their sinful state. Paul began to signal a shift of circumstances from the past to present with the conjunction "but" (δέ). Paul began (2:4a) by highlighting the one who brought about the change—"God" (θεός). God had stepped into a seemingly helpless situation and turned it around.

Spiritual Transformation in the Jewish and Greco-Roman Worlds

The OT gave glimpses into God's provision of a dramatic spiritual renewal for Israel (the vision in the valley of dry bones in Ezek. 37 and the promise of a Messianic Branch emerging out of lifeless Israel in Isa. 11:1; Jer. 23:5; 33:15; Zech. 3:8; 6:12) and the hope of life beyond the grave (Ps. 16:8–11; Isa. 26:19; Dan. 12:2; Hos. 6:2). The Maccabean martyrs found courage in the hope of resurrection after death (2 Macc 7:1–42). Language in the Psalms of Solomon (first or second century B.C.) offered hope for unending life with God (Pss. Sol. 14:2–3, 7). In the Greco-Roman world, mystery religions in particular promised experiences of profound spiritual renewal and rising from the dead. Initiates into the famous Eleusinian mysteries sought experiential insight into the afterlife and rebirth from the goddess Demeter and her daughter Kore (Persephone), who was believed to ascend from the underworld for eight months each year, mirroring the agricultural cycle (cf. Ferguson, 2003, 254–56). In another mystery cult, through secret initiations and rites involving food, drink, and the spilt blood of animals, devotees to the Phrygian (cf. Acts 16:6; 18:23) god Attis could undergo a new birth (Wright, 2013, 265). Cicero spoke about the possibility of gaining both joy in the present life and hope for life after death through participation in mystery rites (*De legibus*, 2.36; cf. Rives, 2007, 174). Paul proclaimed that there was only one way to receive new and eternal life: Jesus Christ was God's provision who made revived spiritual life and resurrection possible for Jews and Gentiles.

Paul made God's motivation clear (2:4b)—"he is rich in mercy" (πλούσιος ὢν ἐν ἐλέει). God's "mercy" (ἔλεος) was an attribute that described his deep concern for distressed people's well-being. Paul's point in this verse resembled what he wrote in Romans 9:15–18: God's mercy was neither prompted by human worthiness nor provoked by human manipulation. God had extended his mercy because of the excellence of his own character and his loving concern for sinners. Paul reiterated this point in Ephesians 2:4c by identifying the reason (prep. διά, followed by acc. noun) for God's saving intervention as "his great love" (ἡ πολλὴ ἀγάπη). God's great love was not an abstract sentiment but was made manifest in his actions. His great love was the love "with which he loved us" (ἣν ἠγάπησεν ἡμᾶς), with the repetition of "love" words reinforcing the prominence of love in God's life-giving actions (BDF §153; Moule, 1960, 32). In this wording Paul recalled God's definitive revelation of love through the sacrificial death of Christ on the cross, which Paul drew a direct line to elsewhere in the letter (Eph. 1:7; 2:13; 5:2, 25).

A Merciful and Loving God

The foregrounding of God's mercy and love recalled God's dramatic revelation of himself to Moses as a merciful and loving God (Exod. 34:6–7). This pivotal passage reverberated throughout the rest of the OT (Num. 14:18–19; Neh. 9:17;

Ps. 86:5, 15; 103:8–9; 145:8–9; Joel 2:13; Jon. 4:2) as a hope-filled pronouncement of God's unchanging character. At the dawn of the new covenant era inaugurated in Christ, Paul powerfully connected the merciful and loving God of the OT with the climactic, life-giving work of Christ.

Paul had prepared his readers for the big reveal of what God had done for them, but he returned briefly to a previous point to heighten the effect of God's saving work. He repeated almost verbatim (2:5a) his initial point from verse 1: they all, Paul included, had been dead in their transgressions (καὶ ὄντας ἡμᾶς νεκροὺς τοῖς παραπτώμασιν, "and we, being dead in our transgressions"). This reminded the readers once again of how dire their situation had been before God's merciful intervention. The stark contrast between a loving God and helpless sinners set the stage for salvation's grand entrance onto the scene (cf. Rom. 5:6–8).

Notable Occurrences of συν-prefixed Terms in Ephesians		
Verse	**Greek term**	**Meaning for Paul's Readers (with Greek term in bold)**
2:5	συνεζωοποίησεν	God had **made them alive with** Christ
2:6	συνήγειρεν	God had **raised them with** Christ
2:6	συνεκάθισεν	God had **seated them** in the heavenly places **with** Christ
2:19	συμπολῖται	They were **co-citizens with** other believers in the household of God
2:21	συναρμολογουμένη	They were **joined together** as part of God's building project
2:22	συνοικοδομεῖσθε	They were **built together** into God's dwelling place
3:6	συγκληρονόμα	They (as Gentiles) were **co-heirs with** Jewish believers
3:6	σύσσωμα	They (as Gentiles) were **co-members of one body with** Jewish believers
3:6	συμμέτοχα	They (as Gentiles) were **co-partakers with** Jewish believers in God's promised blessings
4:16	συναρμολογούμενον	They were **joined together** in the building up of the body of Christ
4:16	συμβιβαζόμενον	They were **held together** in the building up of the body of Christ

Paul unveiled what a merciful and loving God had done for helpless sinners (2:5b). God had "made" Paul and the readers "alive together with Christ" (συνεζωοποίησεν τῷ Χριστῷ). The divine gift of life reversed the bleak state of death from Ephesians 2:1. God was in the business of bringing life out of death (cf. Ezek. 37; Rom. 4:17; 1 Cor. 15:22, 45; 2 Cor. 3:6). Paul contended that his readers were experiencing resurrected life in a spiritual sense now, in anticipation of the full, resurrected life in store for them when Christ returned (Rom. 8:11). In the current verse, Paul communicated similar ideas using one of his favorite grammatical constructions. By virtue of his readers' union with Christ, the eternal, resurrected life of Christ also animated them. Paul's readers participated in the divine life of Christ (cf. Campbell, 2012, 233). Because Jesus lived, they too now lived. Paul explored the additional implications of this startling fact in the next verse.

Spiritual Participation

Paul often used "together with" (a συν- prefix with a verb or noun) to communicate the notion of believers participating in someone else's action or result (cf. Rom. 8:17; Gal. 2:19–20; Eph. 1:6; 2:5, 19–22; 3:6; 4:16; Col. 3:1). Sometimes, as in Ephesians 2:5–6, believers shared in Christ's experience, while other times Jewish and Gentile believers corporately shared in the same outcomes. The construction typically tapped into the deep implications of believers' common union with Christ and communion with him and one another.

First, though, Paul offered a preliminary conclusion to what he had said so far about God's powerful work: it was "because of grace" (χάριτι; dat. of cause; Wallace, 1996, 167–68) that they had been saved. God's grace was the sole basis for the readers' salvation. Paul put God's "grace" (χάρις) at the beginning of the sentence for emphasis, acknowledging its decisive role in the readers' salvation. Here and in other places in Ephesians (1:13; 2:8; 5:23; 6:17), Paul used language of salvation and being saved to depict liberation from the degrading and enslaving effects of sin, along with rescue from God's righteous judgment against sinners. Paul underscored the assurance of God's saving intervention with an interesting construction that can be translated "you are saved," "you have been saved," or "you are and have been saved" (ἐστε σεσῳσμένοι). With the construction Paul avoided limiting salvation to a discrete event in the past, envisioning the ongoing reality of a state of affairs that had resulted from God's action in the past. The passive voice of the participle (σεσῳσμένοι) reinforced the idea that Paul's readers were the beneficiaries of God's gracious deliverance.

2:6. Paul had established the point that because of believers' union with Christ, God had made Paul and his readers alive together with Christ (2:4–5). Paul proceeded to target two other benefits that followed from being united with the living Christ. God had "raised [them] up" (συνήγειρεν) and had "seated [them]" (συνεκάθισεν) "in the heavenly places" (ἐν τοῖς ἐπουρανίοις) together "with" (συν- prefix) Christ as well. These blessings were experienced "in Christ Jesus" (ἐν Χριστῷ Ἰησοῦ), or because of the readers' union with Christ Jesus. God's regenerated children had received all of God's generous blessings within the context of their ongoing and unbreakable communion with Jesus.

This pairing of being raised up and seated powerfully echoed the truths about Christ's resurrection and exaltation that had been driven home in Ephesians 1:20. Christ's resurrection produced a spiritual resurrection for those united with him (cf. Rom. 6:4; Col. 2:12; 3:1), and his exaltation ushered believers into the presence of God. These stunning realities, while experienced spiritually in believers' current lives, guaranteed the future bodily resurrection and complete glorification of believers at the return of Christ (Rom. 6:5; 8:11; Eph. 1:14).

Blessings Already in Christ

Many commentators have observed the strong strain of what is known as "realized eschatology" (which accentuates believers' current possession of God's ultimate blessings) in the letter of Ephesians. More so than in most other letters (Colossians is similar to Ephesians), Paul spoke of believers having already attained the full range of blessings that God dispensed through Christ Jesus (Eph. 1:3). This strong note of realized eschatology reached a crescendo in Ephesians 2:6. Believers, even in their current lives, were raised up with Christ and seated with him in God's presence! Far from introducing this shocking claim out of the blue, Paul simply followed the logic of believers' union with Christ to its fullest implication. If Paul's readers were "in Christ," and Jesus had been raised and seated with God, then believers must have been raised and seated in the heavenly places as well. Of course, they still carried out their lives in a fallen world, awaiting a final redemption and inheritance (Eph. 1:13–14, 18; 4:30; 5:5). But Paul wanted them to draw on the full spiritual resources that they already possessed in order to walk faithfully with God and counteract the schemes of the devil in their present lives (Eph. 5:15–18; 6:10–13). These teachings on "realized eschatology" fit comfortably within Paul's theological vision and serve as support for Paul's authorship of the letter.

2:7. God's gracious and abundant salvation for Paul and his readers served a specific purpose (ἵνα, "in order to"). God had acted in order to "demonstrate" or "make a public display" (ἐνδείκνυμι) of his character. Elsewhere God "demonstrated" (ἐνδείκνυμι) his power through raising up and judging Pharaoh (Rom. 9:17), and demonstrated his patience by saving a violent persecutor such as Paul (1 Tim. 1:16). Additionally, Paul twice used the cognate noun "demonstration" (ἔνδειξις) to refer to God's demonstration of his righteousness by justifying sinners through the sacrificial death of Christ (Rom. 3:25–26). Earlier in Ephesians (cf. Lincoln, 1990, 109), Paul had noted that God's redemptive blessings declared his glory (1:12, 14) and his glorious grace (1:6).

God exhibited "the surpassing wealth of his grace" (τὸ ὑπερβάλλον πλοῦτος τῆς χάριτος αὐτοῦ). Paul credited God's grace for creating the drastic turnaround in the readers' lives (2:5), so this attribute naturally took the spotlight for the display of God's character. Just as Paul had highlighted the surpassing greatness of God's power (Eph. 1:19; cf. 3:19), he magnified the loftiness and incomparability of God's grace with the descriptor "surpassing" (adj. ptc. from ὑπερβάλλω).

Paul stated the time frame of the exhibition of God's grace. God carried out his saving acts in order to reveal his grace "over the course of the coming ages" (ἐν τοῖς αἰῶσιν τοῖς ἐπερχομένοις). Paul normally operated with a distinction between the present age and the age to come (as in Eph. 1:22), but here he may have had in mind both the near-term and far-term future with the plural "ages" (Hoehner, 2002, 337–38; Bock, 2019, 67). During the present, corrupt age the full magnitude of God's glorious grace was not yet completely revealed (1 Cor. 1:20; 2:6; Gal. 1:4; Titus 2:11–14). Still, when Paul and his readers became seated with Christ in the heavenly realms they began to participate in the blessings of the age to come (1 Cor. 10:11; Eph. 1:3), even while they continued to live in a fallen world. And later in Ephesians 3:10, Paul stated that even now God's redeemed and unified people were a testament of his wisdom to rulers and authorities in the heavenly realms. Similarly, God's grace began to shine publicly as soon as his life-giving work transformed believers (Eph. 2:4–7). In the age to come, which would be set in motion by Christ's return, believers' full, glorious status would become evident to the universe (cf. Rom. 8:18–19; Col. 3:3–4).

Just as Jesus had instructed the disciples to pray that God's kingdom would be made known as fully on earth as it already was in heaven, Paul anticipated a future time period in which an audience of all creation and all powers would fully acknowledge the goodness and greatness of God's rule. Similar to the parable of the mustard seed (Matt. 13:31–32), God's kingdom was easily dismissed as inconsequential in this age, but that would change in the future. In the ages to come, God promised to reign in heaven and on earth, through Christ. But even now, Christ's redeemed people, an unlikely assortment of former enemies of God from various backgrounds and nations, were designed to be a striking testimony to God's forgiving and life-giving grace.

God put his grace on public display by means of directing his "kindness" (χρηστότης) towards Paul and his readers. God's kindness consisted of his benevolent actions towards the recipients of his salvation. Paul included in this kindness all of the spiritual blessings made possible through Christ Jesus and believers' union with him (ἐν Χριστῷ Ἰησοῦ, "in Christ Jesus"). These kind actions testified to the surpassing wealth of God's grace.

God's Grace Brings Salvation and Enables Good Works (2:8–10)

God's grace, not human works, brought salvation, through which newly re-created believers carried out God's good works.

2:8–9. Paul further explained (γάρ, "for") God's grace by repeating his affirmation about grace's role in salvation (2:8a): "by grace you are and have been saved" (χάριτί ἐστε σεσῳσμένοι). Paul likely returned to this because it revealed a central facet of the gospel and helped cultivate gratitude and humility among his readers. In Romans 11, Paul expounded on God's saving plans with Jews and Gentiles, in part to help Gentiles appreciate the mercy God had shown them and recognize the hope that persisted for Jews who were not yet reconciled to God. In Ephesians 2:1–10, Paul reminded the readers of a similar truth by driving home the themes of human sinfulness, God's initiative, and God's mercy and grace apart from human merit.

Paul's readers had experienced the saving grace of God "through faith" (διὰ πίστεως). Paul's mention of faith most probably recalled the readers' faith rather than Christ's faithfulness to God. The readers had benefitted from God's saving work as they had responded in faith to the good news of Christ. In chapter 1, Paul had recounted that the readers had been spiritually integrated into God's family when they heard and believed the good and true message of God's salvation (Eph. 1:13). Paul consistently identified faith as the entryway into new life with God (Rom. 3:28; 4:4–5; 5:1–2; 10:9; Gal. 2:16; Phil. 3:9; Col. 2:12). Faith was the fitting response to God's grace and in no way detracted from God as the sole cause and means of salvation. Faith meant relying upon Christ to do what humans could not do for themselves. His sacrifice for sins and triumph over the grave provided forgiveness and eternal life for previously helpless sinners.

Paul ensured that his readers did not miss the significance of God's grace in salvation by providing additional elaboration (καί, "and"). Paul noted (2:8b) that "this" (τοῦτο), referring broadly to being granted salvation by grace through faith, could not be credited to the readers' doing (τοῦτο οὐκ ἐξ ὑμῶν, "this [is] not from you"). No goodness originating in humans was able to set salvation in motion. Credit for salvation belonged to God, whom Paul spotlighted by putting him at the beginning of the next brief sentence (2:8c). God rescued and redeemed believers solely as a gift—salvation was "a gift from God" (θεοῦ τὸ δῶρον). Words related to "gift" were linked to grace in other passages in which the free nature of God's salvation blessings were highlighted (Rom. 3:24; 5:15–17; 2 Cor. 9:14–15).

To further reinforce his point, Paul stated the contrasting negative point to salvation being God's gift (2:9a): salvation was "not by works" (οὐκ ἐξ ἔργων). In his letters, Paul targeted human works both narrowly and broadly as insufficient for salvation. Jews who relied on old covenant practices such as circumcision and food laws to secure permanent good standing with God and spiritual superiority to Gentiles had missed God's new provision of grace in Christ, through faith (Rom. 3:27–31; 9:30–32; 11:6; Gal. 2:11–21; 3:10–13). More universally, no person, regardless of religious and cultural background could carve out a saving relationship with God through his or her own righteous acts (Rom. 3:20; 4:4–6; Phil. 3:9; 2 Tim. 1:9; Titus 3:4–7).

Next, Paul drove home the unmistakable and intended result (ἵνα, "so that") of God's disarming grace for salvation (2:9b): "so that no one can boast" (ἵνα μή τις καυχήσηται). Paul used language of boasting to depict one's sense of spiritual identity and confidence before God (Rom. 3:27; 1 Cor. 1:28–31; Gal. 6:14). People who sought to define themselves spiritually by appealing to their own spiritual résumés had deluded themselves into thinking that they had the resources to forge a friendly relationship with God. God's grace eliminated any human source for boasting.

Paul understood that the proper response to knowing God through Christ was gratitude, not pride.

2:10. Paul explained (γάρ, "for") what God's grace and initiative led to when he wrapped up this section of discourse. Paul and his readers were God's creation or workmanship (2:10a). Paul first reiterated that God was the sole actor in obtaining salvation for believers. Paul and his readers were the product of "his" (αὐτοῦ) grace, which brought them into a new state of being (ἐσμέν, "we are"). Specifically, they were his "workmanship" or "handiwork" (ποίημα), a term Paul used in Romans 1:20 to describe the natural world that God made. Thus, believers' new lives in Christ arose from another instance of God's creative work of bringing something out of nothing (cf. Rom. 4:17; Heb. 11:3).

Accordingly, Paul said that they were "created" (κτισθέντες) by God (2:10b), or refashioned and renewed according to God's perfect design (cf. Eph. 4:24). In sum, believers were a new creation (2 Cor. 5:17; Gal. 6:15) because of a divine act that paralleled God's original work of creation. In Ephesians 2:10, as in the famous passage 2 Corinthians 5:17, believers experienced this new creation reality "in Christ Jesus" (ἐν Χριστῷ Ἰησοῦ). Their salvation and ongoing growth as disciples emerged within the context of believers' connection to Christ Jesus and his divine life. God did not simply wipe the slate clean of all of believers' sins; he made them alive in Christ and equipped them by the indwelling Spirit to live spiritually productive lives. God had promised to bring about this inner transformation as part of his new covenant relationship with his people (Jer. 31:31–34; Ezek. 36:24–28). God delivered on this promise in Christ Jesus.

God's project of new creation had a purpose (or *telos*; BDAG, s.v. "ἐπί" 16, p. 366).[2] Paul and his readers had been created anew in Christ "for good works" (ἐπὶ ἔργοις ἀγαθοῖς). Though Paul discarded good works as pathway to salvation, he commended good works as an expected result of salvation. The "normal" Christian life was marked by pleasing God and providing tangible love and service to others. Paul showed a constant high regard for good works in his letters (2 Cor. 9:8; Col. 1:10; 2 Thess. 2:17; 1 Tim. 6:18; 2 Tim. 2:11; Titus 2:14; 3:1, 8). Despite the accusations of some of Paul's uninformed critics at the time, who suspected that Paul was preaching a life in Christ that was devoid of any holy or righteous behavior (cf. Rom. 3:8, 31; 6:1, 15), Paul always expected lives of fruitfulness from believers. Good works had always been part of God's master plan as well.

God created Paul's readers for good works, "which he arranged in advance" (οἷς προητοίμασεν ὁ θεός) to be the outcome of true life in Christ (2:10c). From the beginning of time God had planned both for believers' salvation (Eph. 1:4–5; 11) and sanctification in Christ (Eph. 2:10). In these passages Paul employed the pronoun and prefix "pre-" (προ) to convey the idea of God plotting his perfect plans for believers before implementing his great acts of creation, redemption, and new creation (cf. Lincoln, 1990, 115).

Paul and his readers did not have to manufacture these good works, since God had given them the means and motivation, through union with Christ and enablement by his Spirit, to carry them out. God reanimated spiritually dead people and fit them for a life of good works "in order that they might walk in them" (ἵνα ἐν αὐτοῖς περιπατήσωμεν). Paul and his readers, who had once been mired in a bog of sin, slavery, and disobedience, could exchange walking in sin (Eph. 2:1–2) for walking in good works (Eph. 2:10d), all because of the gracious salvation of a God who loved them and had mercy on them.

2 This rarer force of the preposition (ἐπί) followed by the dative surfaces some in Paul's other letters (Gal. 5:13; 1 Thess. 4:7; 2 Tim. 2:14; cf. Moule, 1960, 50).

THEOLOGICAL FOCUS

The exegetical idea (though Paul and his readers were formerly doomed and helpless sinners, God graciously saved them and re-created them by uniting them with Christ's resurrected life and spiritual resources) leads to this theological focus: *God's grace brings salvation and new life in Christ to doomed and helpless sinners.*

This passage regularly highlights God's grace (vv. 5, 7, 8) and the related attributes of mercy (v. 4), love (v. 4), and kindness (v. 7), as the driving force behind God's actions. God's grace motivated him to act generously and powerfully on behalf of undeserving sinners (vv. 5, 8). God's grace shined through in his saving work, so that the whole seen and unseen world might witness the magnitude God's grace, now and forever (v. 7). God's grace, freely given, removed any grounds for believers' boasting (vv. 8–9).

God's grace brings salvation and new life in Christ. God's salvation delivers sinners from the judgment they deserve (v. 3), and the new life he bestows reverses sinners' condition of spiritual death (v. 1). God brings this salvation and new life to sinners in and through Christ Jesus. Believers become united with Christ in his life, raised with Christ in his resurrection, and seated with Christ in God's presence (vv. 5–6). God forms believers into a new creation in Christ, so that their lives bear the fruit of good works that God designed them to carry out (v. 10). Christ Jesus thus in every way becomes the defining mark of believers' identity and destiny.

God's gracious salvation in Jesus Christ rescues doomed and helpless sinners from death and judgment. The destructive workings of sinful desires (v. 3), worldly values (v. 2), and satanic spiritual activity (v. 2) feed upon one another and collude to keep humans spiritually derailed and enslaved to sin. This results in humans being spiritually dead (v. 1) and subject to God's righteous judgment (v. 3b). But God's intervention in Christ Jesus results in a dramatic turnaround for sinners who by faith (v. 8) receive God's gift of salvation and new life.

PREACHING AND TEACHING STRATEGIES

Exegetical and Theological Synthesis

In stark categories, Paul contrasted the human conditions without Christ and with Christ: dead but now alive; under the sentence of God's wrath but now the recipients of his grace; following the forces of evil but now walking in good works. The joyful message of 2:1–10 spoke of a gift made possible by something in God—his mercy, not something in humanity—our merit. Paul emphasized that the believer's faith in Christ enables us to share his resurrection life, and as a result we have the motivation and ability to please God with good works: "We are created in Christ Jesus *to do good works*" (v. 10).

Preaching Idea

We were the walking dead; now we're alive in Christ.

Contemporary Connections:

What does it mean?

What does it mean to be the "walking dead"? It means that we were spiritually flatlined, unresponsive to God. Before being "saved through faith" (v. 8), our consciences were not sensitive to the Holy Spirit; we did not care about God's values, we indulged in the passions of the flesh (v. 3), and we did not delight in worshipping him.

The walking dead—zombies—are dead and decaying people, even though they still walk around. They wreak havoc with the living. The walking dead in the movies sometimes devour people. Sometimes they persecute the living. They contribute nothing to society. And yet, unlike the movies where there is no hope of reviving a zombie, there is hope for people who are spiritually dead.

The story of Paul (also called Saul) illustrates this (Acts 9:1–19; 1 Tim. 1:12–17). In his zeal, he seemed to be alive to God, but then God showed him that he was simply the walking dead—a blasphemer, persecutor, and opponent (1 Tim. 1:13). Other biblical examples illustrate the same turnaround: Manasseh (2 Chron. 33:1–20), the sinful woman who anointed Jesus (Luke 7:36–50), and the prodigal son (Luke 15:11–32). The sidebar offers an illustration of repentance, forgiveness, and new life.

New Life

Melvin Burns had suffered a string of robberies from his organic farm in Nova Scotia, including $1,000 worth of tools and $5,000 worth of animals. So, he used Facebook to offer this incentive: if the thief would turn himself (or herself) in, Burns would give him a job on the farm and teach him agricultural skills. Burns held out the hope to the unknown thief that the farmer's personal training would make him employable and bring him respect. Burns wrote, "Please, if you need money and are close to our farm . . . I will offer you much for free and better things to do with your time, and that's no bull." Burns's grace on the undeserving illustrates God's grace on those who were dead in sins. It also illustrates how grace leads to behavioral change. (Ben Johnson, "To Recover His Stolen Tools, This Farmer Is Offering Bacon and Work," Acton Institute Transatlantic Blog [August 10, 2017]).

Is it true?

Is it true that people who are outside of Christ are the walking dead? This seems to run counter to everyday experience where we see lost people who are very much alive—the vigorous athlete, the creative artist, the vivacious celebrity—but this passage is dealing with spiritual life. Lost people may be alive physically and emotionally, but they are dead where it matters most—in the soul. The story of Chuck Colson (sidebar) illustrates how a spiritually dead person can be made alive in Christ.

Spiritually Dead, Now Alive

Charles Colson was special counsel to President Richard Nixon, and a chief instigator of the low moral climate of the White House in the early '70s. He described himself as "Nixon's hatchet man," and in an internal memo he said that he would "walk over my grandmother for Richard Nixon." Watergate brought his world to a sudden and humiliating crash, but it also brought Colson to see his sin. He cried out to God and was born again. That phrase "born again" become the title of his best-selling autobiography of conversion. Even though the evidence against him was thin, he pled guilty, spent seven months in jail, and flourished like a tree planted by streams of water. He read voraciously, started discipleship groups, and eventually founded Prison Fellowship, now reaching 120 countries. In 1993, he received the prestigious Templeton Prize for Religion and donated the $1 million award to charity. As an article in *Christianity Today* stated, that transformation was possible because "[A]midst the earthquake of Watergate he heard the still small voice of God's call. He obeyed it and stayed faithful to it. As a result he has become a shining example of the transforming power of the Holy Spirit and the redemptive blessings of God's grace. As many of his fellow Christians will say about him, God changed Charles Colson and used him for good." (Jonathan Aitken, "Remembering Charles Colson, a Man Transformed," *Christianity Today*, April 21, 2012)

The Bible's insistence that the walking dead are under the wrath of God (v. 3) may be unappealing for modern audiences. They might be helped by distinguishing divine wrath from the way that emotion is manifested in humans. Divine wrath is not abusive, selfish, or cavalier. Furthermore, wrath is the natural corollary of love. When we deeply love someone such as our children, or even an object such as a work of art, we are properly angry when those things are threatened or spoiled. If a man took a hammer to

Michelangelo's *Pietà*, the public would raise an outcry. That very thing happened in 1972 when a deranged man leaped over the partition in St. Peter's Basilica, Vatican City, and struck the *Pietà* fifteen times with a hammer.[3] Humans are God's "work of art," created to display his glory. So when the walking dead wreak sinful havoc in families and society, they make themselves "objects of God's wrath." C. S. Lewis makes this case in *The Problem of Pain* (1940, 35):

> You asked for a loving God: you have one . . . not a senile benevolence that drowsily wishes you to be happy in your own way, not the cold philanthropy of a conscientious magistrate, not the care of a host who feels responsible for the comfort of his guests, but the consuming fire Himself, the Love that made the worlds, persistent as the artist's love for his work, . . . provident and venerable as a father's love for a child, jealous, inexorable, exacting as love between the sexes.

While some listeners may object to the first part of the preaching idea, other listeners may object to the second part—that spiritual zombies can be forgiven and made alive. If salvation were given by moral reform, they would have a strong case, but this passage says that salvation is a gift of grace, not of works (vv. 8–9). God's grace can be hard to accept when the lesson has been drilled into us from childhood that rewards follow performance. The student who studies hard makes straight As; the salesperson who works long hours receives the bonus; the musician who practices makes first chair. We live in a "meritocracy." This cause-effect system can be heard in the movie *The Sound of Music* when Maria (played by Julie Andrews) discovers the love of a good man. She can't believe her good fortune! Why is she so lucky? She muses that nothing comes from nothing and thus concludes, "So somewhere in my youth or childhood / I must have done something good."

The preaching idea might be upheld with a personal example of a time when a friend forgave you when you were at fault, or a generous benefactor stepped in when you were at your wits' end. You were "dead," but grace stepped in and gave "life." The sidebar offers a contemporary story about death, life, and grace, but grace is not cheap. Turning dead people into living people cost Jesus everything.

Bryan Chapell Illustrates Jesus's Costly Sacrifice

Bryan Chapell's hometown is on the banks of a great river that is regularly dredged to keep it open for commerce. Huge piles of sand line the banks of the river. Of course, few things are so enticing to children as a mountain of sand, but few things are also so dangerous. When the sand piles dry they leave a rigid crust on top, but sometimes caverns are formed below by escaping water. If you walk on the crust, you could easily break through, and you would find yourself in the cavern with the sand above rushing in to fill the void. And that's exactly what happened. Two brothers were playing on a sandpile when it gave way and the sand rushed in. When the brothers didn't return home for dinner, family and neighbors organized a search party. They found the younger brother. Only his head and shoulders were sticking out of the sand, and he was unconscious because of the pressure of the constricting sand. When they dug down to his waist, he revived and they shouted, "Where is your brother!" The boy replied, "I'm standing on his shoulders." With the sacrifice of his own life, the older brother had lifted the younger to safety. With similar selflessness, the one who is not ashamed to call himself our brother (Heb. 2:11), the one who is

3 To see an example of this, search YouTube for "Laslo Toth attacking Michelangelo's *Pietà* with a hammer."

rich in mercy, saved us while we were helpless and doomed. Amazing grace. (Adapted from Bryan and Kathy Chapell, *Each for the Other* [Grand Rapids: Baker, 2006], 14–15)

Now what?

If the walking dead can have new life, what can we do to participate in that miracle? Perhaps consider the homeless. Sometimes homeless people are seen as zombies, nameless pariahs on society. Other overlooked people might be illegal immigrants or prisoners. Many churches, parachurch organizations, and foundations have programs to bring practical help to those who need it, offering God's grace in tangible ways like tutoring and befriending. An organization like Big Brothers Big Sisters of America helps young people find a new outlook and path, and when that kind of help is offered, doors open for conversations about spiritual life in Christ.[4]

Many Christians are too shy or scared to witness to the grace of God, or perhaps they don't know how. If your organization provides training on how to share the hope of the gospel, you might offer that training concurrently with preaching this passage. Alternately, simple and engaging training is available on YouTube.[5]

Creativity in Presentation

The YouTube video above is just one in a series produced by Living Waters University. The videos are short and well done and could be used to complement a sermon.

In smaller churches, spontaneous testimonies could drive home the truth that God makes dead people alive, or in larger churches planned testimonies could do the same. Similarly, testimonies could show how serving the "walking dead" changed not only the ones being served but also the ones doing the serving.

Somewhere in the church service, or perhaps within the sermon itself, the hymn "Amazing Grace" could be used in either its traditional or contemporary versions. Written by former slave trader John Newton, the story behind the hymn nicely illustrates this passage—being dead in trespasses and sins, then being made alive in Christ because of grace and mercy, leading to good works. Enslaved persons are like the walking dead, but Newton came to see that *he* was the one who was dead, and then God gave life.[6]

The following quotation from musician and humanitarian Bono may also illustrate the grace of God:

> I'd be in big trouble if Karma was going to finally be my judge. . . . I'm holding out for Grace. I'm holding out that Jesus took my sins onto the Cross, because I know who I am and I hope I don't have to depend on my own religiosity. . . . The point of the death of Christ is that Christ took on the sins of the world, so that what we put out did not come back to us, and that our sinful nature does not reap the obvious death. That's the point. [Grace] should keep us humbled. It's not our own

4 Helping others find new life changes us too. Perhaps share Tim Denning, "10 Life Changing Lessons That Helping Homeless People Taught Me," Addicted2Success, September 8, 2015, https://addicted2success.com/success-advice/10-life-changing-lessons-that-helping-homeless-people-taught-me.

5 To see an example of this, search YouTube for videos on sharing the gospel and training to share the gospel.

6 "John Newton," *Christianity Today*, http://www.christianitytoday.com/history/people/pastorsandpreachers/john-newton.html; Wikipedia contributors, "John Newton," *Wikipedia*, last revised August 31, 2020, https://en.wikipedia.org/wiki/John_Newton.

good works that get us through the gates of heaven.[7]

The following illustration could be used to talk about how God rescued us:

> In July of 2016, seven-year-old Chloe Smith spotted a discarded Olympic gold medal in a pile of trash while on a walk with her father. The medal had been stolen in June from the car of Joe Jacobi, winner of the men's canoe double slalom at the 1992 Olympics in Barcelona. The girl quickly grabbed the misplaced medal and sought out its rightful owner. Finding some social media posts from Jacobi, she soon discovered that he was the owner, and was able to return the medal to a very pleased former Olympian. In the same way, Christ finds us in our mess, defaced and discarded by the devil, and restores us to our rightful place with God.[8]

The preaching idea picks up the flow of thought in the passage with contrast (what we *were* by nature and what we *are* by grace) and causality (being raised with Christ is possible *because of* the grace and power of God, and *results in* good works). This figure could be drawn on a flip chart while teaching the passage or projected on a screen one element at a time as part of a sermon outline.

Whatever creative methods we use, we will want to stress the main idea that God has included us in Jesus's death and resurrection, so now we can live in ways that please him. We were the walking dead; now we are alive in Christ.

This outline could work with the figure above:

- Before Christ, we were dead, enslaved, and condemned (vv. 1–3).
  Draw the first part of the preaching idea—"walking dead."
- Now in Christ we are alive and seated in the heavenly places (vv. 4–7).
  Draw the second part of the preaching idea—alive in Christ.
- This is possible because of the grace of God, not our good works (vv. 8–9).
  Draw the third part—grace.
- Therefore, we walk in good works (v. 10).
  Draw the last part here—we walk in righteousness.

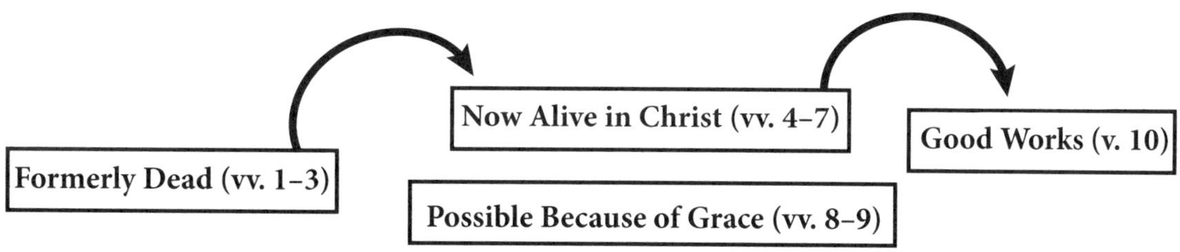

The Progression of Ephesians 2:1–10

7 Bono, *Bono: In Conversation with Michka Assayas* (New York: Riverhead Books, 2005), 226–27.
8 Catherine Thorbeck, "6-Year-Old Girl Finds Olympic Gold Medal, Returns It to Owner," July 5, 2016, ABC News, https://abcnews.go.com/US/year-girl-finds-olympic-gold-medal-returns-owner/story?id=40344677.

DISCUSSION QUESTIONS

1. Ephesians 2:1 says that people are "dead" before they are in Christ. What does that mean?

2. Didn't God give us desires? In what sense are the "desires of the flesh (body)" wrong (v. 3)?

3. How did God make us "alive with Christ," and what does that mean (v. 5)?

4. What does being "raised with Christ and seated in the heavenly places" (v. 6) mean? Why don't we always experience this reality in our daily experience?

5. Why does it take mercy on God's part to save us (v. 4)?

6. Ephesians 2:8 says that we are saved "not by our own doing." Does that mean that humans have no part whatsoever in salvation? Why or why not?

7. What are some of the good works that Paul might have had in mind in verse 10?

8. What specific good works do you sense God is preparing for you in your life right now?

Ephesians 2:11–22

EXEGETICAL IDEA
Through Christ's sacrifice former spiritual outsiders, the Gentiles, along with spiritual insiders, the Jews, had become part of a new, unified, and reconciled people who experienced the Father's presence in the Spirit.

THEOLOGICAL FOCUS
Jesus Christ brings diverse people together into a right relationship with God and one another, in the Spirit.

PREACHING IDEA
God has torn down the walls, so let the walls come down!

PREACHING POINTERS
During Paul's time, religious and cultural barriers separated Jews from Gentiles. The Jews' monotheistic worldview, practice of circumcision, observance of dietary laws, and celebration of distinct religious festivals set them apart from their Gentile neighbors. A literal wall even kept the Gentiles from entering the inner courts of the Jerusalem temple. The Jews, who were in a covenant relationship with God, were spiritual insiders, while people from all other nations (the Gentiles) were spiritual outsiders. Now, upon the arrival of Jesus, God sorted people into new categories according to their response to Christ Jesus. Many Gentiles had entered into a relationship with God through faith in Jesus, and Paul wrote this passage to help them recognize what a stunning gift God had given them by making them insiders through Christ. Likewise, the Jews needed to realize that God had sent Jesus to restore them to a right relationship with God and secure for them permanent insider status as well. Jews and Gentiles together were now part of something new, and Christ had brought them into this new relationship in the same way—by shedding his blood for them.

Barriers continue to divide people. Some barriers are literal, like the one that once divided East Germany from West Germany, or the Great Wall of China that was originally constructed to divide a newly consolidated empire from northern invaders. Other barriers are ideological, evident during radio and television talk shows, on social media posts, and in speeches. People tend to demonize the "other." Demonization can even occur in the church when we separate from one another over secondary doctrinal issues, but through Jesus, unity exists with diversity. That theological indicative is the basis of the moral imperative in 4:3, "Maintain the unity of the Spirit in the bond of peace." Because God has torn down the walls, let the walls come down!

CHRIST RECONCILES SINNERS TO GOD AND TO EACH OTHER (2:11–22)

LITERARY STRUCTURE AND THEMES (2:11–22)

As with the previous passage, in 2:11–22 Paul began with the problem of his readers' former separation from God, highlighted God's gracious intervention through Christ, and then celebrated the change in spiritual status that resulted. But this time Paul expanded his focus, moving from the salvation of individual sinners in 2:1–10 to the reconciliation of both Jews and Gentiles to God and each other in 2:11–22.

There are four movements in the passage. First, Paul presented Christ as the resolution to the gloomy reality of his Gentile readers' alienation from God and God's family (2:11–13). Second, Paul announced a central feature of Christ's work—he had gathered together Jewish and Gentile believers in Christ to become a new, unified, and reconciled people of God (2:14–16). Third, this fulfilled the OT vision of God making a proclamation of peace between himself and those who were both near and far from him (2:17–18). Finally, believers were not just brought near to God, they were integrated into a holy building project, in which God incorporated both Jews and Gentiles who followed Christ into his sacred dwelling (2:19–22).

Paul repeated words such as "peace" and "one" to make clear his interest in God's saving project for Jews and Gentiles. As a new humanity in Christ, Jews and Gentiles were reconciled to one another and to God. Paul also repeatedly returned to Christ's sacrificial work on the cross as the key to carrying out God's work among Jews and Gentiles. In addition, especially toward the end of the passage Paul offered glimpses into the Trinitarian contours of believers' lives with God. Through Christ's ministry and in the Spirit, believers experienced God's ongoing presence as Father.

- ***Former Outsiders Are Now Part of God's Family (2:11–13)***
- ***Christ Brings Peace and Unity to Formerly Divided and Condemned Gentiles and Jews (2:14–16)***
- ***Christ Brings Peace and Relational Access to the Father in the Spirit (2:17–18)***
- ***United Believers Are Built into a Sacred Dwelling for God (2:19–22)***

EXPOSITION (2:11–22)

In this passage, Paul wanted to highlight the sacrificial ministry of Jesus Christ that brought former outsiders, the Gentiles, and former insiders, the Jews, into reconciled relationships with God and with one another. Those who were in Christ and had been reconciled through Jesus's death on the cross had entered into a relationship of unity and peace that broke down walls. These walls had separated Jews and Gentiles for many centuries, and they spanned multiple areas of religious and cultural life. The daily choices both Jews and Gentiles made about what and with whom to eat, what feasts or festivals to observe, and what days to work and rest confirmed the presence of these walls. Behind these daily customs were fundamental differences in worship and belief, centered in the fact that God had chosen Israel to know and worship him alone, rather than the many gods and idols in the surrounding world. Paul explained that God had destroyed dividing walls by inviting both Jews and Gentiles to be recipients of his presence and promises in the person and work of Christ Jesus.

Former Outsiders Are Now Part of God's Family (2:11–13)

Paul's Gentile readers had been formerly excluded from the blessings and hope of being part of God's family, but now they were included in God's family through Christ's sacrifice.

2:11. Paul transitioned (Διό, "therefore") to a new but related topic. Paul summoned his readers to "remember" (μνημονεύετε, impv.) some vital spiritual truths about their past (ποτέ, "formerly") spiritual condition. Paul then signaled exactly what he wanted his readers to remember (ὅτι, "that"). First, though, Paul broke his train of thought (picking it up again at the beginning of verse 12 with a second occurrence of ὅτι) to address and describe his audience.

Paul addressed his readers directly as "you" (ὑμεῖς), before identifying them as Gentiles (τὰ ἔθνη). In Paul's Jewish context, the Gentiles were simply people from other, non-Jewish nations (ἔθνος indicated people belonging to other ethnic groups or nations). But the Jews did not view the Gentiles simply as neighbors who lived alongside them as equals. First and foremost, Gentiles were non-Jews; they were spiritual outsiders: "Don't forget that you Gentiles used to be outsiders" (NLT). There were clearly defined beliefs and practices that separated Jews from Gentiles.

> **How Jews Were Distinct from Gentiles**
>
> As Jews in Asia Minor and other communities outside Judea coexisted alongside non-Jews, they continued to draw their sense of identity from historic beliefs and practices rooted in the Scriptures. The Jews worshipped the God who had called them into a covenantal relationship with himself. They were to worship YHWH alone and reject all idols. This holy God called them to be holy as well (Lev. 11:44, 45; 19:2; 20:7, 26: 21:8) and to learn how to distinguish between the holy and common, the clean and unclean (Lev. 10:1–10; Ezek. 22:26; 44:23). Practices emerging from these beliefs helped keep Jews distinct from Gentiles. These special practices included having males adopt the covenant sign of circumcision, following specific dietary codes according to the Jewish food laws, engaging in ceremonial practices such as ritual baths, and celebrating the Sabbath and Jewish festivals. Jewish identity was also reinforced through expectations of marrying only other Jews and the intentional training of both proselytes (Gentile converts to Judaism) and children in the beliefs and practices of the Jewish people (Barclay, 1996, 408–13).

As he recognized this common understanding of Gentiles, Paul added "in the body" (ἐν σαρκί) as a modifier to "the Gentiles." This modifier served several purposes. First, the qualifier "in the body" marked Paul's Gentile readers as outsiders in one sense, but not in the most important sense. Though they belonged to "the nations" and not Israel, this was true only in a physical sense. These categories of Jews and Gentiles were secondary to the new category that Paul would soon introduce. Because of Jesus Christ, the very label of "Gentiles" would soon lose its importance. Second, "in the body" drew attention to the physical practice of circumcision as a convenient way to identify how people were sorted into these insider and outsider groups. Paul made this clear in the second half of verse 11. A third possible reason Paul used "in the body" to describe the Gentiles was that their physical status of being Gentiles paled in comparison to what Christ achieved in *his* physical body (since Paul used σάρξ, "body," to describe Christ's bodily sacrifice later in the passage). Christ's body made the bodily distinctions and the insider/outsider categories based on them irrelevant.

Paul further identified the Gentiles (app. phrase beginning with οἱ λεγόμενοι) by noting that the Gentiles' uncircumcised status made them outsiders, particularly from a traditional Jewish perspective. The Gentiles were "the uncircumcised" (from ἀκροβυστία); at least, that is how they were labeled (οἱ λεγόμενοι, "the so-called," conveys the idea of labeling) "by those who identified themselves as the circumcised group" (ὑπὸ τῆς λεγομένης περιτομῆς). Paul used the terms "uncircumcised" (ἀκροβυστία) and "circumcised" (περιτομή) to reflect the Jewish understanding of how God viewed people. This sorting of people into groups of circumcised insiders and uncircumcised outsiders reflected the value the Jews placed on circumcision as a sign of God's original covenant with them (cf. Gen. 17). According to the Jews, the Gentiles' uncircumcised status reflected their exclusion from the blessings of belonging to God's special people.

Paul distanced himself from this simplistic sorting of Jews and Gentiles with another reminder that circumcision was still just "in the body" (ἐν σαρκί). And as a final way of minimizing the significance of the categories of the circumcised and uncircumcised, Paul pointed out that the Jews' circumcision "resulted from the work of human hands" (χειροποίητος) rather than from divine intervention. These final points reflected Paul's view elsewhere that a metaphorical, Spirit-implemented circumcision of the heart had eclipsed physical circumcision as the identifying mark of God's people (Rom. 2:29; Col. 2:11; cf. Deut. 30:6).

2:12. Next, Paul returned to his original thought by repeating "that" (ὅτι), which reintroduced the content of what he wanted the readers to remember. Likewise, Paul specified that it was "at that time" (τῷ καιρῷ ἐκείνῳ), or the time before God had included them in his family through Christ (2:13), that certain things had been true of his Gentile readers. At that time Paul's readers had belonged neither to God's chosen people nor to the Christ who would secure a bright future for God's people. Paul used the verb "you were" (ἦτε) to make five points about his Gentile readers' formerly deficient spiritual status.

First, Paul's Gentile readers in the past had been "separated from Christ" (χωρὶς Χριστοῦ), meaning that they had no connection to the promised Messiah of Israel in their history. Before they had heard about Christ and believed in him (Eph. 1:13), Paul's Gentile readers had lacked any direct association with the centerpiece of God's saving plans for the world. God had promised to send his anointed King for Israel (2 Sam. 7:8–16; Ps. 2; Isa. 9:6–7).[1] In fact, Jesus had come "to the Jews first" (Rom. 1:16). If God had not extended his mercy to them, Paul's Gentile readers would have had no share in any of the blessings God had designed for his people (Eph. 1:3). Paul wanted them to remember that they had not always been "in Christ" (2:13). There was a time when they had been separated from him.

Second, Paul's Gentile readers had been "excluded from citizenship in Israel" (ἀπηλλοτριωμένοι τῆς πολιτείας τοῦ Ἰσραήλ).[2] The term for "excluded" (ἀπαλλοτριόω) in this context viewed the Gentiles as being separated from something desirable (BDAG, s.v. "ἀπαλλοτριόω," p. 96). Paul acknowledged "citizenship" (πολιτεία)in Israel as an advantage in past history. God had appointed Israel as his "treasured possession," his "kingdom of priests," and a "holy nation" (Exod. 19:5–6). God had chosen Israel for himself, to both know him and represent him to the world. God had selected Israel for this honor, in distinction from the Gentiles, the

1 Some Jewish writings during the Second Temple period (1 Q28a; 4Q174; 4Q246; Pss. Sol.) demonstrated the continued expectation of a coming Davidic Messiah among some of the Jews (Bateman, 2012, 321–25).

2 The participle "you were excluded" (ἀπηλλοτριωμένοι) functions adjectivally as the complement of the subject "you" (ὑμεῖς) from verse 11.

inhabitants of other nations. Though God had intended for the Gentiles to receive blessings through Abraham's family (Gen. 12:3), the Gentiles had mostly remained on the outside looking in.

Citizenship

People in the ancient Roman world highly valued citizenship. Only some residents in the empire were counted as citizens of Rome. Legal benefits that accompanied citizenship included rights of appeal and requests for specific trial locations, along with protection from especially harsh punishments (Acts 22:25–29; 25:11; 26:32; cf. *DPL*, 140; Polhill, 1999, 15–16). People gained citizenship through a variety of means, including services or gifts to the empire or being born to parents who were citizens (Ferguson, 2003, 62–63). Cities granted citizenship as well. Paul was both a Roman citizen (Acts 16:37–38; 22:25–29) and a citizen of his hometown Tarsus (Acts 21:39). Paul took the idea of citizenship and used it as a metaphor for membership in Israel. Citizenship in Israel connoted belonging to the people that God himself had chosen and established. The people of Israel had played a special role in God's saving plans for the world. The Gentiles (with a few exceptions) had not gained membership in this special people or special plans, before Jesus arrived on the scene.

Paul's third point about his Gentile readers was closely related to the second. They had been "foreigners to the covenants of the promise" (ζένοι τῶν διαθηκῶν τῆς ἐπαγγελίας). They used to have no claim on the abundant future promised by God to his covenantal people. Paul enlisted the word "foreigners" (ξένοι) to describe the Gentiles' lack of access to this promised future. Interestingly, Paul used the singular "promise" to modify the plural "covenants" (cf. Rom. 9:4). God had made and reaffirmed covenants with Abraham and his descendants (Gen. 12, 15, 17, 22, 26, 28; Exod. 3; 2 Sam. 7; Jer. 31) that promised to benefit the people of Israel. Though these covenants had contained specific promises of land, descendants, security, and God's presence, the phrase "the covenants of the promise" likely envisioned multiple covenants(the Abrahamic, Davidic, and new covenants) pointing toward a single promised future (cf. Lincoln, 1990, 137; Arnold, 2010, 155). The individual covenants fed into the ultimate promise of God dwelling with his people in a fruitful and secure land. Gentiles had been outsiders to this promise, apart from the dramatic reversal of fortunes Paul prepared to unveil in the next verse. But first, Paul offered two more descriptions.

Fourth, Paul's Gentile readers "had been without hope" (ἐλπίδα μὴ ἔχοντες). Unlike the people of Israel, the Gentiles had received no promised future to look forward to. "Hope" (ἐλπίς) in its fullest sense depended on an assured future. The Gentiles had possessed no direct claim on the blessings that had been promised to the people of Israel through the Abrahamic and Davidic covenants. In the absence of covenantal promises from God, people were left with only wishful thinking. Prior to Christ Jesus's ministry, the Gentiles had possessed no guarantee from God about their future and thus had looked forward to no ultimate hope (1 Thess. 4:13).

Paul completed his list of characterizations of his Gentile readers' past spiritual condition by noting that they were "without God" (ἄθεοι) in their worldly existence (ἐν τῷ κόσμῳ, "in the world"). Paul's readers had not experienced God's supportive presence in their daily lives (BDAG, s.v. "ἄθεος" 1, p. 24). Israel had known what it was like to have God dwell in their midst. In fact, at the heart of God's covenants with Israel was his provision of a way for Israel to experience his presence in an ongoing relationship (Lev. 26:11–12; Jer. 31:33–34). Significantly, the book of Revelation presented God's permanent dwelling with his people as the climax of the biblical story (21:3–4). Once again, the

Gentiles were formerly excluded from this privilege, and they had been helpless to do anything to change their own situation.

2:13. Paul had set the stage for Christ Jesus's dramatic entrance. Paul contrasted (δέ, "but") the past with the present (νυνί, "now"). Verse 13 contrasts two ways in which God's intervention had changed the Gentile readers' situation. Because they were now "in Christ Jesus" (ἐν Χριστῷ Ἰησοῦ), the readers had experienced change in their proximity to God. Though the readers had existed among "those who were once far from God" (οἵ ποτε ὄντες μακράν), now "they had been brought near" (ἐγενήθητε ἐγγύς) to him. It was God who had acted on behalf of the Gentiles (divine pass. of γίνομαι). It was God who had brought them "near" (ἐγγύς) to him.

The source of Paul's "near" (ἐγγύς) and "far" (μακράν) language became clearer when the readers reached 2:17, where Paul alluded to language from Isaiah 57:19. In the context of 2:13, the main idea was the contrast between remoteness and closeness. This also prepared the way for Paul's pronouncement (v. 18) that believers were brought so near that they were now granted access to God's fatherly presence. Paul highlighted the reason for this change—Christ had shed his blood for them in his death on the cross. The prepositional phrase "by the blood of Christ" (ἐν τῷ αἵματι τοῦ Χριστοῦ) indicated the means by which the readers had been brought near to God. Through the blood of Christ (cf. Eph. 1:7), Paul's Gentile readers experienced a complete reversal of their spiritual standing with God.

Christ Brings Peace and Unity to Formerly Divided and Condemned Gentiles and Jews (2:14–16)

Formerly divided and condemned Gentiles and Jews now had peace with God, since they had become a new, unified, and reconciled people through Christ's sacrifice.

2:14. Paul kept the focus on Christ, introducing additional explanation of Christ's work with the connective "for" (γάρ). First, Paul affirmed that "he [Christ Jesus] is our peace" (αὐτος ἐστιν ἡ εἰρήνη ἡμῶν). Isaiah 9:6–7 identifies the promised Davidic king as "prince of peace" and highlighted the centrality of peace to his rule (cf. Stuhlmacher, 1986, 187). Paul's sentence (using the verb ἐστιν, "is") functioned as a compact way of simultaneously identifying Christ as the securer of divine peace for the believer and acknowledging the deeply personal way that Christ secured it. When Paul shifted the pronouns to first person with "our" (ἡμῶν), it notified the reader that Paul no longer described the Gentiles alone. This aspect of Christ's work applied to both Jews and Gentiles. The peace that resulted from Christ's work was a product of reconciled relationships.

Christ's Ministry of Peace

Paul made peace his central emphasis in 2:14–18. In this context, peace meant "right, harmonious relationships with God and others" (cf. BDAG, s.v. "εἰρήνη" 1b, p. 287). Paul discussed peace alongside the related concepts of unity and reconciliation, since Christ created peace in relationships that had been marked by division and estrangement. The Greek term for "peace" (εἰρήνη) corresponded to the Hebrew idea of *shalom* (שָׁלוֹם), with its semantic range that included the absence of conflict, the presence of human flourishing, and salvation from God (HALOT 2:1506–10). The book of Isaiah in particular inspired Paul's notion of peace, and Isaiah displayed an eschatological peace in various places (9:6–7; 52:7; 53:5; 54:10; 57:19; 66:12). This proclaimed peace that God promised to secure and deliver affected the entire existence of God's people, including their relationship with him and the nations around them. According to Paul in Ephesians 2:14–18, this ultimate peace arrived in the person and ministry of Jesus.

Paul unpacked the way that peace was found in Christ Jesus by indicating two ways (using two parallel ptc. phrases) in which Christ had obtained peace for all believers. First, Christ "had made the two groups into one" (ὁ ποιήσας τὰ ἀμφότερα ἓν). Paul's term for "two" (ἀμφότεροι), which appeared three times in 2:14–18, meant "both," which indicated that the two parts (Jews and Gentiles) made up the whole of (the old) humanity. Christ had now joined the two together into one new people. Paul sprinkled in three more references to the oneness of Jews and Gentiles in Christ in verses 15–18.

Second, Christ "had broken down the dividing wall" (τὸ μεσότοιχον τοῦ φραγμοῦ λύσας) that kept the two groups apart. "The dividing wall" (τὸ μεσότοιχον τοῦ φραγμοῦ) had stood between Jews and Gentiles, dividing them from one another. Paul used the image of a dividing wall metaphorically, to paint the picture of an insurmountable barrier between the two groups. Paul revealed that Christ had decisively eliminated the barrier when he "broke down" the wall (ESV, NASB, NRSV, NKJV, NLT), "destroyed" it (NIV, NET) or "tore [it] down" (CSB). The dividing wall had been accompanied by the "hostility" (ἔχθρα), or antagonism, that existed between the two groups.

The Dividing Wall

An actual wall kept Gentiles out of the inner courts of the temple in Jerusalem. Josephus described this wall and mentioned multiple inscriptions that forbade Gentiles from entering (*Ant.* 15. 417, *J.W.* 5.194; 6.124–126). Two surviving temple stones with an inscription written in Greek can be found in Istanbul's Archaeology Museum (see image 6) and Jerusalem's Israel Museum (Cotton, 2010, 42–45). Paul had even been accused of bringing the Gentile Trophimus (who was from Ephesus) into forbidden areas of the temple complex (Acts 21:27–29). Paul may have had this wall in mind with his metaphor in Ephesians 2:14 (Arnold, 2010, 159–60; Cohick, 2010, 76), though some scholars are not convinced (Hoehner, 2002, 369; Thielman, 2010, 165). The wall was a visible reminder of the Gentiles' exclusion from citizenship in Israel (2:12), and it prevented the Gentiles from drawing near to God's glorious presence (2:18). Paul's use of the language of "near" and "far" also supported the spatial image of differing degrees of nearness to God's presence. Though Paul used different wording for the "wall" (μεσότοιχον) than what appears in the inscriptions and Josephus's description of the wall, his language corresponded well to the realities of that dividing wall in the temple and the broader divisions between Jews and Gentiles that the wall represented.

Jerusalem Temple Inscription.
Courtesy of Istanbul Archaeological Museum Istanbul Archaeology Museums / CC BY-SA (https://creative-commons.org/licenses/by-sa/3.0).

Christ had destroyed this dividing wall of hostility "in his body" (ἐν τῇ σαρκὶ αὐτοῦ). The reference to "body" (σάρξ) complemented the prior mention of Christ's blood in verse 13 to serve as shorthand for the sacrificial death of Christ for sinners. Paul presented Christ's physical body as the focal point of God's victorious work over sin and its destructive effects (cf. Rom. 8:3; Col. 1:22). Christ resolved the problem of division and hostility, not by acting against the Jews and Gentiles and their sinful practices but by offering his own body in death on their behalf.

TRANSLATION ANALYSIS: The phrase "in his body" (ἐν τῇ σαρκὶ αὐτοῦ) probably fits better with the second participle in verse 14 (λύσας, *"has broken down"*) than with the participle in verse 15 (καταργήσας, "setting aside"). Thus, Paul was saying that Christ had broken down the dividing wall in his body (through his sacrificial death). In verse 16, Paul said something similar with "putting to death the hostility in him" (ἀποκτείνας τὴν ἔχθραν ἐν αὐτῷ), just in a crisper way. English translations supporting this first option (that "in his body" is connected to verse 14) include the ESV, NRSV, and NLT (cf. Thielman, 2010, 168), while the NIV, NASB, NKJV, NET, and CSB prefer the second option (that "in his body" is connected to verse 15; cf. Hoehner, 2002, 373). Paul could also have inserted "in his body" as an unattached addendum, as another reminder of the centrality of Christ's physical death to God's whole operation of creating peace (Arnold, 2010, 161–62).

2:15. Paul proceeded to unpack the metaphor of the vivid destruction of a dividing wall by identifying the means of this destruction (ptc. phrase ending in καταργήσας). Christ had broken down the dividing wall by taking action against "the law, with its commandments in the form of binding decrees" (ὁ νόμος τῶν ἐντολῶν ἐν δόγμασιν). When the law's commandments were considered in their official, binding form (cf. Col. 2:14), as part of Israel's relationship with God under the old covenant, they became grounds for condemnation against people (cf. 2 Cor. 3:9). This created a problem that Jesus resolved in his sacrificial ministry. Paul understood the law as a whole as God's gift (Rom. 7:12; 9:4), but a fixation on the observance or non-observance of the law diverted attention away from God's radical provision of grace and righteousness in Christ (Rom. 3:21–31; 9:30–10:4; Gal. 2:21; 3:21–25). Christ had confronted and defeated the condemning effects of sin under the law (Eph. 2:16; cf., Rom. 8:1–4; Gal. 3:13; Col. 2:14) and thereby obliterated the dividing effects of the law and its demands (Eph. 2:14–15; cf., Gal. 3:23–28). The universal problem of sin called for a universal, God-initiated solution that reconciled both Jews and Gentiles to God (cf. Stuhlmacher, 1986, 189–90).

Specifically, Christ had "set aside" (καταργέω) the law, with its commandments and binding decrees. This participle (καταργήσας) most likely related back to the immediately preceding participial phrase (τὸ μεσότοιχον τοῦ φραγμοῦ λύσας), giving additional insight into the means by which Christ destroyed the dividing wall. The word for "set aside" (καταργέω) could relay a meaning as strong as "destroy" or "abolish" or as moderate as "set aside" or "nullify" (BDAG, s.v. "καταργέω," 525–26). When applied to the law, as in this case, "set aside" (NIV) or "make something unbinding" (cf. CSB, NET) seems more appropriate than "abolish" (ESV, NASB, NRSV, NKJV). Christ had not carried out destructive attacks against God's law but rather had ushered in a new covenant that set aside the law as a comprehensive, judgment-inducing system (cf. Col. 2:14) and empowered believers to fulfill the truest goals of the law—to love God and others (Mark 12:28–31; Rom. 8:3–4; 13:8–10), thus carrying out the "law of Christ" (1 Cor. 9:21; Gal. 6:2).

With a marker of purpose (ἵνα, "in order that"), Paul examined two goals for Jesus's action to set aside the law and its binding commandments. First, Christ took the two, formerly divided groups and created in himself one new humanity. The "from-two-to-one" pattern resurfaced from verse 14. Those who started as two groups (τοὺς δύο, "the two") turned "into one" (εἰς ἕνα), by Christ's action. The old paradigm of sharp distinction between Jews and Gentiles was being eliminated.

Christ's purpose was to "create" (κτίζω) a new entity through his work on the cross. This language added to the growing list of instances of "new creation" ideas in the letter (Eph. 2:10 had previously used κτίζω in reference to believers). Everything would culminate in the final work of God gathering and uniting all things in Christ (Eph 1:10; cf. *CNTUOT*, 814). Christ had accomplished this new creation "in himself" (ἐν αὐτῷ), as a natural extension of his own new creation existence (cf. 2 Cor. 5:16–17). Believers had found their new creation identity only as part of their union with Christ, which they shared together with other believers. Christ Jesus created within himself "one new humanity" (εἰς ἕνα καινὸν ἄνθρωπον). This one new humanity arose in stark contrast to the long-standing divided humanity of Jews and Gentiles seen throughout salvation history. Jesus's creation of this new, unified humanity brought salvation history a crucial step closer to all things being made new and united in him (Eph. 1:10). Paul would later springboard from this idea of newness in Ephesians 4, when he instructed believers to leave behind the old way of living and to embrace the new way (Eph. 4:20–24).

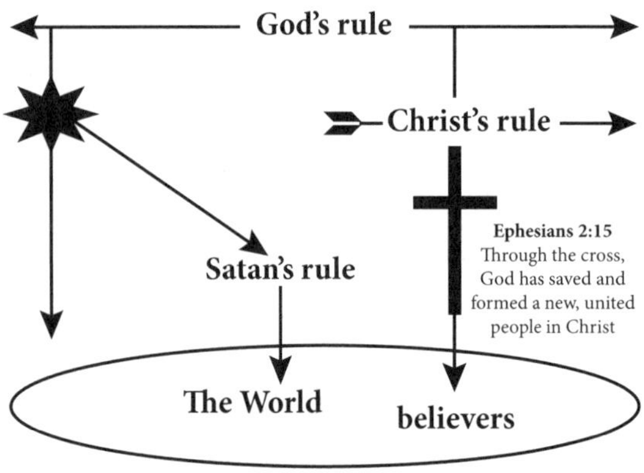

Through the Cross, God Saves and Forms a New Humanity

TRANSLATION ANALYSIS: The term "man" (ἄνθροπος) is difficult to translate in this context, since the "one new man" related both to an individual man (Jesus, who creates the new man "in himself") and to a group (consisting of a new type of person, neither Jew nor Gentile). The translation "man" (ESV, NASB, NET, NKJV, CSB) accords with the new man being constituted in Jesus Christ. The translations "humanity" (NIV, NRSV) and "people" (NLT) recognize the corporate nature of the new humanity.

Before moving on to Christ's second purpose for nullifying the law, Paul returned to the theme of peace. Christ's work of creating a new humanity out of Jews and Gentiles had resulted in peace (ποιῶν εἰρήνην, "making peace," adv. ptc. of result; Wallace, 1996, 639). After introducing Christ as believers' peace (2:14a), Paul had explored what this looked like for the common life of Jews and Gentiles in Christ. This unity in Christ was not simply the absence of division but was the positive generation of peace. Believers could celebrate both unity and peace as Christ's doing. He had already secured these things for both Jews and Gentiles, so that unity and peace were part of the believers' DNA as a new humanity in Christ. When Paul later called his readers to promote unity and peace in their relationships with one another, he asked only that they keep or preserve the unity and peace that Christ had already established (Eph. 4:3).

2:16. Christ's work on the cross, as introduced in verse 14, served two purposes (both governed by ἵνα, "in order that," from verse 15b). The first purpose had been to bring Jews and Gentiles together as one in Christ. The second purpose was "to reconcile" (ἵνα . . . ἀποκαταλλαξῃ) these Jews and Gentiles to God. If the first component of Christ's work achieved peace among people, the second component achieved peace between people and God (cf. Rom. 5:1–11; Col. 1:19–22). We can refer to these components as "horizontal and vertical reconciliation." Paul implied that both Gentiles and Jews needed this vertical reconciliation with God through Christ, in addition to horizontal reconciliation with one another.

Most commentators suspect that with "reconcile" (ἀποκαταλλάσω), Paul crafted a previously unknown variation of the common word for "reconcile" (καταλλάσσω) in order to communicate the extraordinary nature of this divine reconciliation. When Paul used the innovative term for reconciling here and in Colossians 1:20–22, he took the basic meaning of restoring peace between two parties but likely intensified it. This intensification captured the divine wonder of God being one of the parties, as well as the expansive reach of the reconciliation. God had reconciled individuals to himself, but within a larger reconstructive work that touched the whole body of Christ and even the entire universe (Col. 1:20; cf. Eph. 1:9–10).

Christ had reconciled the two groups (τοὺς ἀμφοτέρους, "both of them") together to God. Since Jews and Gentiles who had faith in Christ Jesus had been made into one new humanity because of Christ's work, it was only logical that they were reconciled to God as a unit. This newly created humanity of believers had been constituted as one new entity "in one body" (ἐν ἑνὶ σώματι)—*Christ's* body. Jesus Christ gave his body sacrificially to create a new body of believers, and as head of this new body, he led his new people into a renewed relationship with humanity's creator.

As part of his steady drumbeat in this passage, Paul pointed to the cross (διὰ τοῦ σταυροῦ, "through the cross") as the means by which God had made peace and reconciliation possible. It was the death of Jesus that marvelously created wholeness to the relationship between God and his newly formed people (cf. 1 Cor. 1:17–25; Col. 1:20).

Crucifixion

The Romans carried out crucifixions as public, painful, and humiliating executions of condemned criminals. Death on a cross typically followed tortures such as flogging (Hengel, 1977, 27–32). Cicero described the cross as "an accursed thing" (*In Verrem* 2.5.162) and the practice of crucifixion as "that most cruel and disgusting penalty" (*In Verrem* 2.5.165). Josephus viewed crucifixion as "the most pitiable of deaths" (*J.W.* 7.202–203). Jesus willingly took on this painful and degrading form of death in order to bring peace and reconciliation to sinners.

Christ had brought reconciliation by means of "putting to death" (ἀποκτείνας) the obstacle to reconciliation. Paul deftly moved from the jarring image of the infliction of death on a cross to the recognition that Jesus's death on the cross had entailed the "killing" of something. What Jesus had put to death was the aforementioned "hostility" (τὴν ἔχθραν). This recalled the hostility first introduced as the barrier between Jews and Gentiles (v. 14). But now that Paul had added the component of vertical reconciliation to the discussion, the hostile breach between God and sinful humanity had been destroyed as well (Stuhlmacher, 1986, 190; Thielman, 2010, 172). God forgave the sins that had separated both Gentles and Jews from Christ (Isa. 59:2; Moritz, 1996, 41).

Christ eliminated these two dimensions of hostility "in himself" (ἐν αὐτῷ), meaning in his body. This reemphasized the personal nature of Jesus's work on the cross, as already highlighted with the wording "in Christ Jesus" (2:13), "in the blood of Christ" (2:13), and "in his body" (2:14). Christ's body was the focal point for the destruction of sin and barriers to reconciliation as well as for the formation of one new and reconciled body of believers ("in him," verse 15; "in one body," verse 16).

Christ Brings Peace and Relational Access to the Father in the Spirit (2:17–18)

In his earthly ministry Christ had proclaimed and secured peace for both those far from and near to God, meaning that both Gentiles and Jews now had relational access to the Father in the Spirit.

2:17. Paul tied this new subsection to the previous one with the connective "and" (καί). Paul summarized Jesus's earthly ministry by commenting that he "came and preached good news of peace" (εὐηγγελίσατο εἰρήνην). Christ had proclaimed this peace to Paul's Gentile readers (ὑμῖν, "to you"), or "to those who were far" (τοῖς μακρὰν) from God, as well as peace to the Jewish people, or "to those who were near" (τοῖς ἐγγύς). While in verse 13 Jesus brought the far-off Gentiles near to God, this verse reminded the readers that both the outsider Gentiles and the insider Jews had needed Jesus's peace-bringing ministry.

The picture of Christ proclaiming good news of peace struck several chords at once. First, it supported the theme of peace interwoven throughout Ephesians 2:14–18. Second, it corresponded to a central focus of Jesus's ministry in the Gospels—to proclaim the good news of the kingdom of God (Matt. 4:23; 9:35; Mark 1:1–14; Luke 4:43; 8:1; Acts 10:36). Third, it picked up an ancient prophecy from Isaiah 57:19, supplemented by Isaiah 52:7, and showed its ultimate fulfillment in the ministry of Christ. In view of this third point, the verse had a timeless quality to it. It connected the entirety of Christ's "coming" (ἐλθῶν) and the Spirit-empowered advance of his mission through the apostles to the arrival of the eschatological good news championed in Isaiah (cf. Barth, 1974, 295; Moritz, 1996, 44–45; Klein, 2006, 79). The emphasis was less on specific events in history unfolding and more on an overall vision of peace being realized. Christ's ministry and its enduring legacy fulfilled the story put forward in the OT.

Isaiah's Gospel of Peace

Isaiah 57:15–19 promised God's future healing, leadership, restoration, and comfort of his people. The prophet poetically depicted the Lord announcing "peace, peace, to the far and to the near" (εἰρήνην ἐπ' εἰρήνην τοῖς μακρὰν καὶ τοῖς ἐγγὺς οὖσιν, LXX). When Paul alluded to the passage, he highlighted the proclamation of peace to both Gentiles and Jews. Additionally, Paul introduced the proclamation of peace with wording reminiscent of Isaiah 52:7 (cf. Eph. 6:16; Rom. 10:15), where heralds of God's reign were shown "proclaiming good news" (εὐαγγελίζομαι) of "peace" (εἰρήνη) that accompanied the announcement of God's return to Zion and the arrival of his kingdom in their midst. God's eschatological salvation, as described in Isaiah 40–66, consisted of God actually showing up in the world as King (cf. Isa. 40:9–11). According to Paul, God, in the person of Jesus, "came" (ἐλθών) and proclaimed good news of peace to all peoples of the world, whether Gentile or Jew, fulfilling the hope of God's saving presence in the world. All of this also recalled Isaiah's prophecy that God would bring both the exiles of Israel and "still others"—foreigners from the nations—into his holy house (Isa. 56:6–8; Moritz, 1996, 41). Jesus embodied the peace of God and brought peace and healing in his own body, on the cross (cf. Isa. 53:5).

2:18. Paul expounded upon the peace trumpeted by Christ by introducing some of the substance (ὅτι, "that") of the good news of peace. Christ had brought the message that through him, both the "far off" Gentiles and the "close by" Jews had relational access to the Father in one Spirit. Paul switched to first-person plural verb endings again, since "the two" (οἱ ἀμφότεροι), Gentiles and Jews, were one new humanity and thus enjoyed God's blessings together. Specifically, Jews and Gentiles together "have access to the Father" (ἔχομεν τὴν προσαγωγὴν . . . πρὸς τὸν πατέρα). This "access" (προσαγωγή) amounted to an opportunity to approach God's presence as dearly loved children and be in communion with him as their Father (cf. Eph. 3:12).

This relational access was made possible by the reconciling work of Christ (δι' αὐτοῦ, "through him"). The one who proclaimed peace was the one who secured peace and access through his sacrificial ministry. Earlier in the chapter, Paul had described believers as being made alive with Christ, raised with him, and seated in God's presence with him (Eph. 2:5–6). Accordingly, Paul and his readers did not need to seek an audience with the Father; they already "have" (ἔχω) this access, since they were already in the Father's presence. The readers' access to God was also experienced "in one Spirit" (ἐν ἑνὶ πνεύματι). Both Jews and Gentiles enjoyed an existence through Christ and in the Spirit that provided ongoing communion with the Father. This verse powerfully reflected the Trinitarian nature of the believer's experience. The main sentence ("the two have access") was modified by three prepositional phrases:

- "through him [Christ]"
- "in one Spirit"
- "to the Father"

All who had been reconciled to God in Christ had been ushered in the Spirit into the presence of God. Paul insisted on the significance of this idea by restating it at the end of the current passage (2:22; cf. 4:4).

United Believers Are Built into a Sacred Dwelling for God (2:19–22)

Jewish and Gentile believers who were united in Christ were being built into a special dwelling for God in the Spirit and on the foundation of Christ.

2:19. As a consequence (ἄρα οὖν, "consequently") of all that Christ had done for them, Paul's Gentile readers had experienced a dramatic turnaround in their spiritual position. Paul returned to second-person language to reemphasize what God had achieved for the Gentiles through Christ. He reiterated two things that were "no longer" (οὐκέτι) true of their spiritual standing. They were no longer "strangers and outsiders" (ξένοι καὶ πάροικοι) to God's covenantal family. Paul had previously noted that the Gentiles were "strangers" to the covenants of God's promise (2:12). That label no longer applied to them. Neither did the label "outsiders." The term "outsider" (πάροικος) was more typically understood as "alien" or "foreigner," but "outsider" captures more of the sense of separation from a desired group. In this case, the Gentile readers had been outsiders to the household of God. With the compound term "outsider" (πάροικος), Paul began a series of terms that contained the root syllable related to "household" or "dwelling" (οἰκ-).

In contrast (ἀλλά, "but") to their former status of strangers and outsiders, Paul's Gentile readers were now co-citizens with Jewish believers and members of God's household. Paul's term for "co-citizens" (συμπολίτης) adeptly recalled verse 12, where the Gentiles had been recognized as "estranged from citizenship" (ἀπηλλοτριωμένοι τῆς πολιτείας) in Israel. Here, Paul used the prefix "co-" (συν-), meaning "together with," to express the Gentiles' equal standing with Jewish believers in Christ. Paul elsewhere used the "together with" (συν-) prefix to join believers with Christ (Rom. 6:5–8; 8:17; Gal. 2:19–20; Eph. 2:5–6; Col. 3:1), but the concept of union with Christ allowed for the natural extension to shared blessings among believers, as in Ephesians 2:19.

Paul asserted that his Gentiles readers were co-citizens with the "saints" (τῶν ἁγίων; gen. of association; Wallace, 1996, 128–30). The term "saints" (ἅγιοι) was the noun form of the adjective "holy" (ἅγιος). It thus communicated the idea of being set apart for God's family. Since Paul called all of his readers "saints" in Ephesians 1:1, he likely understood that Gentile believers shared in a moniker that had first applied to the Jewish believers in the early church. These Gentiles, along with the Jews as their fellow believers, were "members of the household of God" (οἰκεῖοι τοῦ θεοῦ). Former "outsiders" (πάροικοι) were now "members of the household" (οἰκεῖοι) of God. The term "member of a household" (οἰκεῖος) had the connotation of deep belonging, of being a permanent insider in the family (cf. Gal. 6:10; BDAG, s.v. "οἰκεῖος" b, p. 694). With the reappearance of a root (οἰκ-) that supported both household and building images, Paul made a more overt turn towards a temple metaphor, proclaiming that Jews and Gentiles in Christ did not simply form a new group but constituted a people with a holy purpose.

2:20. Gentiles who were now part of God's household had been "built upon" (ἐποικοδομέω) a well-laid foundation. They had been built "upon the foundation" (ἐπὶ τῷ θεμελίῳ) that had already been initiated as part of a holy building project. Paul pivoted from the image of a family household to a building structure at this point, which was made easier by the flexibility of the "household" or "dwelling" (οικ-) word group and the fact that people were the building materials for the metaphorical structure.

The already-existing foundation consisted of "the apostles and prophets" (τῶν ἀποστόλων καὶ προφητῶν). These two groups were viewed in close association to one another, as indicated by the single article that governed the two groups. The ministries of apostles and prophets were not always sharply distinguished from one another. Silas, for instance, was called a prophet (Acts 15:32) and an apostle (1 Thess. 2:6). Together, apostles and prophets in the early church used their spiritual gifts to help establish a movement and body of believers that would begin to spread around the world.

The apostles' marching orders had been to testify truthfully about the identity and ministry of Jesus, placing a particular emphasis on his resurrection (Acts 1:21–22). Paul could use the label "apostle" either narrowly, to speak about himself and other believers who had witnessed firsthand the resurrected glory of Christ (1 Cor. 9:1; 15:3–11), or more broadly, to refer to those serving in ministry in coordination with the apostles (Rom. 16:7; 1 Cor. 4:6–9; 1 Thess. 2:6). Apostles proclaimed the authoritative message about Christ and guarded the integrity of that message against all attempts to undermine it.

The prophets Paul mentioned were quite likely prophets in the early church, rather than the ancient prophets of Israel (Eph. 3:5; 4:11; 1 Cor. 12:28–29). The apostles were listed before their contemporaries the prophets, and if Christ was the cornerstone of the church (Eph. 2:20b), the apostles and prophets of the early church radiated from that cornerstone. These early church prophets were seen in action in several places in Acts (11:27–28; 13:1–3; 21:10–11), and Paul commended their ministry, provided that other believers weighed and evaluated their prophecies (1 Cor. 12–14; 1 Thess. 5:20–22). The Spirit had equipped these prophets to speak words of strengthening and encouragement for the church (1 Cor. 14:3–4), and the words were powerful enough that people outside the church could feel convicted upon hearing the message (1 Cor. 14:24–25).

In the final part of verse 20, Paul completed the picture of the foundation (ὄντος ἀκρογωνιαίου αὐτοῦ Χριστοῦ Ἰησοῦ; gen. abs. construction) before moving on to his next idea. In God's sacred dwelling that consisted of his people, Christ Jesus was the cornerstone of the foundation (cf. 1 Cor. 3:11). Paul underscored Jesus's identity as the cornerstone with the emphatic use of "himself" accompanying "Christ Jesus" (αὐτοῦ Χριστοῦ Ἰησοῦ). The image of a "cornerstone" (ἀκρογωνιαῖος) stressed the centrality of Christ to both the foundation and the building constructed upon it.

2:21. When Paul paused to highlight Christ as the cornerstone, this reminded the readers of Christ's supremacy in the church, but it also directed their attention to their connection to Christ. By using a relative pronoun within the prepositional phrase "in whom" (ἐν ᾧ), Paul linked what he said about believers in verse 21 back to what he said about Christ in verse 20. For Paul, believers were part of the holy structure that extended from Christ himself. In Christ Jesus, all household members, as they were joined together, grew up into a holy temple. Since believers were united with Christ, the cornerstone, they became part of this metaphorical "building" (οἰκοδομή) as well (cf. 1 Cor. 3:9). Paul declared that "the whole building" (πᾶσα οἰκοδομή) was in the process of growing (αὔξει, "grows"). This growth occurred as God integrated believers into the building and joined them closely with the other people around them (συναρμολογουμένη, "joined together"; temp. or instr. ptc.). The term "join together" (συναρμολογέω, also in Eph. 4:16) meant "to join together so as to form a coherent unity" (BDAG, s.v. "συναρμολογέω," 966). With the wording in the verse so far, Paul reminded readers of their corporate identity as a single building but also of their individual assimilation into the structure.

The spectacular result (signaled by εἰς, "into") was a "holy temple" (εἰς ναὸν ἅγιον). The term "temple" (ναός) denoted a site in which God's divine presence dwelt (2 Sam. 22:7; Ps. 11:4; 27:4; Hab. 2:20) and sometimes corresponded specifically to the inner holy place and most holy place of YHWH's temple (Heb. 9:2–3). Paul employed "temple" (ναός) to describe God's people as God's holy dwelling (cf. 1 Cor. 3:16–17; 6:19; 2 Cor. 6:16; BDAG, s.v. "ναός" d, p. 666; Hoehner, 2002, 410–411; Talbert, 2007, 84–85). In Christ, all household members, joined together, grew up into a special building that housed God's divine presence, fulfilling the original purpose of the temple in Jerusalem (2 Chron. 7:1–3; cf. Ezek. 43:5). The adjective "holy" (ἅγιος) further accentuated the sacred nature of the temple, preparing the way for the explicit assertion in verse 22 that God himself dwelt in this new temple. In the new covenant era, God chose to dwell within and among his people rather than in actual structures.

The final prepositional phrase in the verse, "in the Lord" (ἐν κυρίῳ), referred to Christ. The phrase likely modified the immediately preceding "holy temple" and said something about believers' close association with the Lord in their existence as a temple. The phrase retained the close connection between Christ and his people and set up a smooth transition into verse 22.

2:22. As a conclusion to the passage, Paul affirmed that in Christ, even his Gentile readers were being built up (together with Jewish believers) into a dwelling place for God. A repetition of the phrase "in whom" (ἐν ᾧ) facilitated a continued focus on Christ as the key to a believer's incorporation into this temple for God. Paul ensured that his Gentile readers caught this truth and understood its relevance to their situation by addressing them directly with "you also" (καὶ ὑμεῖς). Paul again attached the prefix meaning "together with" (συν-) to a verb to depict an experience that the Gentiles shared with Jewish believers in Christ. Paul told his Gentile readers that "together (with the Jews) you are being built up" (συνοικοδομεῖσθε) to fulfill God's purpose. Believers experienced this expansion corporately, as a unified body.

The outcome (εἰς, "into") of this construction was that the believers became "God's dwelling place" (κατοικητήριον τοῦ θεοῦ). The metaphor of believers becoming God's dwelling place tied together the various ideas that had surfaced in the passage—that believers in Christ were reconciled to God and each other, had relational access to his fatherly presence, and were being formed into his temple. Paul affixed the prepositional phrase "in the Spirit" (ἐν πνεύματι) to create one final picture of what it looked like for God to dwell among his people in the current age. The Spirit provided the spiritual arena in which believers together experienced the presence of God. The Spirit was "the mortar which bonds [believers] as the bricks of the new temple of God" (Dunn, 1998, 425). The readers' reception of the Spirit (Eph. 1:13) prepared them for an ongoing spiritual communion with God, in anticipation of a fuller encounter with the glory of God when Christ returned.

THEOLOGICAL FOCUS

The exegetical idea (through Christ's sacrifice former spiritual outsiders, the Gentiles, along with spiritual insiders, the Jews, had become part of a new, unified, and reconciled people who experienced the Father's presence in the Spirit) leads to this theological focus: Jesus Christ brings diverse people together into a right relationship with God and one another, in the Spirit.

Jesus is once again at the center of the passage, as indicated by the "in Christ" and "in him" statements at key places. Believers experience the gracious work of God in their lives as a result of their union with Christ. Christ functions as the chief cornerstone of the ever-expanding temple of God (v. 20). The temple is built upon him and grows as believers remain united with him. Alongside these emphases the passage highlights the sacrificial ministry of Christ. God accomplishes his purposes through the blood of Christ (2:13), the cross (2:16a), and in Christ's own body (2:14, 16b).

Christ's ministry rescues all types of people, including people from various nations and backgrounds throughout history. Though many cultural and religious barriers divide people even today, a central barrier in the story of salvation has been the one between Jews and non-Jews. God chose the Jews as his special people, promised a wonderful future for them, and blessed them with his own presence in their midst. The Gentiles knew of no such experience or hope. But Christ's death on the cross brought peace to both Jews and Gentiles. That means that anyone can experience right relationships with both God and with other believers, whether Jew or Gentile. Christ has removed barriers to fellowship among believers, so all are united in him. All other labels and identities become secondary to the common privilege of becoming part of the one new humanity that Christ has created.

Having a right relationship with God is an opportunity to enjoy the relational presence of the Father (v. 18). Believers together become a sacred dwelling for the God of the universe (v. 22), who can never be confined to temples but graciously grants access to those who come to him through Christ. Believers are incorporated into Christ's own body (v. 15) and ushered in the Spirit into God's presence (v. 18). As cherished children who have been adopted into God's family (Eph. 1:5), believers draw near to God and by the Spirit can address God with the affectionate words, "Abba, Father" (Rom. 8:15; Gal. 4:6). Thus, Christ has made the way for believers to enjoy relationships with God and other believers that are marked by God's generous peace and his loving presence in the Spirit.

PREACHING AND TEACHING STRATEGIES

Exegetical and Theological Synthesis

In this rich passage Paul depicted humanity, Gentiles in particular, in spiritually desperate terms: separated from Christ, excluded from Israel (God's chosen people), foreigners to his covenants, without hope, and—most encompassing of all—without God. Paul also implied that the Jews, not just the Gentiles, needed to be reconciled to God. The Jews looked down on the Gentiles and meticulously separated from them. Likewise, the Gentiles with their polytheistic-superstitious religions and licentious lifestyle had little common ground with the Jews. Thus, for Paul, humanity needed to be reconciled vertically to God and horizontally to each other.

God's response to humanity's plight was the sacrificial work of Jesus on the cross, applied by the Spirit who made the two groups into "one new humanity" (v. 15). With mighty power and great grace, God made peace through the blood of the cross; and that all-important theological fact had social implications as well. God made peace between Jews and Gentiles, forming them into one household and one temple. The Trinitarian nature of this great work of reconciliation can be seen in that the Ephesian believers, whether Jew of Gentile, were given access *to* the Father, *through* the blood of Christ, *in* the Spirit (v. 18).

Preaching Idea

God has torn down the walls, so let the walls come down!

Contemporary Connections

What does it mean?

What does it mean that God has torn down the walls? Walls are physical reminders of spiritual, social, and ethnic divisions. Paul had in mind the literal wall in the temple confines and used that image to speak about the metaphorical wall between Jewish and Gentile believers. The motive for building a physical wall might be to mark one's territory, to keep animals or people inside, to keep others outside, or to protect ourselves from the "other." The Great Wall in China was built to keep nomadic tribes and other states from invading. The Berlin Wall was built to keep East Berliners in their place. The wall along the southern border of the United States is intended to keep people from illegally entering from Mexico. But there are metaphorical walls as well. Walls of prejudice or nationality as between Pakistan and India. Some walls serve good purposes. Other walls are worth tearing down, whether they be literal or metaphorical. In parts of the Southern United States, one way to separate people used to be with drinking fountains—"whites only" and "blacks only." God has done torn down such repugnant walls. The wall of hostility between Jews and Gentiles, men and women, young and old, conservative and progressive, and majority race and minority is demolished when we look to Jesus who unites believers in himself.

The peaching idea captures the social implications of the spiritual truth: reconciliation with God results in reconciliation with each other. One way to explain that idea could be with cross-references from Isaiah to expound the full-orbed sense of "shalom." Another way might be through contrast, describing what is *not* meant. Perhaps something like this:

> "Peace" is not simply the absence of war, it is the presence of goodwill; it is not simply laying down one's arms, it is picking up tools to rebuild. At the end of World War I, the armistice created a kind of peace, but that peace was thin, temporary, and resented. You see, Germany was humiliated by the so-called peace and bided it's time to retaliate. And retaliate they did in World War II. The guns may have ceased, but animosity in the heart had continued. Biblical peace is much more than cessation of hostility. It is friendship, harmony, and accord. It is not the armistice of World War I; it's more like the unification of Germany when the Berlin Wall crumbled. Two countries became one—one people, one language, one economy, one future.

The preaching idea might also be explained by showing a picture of the "the dividing wall" (v. 14). See Creativity in Presentation for a contemporary visual device.

The dismal depiction of people outside of Christ (five phrases in v. 12) might be illustrated with some data about solitary confinement (Weir, 2012). Prison systems use two types: "disciplinary segregation" and "administrative segregation." The first is used as punishment and the second is used when the prisoners are deemed a threat to the guards or other inmates. In that case, the prisoner is completely isolated for months or even years, and the results can be devastating. This kind of solitary confinement can lead to mental health problems such as anxiety, panic, insomnia, paranoia, aggression, and depression. We were created for connection with other people and God himself, so the depiction in verse 12 is indeed dismal—separated from Christ, alienated from Israel, strangers, no hope, and without God.

Is it true?

Has God truly torn down the wall and made us one? The track record of the church can argue against this with our denominationalism, tribalism, and factions. One way to address skepticism could be by employing restraint, humbly admitting that the church is divided, but then by holding out hope. If God made peace between the Jews and Gentiles where severe hostility existed, then surely he can tear down walls between political parties, races, and people who separate from each other because of secondary doctrinal issues. Labels that that divide take a back seat to our primary identity—followers of Jesus.

A concrete example of how God has torn down walls can be seen in the ministry of Bryan Loritts, former pastor of the Abundant Life Church Fellowship in Mountain View, California, currently a pastor of The Summit Church in Raleigh/Durham, North Carolina, and president of the Kainos Movement dedicated to diversity and reconciliation. When he delivered a message on Ephesians 2 several years ago at Wheaton College's Inhabit Conference, he was then part of a pastoral staff and congregation that was multiethnic.[3] Loritts tells a story of visiting England and then Australia in quick succession. He was struck that Australia, far distant from England, looked so much like England: tea each afternoon at 3:00, driving on the "wrong" side of the road, and a group of Aborigines playing cricket. The reason for this mirroring of culture is, of course, that England colonized Australia. They took the culture, customs, and practices of England to the other side of the globe and made the foreign land into a little England. Loritts uses this as an analogy: we are citizens of heaven, a place that is multicultural as revealed in Revelation 7:9. Pastor Loritts says, "We exist to take the culture, customs, and practices of a faraway place called 'heaven' and inject them into a place called earth."

Now what?

In light of the fact that God has torn down the walls that divide, how can we tear down walls? Perhaps we might partner with an inner city (or suburban) church in a tutoring program, join another church in their evangelistic ministry, or invite a pastor who is different than we are to fill the pulpit. In my (Jeffrey's) home area, a consortium of churches called the North Shore Gospel Partnership has come together. Seven churches have covenanted to support, bless, and aid each other to reach our area of the country. The churches range from nondenominational "low church" to Anglican "high church." Some are egalitarian in regard to the role of women in ordained ministry, and some are complementarian. Some practice infant baptism and some believers' baptism, but they are united in the gospel. This unity is fueled by the virtues listed in Ephesians 4:1–3—humility, gentleness, patience, bearing with one another, and being eager to maintain the unity of the Spirit. God has created unity that these churches display and maintain by thinking the best of others and thinking little of themselves.

Another way to tear down walls could be with a time of confession. Nothing disarms hostility like humbly admitting that we are wrong, asking for forgiveness, and then forgiving one another. The time of confession could be part of a pastoral prayer, a "sacred assembly" as

3 To listen to Dr. Loritts teach on Ephesians 2, see https://vimeo.com/82747958. In that message Loritts states: "The great tragedy of American history is that we have tried to resurrect what God has torn down, the dividing wall."

described in Nehemiah 8, or a planned testimony. A Caucasian person might confess how he or she has let racial prejudice ruin work relations in the small office where they work. A rich person might confess how he or she has overlooked the poor and deliberately shunned them.

Creativity in Presentation

Ronald Reagan's "Tear Down This Wall" speech could provide a historical example. When the Berlin Wall came down, two nations became one. Delivered at the Brandenburg Gate in West Germany with the Berlin Wall behind him, Reagan said, "General Secretary Gorbachev, if you seek peace, if you seek prosperity for the Soviet Union and Eastern Europe, if you seek liberalization, come here to this gate. Mr. Gorbachev, open this gate. Mr. Gorbachev, tear down this wall." The entire speech (26 minutes) is easily found on YouTube.

Ephesians 2:11–22 is packed with metaphors that can suggest illustrations. The following one (from Larsen, 2019, 53) might be used to demonstrate how God has built the church on the foundation of the apostles and prophets with Christ Jesus as the cornerstone (v. 20). The John Hancock Center on Michigan Avenue in Chicago, one of the tallest buildings in the United States, would not stand without a good foundation. The soil there is sandy loam, so it rests on 239 giant steel and concrete caissons that extend far below the surface into the bedrock under the city. The majority of the caissons—181—go down 100 feet; 58 go down 200 feet. We are anchored in Christ.

Other metaphors in the passage come from the worlds of society (we are fellow citizens, v. 19), family (we are members of one household, v. 19), the body (v. 16), and the temple (the dividing wall is destroyed, we are built on the foundation of the apostles and prophets with Christ himself as the cornerstone, vv. 14, 20–22). These metaphors could stand alone as visual aids, or they could be combined into one long depiction that runs throughout the message.

For another visual illustration, place a "wall" (perhaps stones or a fence) in the middle of the stage. Using a volunteer to stand at one side of the wall, you might describe the plight of the Gentiles. They are far from God and alienated from God's people, Israel. They have no hope. Then, using a volunteer to stand at the other side of the wall (a person from a different age group or gender), you might describe the hostility between Jews and Gentiles in Paul's day and draw parallels with social discord today. Then the two volunteers could come out from behind the wall and move slowly to a cross in the middle of the stage. The cross reconciles us vertically and horizontally. The longer beam of the cross (the vertical one) represents the more difficult and astounding accomplishment—reconciliation with God. The shorter beam rests on the longer one. Horizontal reconciliation with each other is possible because he has made us one in Christ Jesus.

To illustrate how Christ-followers are members of one household (v. 19), perhaps use this story reported by NPR:

> In 2016, a NASA Mars mission crew returned from a yearlong trip, but in fact they had never left earth. For a year they had lived in Hawaii in a simulator called the Hawaii Space Exploration Analog and Simulation (HI-SEAS). According to NPR's report, "The goal of HI-SEAS is to test what it would be like for people to live on Mars, and what the project designers call 'team performance and cohesion'—or how a group of strangers might handle being stuck together for 12 months." The crew of six lived together in a "1,200-square-foot, solar-powered dome on the side of a Hawaiian volcano" in order to simulate the feel of a Mars base. As you can imagine, getting along with crewmates can be a challenge in such tight quarters. According to one of the members, the "biggest enemies"

> (in addition to boredom) are "the rest of the crew." Most followers of Christ won't be packing for a yearlong space simulation anytime soon, but we will be called into situations and relationships that test our patience. That's when we need to remember that we are fellow citizens and members of the household of God (v. 19).[4]

Robert Frost's poem "Mending Wall" (in *North of Boston* [London: David Nutt, 1914]) explores how humans seem to have simultaneous, contradictory impulses. On the one hand, as his neighbor says, "Good fences make good neighbors," but on the other hand, Frost feels that "something there is that doesn't love a wall." Here is a portion of the poem:

> [The neighbor says,] "Good fences make good neighbours."
> Spring is the mischief in me, and I wonder
> If I could put a notion in his head:
> "*Why* do they make good neighbours? Isn't it
> Where there are cows? But here there are no cows.
> Before I built a wall I'd ask to know
> What I was walling in or walling out,
> And to whom I was like to give offence.
> Something there is that doesn't love a wall,
> That wants it down."

The Church of Reconciliation

The Berlin Wall was a double wall with a no-man's-land between. When the wall was made through the city of Berlin in 1961, they demolished everything between the walls—buildings, houses, roads, everything except one thing—a church, the Church of Reconciliation built in 1885. No one knows why they permitted the church to stand, but there it stood among the flood lights, barbed wire, upturned spikes, and mines. It became a symbol that the gates of hell will not prevail against the church. But the gates of hell also know the power of symbols, so in 1985 it was torn down.

As the members of the parish watched the church fall, they staged their own symbolic act. They danced on the wall. That was how they said farewell to their church. But the story wasn't over yet. In 1989, the wall came down, and the people of the parish started looking for the remains of their church. They discovered it piece by piece—the altar, the bells, the statue of Jesus Christ, the cross (now distorted in shape). The new united country of Germany gave the parish the right to repossess the ground, and the people rebuilt. Today you can visit the Chapel of Reconciliation.

For pictures of the church, see Google Images, "Church of Reconciliation, Berlin"

Our creative illustrations and demonstrations will want to highlight how God has made us one in Christ and how we can respond to that fact. So let's focus the sermon on this: God has torn down the walls, so let the walls come down!

A possible outline:

- We were far from God (vv. 11–12).
- But he brought us near to himself through the cross (v. 13)
- Therefore, he has torn down the walls between us (vv. 14–22).
- So let the walls come down!

4 Rebecca Hersher, "'Mars Mission' Crew Emerges from Yearlong Simulation in Hawaii," August 29, 2016, https://www.npr.org/sections/thetwo-way/2016/08/29/491794937/mars-mission-crew-emerges-from-yearlong-simulation-in-hawaii.

DISCUSSION QUESTIONS

1. Why were Gentiles far from God, and why, in a sense, were the Jews also far from God?
2. Why were Jews and Gentiles hostile toward each other? What prompted Paul to write this passage?
3. How has God made peace *with* Jews and Gentiles and *between* Jews and Gentiles?
4. What does the "dividing wall of hostility" mean?
5. Where do we see similar hostility in our country?
6. Where do we see similar hostility in our church?
7. How might the death of Jesus and our common access to the Father impact that hostility?
8. What are some benefits described in the passage of being a unified people in Christ?
9. What are some things that believers could accomplish together if we lived out that unity?

FOR FURTHER READING

Colson, Charles W. 1977. *Born Again.* Old Tappan, NJ: Spire Books.

Demarest, Bruce. 1997. *The Cross and Salvation: The Doctrine of Salvation.* Foundations of Evangelical Theology. Wheaton, IL: Crossway.

Furman, Gloria. 2017. *Alive in Him: How Being Embraced by the Love of Christ Changes Everything.* Wheaton, IL: Crossway.

Stott, John R. W. 2006. *The Cross of Christ.* 20th Anniversary ed. Downers Grove, IL: InterVarsity.

SUFFERING FOR THE GOSPEL AND PRAYING FOR GOD'S PEOPLE (3:1–21)

In this chapter, the third major section of the letter, Paul opened a window into how he fulfilled his God-given calling in two areas. First, even in the midst of suffering Paul proclaimed the revealed mystery that the good news of Christ was for the Gentiles in addition to the Jews (3:1–13). Second, Paul carried out his calling by praying that his readers would grasp the abundant power and love of Christ (3:14–21).

For the third major section, Suffering for the Gospel and Praying for God's People (3:1–21), there are two preaching units: "Suffering for a Great Cause" (3:1–13) and "A Prayer to Experience God's Power and Love" (3:14–21).

Ephesians 3:1–13

EXEGETICAL IDEA
Paul's imprisonment was nothing compared to his God-given opportunity to reveal the mystery of God's eternal plans to put his wisdom on display in Christ and through a unified church.

THEOLOGICAL FOCUS
Participating in this groundbreaking era of God's story is well worth the sacrifice.

PREACHING IDEA
God's messenger might be chained, but God's message is unchained.

PREACHING POINTERS
Paul's readers lived during uncertain times. They participated in a fledgling spiritual movement whose ultimate success still seemed in doubt. They had received encouraging reports about the progress of the gospel in various parts of the Roman Empire, but they also continued to hear unsettling news about the hardships of Paul, a respected apostle and visible leader in the early church. Roman authorities had imprisoned Paul for years in Caesarea and Rome, after his initial arrest in Jerusalem (Acts 21:26–28:31). Incarceration was considered shameful in the Roman world, since it marked the prisoner as a criminal in the eyes of society. What should the readers make of this distressing setback? Was Paul's mission worth the sacrifice? If authorities regarded Paul as a shameful criminal, what would become of the readers' own standing in broader society? Friends and acquaintances of a once-respected prisoner would feel tempted to distance themselves from him. Paul's readers needed a healthy dose of the eternal perspective that inspired Paul's ongoing willingness to endure persecution.

We face setbacks today too. In many parts of the world Christians are persecuted for the faith. The persecution can range from "mere" shaming to outright physical hostility. While no one can predict the future, it seems that the post-Christian West may be moving toward the ill-treatment known in parts of Asia, the Middle East, and Africa. For Western Christians, lesser forms of "persecution" exist even today—the employee is passed over for promotion because she won't play ball with the company's unethical practices, an applicant to graduate school is rejected because he included a statement about his belief in objective truth, or a family member feels the cold shoulder when arriving at the reunion. When mistreated for the gospel, how can we not lose heart (v. 13)? By adopting Paul's attitude. He had an eternal perspective on both the gospel and his sufferings, and that perspective injects hope into all who suffer for the faith. Ultimately, the hope is that even if the messenger is chained, the message is unchained.

SUFFERING FOR A GREAT CAUSE (3:1–13)

LITERARY STRUCTURE AND THEMES (3:1–13)

Paul turned to a new topic at the beginning of chapter 3. Paul prepared to offer another prayer for his readers, but his mention of his status as a prisoner prompted a discussion about the ministry God had given him. The passage consists of two major sections, 3:1–7 and 3:8–13. Both support Paul's overall message in the passage—that his suffering as a prisoner was for a greater purpose. The introduction to Paul's hardships in verse 1 became resolved in verse 13 with the conclusion that his sufferings were worth the trouble. In between, Paul provided extensive discussion of his calling, the message God revealed to him, and the sweeping plans God had for the world.

Paul placed a strong accent on the ministry God had given him by grace, celebrating "the stewardship of God's grace that was given to me" (3:2), "the gift of God's grace that was given to me" (3:7), and "this grace that was given to me" (3:8). Paul also continued to place Christ at the center of believers' initial and ongoing experience with God, using variations of the "in Christ" wording (3:6, 11, 12) and highlighting Christ's centrality in other ways (3:4, 8, 13). Specifically, Christ's work in and through a unified church featured prominently in God's proclamation of his wisdom to the unseen spiritual powers of the universe.

- ***God Appoints Paul to Help Gentiles Appreciate Their Place in God's Family (3:1–7)***
- ***Paul Suffers but Participates in God's Cosmic Plans (3:8–13)***

EXPOSITION (3:1–13)

In Ephesians 3:1–13, Paul provided the reason for his ongoing ministry of suffering, teaching, and prayer for Gentile believers such as the recipients of this letter to the Ephesians. Passages in which Paul introduced and described his calling and ministry have been characterized as "apostolic apologies" (cf. 2 Cor. 1:12–17; Gal. 1:10–2:21; Col 1:23–29; 1 Thess 2:11–2; Boers, 1975, 153). In apostolic apologies, Paul shared the history and purpose of his calling as a way of clarifying the reason for his devoted service to his readers and his basis for addressing his readers in a spiritually authoritative way. In this passage, Paul's introduction to his calling further served to replace the typical shameful connotations of being imprisoned with the honor and significance of carrying out the glorious ministry God had assigned to him.

God Appoints Paul to Help Gentiles Appreciate Their Place in God's Family (3:1–7)

Paul, the prisoner of Christ, had received God's gracious stewardship to minister to Gentiles and to share with them the mystery, or divinely revealed message, about their full welcome into God's family through Christ.

3:1. With the construction "for this reason" (τούτου χάριν), Paul intended to pivot from the majestic picture of Jews and Gentiles being united and reconciled to God (2:11–22) to a prayer for his readers' comprehension of these truths. Paul eventually repeated "for this reason" (3:14) and offered his prayer (3:14–21), but not until after he had taken a long detour in another direction.

As a prelude to his prayer Paul reviewed the context of his relationship to his readers and clarified the reason for his commitment to them (cf. Philem. 8–10). He served Christ, even to the point of being imprisoned, on their behalf. This helped assure the readers of the sincerity of his genuine concern for them. Paul began with "I, Paul" (ἐγὼ Παῦλος), wording that he sometimes used to reinsert himself into the discussion as part of a switch of topics (2 Cor. 10:1; Gal. 5:2; Col. 1:23; Philem. 19). Paul thus invited his readers to picture him preparing to pray for them.

Mosaic of Paul, Berea. Courtesy of Greg MaGee.jpg

Paul called himself "the prisoner of Christ Jesus" (ὁ δέσμιος τοῦ Χριστοῦ). Paul wrote while under house arrest in Rome (Acts 28:16, 30). Paul identified Christ as the reason for his confinement and perhaps cleverly insisted that he was bound to Christ even more than to a chain (cf. Philem. 1:9). Paul's loyalty to Christ was what distinguished him from a regular prisoner. Enduring opposition from others went with the territory of publicly proclaiming the good news of Christ (cf. 2 Tim. 2:8–9). With this willing embrace of suffering for Christ, Paul began to redefine his imprisonment as a noble rather than shameful situation.

The Shame of Imprisonment in the Roman World

Both Jews and Gentiles lived in a world that reinforced honor and despised shame (deSilva, 2016, 26–27). Being imprisoned branded one as a criminal and thus was especially shameful (Rapske, 1994, 288–98). People sometimes distanced themselves from a prisoner who had once been an acquaintance or friend, in order to protect their own reputation. For instance, when one man was falsely implicated in a crime, he found that "even his erstwhile friends turned their backs upon him" (Lucian, *Tox.* 28 [trans. Harmon]). Seneca noted that artificial friendships could be unmasked in the wake of being imprisoned: "[A]t the first rattle of a chain such a friend will desert him" (*Ep.* 9.9 [trans. Gummere]). In a later imprisonment, some of Paul's acquaintances abandoned him (2 Tim. 4:16). In particular, the once faithful Demas deserted him in order to preserve his status in the eyes of broader society (2 Tim. 4:10).

Paul accepted imprisonment "for you" (ὑπὲρ ὑμῶν), or for the sake of his readers. He served Christ by ministering to them, especially since they were counted among "the Gentiles" (τῶν ἐθνῶν). Paul understood that God had called him specifically to reach the Gentiles (Acts 9:15; Rom. 11:13; 15:15–16; Gal. 1:16; 2:7–9; 1 Tim. 2:7). Paul viewed his readers as a small but representative part of his larger ministry sphere. By framing his imprisonment as a God-ordained by-product of his commitment to his readers, Paul injected a strong note of sincerity into his ministry of teaching his readers and praying for them.

3:2. At this point Paul interrupted his train of thought with "if indeed" (εἴ γε), which indicated a change of direction by pausing to give an already-introduced idea further consideration. Now that Paul had linked his imprisonment to his commitment to his Gentile readers he recognized the need to reassure his readers that his ministry to them was worth the sacrifice. This sparked an extended digression into the origins and focus of Paul's Gentile-oriented ministry. Since Paul's recipients included people (from many churches across Asia Minor) who didn't know him personally, he indicated that he could not presume that they had already "heard" (ἀκούω) the full story of his calling to ministry. Even more, as relatively new arrivals into God's family Paul's Gentile readers may not yet have fully fathomed that they had entered this family at a climactic time in salvation history.

Paul took the opportunity to catch his readers up to speed on "his gracious stewardship from God" (τὴν οἰκονομίαν τῆς χάριτος τοῦ θεοῦ; obj. of ἠκούσατε). The term "stewardship" (οἰκονομία) in this context, when it referred to Paul's ministry (unlike the case in its other occurrences in Eph. 1:10; 3:9), meant a "stewardship" (ESV, NASB, NET), "commission" (NRSV), or "administration" (NIV, CSB), as in a significant administrative responsibility to carry out on God's behalf (BDAG, s.v. "οἰκονομία," 1b, p. 697). The related noun (οἰκονόμος) meant "steward" (cf. 1 Cor. 4:1), capturing the idea of handling a responsibility or valued possession to the satisfaction of the one who entrusted it. The modifier "of God's grace" (τῆς χάριτος τοῦ θεοῦ; attrib. gen. phrase) specified that Paul had received this stewardship by God's grace (Eph. 3:7, 8; cf. Rom. 12:3; 15:15; 1 Cor. 3:10; 15:10; Gal. 1:15; 2:9).

Next, Paul reiterated that God had given him this gracious stewardship for the benefit of his readers. Paul's ministry assignment "was given to me" (τῆς δοθείσης μοι) and it was "for you" (εἰς ὑμᾶς). Paul used the wording "was given" (pass. voice, δίδωμι) three times in this passage (also in 3:7, 8), reminding the readers that he had embarked on his ministry in response to God's appointment, not on his own initiative. Paul himself had been a beneficiary of God's giving nature, and he gratefully fulfilled his calling by serving his readers.

3:3. Paul announced that the message he proclaimed "was made known to me" (ἐγνωρίσθη μοι). Paul's use of "was made known" (pass. voice, γνωρίζω) further presented him as a recipient of God's purposeful actions. Truth had been made known to Paul "by way of revelation" (κατὰ ἀποκάλυψιν), with the preposition "by way of" (κατά) likely conveying the mode by which God made known his message to Paul. God had divulged truths to Paul, and he shared these teachings with his churches. By "revelation" (ἀποκάλυψις), Paul likely referred to the initial revelation he had received on the road to Damascus (cf. Gal. 1:12–17). Paul's experience of encountering the resurrected Jesus that day had set the course for his entire ministry and theology.

Christ's Revelation to Paul

Jesus disclosed the essential pieces of Paul's teachings and ministry when he appeared to Paul on the road to Damascus. Jesus, the one Paul had opposed so zealously, confronted Paul in a multisensory experience that overwhelmed him (note Ananias's God-given instructions to Paul to report what he had "seen and heard" in Acts 22:15). Jesus demonstrated his resurrection from the dead (1 Cor. 9:1; 15:8; cf. Acts 26:22–23), vindicated his identity as the promised Messiah (Acts 9:20–22), affirmed his intimate bond with his people (Acts 9:4–5; 22:7–8; 26:14–15), and assigned Paul with the task of preaching a message of forgiveness and deliverance to both Jews and Gentiles (Acts 26:16–18, 22–23; Gal. 1:16). Paul grouped these topics together in the introduction of his letter to the Romans (1:1–6). These were some of the main themes Paul unpacked in Ephesians as well.

Paul called the content of God's revelation "the mystery" (τὸ μυστήριον), which in the Christian era meant divine truths that were formerly concealed but had now been disclosed in Christ (cf. Rom. 16:25–27; 1 Cor. 2:7–10; Col. 1:25–27). Frequent mentions of "mystery" (μυστήριον, LXX) in Daniel (2:18, 19, 27–30, 47) shaped many uses of the term in the NT. Paul spent much of the rest of the passage unfolding the substance of this revealed mystery. Paul's use of the article before "mystery" referred back to his prior mention of mystery in Ephesians 1:9–10. With the clause, "just as I wrote you before, briefly" (καθὼς προέγραψα ἐν ὀλίγῳ), Paul made this connection explicit. Paul had simply introduced the topic of the divine mystery earlier as part of his thesis statement for the letter, but now he intended to go into greater detail about it and relate it to both his calling to serve Christ and the divine project of reconciliation he had unfolded in Ephesians 2:11–22.

3:4. By referring to what (πρὸς ὅ) Paul had already begun to write in the letter, believers under Paul's care were privy to the contents of the mystery that God had revealed to Paul. God had called Paul to serve as a vehicle of divine revelation to his readers. They too "are able to develop an understanding" (δύνασθε . . . νοῆσαι) of the insights God had made available to Paul. The term "understand" (νοέω) carried the sense of understanding acquired through patient reflection (BDAG, s.v. "νοέω" 1b, p. 674). In this case, the readers developed their understanding and became familiar with Paul's divinely received perspectives "when they read" (ἀναγινώσκοντες; contemp. temp. ptc.) Ephesians, Paul's letter to them. Paul's letters provided valuable instruction for his readers when he could not visit them in person.

TRANSLATION ANALYSIS: The verb "to read" (ἀναγινώσκω) can indicate a public reading of Scripture or another document (cf. BDAG, s.v. "ἀναγινώσκω" b, p. 60). Paul often used the passive voice of this verb to communicate the idea of a congregation hearing a letter or passage of Scripture read to them (2 Cor. 3:15; Col. 4:16a, 16b; 1 Thess. 5:27; cf. Acts 13:27; 15:21). Even in its active form, though, the verb may still denote a public reading (Col. 4:16c; Acts 15:31). The use of the active form in Ephesians 3:4 probably denoted a public reading of the letter among the recipients of Paul's letter (Lincoln, 1990, 176; Arnold, 2010, 188). That would mean that many of Paul's "readers" were actually "hearers" instead.

By reading the letter, the recipients benefited from "Paul's received insight into the mystery of Christ" (τὴν σύνεσίν μου ἐν τῷ μυστηρίῳ τοῦ Χριστοῦ). Paul wanted the readers to understand his "insight" (σύνεσις), meaning the content of the revelation Paul received, not any innate ability he had to grasp deeper truths. God had disclosed his truths to Paul so that Paul could relay them to others. Paul wanted to make sure that his readers grasped this crucial summary of God's plan for the world. Before he moved to practical teaching in Ephesians 4–6, Paul wanted to situate his readers within God's grand story for the world. The readers needed to know where they fit so that they could live faithfully within that story.

Paul clarified that he wanted to share with them his insight "into the mystery of [the] Christ" (ἐν τῷ μυστηρίῳ τοῦ Χριστοῦ). Paul called God's revelation to him the mystery regarding Christ (Best, 1998, 304; Thielman, 2010, 196–97), displaying his conviction that Jesus, the promised Messiah, was the cornerstone of God's saving plans for the world and his church (Eph. 1:9–10; 2:20–22). In Colossians 2:2, Paul directly pinpointed Christ as the mystery (Col. 1:26–27; 4:3; 1 Tim. 3:16). As the Messiah, Jesus completed the unfinished story of the OT and perfectly brought together all of the pieces of God's plans that were waiting to be united.

3:5. Paul wanted his readers to appreciate this momentous period in salvation history (cf., 2 Cor. 6:2). The mystery Paul imparted to them was one that (introduced by the relative pronoun ὅ) "in other generations" (ἑτέραις γενεαῖς) before them "was not made known to humans" (οὐκ ἐγνωρίσθη τοῖς υἱοῖς τῶν ἀνθρώπων). Paul emphasized the divine quality of the mystery, since the mystery consisted of knowledge inaccessible ("not made known," pass. voice) "to humanity" (lit., "to the sons of men," τοῖς υἱοῖς τῶν ἀνθρώπων) apart from God's choice to disclose it. During prior generations God had exercised his sovereign right to withhold this divine knowledge from humans. Though various patterns and signposts in the OT, including the passages from Isaiah that Paul drew upon in Ephesians 2:11–22, pointed forward to a future consummation of salvation history, the intricacies and full repercussions of that fulfillment remained obscured from human view (cf. Rom. 11:25–27; 1 Peter 1:10–12).

Fulfillment and Mystery

How could Paul characterize Jesus's ministry as both eagerly expected and dramatically new? On the one hand, Paul could portray Jesus's arrival as the fulfillment of the OT, whether of the overall narrative arc of the Scriptures (Rom. 1:1–3; 3:21; 1 Cor. 15:3–4; 2 Tim. 3:15), or of specific passages that foreshadowed Christ's intervention (Eph. 2:13–18 and many other examples). On the other hand, by God's own design, Jesus's ministry had been groundbreaking and in many ways unanticipated. Paul described this revelation of a previously hidden mystery in various places (Rom. 16:25–26; 1 Cor. 2:7–10; 4:1; Eph. 1:9; 3:3–4, 9; Col. 1:25–27). D. A. Carson speaks of a mystery that was often "hidden in plain view," since the major pieces of God's culminating work in Christ were interspersed across the OT, yet only upon the appearance of Christ Jesus did those assorted pieces begin to fit together (Carson, 2004, 427; cf. Ridderbos, 1975, 50–51; Bockmuehl, 1990, 148–56). And while God had previewed in the OT his plans to fulfill his covenants to his people and impact even the nations through his Messiah and by his Spirit, the exact implementation and full ramifications of this salvation were not readily apparent (Grindheim, 2003, 547–48). The newness of Paul's dramatic encounter with Christ supplemented his preexisting knowledge of the Scriptures to forge his understanding of God's activities in the world.

The situation was now quite the opposite. Using a marker of comparison (ὡς, "as") following the negation of the prior verb (οὐκ ἐγνωρίσθη, "was not made known") Paul showed that by contrast, God had "now" (νῦν) made these divine plans available to people of this generation. Some, such as Paul, had received this revelation directly from Jesus. Others, such as Paul's readers, relied on God's designated messengers to report God's teachings to them. Paul was among the initial recipients of God's revelation.

This truth "was revealed [by God]" (pass. voice; ἀπεκαλύφθη) to a group of God's special ministers. Paul identified these ministers as the "apostles" (ἀπόστολοι) and "prophets" (προφῆται). In Ephesians 2:20, Paul had identified the apostles and prophets as the foundation of God's new temple (with Christ as the cornerstone). In both places, these were authoritative eyewitnesses of Christ's ministry and resurrection (apostles) and proclaimers of divinely sourced directives and messages for the churches (prophets).

Paul added two modifiers to these ministers in this passage. First, the apostles and prophets were "holy" (ἅγιος). With this term, Paul highlighted their special appointment rather than their stellar character or elevated status. The meaning "set apart" or "consecrated to the service of God" (BDAG, s.v. "ἅγιος" 1, p. 10) functioned similarly to the substantive use of "saints" (ἅγιοι), which Paul applied to all believers (Eph. 1:1, 15; 3:8; 4:12; 5:3; 6:18).

Second, these apostles and prophets were "his" (αὐτοῦ), likely referring to God, since the two verbs in the verse envisioned him as the subject (Lincoln, 1990, 178–79; Hoehner, 2002, 442–43). This pronoun coordinated with "holy" to stress that the ministers had been selected by God and thus answered to him for their service.

God had revealed the mystery to the apostles and prophets "by the Spirit" (ἐν πνεύματι). The Spirit's guidance operated in tandem with the eyewitness testimony of the apostles to propagate and preserve the integrity of the early Christian message (John 14:26; 1 Cor. 2:6–13). In addition, both Old and New Testaments attested to the Spirit's role in prophecy (Num. 11:25–26; Joel 2:28–32; Acts 2:16–21; 1 Cor. 12:7–11; 2 Peter 1:21; Rev. 19:10). In this context, Paul's emphasis on the Spirit's supernatural assistance in revelation paired well with a message of divine origins that was long hidden from human awareness (cf. 1 Cor. 2:7–10).

3:6. Paul introduced the substance of the revealed mystery with a construction (inf., εἶναι) that gave information about the full equality of "the Gentiles" (τὰ ἔθνη) alongside the Jews in Christ Jesus (cf. Gal. 3:28; Col. 3:11). The insertion of "namely" (NET) or "to be specific" (NASB) helped associate the construction (appositional inf. beginning with εἶναι) with the mystery of verse 4. Paul thus highlighted a central feature of God's saving plans as well as a truth that would resonate powerfully with his Gentile readers.

A Different Climactic Chapter

As N. T. Wright (2013, 121–39) observes, it was common for Jewish writings during the Second Temple period to retell the story of God's work in history. By discerning how God was at work with his people from one era to another, the Jews could seek to discern where the story was going in the future and what would be the climactic chapter. The climactic chapter sometimes consisted of God delivering his people from the evil Gentile kingdoms (3 Macc, Wis, Pss. Sol.). In Ephesians 3, Paul's revealed mystery pointed to a climactic chapter of God's story that the other stories never considered. Through the ministry of Jesus, the Messiah, God had welcomed the Gentiles into his family as full equals with the Jews. Gentiles had become co-heirs, co-members of one body, and co-partakers in the promise from God to finally restore his people and give them full access to his presence. God had formed this new humanity in anticipation of one day restoring all things under the reign of Christ (Eph. 1:10).

Paul noted three spiritual privileges that the Gentiles now shared in common with Jewish believers in Christ, in each case using a word with the prefix "co- " (συν-) to emphasize the Jews' and Gentiles' equal standing in God's family and kingdom. First, they were "coheirs" (συγκληρονόμα) with the Jews in Christ (the NIV adds "with Israel" as the inferred fellow recipients of the inheritance; cf. NLT). Elsewhere in the letter Paul commented on believers' inheritance (Eph. 1:14, 18; 5:5), and the related word ("co-heirs") here likewise imagined the entirety of believers' eschatological blessings in the final kingdom of God (cf. 1 Cor. 6:9–10; 15:50; Gal. 5:21).

Second, Gentile believers in Christ were "co-members [with Jewish believers] of one body" (σύσσωμα). This fit nicely with Paul's development of the theme in Ephesians of the church being Christ's body, with the image flowing smoothly from the ideas introduced in Ephesians 1:23 and 2:16. Though this creatively constructed term (σύσσωμος), which added the co- prefix (συν-) to "body," appears nowhere else in the NT, passages such as 1 Corinthians 12:27 and Ephesians 5:30 put forward similar concepts.

Third, Gentile believers were "co-partakers (with Jewish believers) in the promise" (συμμέτοχα τῆς ἐπαγγελίας). Paul used the compound term "co-partakers" (συμμέτοχα) again in Ephesians 5:7 but nowhere else in his letters. In this verse, it perfectly captured the idea of the Jews' and Gentiles' shared reception of God's promised blessings. Again, as in Ephesians 2:12, the promise was singular (rather than "promises"), suggesting that Paul perceived primarily the singular fulfillment of God's covenantal assurances (in the Abrahamic, Davidic, new covenants) in Christ and by the Spirit, as portrayed in Ephesians 2:14–22 (cf. Gal. 3:7–29, where Paul spoke of a singular "promise" in conjunction with an inheritance, the Spirit, and Jews and Gentiles being united in Christ; Hoehner, 2002, 447; Thielman, 2010, 205).

The phrase "in Christ Jesus" (ἐν Χριστῷ Ἰησοῦ) probably modified all three of the spiritual blessings in the verse. In Ephesians, Paul consistently used "in Christ" (and its equivalents) as a way to keep all of God's works and believers' experiences revolving around the central axis of Christ's person and ministry. In this verse, then, Gentiles experienced all three advantages because of their incorporation into Christ Jesus and their sharing in his exalted status (cf. Eph. 2:5–7). Paul attached one more modifying prepositional phrase, "through the gospel" (διὰ τοῦ εὐαγγελίου), to specify that the gospel, or the events and proclamation of Christ's death and resurrection, was the means by which participation in God's family and kingdom became possible. When the gospel was responded to with sincere faith, people from all backgrounds entered into a permanent, abundant existence with Christ and other believers. Paul's Gentile readers had begun to taste and see the benefits of this good news.

The Gospel of the Reign of Augustus

Paul and other early believers continued to use "gospel" terminology that was prominent in Jesus's ministry and grounded in the Septuagint's inclusion of "proclaim good news" (εὐαγγελίζω) in several eschatological passages in Isaiah (cf. Rom. 10:14–15). In addition, though, the term also surfaced in interesting places in the broader Roman world. One famous Greek inscription found in the ancient city of Priene (not too far from Ephesus) used "gospel" (εὐαγγέλιον) and other elevated language to venerate the Emperor Augustus. The residents responsible for the inscription displayed their loyalty to Rome and its ideals by calling Augustus a "savior," "benefactor," and "god," acknowledging the touch of the divine they discerned in his leadership. The residents honored his birth and ongoing presence in the world as "good news." Gospel language could carry with it a celebratory and victorious tone both inside and outside the Bible, but in Paul's estimation only Jesus's triumphant ministry aptly reflected the ultimate good news for this world.

3:7. In the final verse of the subsection (Eph. 3:1–7), Paul revisited the idea (from Eph. 3:2) of the stewardship that God had entrusted to him. Paul referred to the aforementioned "gospel" (οὗ, "of which") to link his service to the cause of the gospel (cf. Col. 1:23). As a "servant" or "minister" (διάκονος) of the gospel, Paul "became" (ἐγενήθην) a modest intermediary in a great project. The gospel was God's priceless gift to humanity, and Paul had received the amazing privilege and responsibility of proclaiming it (Rom. 1:1; 1 Thess. 2:4; 2 Tim. 1:10–11).

Paul had become a minister of the gospel "by the gracious gift of God" (κατὰ τὴν δωρεὰν τῆς χάριτος τοῦ θεοῦ). This return to a familiar theme (cf. Eph. 3:2) supported the idea that God superintended both his global plans and his enlistment of Paul into those plans. Paul knew from his own experience on the road to Damascus that his call to ministry had resulted solely from God's orchestrations, apart from any of Paul's initiative and even in spite of it. Paul further highlighted God's supernatural intervention in his life by noting that this gracious gift "was given to me by God's powerful action" (κατὰ τὴν ἐνέργειαν τῆς δυνάμεως).

The God who "exercised" (ἐνεργέω) his power to achieve his purposes over all creation (1:11) in the resurrection of Christ (1:20), and in the lives of believers (1:19; 3:20), had worked similarly to recruit Paul for ministry. God exercised his "power" (δύναμις) to bring his perfect plans to fruition. Paul continued to explore the scope and magnitude of these plans in the section that followed.

Paul Suffers but Participates in God's Cosmic Plans (3:8–13)

Paul's sufferings paled in comparison to being invited to participate in the great plans that God was now carrying out in Christ and through the church, in full sight of spiritual entities.

3:8. Paul's reflection upon the way that God had graciously and powerfully appointed him to ministry (3:7) sparked the admission that this calling had been completely undeserved. Paul turned his attention to his unworthiness with a new sentence that began with "to me" (ἐμοί) and was followed by a self description of his spiritual standing before his initial encounter with the resurrected Christ. Paul depicted himself as "the very least of all believers" (τῷ ἐλαχιστοτέρῳ πάντων ἁγίων). Paul acknowledged that his past persecution of Christians made him the most unlikely of candidates to serve on God's team. Paul also reveled in God's gracious calling against the backdrop of his adversarial past in Galatians 1:13–16 and 1 Timothy 1:12–16. In 1 Corinthians 15:9–10, Paul had pinpointed his regrettable history as the reason for his lowest standing among the apostles (ὁ ἐλάχιστος τῶν ἀποστόλων, "the least of the apostles"). In Ephesians 3, Paul intensified the comparison ("very least" instead of "least") and widened the group (from the apostles to "all of the saints," or all believers) in which he ranked last. Paul appreciated God's outreach to him all the more when he considered how unfit he had been to receive it.

Once again, Paul used the phrase "this grace was given" (ἐδόθη ἡ χάρις αὕτη; pass. voice) to describe God's gracious initiative in calling him. The wording identified Paul as the recipient, not the actor. Paul mentioned "this" (αὕτη) grace, since he had just referred to the grace or privilege of serving God in the previous verse. The God who saved believers by his grace (2:8–9) also invested their lives with meaning by his grace (2:10).

Two infinitive phrases stood in apposition to "this grace" (ἡ χάρις αὕτη) and thus further defined this wonderful ministry. The first aspect of the gracious ministry Paul had received consisted of "proclaiming good news to the Gentiles" (τοῖς ἔθνεσιν εὐαγγελίσασθαι), who would otherwise be oblivious to the fact that God had now acted decisively to rescue and restore the people of the world (cf. Gal. 1:16). Paul's Gentile readers were thus among the beneficiaries of God's gracious appointment of Paul to his service. Paul exhibited his characteristic fondness of gospel language (cf. the verbal form in 2:17 and the noun forms in 1:13; 3:6). Paul fulfilled a ministry of proclamation (εὐαγγελίσασθαι, "to proclaim the good news"), with a message focused on how God's good plans for the world were coming to fruition in Christ.

Paul touted the good news of "the unfathomable richness of Christ" (τὸ ἀνεξιχνίαστον πλοῦτος τοῦ Χριστοῦ). The term Paul enlisted (ἀνεξιχνίαστος) meant "unfathomable" (NASB, NET), "unsearchable" (ESV, NKJV), "boundless" (NIV, NRSV), or "incomprehensible" (BDAG, s.v. "ἀνεξιχνίαστος," p. 77). The word appeared several times in Job in the Septuagint (Job 5:9; 9:10; 34:24), and Paul employed the term to describe God's unsearchable judgments in Romans 11:33. The term aligned well with Paul's discussion of a mystery beyond human grasp, apart from divine disclosure. It approximated the word for "all-surpassing" (ὑπερβάλλω) that modified "richness" in Ephesians 2:7 (cf. 1:19), and it prepared the way for Paul's prayer that his readers would know a love that surpassed knowledge in Ephesians 3:19. Earlier Paul had used language of "riches" or "richness" (πλοῦτος) as a descriptor of God's grace (1:7; 2:7), glorious inheritance (1:18), and God's mercy (2:4). This time, Paul spoke of "the riches of Christ" in more of a summary fashion, to mean "the riches found in Christ" (cf. Eph. 1:3). God had commissioned Paul to announce these riches in Christ to Gentile audiences such as his readers.

3:9. Paul identified the second feature of his gracious ministry (connected with the first by καί, "and") as the responsibility to "enlighten" (φωτίσαι) people about God's plans. The imagery of light captured the beauty and power of God's truth (Eph. 1:18; 2 Cor. 4:4–6; Matt. 4:16; Luke 2:32; John 1:9; Acts 26:18). With this picture, Paul may have even recalled his own illuminating encounter with Christ (Acts 9:3; 22:6; 26:13; Stott, 1979, 121). Paul and the early Christians had not reduced salvation to spiritual enlightenment alone, but Paul did see Spirit-aided illumination about God's deeper truths as an important component of ongoing spiritual growth in Ephesians (Eph. 1:18; cf. 1 Cor. 2:9–16). Whether Jew or Gentile, "all people" (πάντας) needed exposure to the splendor of God's all-encompassing program for the world (Eph. 1:9–10).

Having already expressed the "what" of the mystery in verse 6, Paul turned his gaze to God's method or plan for implementing the mystery (τίς ἡ οἰκονομία τοῦ μυστηρίου, "what is the administration of the mystery"). Paul used the term for "implementation" or "administration" (οἰκονομία) flexibly in Ephesians, earlier applying it to God's oversight in directing salvation history to its final destination (Eph. 1:10) and to Paul's own commission, given by God (Eph. 3:2). In this context, the implementation denoted Christ's reconciling work, as depicted in Ephesians 2:13–18 and touched on in 3:11. God had authorized Paul not only to proclaim the depths of the good news of Christ but also to frame that good news within the grander scope of God's unfolding plans.

The mystery now revealed to and through Paul "had been kept hidden" (ἀποκεκρυμμένου) from people of earlier eras. This reminder of past hiddenness cohered well with the overall idea of mystery. The truth of the mystery had been withheld "from people of other [earlier] eras" (ἀπὸ τῶν αἰώνων), namely, because the time had not yet been right for Jesus's decisive arrival (Gal. 4:4; Mark 1:15). God had kept this mystery to himself (ἐν τῷ θεῷ, "in God") in the meantime. The God who was sovereign in creation was also sovereign in revelation. The God "who created all things" (ὁ τὰ πάντα κτίσαντι) as part of a good creation (Gen. 1) now revealed, through Paul, the good news of how he was perfectly re-creating believers in Christ (Eph. 2:10) and had re-created Jews and Gentiles together into one new humanity (Eph. 2:15).

3:10. Paul noted the purpose (ἵνα, "in order that") of God's past concealment of the mystery. God had kept this mystery to himself in order that "now" (νῦν), with everything having been arranged, certain truths could "be made known" (γνωρισθῇ). Specifically, "God's multifaceted wisdom" (ἡ πολυποίκιλος σοφία τοῦ θεοῦ) was now put on display. An emphasis on God's wisdom coordinated well with God's method for accomplishing his will (from verse 9). God carried out his eternal plans masterfully, creatively, and comprehensively (thus displaying his "multifaceted wisdom"), reconciling sinners to himself in Christ and creating a new humanity of diverse but united people in Christ.

TRANSLATION ANALYSIS: The intensified term "multifaceted" (πολυποίκιλος) is a compound term that adds "much" or "many" to the more standard word "diversified" or "manifold" (ποικίλος). The resulting compound term can be translated as "manifold" (NIV, ESV, NASB,

NKJV), "multifaceted" (CSB, NET), or even "in its rich variety" (NRSV, NLT). Paul enlisted the term to highlight the greatness and complexity of God's wisdom, which was being revealed to a watching universe.

It was through this one new diverse body of believers, "through the church" (διὰ τῆς ἐκκλησίας), that God revealed his great wisdom. The church thus had become "exhibit A" of God's plans to unite all things in heaven and on earth in and under Christ Jesus (Eph. 1:9–10). If Jews and Gentiles could become reconciled to God and one another, enjoying full life and an unhindered relationship with the Father together in his presence, then nothing would stop the eventual arrangement of all things under Christ's perfect governance.

God had an audience in mind for this broadcast of his wisdom. God determined to make his plans known "to the rulers and authorities in the heavenly places" (ταῖς ἀρχαῖς καὶ ταῖς ἐξουσίαις ἐν τοῖς ἐπουρανίοις). The appearance of this expansive and otherworldly audience continued Paul's focus in Ephesians on the cosmic setting of God's work (Eph. 1:3, 9–10, 20–23; 2:6–7). Astonishing and magnificent plans deserved an unparalleled audience. An ever-expanding audience from verse 8 to verse 10 was witnessing the triumph of God's work. Paul preached the good news of Christ to the Gentiles (3:8), then shed light about God's plans to all people (3:9), as part of God's greater intent to declare his wisdom to the unseen powers of the universe (3:10).

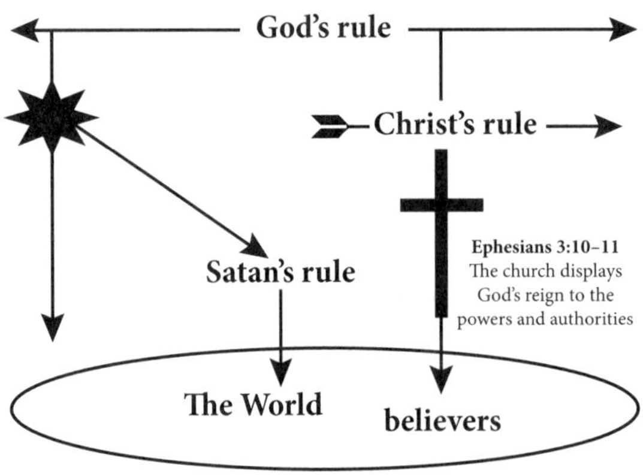

The Church Displays God's Current Reign within a Fallen World

The "rulers" (ἀρχαί) and "authorities" (ἐξουσίαι) were likely hostile spiritual powers (*DPL*, 539), in league with the current ruler of the world (Eph. 2:2) for the purpose of opposing God and harassing his people (Eph. 6:12). Accordingly, this display of God's wisdom to evil powers carried a note of vindication, as these enemies of God had to acknowledge the creativity and effectiveness of the way God had carried out his cosmic-scaled plans, as well as the certainty of their own eventual defeat in view of the work God had set in motion (cf. Phil. 2:9–11).

The Drama Portrayed

John Stott (1979, 123–24) captures God's cosmic work beautifully: "It is as if a great drama is being enacted. History is the theatre, the world is the stage, and church members in every land are the actors. God himself has written the play, and he directs and produces it. Act by act, scene by scene, the story continues to unfold. . . . [T]he cosmic intelligences, the principalities and powers in the heavenly places" are the "spectators of the drama of salvation."

3:11. God had not made an arbitrary decision to finally reveal his plans but did so "according to his eternal design" (κατὰ πρόθεσιν τῶν αἰώνων). God had now disclosed his wise program for salvation, guided by his eternal, foreordained plans and timetable (cf. Rom. 16:26). With "design" (πρόθεσις), Paul returned to the pre- (προ-) prefixed words that he had employed liberally in Ephesians 1:3–14 to describe God's forethought in his actions (Eph. 1:9, 11; cf. Rom. 8:28; 9:11). God worked purposefully in all that he did, crafting a perfect plan and bringing it to completion at the right time and in the right way.

Next, Paul specified how God "accomplished" (ἣν ἐποίησεν) these plans. In this context, the term "he did" (ἐποίησεν) means "he accomplished" (during the time frame of Christ's incarnational ministry) rather than "arranged" or "hatched" (from eternity past). God brought these carefully formed plans to fruition "in Christ Jesus our Lord" (ἐν τῷ Χριστῷ Ἰησοῦ τῷ κυρίῳ ἡμῶν). God's implementation (cf. οἰκονομία, from verse 9) of his eternal plans corresponded to the climactic ministry of Jesus, the Messiah. Alongside the earlier reminder of the centrality of Jesus Christ in the passage (3:4), this verse anchored God's program for the nations in Jesus's identity and ministry as the Christ (cf. Thielman, 2010, 218). The addendum of "our Lord" to "Christ Jesus" grouped Paul and his readers together ("our") and injected a tone of exalted authority to Christ ("Lord"). This title did justice to Christ's preeminence in a grand undertaking that had cosmic reverberations.

3:12. Next, Paul pivoted from the achievement of God's purposes in Christ to the resulting outcomes for believers in Christ. The Lord Jesus Christ was the one "in whom" (ἐν ᾧ) believers attained these spiritual outcomes. In particular, Paul announced to his readers that "we have boldness and confident access" (ἔχομεν τὴν παρρησίαν καὶ προσαγωγὴν ἐν πεποιθήσει) in Christ Jesus. Though Paul at times used the term "boldness" (παρρησία) to refer to his own and his associates' ministry posture (as in Eph. 6:19; 2 Cor. 3:12; Phil. 1:20), the first-person plural ("we") in this case continued from "our" Lord in the previous verse and described all believers' open approach to God. This corresponded well to the related concept (linked by καί and a shared article) of "confident access" (προσαγωγὴ ἐν πεποιθήσει) to God. Paul did not specify that their access was to God in particular (as in Eph. 2:18), but this was implied. Paul and his readers drew near to God with the confidence of a trusting child enjoying a loving father's presence.

Boldness and Confident Access

The boldness and confident access Paul's readers now enjoyed with the Father was strikingly different from both traditional Jewish and Roman religious experiences. God set apart Aaron, his sons, and the Levitical priests to represent the Israelites before Yahweh (Exod. 28–29; Lev. 8; Num. 3:5–39; 8:5–26). They were entrusted with a special access to God that was withheld from the rest of the people (cf. Lev. 16). The priests' ceremonial practices were expected to be carried out carefully and in exacting detail (Lev. 1–7; 10:1–11). Ferguson (2003, 171) describes the precision needed in Roman religious ceremonies: "If a mistake was made, the ceremony had to be done over from the beginning." Paul's readers, in contrast, relied on the perfect sacrificial work that Christ completed on their behalf (Eph. 1:7; 2:13–18). This gave them a wonderful access, by grace, into the Father's presence.

Believers experienced this boldness and confident access "through faith in him" (διὰ τῆς πίστεως αὐτοῦ) referring to faith in Christ. Receiving God's blessings through a trusting response to the preached message about Christ was consonant with Paul's teaching earlier in the letter (Eph. 1:13, 19; 2:8–9; cf. Eph. 3:17). Though grammatically possible, the idea of Christ's own faithfulness being the pathway to enjoying God's presence would surface too suddenly to be the probable meaning. Paul connected the believer's faith and access to God's grace in Romans 5:1–2 as well.

TRANSLATION ANALYSIS: The NET translation has "by way of Christ's faithfulness" (διὰ τῆς πίστεως αὐτοῦ) rather than the more common "through faith in him [Christ]." Grammatically, the genitive noun "of him" may serve as either the object or subject of faith. If the object (Lincoln, 1990, 190; Schnackenburg, 1991, 142; Arnold, 2010, 199; Thielman, 2010, 219; Bock, 2019, 103), then Christ was the object of the believer's faith. If the subject (Barth, 1974, 347; Wallace, 1996, 114–16; Foster, 2002, 84–95; Gombis, 2004, 322; Talbert, 2007, 100; Witherington, 2007, 268), then Christ exercised the faith (or faithfulness) toward God, for the believer's benefit. Scholars regularly debate the exact meaning of phrases similar to this in other places in Paul's letters (Rom. 3:22, 26; Gal. 2:16; 3:22; Phil. 3:9). Most likely, these phrases referred to believers' faith in Christ.

3:13. Paul concluded (διό, "therefore") his long digression of Ephesians 3:1–13 with a practical, pastoral directive to his readers, using "I ask" (αἰτοῦμαι) rhetorically to introduce his counsel as a request. Paul advised his readers "to not lose heart" (μὴ ἐγκακεῖν) about his imprisoned state. Elsewhere Paul spoke about "not losing heart" when he hoped to promote tenacity in serving Christ (2 Cor. 4:1; Gal. 6:9). Paul did not want them to lose heart "because of my afflictions" (ἐν ταῖς θλίψεσίν), or what Paul had suffered in the course of this God-given ministry. Paul spoke of his "afflictions" (θλῖψις) endured during the course of ministry in various other places (2 Cor. 1:4–8; 4:17; 6:4; 7:4; Phil. 1:17; 1 Thess. 3:3–7). The imprisonment of a prominent ministry leader such as Paul had the potential to unsettle Paul's readers, who may have wondered what this meant for the overall progress of the church and their broader standing in society. Paul wanted to intervene before any feelings of discouragement took root. This suggests that at least part of Paul's purpose in this whole section was to direct readers' attention away from any sense of shame from suffering to the grandeur of the ministry that Paul carried out for them (cf. Gombis, 2004, 316, 323; Sherwood, 2012, 106–8).

Paul further reassured his readers that his adversity served to advance the greater good of his readers. Coming full circle from where he began (Eph. 3:1), Paul observed that he suffered "for your sake" (ὑπὲρ ὑμῶν), so that they and other Gentiles who believed in Christ could participate in the full extent of the blessings God had designed for his adopted children. Whatever struggles Paul confronted, Paul told his readers, they "were for your glory" (ἥτις ἐστιν δόξα ὑμῶν). The word "glory" (δόξα) could have a range of possible meanings, but in the context of Ephesians, which imparted a sweeping vision of the magnificent reality that God had opened up to believers, the term likely carried an eschatological meaning that captured the totality of believers' current and future spiritual assets in Christ. Paul presented the hope of glory as comfort for believers who suffered (Rom. 5:1–5; 8:18; 2 Cor. 4:16–18), and he believed that his Gentile readers gained admittance into a glorious existence with God partially as a result of his own ministry of suffering (2 Cor. 1:6; 4:11–12; 6:10; 12:15; Col. 1:24). Paul closed the passage on this note, guiding his readers about how to process ongoing concerns about Paul's hardships and any other news of setbacks to the church's progress. They should take courage in the fruitful results of the eternally meaningful ministry in which Paul participated.

TRANSLATION ANALYSIS: Some scholars believe that the clause "which are for your glory" (ἥτις ἐστιν δόξα ὑμῶν) pictures Paul's sufferings instilling a healthy sense of pride (δόξα in the sense of "boast" or "honor") among Paul's readers (NLT; Muddiman, 2001, 164; Hoehner, 2002, 470; Bock, 2019, 104). Less likely, the phrase could be rendered "which is to your credit," which would imply that Paul's readers should take pride in refusing to adopt a pessimistic attitude about Paul's adversities (an option suggested by the verse note in the NET). In view of what Paul just shared about the momentous realization of God's cosmic plans in Christ, an eschatological sense of believers' glory fits much better (with Lincoln, 1990, 192; Best, 1998, 332;

Arnold, 2010, 200; Thielman, 2010, 222; Roberts, 2016, 99). Paul's description in 1 Corinthians 2:7 of a mystery, eternally prearranged by God, culminating in believers' eschatological glory in Christ, also offers strong support for a similar meaning of "glory" in Ephesians 3:13.

THEOLOGICAL FOCUS

The exegetical idea (Paul's imprisonment was nothing compared to his God-given opportunity to reveal the mystery of God's eternal plans to put his wisdom on display in Christ and through a unified church) leads to this theological focus: *Participating in this groundbreaking era of God's story is well worth the sacrifice.*

This passage describes the groundbreaking era in which followers of Christ participate. Christ Jesus has ushered in a decisive moment in salvation history. Believers can fathom the magnitude and hope of this new era because God has now disclosed his amazing, once-hidden plans ("the mystery") through his apostles and prophets (vv. 4–5). Because of Christ's climactic ministry the world has entered into a highly significant era in which people from all backgrounds, Jew and Gentile, can now be reconciled to God and enjoy his presence (v. 6; cf. 2 Cor. 6:1–2). God is restoring first a people and then the world to himself. God's creation of a spiritually alive and unified church consisting of people from different nations testifies to God's eventual reuniting of all things under Christ's glorious rule (Eph. 3:10; 1:9–10). In Christ Jesus, believers enjoy unhindered access to God (3:12) and are on a path to a final, perfect, and permanent encounter with God in his full glory (v. 13).

Believers who suffer for Christ need not lose heart (v. 13), taking comfort in the fact that their participation in God's story is well worth the sacrifice. Paul knew this, even as the weeks and months of his imprisonments had turned into years. Paul realized that his confinement persisted only because of his unrelenting commitment to serving Christ on behalf of his readers (v. 1). Paul helped his original readers reinterpret the meaning of his imprisonment by reminding them of the remarkable story that was marching forward and coming into focus before their very eyes. In the same way, believers today can gain a renewed vision of the grandeur of God's cosmic purposes in the midst of their gritty and sacrificial service to Christ. Paul's teachings can help believers grow in their appreciation of the full import of God's reconciling work in this world. Such a prized opportunity puts all hardships and inconveniences into their proper perspective.

PREACHING AND TEACHING STRATEGIES

Exegetical and Theological Synthesis

In a sweeping description of the gospel (v. 7)—the mystery of God's eternal plan—Paul put things in perspective. He may have been a prisoner for Christ Jesus (v. 1), but he did not lose heart, and he asked the Ephesians to take the same attitude (v. 13). The gospel was given to Paul as a stewardship (v. 2) to announce God's long-hidden plan to include the Gentiles as members of the same body with the Jews (vv. 3–6). That mystery was hidden for ages (v. 9) but then was revealed by Paul's ministry. The Ephesians weren't the only ones to hear the announcement; the rulers in the heavenly places also were made aware of God's plan (v. 10). No wonder Paul was bold (v. 12) and did not lose heart even though he was a prisoner.

Preaching Idea

God's messenger might be chained, but God's message is unchained.

Contemporary Connections

What does it mean?

What does it mean that God's messenger might be chained? Background material on Paul's house arrest could be shared, including pictures (e.g. a Roman soldier), objects (e.g. chains), or maps (e.g. the locations of Ephesus and Rome). A bridge could be made to the twenty-first century with a story and pictures of modern persecution such as the 2019 Easter bombings of a church in Sri Lanka.[1] Going back a few decades, the story of Richard Wurmbrand (1909–2001) could explain how God's messengers are sometimes chained. See Wurmbrand's story below in the "Creativity in Presentation" section.

The second half of the preaching idea—God's message is not chained—means that the good news of Jesus is spreading and cannot be contained by persecution. In this passage, the focus of the good news is on the fact that God is forming the Gentiles and Jews into one body. Previously that announcement was a "mystery" (vv. 3, 4, 6). Paul used the term "mystery" in a way that may be unfamiliar to some listeners. The following suggestions might help explain the concept.

- We might first employ the term as it is commonly understood today with examples of mystery novels such as Sherlock Holmes.

- Then we might deconstruct the modern usage of "mystery" by pointing out that Paul's concept differed. It was not something that clever detectives figured out; it must be revealed by an all-knowing guide who simply explains to Sherlock Holmes "whodunit."

- Then we could further clarify the concept with a cross-reference to Daniel, where the term described the secret plan of God that Nebuchadnezzar had seen in a dream but which Daniel could explain only when God gave him insight.

Another idea that supports the preaching idea might also need clarification: "rulers and authorities in the heavenly places" (v. 10).

Is it true?

Is it true that God's messenger might be chained, but God's message is unchained? While persecution in North America does not reach the levels seen in other parts of the world or other eras of time, it nevertheless exists, and can often be considered a hostile climate.

Because God's message of the gospel is not chained, we should not lose heart. But maintaining hope can be difficult when facing persecution. Family members might roll their eyes and label the sincere believer a "fanatic" and "intolerant." That will cut the heart out of anyone! The supervisor at work might reject the promotion of the believer who is striving to be salt and light. Ouch. Of course, Paul's sufferings and the sufferings of fellow believers in many parts of the world were much worse that these forms of "persecution," yet Paul was not discouraged, and he asked the believers in Ephesus (and by extension, he asks us also) to not lose heart. We keep up our courage when we see the good news advancing despite our suffering or even because of it.

Now what?

If it is true that God's messenger might be chained, but God's message is unchained, how should we respond? We might give people a

1 Bernadette Tuazon, Sean O'Key and Darran Simon. Cody McCloy, Natalie Yubas, Henrik Pettersson, Ignacio Osorio and Padraic Driscoll, "Terror in Sri Lanka," CNN.com, April 2019, https://www.cnn.com/interactive/2019/04/world/sri-lanka-attacks. For a discussion of current persecution and a map of the world where persecution is worst, see Sarah Eekhoff Zylstra, "The Top 50 Countries Where It's Most Dangerous to Follow Jesus," *Christianity Today*, January 10, 2018, https://www.christianitytoday.com/news/2018/january/top-50-christian-persecution-open-doors-world-watch-list.html.

chance to share their stories of facing opposition because of their faith in Christ. This could help them take heart as they discover that they are not alone. Furthermore, to help people to continue sharing the gospel even when times are tough, we might point out that the message is from God himself. The passive verbs suggest this. The gospel "was given" (v. 2), has been "made known" (v. 3), and Paul "was made" a messenger (v. 7). In other words, we did not invent this message. That reminder can build confidence. The gospel is an astounding and gracious announcement of good news from God, and it is not chained.

We might encourage the listeners to take one small step in sharing the good news—pray for someone close to you who needs to hear of God's love. Prayer could be made every night at dinner time, or as the last thing at night before turning out the light. We might pray for our neighbors as we walk the dog. Not only does prayer affect those we pray for, but it also affects us by aligning our values with God's.

A sermon from this passage could also be coupled with an evangelistic outreach. Perhaps we might schedule the sermon just before the start of an Alpha or Christianity Explored course. This would give people a way to respond to the preaching idea by inviting their friends to hear the good news.

Creativity in Presentation

The form of this passage—first-person account expressed with multiple word pictures—suggests some genre-sensitive ways that could be used to present the sermon. One is testimony. We might borrow Paul's own "technique" of self-disclosure. You could share your own testimony or ask a member of the church to do so. If someone in the congregation has undergone hardships in God's service, their testimony might follow the sermon; or perhaps they could give you permission to share their story during the sermon. Interview could be used similarly, asking questions such as these: "Have you suffered for the gospel? How did you feel at the time? Did you see the gospel advance because of your suffering?" As mentioned above, the story of Richard Wurmbrand could be used. He was a pastor in Romania and was imprisoned and tortured for fourteen years under Communist rule. His most famous book is *Tortured for Christ*, and a film by the same name was made in 2019. He was burned, locked in a large icebox, and the soles of his feet were beaten until the flesh was torn off.[2]

This passage also uses word pictures that could become actual pictures in the sermon. Jews and Gentiles are "one body"; God's grace is a "gift" of "unfathomable riches"; God has "enlightened" people to his message; and we have "access" to God. These could be illustrated with pictures or objects. For example, to illustrate "access" we might pull out a large ring of keys, trying some of them unsuccessfully on a padlock. But then, *eureka*! We find the right key and gain access.

To include young people in the teaching, the term "mystery" could be illustrated with a game often found in children's materials: embedded into a line drawing of, say, a sunset, might be a shoe, a duck, a fountain pen, and a beach ball. Those objects are hiding in plain sight just as God's plan of salvation was present for millennia in the Hebrew Scriptures. The young person might be invited to circle or highlight the objects. This illustrates that the plan was there all along, but only after someone reveals it do we see it plainly.

The metaphor of "chains" in the preaching idea could also be leveraged by displaying some chains. You might even "bind" yourself with the chains as you talk about the first part

---

2 Wikipedia contributors, "Richard Wurmbrand," *Wikipedia, The Free Encyclopedia*, last revised September 3, 2020, https://en.wikipedia.org/wiki/Richard_Wurmbrand.

of the preaching idea (God's messenger may be chained), and then set them aside for the second part (God's message is unchained). These visual aids could be woven into the outline below.

In all of our creativity, we will want to emphasize the main idea: God's messenger might be chained, but God's message is unchained.

A possible outline:

- God's messenger might be chained.
    - Historical background on Paul's house arrest
    - Current examples of suffering for the gospel

- God's message is unchained.
    - It is a mystery revealed.
    - It is good news.

- Conclusion: Therefore, we do not lose heart.

DISCUSSION QUESTIONS:

1. What was the significance of Paul's circumstances when he wrote this passage?

2. What does "mystery" mean in this passage? How is it different than our concept of a "mystery story"?

3. What did stewards do in Paul's day? How are we stewards of the gospel? Do you consider yourself a steward?

4. In what way is the church significant to God's plans for the world? How should that shape our estimation of the church's value and mission?

5. According to this passage, why should we not lose heart when we experience opposition to the gospel?

Ephesians 3:14–21

EXEGETICAL IDEA

Paul praised God and prayed confidently that the all-powerful Father, by his Spirit, would empower Paul's readers to know and experience the abundant love of Christ in their hearts.

THEOLOGICAL FOCUS

Believers can pray that God's Spirit will empower them and help them to experience the love of Christ in deep and personal ways.

PREACHING IDEA

God, empower us to know your unknowable love.

PREACHING POINTERS

Many of Paul's readers had emerged from a pagan background in which the Greco-Roman gods were distant, demanding, and unpredictable. These new followers of Christ were beginning to understand the idea that a loving God had made a personal relationship with him possible, but deeply experiencing this truth was another matter. Paul's consequential teachings about the good news of Christ could easily remain on the surface of the lives of Paul's readers. These truths needed to sink in deeply at the heart level so that the message of God's love could shape the readers' identity and permeate their attitudes, actions, and affections. The readers could not manufacture this outcome on their own. They needed God's Spirit to knit Christ's personal and ongoing ministry of love within their hearts. Paul assured his readers of his commitment to intercede for them before the Father, who was able and willing to meet their need to experience his love inwardly and genuinely.

Likewise, for some people today God can seem distant, demanding, and unpredictable. He is like a divine watchmaker who creates the universe, winds it up, and lets it go, rarely touching human concerns again. Historically that has been called "deism," and it is alive and well today according to sociologists Christian Smith and Melinda Lunquist Denton. In *Soul Searching: The Religious and Spiritual Lives of American Teenagers* (2005), the authors conclude that many young adults view God in terms of "moral, therapeutic deism." In contrast to the deistic God who makes few demands on us, some world religions and even some branches of Christianity picture the Almighty as a glowering drill sergeant or disapproving governess. Garrison Keillor pokes fun at such a church in the fictitious town of Lake Wobegon, Minnesota, a parish that he names Our Lady of Perpetual Responsibility. This passage from Ephesians proclaims the true God, neither distant nor glowering, but full of love. The prayer Paul made for the Ephesians applies to all of us: God, empower us to know your unknowable love.

A PRAYER TO EXPERIENCE GOD'S POWER AND LOVE (3:14–21)

LITERARY STRUCTURE AND THEMES (3:14–21)

In Ephesians 3:1–21, Paul resumed the prayer he had prepared to begin in Ephesians 3:1. Paul's prayer built upon theological concepts that he had already covered in the letter but now applied them in a personal and experiential direction. Paul prayed that believers would lean fully into their union with Christ, their admittance into God's presence by the Spirit, and their freely received insights into God's plans. Paul asked God to imprint his truths into the readers' lives so that Paul's teaching would be internalized and result in deeply formed identities in Christ.

The passage consists of the main substance of the prayer (Eph. 3:14–19), followed by a brief doxology (Eph. 3:20–21). In keeping with Paul's style in Ephesians so far, the body of the prayer is covered in one long sentence with multiple subordinate clauses and phrases. Though the syntactical structure is not easy to trace, the intricate weaving together of complementary ideas makes Paul's central goals clear. With eyes fixated on the power and goodness of God, Paul prayed with confidence that the Father would by his Spirit strengthen Paul's readers to know and experience the abundant love of Christ.

- ***Being Filled with the Abundant Love of Christ (3:14–19)***
- ***Praise to a Glorious God Who Exceeds All Expectations (3:20–21)***

EXPOSITION (3:14–21)

In this passage Paul composed a short but profound prayer for his readers. The prayer took only a minute to read out loud, but it painted a rich picture of the spiritual and relational intimacy with God that was now available to Paul's readers. This access to intimate communion with a loving God stood in stark contrast to many of Paul's readers' past experiences with Roman religion. Roman religion consisted of people seeking, with the help of priests and other religious guides, knowledge about unpredictable deities that would shed light on a person's or community's obligations to the gods and goddesses. Through discerning and fulfilling their duties, the people could secure the deities' favor and intervention for each new uncertainty and trouble that arose in life (Ando, 2003, 4–5, 10–13). Paul, on the other hand, proclaimed that a God of love had invited Paul's readers into an ongoing relational communion with him, through Christ and by the Spirit. Paul's readers could take refuge in and experience this intimacy moment by moment.

Being Filled with the Abundant Love of Christ (3:14–19)

Paul prayed that his readers would know and experience the full extent of Christ's great love as the Father strengthened them by his Spirit.

3:14. Resuming his train of thought from Ephesians 3:1, Paul once again introduced his prayer for his readers with "for this reason" (τούτου χάριν), referring back to the dramatic and far-reaching plans of God that had touched the lives of Paul's readers (Eph. 2:1–22) and gave meaning to Paul's ministry (Eph. 3:1–13). Themes already developed in Ephesians bubbled to the surface in this prayer as well.

Paul described his posture of prayer by professing, "I bow my knees" (κάμπτω τὰ γόνατα μου). This physical expression of reverence for God (Acts 21:5; Rom. 14:11; Phil. 2:10) underscored the sincerity with which Paul approached his task. Paul knelt in humility "before the Father" (πρὸς τὸν πατέρα). Paul again opted for this intimate relational term for God, in keeping with the free access God had granted to all believers as his cherished children (Eph. 3:12). Jesus himself had encouraged his disciples to pray to God as "our Father" (Matt. 6:9). Paul's description of his prayerful interaction with God implied a broader habit of praying for his readers' spiritual well-being.

3:15. Paul contemplated the Father to whom he prayed with wording (rel. clause starting with ἐξ οὗ, "from whom") that further described God as Father. God's identity as "Father" (πατήρ) came into greater focus through his relationship to "every family" (πᾶσα πατριά). Paul noted that every family "is named" (ὀνομάζεται) "from" (ἐκ) the Father, with a play on words between "Father" (πατήρ) and "family" (πατριά) in the Greek. Paul pondered the idea that every family (*patria*) owed its name to the original family head (*Patēr)*. In Paul's culture the label "family" encompassed not only narrow family units but also broader groupings of relatives, clans, and nations (BDAG, s.v. "πατριά," p. 788). Paul even included every family "in heaven and on earth" (ἐν οὐρανοῖς καὶ ἐπὶ γῆς) in his description. Paul referred to heaven and earth in its totality with this phrase (cf. Eph. 1:10). Though used in a different way in this context, the wording "in heaven and on earth" had a familiar ring from the prayer Jesus taught his disciples (Matt. 6:10). The mention of families in heaven may have referred to various groupings of spiritual powers in the heavenly realms, or to human families from the past. The existence of all heavenly and earthly families further magnified the worth of the Father to whom Paul prayed.

TRANSLATION ANALYSIS: All family groupings are named "from" or "by" (ἐκ) God the Father. But what does that mean exactly? The preposition (ἐκ) could be translated as "by," so that every family "is named by the Father." That translation would yield a connotation of authority that comes with naming something (NLT; Lincoln, 1990, 203; Best, 1998, 337–39; Arnold, 2010, 208–9; Thielman, 2010, 228; Bock, 2019, 106–7). The interpretation proposed in this commentary is the idea that every family derives its name, or identity, "from" the Father (NIV, NASB, NRSV; Stott, 1979, 134; cf. early Christian commentators such as Theodoret and Jerome [ACCS, 144–45]). This translation better appreciates the wordplay between "father" (πατήρ) and "family" (πατριά) and aligns more readily with the passive voice construction (rather than "the Father, who names every family;" cf. Eph. 1:21; 1 Cor. 5:11). This interpretation does not exclude notions of authority but places greater emphasis on God's exclusive standing as Father of all possible family groupings (note the similar portrayal of God's all-encompassing fatherhood in Ephesians 4:6). Paul inserted this clever wordplay with the goal of sparking his readers' fuller appreciation of the scope and significance of God's status as Father.

3:16. Paul marked the beginning of the content of his prayer (ἵνα, "that") and asked God to "grant" (δῷ) favorable things to his readers. Paul had already recounted God's giving nature in the previous section, in reference to his own ministry and teachings (Eph. 3:2, 7, 8). Now, he prayerfully appealed to God's giving disposition on behalf of his readers (ὑμῖν, "you"). Paul asked God to grant an initial request for his readers (communicated by an infinitive construction with multiple levels of modifying phrases and clauses), in keeping with God's divine generosity. The literal "the riches of his glory" (κατὰ τὸ πλοῦτος τῆς δόξης αὐτοῦ) carried the sense of "his glorious, unlimited resources" (NLT). Paul approached God confidently, knowing that God gave spiritual blessings to believers out of his abundant storehouses of divine gifts, in ways that even exceed human expectations (Eph. 3:20).

Paul asked that God's power would strengthen Paul's readers, or that he would enable them "to be strengthened in power" (δυνάμει κραταιωθῆναι). By placing "power" at the front of the infinitive construction, Paul placed emphasis on that power. Paul desired to see God's power extended to the readers for the purpose of their spiritual formation (cf. Gal. 4:19). Paul did not want his readers to underestimate the divine power at their disposal (cf. Paul's earlier mentions of God's power in Ephesians 1:19; 3:7, and his return to the theme in 3:20). Remembering God's power would motivate Paul's readers to make their own confident appeals to God for their spiritual growth and strength.

Paul envisioned God transmitting this power to his readers "through his Spirit" (διὰ τοῦ πνεύματος αὐτοῦ), which was the way a transcendent God was exercising his personal influence in the lives of his people. The modifier "his" (αὐτοῦ) after "Spirit" provided a glimpse into the life of the Trinity, with the complete association between God the Father and God the Spirit even as the Spirit carried out God the Father's perfect, restorative work in the life of the believer. Along these lines Paul requested God's power for his readers, not to be used outwardly for greater influence over their surroundings, but to strengthen them inwardly, or "in the inner person" (εἰς τὸν ἔσω ἄνθρωπον) for a deeper communion with God. The God who had powerfully created all things (Eph. 3:9) also exercised his power by his Spirit in intimate ways in believers' lives. Paul and his colleagues regularly experienced the renewing effects of God's work in "their inner beings" (ὁ ἔσω ἡμῶν) when they served Christ in exhausting circumstances (2 Cor. 4:16; cf. Thielman, 2010, 230).

3:17. Paul asked for the Spirit to mediate God's presence in his readers' lives in the person of Christ, so that God's spiritual strengthening of his readers would result in "Christ dwelling in your hearts" (κατοικῆσαι τὸν Χριστὸν ἐν ταῖς καρδίαις ὑμῶν). Paul's mention of the "heart" (καρδία) augmented his reference to the inner person from the verse before. Paul prayed that God would make his readers' interior lives the focal point of his spiritual work. Paul raised the powerful image (κατοικῆσαι, "to dwell") of what this interior work would look like: that the Christ who had taken up residence within Paul's readers would cultivate a deepening relationship of intimate fellowship with them.

With "to dwell" (κατοικῆσαι), Paul showed his fondness for the divine habitation metaphor that he had first developed in Ephesians 2:19–22 (using the related word κατοικητήριον, "dwelling place," in 2:22). In the past, God had dwelt in Solomon's temple in Jerusalem (966–586 B.C.) as a preview of the full arrival of his glory, and now Christ's residence in believers' hearts pointed to God's ultimate goal of dwelling fully with his people in the new heavens and earth (Rev. 21–22). Paul revealed his implicit Trinitarian worldview by his instinctive juxtaposition of two complementary ideas about the Spirit and Christ Jesus. He described God's dwelling place, in the Spirit, in Ephesians 2:22 on the one hand, and Christ's indwelling, through the Spirit, in the Paul's readers' hearts on the other hand.

It was "through faith" (διὰ τῆς πίστεως), or through a childlike trust in Christ and reliance upon him for relating to God, that Paul's readers could experience the ongoing indwelling of Christ in their hearts (cf. Eph. 3:12). Christ made his home in the hearts of people who believed in him, as they continued in the faith that had marked the beginning of their journey with Christ (Eph. 1:13; Col. 2:6–7). Paul thus exhibited his assumption that God was accomplishing his work in the lives of spiritually responsive people, who, having been given new life by the Spirit, exercised continuing faith in Christ.

Christ dwelled in readers' lives because they had been "rooted and grounded in love" (ἐν ἀγάπῃ ἐρριζωμένοι καὶ τεθεμελιωμένοι).[1] Paul put "in love" (ἐν ἀγάπῃ) at the front of the phrase for emphasis, and he kept the focus on God's love through Christ in the next two verses. Paul identified being connected to Christ's love as the basis of Christ's indwelling work and previewed the readers' opportunity to cherish the love of Christ as a result. Paul inserted this affirmation to assure believers of this already-secured status (perf. ptc.) that set the stage for Christ's ongoing presence in their lives and made further spiritual growth possible.

The vivid images of being rooted in the soil of love and being constructed upon the foundation of love (cf. the similar pairing in Col. 2:7) worked together to celebrate the pervasive contribution of Christ's love to believers' life and growth. The term "rooted" (ῥιζόω) envisioned lives planted deeply in the soil of Christ's love, prepared for further nourishment by that love. The term "grounded" (θεμελιόω), translated as "grounded" (ESV, NASB, NET, NRSV, NKJV) or "(firmly) established" (NIV, CSB), likewise conceived of a trustworthy initial foundation giving support to believers' maturing lives (cf. BDAG, s.v. "θεμελιόω" 2a, p. 449). This second term revisited Paul's portrayal of believers as a temple, built upon the sturdy "foundation" (θεμέλιος) of the apostles, prophets, and fundamentally, Christ (Eph. 2:19–22).

3:18. Paul stated his desired purpose (ἵνα, "in order that") for his readers' spiritual communion with the indwelling Christ. He prayed that "you would be able to comprehend" (ἐξισχύσητε καταλαβέσθαι) the realities of what God had made available. The verb "be able to" (ἐξισχύω) communicated the ability or capacity to do something (BDAG, s.v. "ἐξισχύω," p. 350). In this case, Paul prayed that God would enable Paul's readers to grasp (καταλαβέσθαι, complementary inf.) the significance of divine truths illuminated to them as believers in Christ. Having stressed the revelatory grace of God in Ephesians 1:9 and 3:2–9, Paul prayed that readers would take advantage of the divine knowledge made available to them.

Paul prayed that his readers' growth in understanding would occur in conjunction "with all of God's people" (σὺν πᾶσιν τοῖς ἁγίοις). Paul's readers were part of a larger, worldwide body of believers who had been called to belong to God and appreciate his ways. While Paul's prayer on the whole imagined individual believers plumbing the depths (and other dimensions) of Christ's love, Paul's inclusion of "with all of God's people" reminded the readers of the corporate nature of growing in understanding about God and life with God in Christ (a theme revisited in Ephesians 4:1–16).

Paul prayed specifically that his readers, and all believers, would be able to grasp "what is the breadth and length and height and depth [of Christ's love]" (τί τὸ πλάτος καὶ μῆκος καὶ ὕψος καὶ βάθος). Surprisingly, Paul never completed the thought but instead left the ultimate object of contemplation to be inferred. Since this sentence was sandwiched between two tributes to the love of Christ, love was the most likely topic intended (Lincoln, 1990, 213; Best, 1998, 346; Muddiman, 2001, 172–73; Hoehner, 2002, 488). Paul painted a picture of a divine love with colossal dimensions worth exploring and savoring with unending devotion. This depicted the love of Christ as much

1 The prepositional phrase "in love" (ἐν ἀγάπῃ) modifies the two participles rather than the infinitive before it.

more than a simple concept to affirm but a rich and complex reality that had all sorts of facets and implications.

Divine Love

Though Paul often used the Greek term for "love" (ἀγάπη) to refer to human love, especially among believers in Christ, this love ultimately proceeded from the love that God had demonstrated in Christ. God's love consisted of his commitment to people's best interests, and it accompanied his covenantal relationship with them. In his incarnational ministry, Jesus both exhibited and proclaimed a love that addressed short-term and especially eternal needs (Mark 2:1–12). Paul not only followed Jesus's example of love but also expounded upon the implications of Christ's love for diverse groups of people (1 Cor. 9:19–23). Besides modeling the love of Christ with tender personal investment (Acts 20:17–38; 1 Thess. 2:1–12) and courageous clarity (2 Cor. 7:8–10), Paul pointed to it in his teaching. Paul located the love of God in two main truths. First God had displayed his love in Christ's sacrifice (Rom. 5:6–11; 2 Cor. 5:14–15; Gal. 2:20; Eph. 5:2, 25), since sinners received forgiveness and reconciliation through Christ's death for them. Second, God extended love through Christ's ongoing mediatorial work that allowed believers to enjoy God's support and blessings, now and in the future, by the Spirit (Rom. 8:28–39; 2 Cor. 13:14; Eph. 1:4; 2:4–7). Since the love of Christ was so expansive in its reach, Paul prayed that his readers would be captivated by the extent and complexity of Christ's love.

3:19. Paul restated the previous result of grasping the extent of the love of Christ by praying for his readers "to know the love of Christ that surpasses knowledge" (γνῶναί τε τὴν ὑπερβάλλουσαν τῆς γνώσεως). Paul artfully paired "to know" (γνῶναι) with a love beyond "knowledge" (γνῶσις) and pondered the paradox of knowing the unknowable. God is eternal and transcendent, so Paul's readers could not know his love, nor his power, grace, or wisdom (Eph. 1:19; 2:8; 3:4–5, 9) by their own ingenuity. But God provided the readers, those who had received forgiveness and new life through Christ, the spiritual resources they needed to know him. Paul's readers could contemplate and experience a love that would otherwise exceed their grasp.

Paul's desired purpose (ἵνα, "in order that") for his readers' realization of the love of Christ was for their full enjoyment of the life that God offered them in his presence and under his care. Paul returned to the "fullness" language of Ephesians 1:23 to express the ideal outcome of drawing deeper and nearer into the love of Christ. A progressively growing knowledge of the love of Christ resulted in being "filled" (πληρωθῆτε) "to the fullest extent of the fullness of God" (εἰς πᾶν τὸ πλήρομα τοῦ θεοῦ). Though being filled "with God" (as with ESV, CSB, NRSV, NKJV) approximates the gist of Paul's prayer, the preposition "to" (εἰς) does not support the actual meaning of being filled "with" God. Paul left unstated who or what would fill his readers. Instead, he highlights the degree to which (εἰς) his readers could encounter the fullness of God in their lives (cf. NIV, NASB, NET). Paul's wording hinted at believers sharing in the divine life of God without directly saying so. Later, Paul associated God's Spirit with his readers being filled (Eph. 5:18). According to Paul, God's fullness included his presence (cf. Eph. 2:18–22; 3:12; Col. 1:19; 2:9) and all of the benefits God extended to his children (Eph. 1:3).

Eternal, Intra-Trinitarian Love

Paul's powerful words about the Father's love shared with believers in Christ and by the Spirit anticipated the concept of the eternal, intra-Trinitarian love that theologians have explored throughout the centuries. In this line of thinking, the Father, Son, and Spirit give and receive love with one another throughout eternity, and believers in Christ have been invited to participate in this loving communion. Jesus articulated his own conception of these ideas especially in John 14–17, where he both described and prayed for his disciples' enduring delight in divine fellowship. Abundant life for believers consists of entering into the loving communion of Father, Son, and Spirit. Glimpses into this experiential enjoyment of the love of the Trinity surfaced in other places in Paul's letters as well (Rom. 5:5; 8:15–16; 2 Cor. 13:14; Gal. 4:6).

Praise to a Glorious God Who Exceeds All Expectations (3:20–21)

God deserved praise and honor in the church, since he was the one who was able to answer prayers beyond what believers could ask or imagine, by the power he activated within believers.

3:20. Paul concluded his prayer with a doxology, or words of praise directed to God. With the transitional particle "now" (δέ) Paul turned to describe the God to whom he prayed. Paul began by acknowledging God's powerful ability (τῷ δυναμένωι, "to the one who is able"). Paul prayed to the God of the universe, whose power in creation and salvation knew no bounds: it was "beyond everything" (ὑπὲρ πάντα). Paul knew that God was able and ready to exercise his power (ποιῆσαι, "to do") on behalf of Paul's readers. God was able to do "immeasurably more" (ὑπερεκπερισσοῦ) "than what" (ὧν) Paul and his readers could "ask or think" (αἰτούμεθα ἢ νοοῦμεν). God was able to surpass the readers' expectations because his limitless power outstripped their understanding of it. Paul underscored this truth by progressing from believers' spoken requests to God to their unspoken hopes for God to intervene. In both cases, Paul affirmed that God was able to exceed all expectations in his dealings with his people.

God supported Paul and his readers in their times of need "by the dynamic power operating in our lives" (κατὰ τὴν δύναμιν τὴν ἐνεργουμένην ἐν ἡμῖν). God "is able" ("has power," δύναμαι) to act for believers by putting his "power" (δύναμις) to work in their lives. Paul described God as always being on the move (ἐνεργουμένην, pres. tense conveys an ongoing activity) in believers' lives. Paul likely pictured God's power in operation not just among the believing community generally but within each believer's inner experience (ἐν ἡμῖν, "in you"), since this had been his focus throughout the prayer. God worked dynamically in believers' inner being (Eph. 3:16), or hearts (3:17), to fulfill the goal of helping them experience Christ's love.

3:21. After describing his powerful God, Paul directed glory to him (αὐτῷ ἡ δόξα, "to him [be] the glory"). By "glory" Paul meant praise appropriate to God's greatness. Paul called for God's greatness to shine "in [and through] the church" (ἐν τῇ ἐκκλησίᾳ) and "in [and through] Christ Jesus" (ἐν Χριστῷ 'Ιησοῦ). God's glorious presence and work permeated the church, so that believers deeply experienced his power and love. God's glory then radiated through this new humanity he had formed, as a testament to his great wisdom (Eph. 2:15; 3:10). Even more fundamentally, God's glory was revealed in and through Christ. God's glory in the church and in Christ was intimately related. Christ was no longer visibly present, having ascended to the right hand of God, but those who were united with him became his agents. Whenever the church proclaimed Christ and bore witness to him through its actions and relationships, God was glorified.

Paul delighted in the thought of God's glory being put on display in and through Christ and the church from one generation to another without end (εἰς πάσας τὰς γενεάς, "unto all generations") until "the culmination of the ages" (τοῦ αἰῶνος τῶν αἰώνων). At that final time, God promised to gather and restore all things under Christ (Eph. 1:9–10) and fill the universe with his presence and glory (1:23). As human history advanced toward its completion in Christ, God was already mightily at work to carry out his perfect purposes in and through his people. When Paul knelt in dependence and reverence to God, he addressed a God who was both able and willing to exercise his power to strengthen and equip his dearly loved people.

Paul concluded the doxology at the end of his prayer with the interjection "Amen" (ἀμήν). Paul and other early Christian writers often used this term to punctuate words of praise or adoration directed to God (cf. Rom. 1:25; 9:5; 11:36; 16:27; Heb. 13:21; 1 Peter 4:11; 5:11; Jude 25; Rev. 1:6). Paul thus closed his prayer with an affirmation of God's majestic character.

THEOLOGICAL FOCUS

The exegetical idea (Paul praised God and prayed confidently that the all-powerful Father, by his Spirit, would empower Paul's readers to know and experience the abundant love of Christ in their hearts) leads to this theological focus: Believers can pray that God's Spirit will empower them and help them to experience the love of Christ in deep and personal ways.

God the Father works by his Spirit to apply the love of Christ to believers' lives. When Paul prayed for believers, he reflected this implied Trinitarian vision, picking up from similar description in Ephesians 1:3–14 and 2:18–22. God the Father, by his generosity and power (vv. 15–16, 20), bestows the blessing of the intimate and loving presence of Christ in believers' lives (v. 17). Believers participate in this amazing communion with Christ through the Spirit's internal work in their lives (v. 16).

This extension of divine fellowship results in spiritual lives centered and encompassed in love. Believers in Christ Jesus initially get rooted in and founded upon the perfect love of the Trinity when they hear and believe in the gospel of Christ (v. 17; cf. Eph. 1:13). But as Paul's prayer makes clear the Spirit opens a vista to a fuller and deepening experience of the love of God in Christ (v. 18). God invites believers to contemplate, explore, and enjoy the love of Christ on an ongoing basis. In the process, they are inwardly strengthened by the Spirit to remain in Christ's love and experience the fullness of God's goodness in their lives (v. 19). Though the Christian faith is a corporate exercise, God draws near to each believer for personal formation and deep communion. This gift is meant to be treasured and appropriated by every believer.

PREACHING AND TEACHING STRATEGIES

Exegetical and Theological Synthesis

With this prayer the theologically rich first half of the book reached a climax. Paul's prayer underscored God's love that "surpasses knowledge" (v. 19), and his power that was able to do "exceedingly more than all we ask or think" (v. 20). Paul's readers had been rooted and grounded in the love of God, and now Paul prayed for a deepening of those roots and a strengthening of that grounding. For the Ephesian Christ-followers, life with God commenced when they had been born again, and then as they walked with God, Paul prayed that they would find treasures yet to be discovered and supplies of strength yet to be tapped. The fact that Paul interceded for the Ephesians implied that they did not fully understand the things requested—knowledge in their "inner being" (v. 16) of the love and power of the triune God. They needed experiential knowledge of God, so Paul prayed that the Ephesians, and by extension the entire church through the ages, would know the unfathomable depths of God's love and power.

Preaching Idea

God, empower us to know your unknowable love.

Contemporary Connections

What does it mean?

What does it mean for us to pray that God would empower us to know his unknowable love? Paul did not pray for something concrete like rain or daily bread; he prayed for something less tangible—that we may be rooted and grounded in divine love and strengthened in the inner person. We have analogies of God's love all around us. For example, one aspect of his love—jealous protection—could be compared to the protective love of a dog for her puppies. Perhaps you have a story of trying to pick up a puppy only to be met with the wrath of the mother. Another aspect of God's love, his tender mercy, could be captured with the true story of Brandt Jean in the Creativity section.

The final scene from *The Last Battle,* the last book of C. S. Lewis's *The Chronicles of Narnia,* might help capture the idea of grasping something that cannot be fully grasped. As the characters run deeper and deeper into Narnia, closer and closer to God, their refrain is, "Come further up, come further in!" That is the prayer of the passage—that we would keep going further and further into experiential knowledge of God's love.

Is it true?

Can humans actually be empowered to know God's unknowable love? Can something that is ultimately unknowable actually be known? What kind of doubletalk is that? Walking through the valley of life is a normal part of worshippers' experience, as illustrated by the fact that about fifty psalms—one-third of the book of Psalms—are laments. The psalms of lament are plaintive cries from people who were in danger, had been betrayed, or faced other trials. They show us that God's people groan. Perhaps that is why Paul prayed this prayer. We might draw on analogy once again: when I (Jeffrey) was a child, I was playing in the snow, trying to climb up a steep bank, and I kept slipping back. Struggling with all my strength, I almost reached the top time after time, only to slide backwards. In despair, I started to cry (lament!), and that is when my father put on his snow boots, slid into the gully with me, and with one swing of his mighty arms heaved me over the top of the gully into a soft bank of snow. I needed someone else to do what I couldn't do myself, and that is why we pray that God would help us know the heights (and other dimensions) of his love.

Now what?

How can we be empowered to know the love of God? Through prayer. Just as Paul prayed for the Ephesians, so can we pray for the people in our circles and for ourselves as well. One way to do this is by praying Scripture—this text—back to God. We might insert the names of our loved ones and fellow church members into Paul's prayer to personalize it. We could also pray the text for ourselves. We might memorize these verses and start each day with them. I (Jeffrey) begin each of my devotional times with silence and meditation, reminding myself (as I breathe in) of the love of God and (as I breathe out) expressing my gratitude to God.

Another way to grow in the knowledge of God is with the study of Scripture. We might journal our thoughts as we read, or share a verse from our daily reading with a friend. Taking notes during Bible teaching can help with the retention of truth and serve as a way to slow down and meditate. Some people are auditory learners and might be encouraged to listen to Scripture with an audio Bible such as the one found at the website Daily Radio Bible.

Spiritual friendships also help us know the unknowable love of God. This is implied when Paul prayed that the Ephesians would be able to comprehend the love of Christ *with all God's people* (v. 19). If your church or organization offers support groups, accountability partnerships, spiritual direction, or counseling, it might be appropriate to showcase those ministries along with the sermon.

Although the full extent of God's love is ultimately unknowable, we might share what we do know with others, perhaps with a ministry to the "least of these" such as immigrants, the homeless, or the sick. Simply visiting people in the hospital and praying with them can be a tangible expression of the love of God, and we may find that sharing love also enhances our own experience of love. An organization like GriefShare could give listeners a concrete way to be the hands and feet of Jesus in extending love. As their website states, "GriefShare is a friendly, caring group of people who will walk alongside you through one of life's most difficult experiences. You don't have to go through the grieving process alone" (griefshare.org). While this kind of ministry is applicable to anyone who grieves, it can be life-giving especially for older people who have lost their spouses.

Another way to be a conduit for the love of God is through foster parenting. My home church is experiencing a remarkable outpouring of love in this way. We pray for organizations that facilitate fostering, and a growing cadre of people in the church, including unmarried women, are stepping forward to be foster parents. The rest of us offer financial, prayer, logistical, and emotional support for them.

Creativity in Presentation

Amber Guyger, an off-duty police officer in Texas, returned to her apartment after work. But it wasn't her apartment. She had mistakenly entered the home of Botham Jean. She thought he was a burglar and shot him. Botham's brother Brandt testified in court (the video is below) and forgave her, saying that he wanted the best for her and that giving her life to Christ would be the best. This is divine love. The video ends with them embracing. Amber experienced mercy, the kind of mercy God gives us. Paul says that God's love surpasses knowledge, but we can glimpse of it in scenes of human love like this.[2]

Creativity might be found by following the text's own form—prayer and doxology. For example, we might pray in the middle of the sermon, not simply at the beginning or end. Or perhaps after each point of the sermon someone in the congregation could pray. Including both genders and multiple age groups might draw in the listeners—a teenager, twentysomething, empty nester, and octogenarian. Similarly, the preacher might compose a written prayer that is placed on the screen or in the bulletin so that it can be prayed corporately. Just as Paul prayed for knowledge of God's love, we can do the same as a body. Even a simple technique like having the congregation respond at certain points with a repeated phrase such as "make it so," or "yes, Lord" might help reproduce the tone and purpose of the text. As we sprinkle the preaching idea throughout the sermon, the congregation could add their own "amen."

A planned testimony of someone praising God in the midst of a trial could cement the idea. This would show that Paul's language is not just "pie in the sky." Knowing the love of God *is* possible. We may be sorrowful, but we also rejoice (2 Cor. 6:10). We may grieve but not as people who have no hope (1 Thess. 4:13). The apostle Paul walked through the valley, but he did not lose heart, because his inner self was being renewed day by day (2 Cor. 4:16–18).

Doxology might also find a home in this sermon. The congregation could sing the Old Hundredth (the traditional "Doxology") as the conclusion of the sermon. We might also try personalizing verses 20–21 for our particular context with a benediction like this:

> Now to him who is able to do far more abundantly than all that we ask or think,
> to him who founded our church in 2004 and who keeps our church in [current date],

2 For an example of this, search for videos of Brandt Jean and Amber Guyger on YouTube.

> to him who looked with favor on Jean and
> Alonzo for the adoption of their new
> daughter Anna,
> to him who rescued our youth group when
> they were stranded for two days on the
> mountain,
> to him be glory in the church and in Christ
> Jesus throughout all generations, forever and ever. Amen.

Paul's poetical language and soaring emotion suggest that the sermon might use a "high style" once or twice to prompt worship. Ephesians 3:14–21 uses parallelism (e.g., the repetition of "in order that" at the beginning of three parallel clauses), metaphor (e.g., "rooted in love"), and wordplay (e.g., "filled to fullness" or "know that which surpasses knowledge"). An expository sermon that mirrors that tone and form might employ its own parallelism and metaphors, perhaps like this:

> May God open our eyes to see through the
> spiritual fog,
> May he unstop our ears to hear the symphony of his love,
> May he bend our knees to bow in worship,
> May he light a fire on the altar of our hearts
> to produce praise, never-ending praise,
> And may he sanctify us through and
> through, so that we, the church,
> will give him glory throughout all
> generations.
> Amen.

Knowing God is knowledge truly worth possessing. It is not like knowing the largest prime number, discovered in 2018, which has 23,249,425 digits. Some of these colossal numbers are called Mersenne primes, named after a mathematician who studied them in the seventeenth century. Smaller Mersenne primes are used in encryption—a very valuable function—but the giant numbers have few practical applications. For the man or woman on the street, memorizing the largest number (if it were possible!) would serve no purpose.[3]

The key idea to articulate is this: the love of God surpasses knowledge, yet we should pursue that experiential knowledge and pray for it. God, empower us to know your unknowable love.

A possible sermon outline:

- [Intercession] May God empower us with his unlimited power (vv. 14–17a).
- [Intercession] May God help us know his unknowable love (vv. 17b–19).
- Conclusion: [Doxology] Glory be to God in the church and in Christ Jesus throughout all generations (vv. 20–21).

---

3 Evelyn Lamb, "The Largest Known Prime Number, *Slate*, January 4, 2018, https://slate.com/technology/2018/01/the-worlds-largest-prime-number-has-23249425-digits-heres-why-you-should-care.html.

DISCUSSION QUESTIONS

1. Have you ever prayed to be strengthened with power? Why or why not?

2. Have you ever prayed to be strengthened to grasp the love of God?

3. If you had a vision of God's power like the one described in this passage, what difference would it make to something you're facing?

4. If you had a vision of God's love like the one described here, what difference would it make to something you're facing?

5. Why did Paul emphasize grasping the love of Christ "together with all of God's people"?

6. Put the phrase "filled to all the fullness of God" in your own words.

FOR FURTHER READING

Bruce, F. F. 1977. *Paul: Apostle of the Heart Set Free.* Grand Rapids: Eerdmans.

Carson, Donald A. 2014. *Praying with Paul: A Call to Spiritual Reformation.* 2nd ed. Grand Rapids, Baker.

Gurevich, Andrew, and Jeffrey Arthurs. 2000. "Theological and Rhetorical Perspectives on Self-Disclosure in Preaching." *BSac* 157: 215–26.

Mitchell, Henry H. 2010. *Celebration and Experience in Black Preaching*, rev. ed. Nashville: Abingdon.

Wilson, Paul Scott. 2008. *Setting Words on Fire.* Nashville: Abingdon.

WALK IN UNITY, A NEW IDENTITY, LOVE, AND LIGHT (4:1–5:14)

Paul moved from deep, Trinitarian doctrine (chapters 1–3) to transformed practice, beginning in chapter 4. First, Paul encouraged readers who shared a common faith but had diverse gifts to grow together toward maturity (4:1–16). Next, he challenged readers to stand apart from the crowd by putting on their new identity in Christ, which would lead to new practices in specific relationships and areas of life (4:17–5:2). Paul concluded the major section by exhorting readers to live consistently with God's kingdom and shine Christ's light in a dark world (5:3–14). Along the way, Paul continued to provide strong theological motivation for carrying out these practical applications.

The letter's fourth major section, Walk in Unity, a New Identity, Love, and Light (4:1–5:14), is comprised of three preaching units: "United in Christ, Equipped to Grow Together" (4:1–16), "A New Identity Brings New Practices" (4:17–5:2), and "Shine Christ's Light in a Dark World" (5:3–14).

Ephesians 4:1–16

EXEGETICAL IDEA

When Paul's readers invested in their relationships with one another, embraced shared beliefs in Christ, and ministered according to the gracious gifts they received from the exalted Christ, they could experience spiritual growth and unity together, with each believer contributing to that growth.

THEOLOGICAL FOCUS

Believers grow and experience unity together in Christ when they invest in their relationships with one another, celebrate shared beliefs, and draw upon Christ's gracious gifts for ministry.

PREACHING IDEA

To live in unity, let's remove our pride, avoid the riptide, and not hide.

PREACHING POINTERS

Paul's Gentile readers were used to unifying around the emperor and Rome, for the glory of Rome. Jewish readers had rallied around God's law and the temple for unity. Now that they were recipients of great blessings in Christ, readers needed to replace the glory of Rome and love for law and temple with an even stronger unifying vision and a more compelling sense of corporate identity and purpose. This new identity and purpose was found in Christ and the church. Paul's readers needed input on pursuing this new identity and purpose as a group because God had made them a united body and had called them to a corporate mission. The prospect of growing together in Christ may have seemed particularly daunting given the complicated relational and religious dynamics between Jewish and Gentile believers in Christ. Added to this, Paul's readers faced the challenges of relating to one another constructively in ordinary interpersonal relationships. But Christ did not leave Paul's readers to fend for themselves. He had supplied the example and the spiritual resources for their success.

Today followers of Jesus are tempted to find identity in culture, politics, and religion. Being a fan of a pop culture idol and finding unity with similar people is sometimes more important than our identity as Christ-followers. Sometimes our national identity overshadows our spiritual identity. Being American (or Canadian, Guatemalan, etc.) overshadows our self-concept more than being Christian. The same can be true of our political parties and religious or denominational identities. But God has not unified us around earthly parties. Following the dense and awesome theology of chapters 1–3, this passage turns to application, urging us to keep the unity of the Spirit. To do that, humility, good teaching, and transparency would be needed. To live in unity, let's remove our pride, avoid the riptide of false teaching, and not hide from one another.

UNITED IN CHRIST, EQUIPPED TO GROW TOGETHER (4:1–16)

LITERARY STRUCTURE AND THEMES (4:1–16)

This passage marks the beginning of Paul's practical instructions for his readers, after the doctrinally rich material of chapters 1–3. Ephesians 4:1–16 is a long passage, but it retains a strong thematic focus and thus works well as a coherent whole. The passage consists of two main sections. In Ephesians 4:1–6, Paul promoted virtues and shared beliefs that preserved unity among believers, and in 4:7–16 he envisioned believers using their Christ-given gifts to cultivate spiritual growth and doctrinal integrity in their churches.

From this point on, Paul highlighted the need for believers to "walk" (περιπατέω) in a distinct and purposeful way that testified to their sincere belief in Christ (see Eph. 4:1, 17; 5:2, 8, 15). Paul's instructions, however, continued to be guided by a robust theological understanding of God's overarching plans and the spiritual resources he had made available to believers. God's calling (Eph. 4:1, 4) motivated believers for unified and hope-filled living. Christ generously supplied his body, the church (Eph. 4:8–11, 15), with the resources necessary for cooperative growth. The unity that Christ had created for the church (Eph. 2:15) was now the church's to preserve, with his help (4:3, 13).

- ***Preserving the Unity Found in a Common Faith (4:1–6)***
- ***The Body of Christ, Equipped for Growth (4:7–16)***

EXPOSITION (4:1–16)

In his typical flowing style, Paul highlighted the generosity of Christ, the unity of the one body of Christ, the goals of growth and edification in the church, and the relational virtues that facilitated growth. This initial section in the second half of the letter reaffirmed that Paul considered practical Christian growth to be a corporate phenomenon that was propelled forward by Christ himself. Paul's vision of unity and growth that was available to all was rooted in the gracious work of God through Christ in the church. This was in contrast to unity orchestrated by human governments and societal peer pressure (as with the imperial cult), or unity that limited participation to one group of people alone (as with common perceptions of Jewish law and identity in the Second Temple period).

Preserving the Unity Found in a Common Faith (4:1–6)

Paul urged his readers to pursue a course of humility, love, and unity with one another, since they were united in a common faith, life, and hope in the Father, Son, and Spirit.

4:1. Paul kept his sweeping survey of God's majestic plans from Ephesians 1–3 in view (οὖν, "therefore") as he made a major turn to the practical exhortation of his readers. Paul urged his readers (παρακαλῶ ὑμᾶς, "I urge you") to adopt the right mindsets, practices, and goals for their Christian growth and relationships with one another. Paul often began his admonitions with the term "I urge" (παρακαλέω; cf. Rom. 12:1; 1

Cor. 1:10; 2 Cor. 6:1), and with it he invited his readers to focus on the specific instructions that followed.

Paul described himself as "I, a prisoner in the Lord" (ἐγὼ ὁ δέσμιος ἐν κυρίῳ), which resembled the presentation of himself in Ephesians 3:1. Paul's environment of being under house arrest in Rome loomed large in his mind. Paul accepted this state of affairs as a necessary by-product of his service for Jesus, his Lord. Paul likely highlighted the connotation of Jesus's authority here with "Lord" (κύριος), since it reminded Paul and his readers that Christ was the one who ultimately controlled Paul's fate, even though the Romans were the ones confining him. Paul mentioned his imprisoned status to heighten the force of his appeal by underscoring the sacrifice he was making in ministry and the sincerity of his commitment to his readers' spiritual well-being.

Paul continuously urged his readers "to walk" (περιπατῆσαι), or to carry out their daily lives, in a particular way. They were to develop a distinct stride in their personal practices, by living "in a manner worthy" (ἀξίως) of God's name. Paul wanted his readers to pursue the excellence that characterized "the calling to which they were called" (τῆς κλήσεως ἧς ἐκλήθητε). Paul doubly highlighted the notion of God's calling by using both the noun "calling" (κλῆσις) and verb "to call" (καλέω) in close succession (cf. Eph. 4:4). In this context, Paul probably pictured this calling as the totality of blessings and responsibilities stemming from his readers' initial call into union with Christ and inclusion in his family. In Ephesians 1:18, Paul had spoken about "the hope of [God's] calling" (cf. Eph. 4:4), in conjunction with the believer's inheritance. In Ephesians 4:1, Paul indicated that the glorious present and future outcome to which believers had been called ought to inform the way they lived each day. Paul wanted readers to aspire toward conduct and practices that reflected the greatness of the story that they had entered into.

4:2. In verse 2, Paul spelled out what it should look like for believers to walk in keeping with their high calling. First, his readers were to walk "with all humility and meekness" (μετὰ πάσης ταπεινοφροσύνης καὶ πραΰτητος). Paul prescribed these virtues in full measure with the addition of "all" (πᾶς). The two related terms "humility" (πραΰτης) and "meekness" (ταπεινοφροσύνη) depicted people who were secure in their own worth and did not need to bolster their egos or assert their superiority over others (BDAG, s.v. "πραΰτης," p. 861; s.v. "ταπεινοφροσύνη," p. 989). Years before (Acts 20:19), Paul himself had served the Ephesians "with all humility" (μετὰ πάσης ταπεινοφροσύνης), which had helped him create a strong bond of affection with the believers there. Paul advocated adopting a posture of "meekness" (πραΰτης) rather than a punitive approach when ministering to others (1 Cor. 4:21; 2 Cor. 10:1; Gal. 6:1; 2 Tim. 2:25; Titus 3:2). Attitudes of humility (Phil. 2:3; Col. 3:12) and meekness (Gal. 5:23; Col. 3:12) contributed to healthy churches and harmonious relationships with others. In this passage, Paul likewise introduced them as essential ingredients for unified Christian communities. These were among the virtues that rose in prominence within the cross-shaped, upside-down context of Jesus's ministry, before the victorious arrival of the kingdom in its full glory.

Second, Paul instructed his readers to walk "with patience" (μετὰ μακροθυμίας), which described a posture of "forbearance" with other people (cf. 2 Tim. 4:2; BDAG, s.v. "μακροθυμία" 2a, p. 612–13). Paul identified this quality of patience as a hallmark of love for others (1 Cor. 13:4, μακροθυμέω). Paul grouped this virtue with the preceding two in Colossians 3:12 as well. Its addition here further described people who interacted with others in respectful and understanding ways. Christ himself exercised patience (1 Tim. 1:16) alongside meekness (2 Cor. 10:1).

Third, Paul encouraged "bearing with one another in love" (ἀνεχόμενοι ἀλλήλων ἐν ἀγάπῃ). This complemented Paul's endorsement of patience in the previous phrase, and created the picture of an ongoing effort (pres. tense ptc., ἀνεχόμενοι). The phrase "bearing with one another" (ἀνεχόμενοι ἀλλήλων) suggested interpersonal tolerance and relational resiliency (BDAG, s.v. "ἀνέχω" 1a, p. 78). Those who bore with one another maintained realistic expectations about others' behavior and knew when to let annoyances pass without complaint. Believers who were humble and meek (v. 1) understood their own flaws and rough edges and were ready to make allowances for others' shortcomings. Paul raised the bar above this minimum standard for tolerance with the modifier "in love" (ἐν ἀγάπῃ). Paul did not want his readers to simply develop a thick skin with others by ignoring or dismissing others. Instead, they were to engage with the people around them with a desire for others' best interests. Paul returned multiple times to the centrality of the virtue of love in the second half of the letter (Eph. 4:15, 16; 5:2, 25, 28, 33).

4:3. For the fourth explanation of how Christians should walk, Paul said that they should "be eager to maintain the unity of the Spirit in the bond of peace" (σπουδάζοντες τηρεῖν τὴν ἑνότητα τοῦ πνεύματος ἐν τῷ συνδέσμῳ τῆς εἰρήνης). The phrase stood in parallel with the previous one by describing actions Paul expected his readers to adopt in their walk with Christ. Paul wanted his readers to live in a worthy manner "by being eager" (σπουδάζοντες, ptc. of means), or showing vigilance, "to preserve" (τηρεῖν) something that Christ has already secured for them (cf. Dunn, 1998, 562). Christ had already created unity by bringing forgiven Jews and Gentiles together as one new entity (Eph. 2:15). Now Paul told his readers to actively "guard that unity" (τηρεῖν τὴν ἑνότητα) in their congregational life and worship. This unity was "of the Spirit" (τοῦ πνεύματος), or forged by the Spirit. The Spirit mediated the presence of the indwelling Christ to all believers (Eph. 3:16–17) and gave shared access to the Father (Eph. 2:18). By his Spirit, God had supernaturally created this unity by connecting believers "in the bond of peace" (ἐν τῷ συνδέσμῳ τῆς εἰρήνης). In other words, the peace that Christ supplied acted as a binding agent, joining people together in unity. Paul associated peace with unity in Ephesians 2:13–17. There and here Christ delivered peace through his sacrificial death on the cross so that people from all backgrounds could be reconciled to God and to one another.

4:4. The image in verse 3 of finding unity in the Spirit provided an opening for Paul to consider the inner workings of the unity God had designed for his people. In the next three verses, Paul spotlighted the basis for Christian unity with succinct and effective language that was perhaps inspired by early Christian confessions of faith. Paul identified common beliefs within the Christian community, but these affirmations were more than beliefs; they reflected the essential makeup of the church as well as its shared experience as a spiritual entity. These beliefs and experiences forged an enduring unity between both Jews and Gentiles who followed Jesus Christ.

The Shared Identity of the Jews in the Roman World

Jews who were dispersed throughout the Roman world during the Second Temple period were united through several major factors. Chief among these were a shared ethnic heritage (Barclay, 1996, 402–13) and the significance of the law and temple to corporate life and identity (Wright, 2013, 90–108). Jews believed in one God, Yahweh (Deut. 6:4–6), who had given his Law through Moses to the people (Exod. 19–24; cf. Josephus, *Ant.* 3.222–223) and was to be worshipped in one temple (cf. Philo, *Spec. Leg.* 1.67; Josephus, *Ag. Ap.* 2.193). Jews living outside of Judea could strengthen their bonds with one another through regular participation in synagogues and by celebrating Jewish festivals such as the Passover, Feast of Tabernacles, the Day of Atonement, or Pentecost (either in their own communities or by going to Jerusalem; cf. Acts 2:1–11; Barclay, 1996, 415–19). Paul wanted his readers, whether Jew or Gentile, to embrace a new common identity centered in the work of God through Christ Jesus.

First, Paul announced that there was "one body and one Spirit" (ἓν σῶμα καὶ ἓν πνεῦμα). Paul began his survey of Christian unity by asserting the fundamental oneness of the body of Christ and the presence of the Spirit of God in its midst. The logic behind these first two affirmations was spelled out more thoroughly in 1 Corinthians 12:13: "For we were all baptized by one Spirit so as to form one body—whether Jews or Gentiles, slave or free—and we were all given one Spirit to drink" (NIV). Paul's vision of redeemed Jews and Gentiles becoming one new humanity in Christ (Eph. 2:15; 3:6) had prepared the way for a similar picture of one body and one Spirit in Ephesians. The body of Christ (cf. Eph. 1:23; 3:6; 4:12, 16; 5:23, 30) was by definition a single unit, connected to Christ as the head. God's Spirit animated the body for believers' enjoyment of God's presence and fruitfulness in ministry.

A loose transition (καθὼς καί, "just as also") continued the theme of oneness. Paul placed focus on the shared hope that his readers and other believers had received because they had been called by God (ἐκλήθητε ἐν μιᾷ ἐλπίδι τῆς κλήσεως ὑμῶν, "you were called in one hope of your calling"). Paul drew upon the same cognate words, "calling" (κλῆσις) and "to call" (καλέω) that he had used in his introductory statement in the section (Eph. 4:1). The pairing of "hope" (ἐλπίς) and "calling" (κλῆσις) recognized that through Christ, God immersed people into a mighty current that led to a single, glorious destination. This single hope was guaranteed by Christ's redemptive work and culminated in Christ's future return. In the meantime, Paul's readers could draw comfort and assurance in their certain and permanent hope in Christ.

4:5. Next, Paul listed three more aspects of spiritual life that formed his readers' shared identity. First, believers confessed "one Lord" (εἷς κύριος). Paul had in mind the Lord Jesus when he used the title "Lord" (see Eph. 1:2, 3, 15, 17; 3:11). This title communicated the idea of Jesus's enduring authority over the church and was one of the most common titles for Jesus in the early church. The Lord Jesus exercised his authority with believers' highest good in mind, demonstrating himself to be a trustworthy and good master. Paul and early Christians often proclaimed the lordship of Jesus with joyful and triumphant tones (see Rom. 10:9; 1 Cor. 8:6; 2 Cor. 4:5; Phil. 2:11; Rev. 22:20). Since both Jewish and Gentile believers shared a common standing in the Lord, Paul naturally put Jesus's sole lordship at the center of his readers' spiritual existence.

A related truth to Jesus's lordship was the presence of "one faith" (μία πίστις) in Paul's readers' lives. The term "faith" (πίστις) had a range of connotations throughout Paul's letters. In this instance, Paul probably intended to highlight the core teachings and traditions about Christ Jesus that had been passed down by the apostles and prophets (Eph. 2:20; 3:5; see also 1 Cor. 11:2; 15:1–4; 2 Thess. 2:15; 3:6; 1 Tim. 6:20; 2 Tim. 1:14) with this mention of "one faith." Jews and Gentiles embraced a common faith in what they heard about the good news of Christ (Eph. 1:13).

The first mild surprise on this list arrived with "one baptism" (ἓν βάπτισμα). Paul had not made direct reference to baptism before this in the letter, but water baptism was a central component of early Christian practice that was inseparable from other major themes that Paul did develop in Ephesians. Paul's "one baptism" likely encompassed both the ritual of water baptism and its spiritual significance. At various points in his letters (Rom. 6:3–4; 1 Cor. 1:12–15; 12:13; Gal. 3:27–28; Col. 2:12), Paul associated baptism with faith, inclusion in the body of Christ, union with Christ, and the activity of the Spirit. Paul understood the ritual of baptism as signifying one's spiritual transfer into the body of Christ. The shared experience of the ceremony of baptism celebrated and reinforced the other spiritually rich themes listed in the passage.

Paul's Teachings on Baptism

Paul viewed baptism as an initiation into a permanent relational connection with Christ and his body, the church. Through faith, believers became united with Christ in both his death to sin and his life in God (Rom. 6:3–4; Col. 2:12). Baptism signified a Spirit-enabled incorporation into the body of Christ through which believers experienced intimate relational bonds with Christ and his people (1 Cor. 12:13; Gal. 3:27–28). Unlike the early church manual known as The Didache (7.1–4), Paul's letters typically bypassed extensive discussion of the practice of baptism (see 1 Cor. 1:13–17). This did not mean that Paul found the physical practice of baptism to be irrelevant. Paul was not a dualist who dismissed the importance of embodied experience in deference to a purely spiritual existence. But Paul rightly recognized that the spiritual realities underpinning water baptism gave the practice its ultimate meaning.

4:6. Paul concluded his brief list of the central features of Christian life with God, which was appropriate, since believers directed their adoration to God, through the Son, and by the Spirit (Rom. 7:25; 11:33–36; 16:27; 1 Cor. 8:6; Gal. 1:5; Eph. 3:21; Phil. 2:11; 4:19–20; Col. 3:17; 1 Tim. 1:17). Paul exalted the "one God" (εἷς θεός), who was also a Father (καὶ πατήρ, "and Father"), and proclaimed that God was "the Father of all" (πατὴρ πάντων). Since the previous titles and concepts modified by "one" in Ephesians 4:4–5 related to believers in particular,

A Baptismal Pool in Ephesus, from the fifth or sixth century. Courtesy of Greg MaGee.

Paul likely acknowledged God as Father of all believers with his initial mention of "one God and Father of all" in Ephesians 4:6a.

Not content to stop at this simple statement of God's fatherhood, Paul proceeded to magnify God as "the one who is over all and through all and in all" (ὁ ἐπὶ πάντων καὶ διὰ πάντων καὶ ἐν πᾶσιν). At this point, Paul likely broadened the scope of God's fatherhood to communicate the ultimate authority and presence of God the Father over all things (ἐπὶ πάντων) (cf. Rom. 11:36; 1 Cor. 8:6; Eph. 1:10–11, 22; 3:9; Col. 1:16–17). As much as Rome and its leaders sought to occupy center stage in people's loyalties and affections, only God had a legitimate claim to be Father over all creation.

Magnifying Caesar Augustus

Paul's readers would have encountered statues, coins, and exalted language that reminded them of the greatness of Caesar Augustus and other emperors. A large building in Ephesus, for instance, was constructed in honor of the goddess Artemis, Emperors Augustus and Tiberius, and the Ephesian people (Schnabel, 2004, 1208). Also in Ephesus, a portion of a Latin inscription on a city gate is translated as follows: "To the

Emperor Caesar Augustus son of a god, the high priest, twelve times consul, twenty times tribune, and Livia, wife of Caesar Augustus" (Wilson, 2012, 217). Augustus had formally received the title "Emperor [Imperator] Caesar son of a god" early in his reign (Ferguson, 2003, 27). A famous history of the exploits of Caesar Augustus was known as *Res Gestae Divi Augustus* (Deeds of the Deified Augustus). An inscription in Priene (also in Asia Minor) even celebrated Augustus as a "savior" and "god" whose appearance was the beginning of "good news" (εὐαγγέλιον) for the world. Within this Roman context, Paul contended that only the God who was "over all and through all, and in all" (Eph. 4:6) was worthy of being magnified and worshipped.

Paul multiplied prepositional phrases to communicate the comprehensive quality of God's fatherhood. First, he was "over all" (ἐπὶ πάντων), which conveyed an overarching authority over all things he had created (Eph. 3:9) and anticipated his kingdom coming on earth as it was in heaven. Second, God was "through all" (διὰ πάντων). Paul probably imagined God being at work through all situations to advance his good and perfect plans in salvation history (cf. Rom. 8:28; Eph. 1:11). Romans 11:36, which had similar doxological language, celebrated that "through God are all things" (δι' αὐτοῦ . . . τὰ πάντα). Finally, God was "in all" (ἐν πᾶσιν), which likely coordinated with the language of the fullness of God found elsewhere in Ephesians (1:23; 3:19; 4:10, 13; 5:18). As in those contexts, God's manifestation of his glorious presence throughout all creation promised to be a final reality once Jesus returned. The repetition of "all" (πᾶς) approached from three different perspectives (over all, through all, and in all) lifted the readers' gazes to a more sweeping fatherhood that would impact every aspect of the new creation. One day the children of God would be revealed, and all of creation would be set free (Rom. 8:19–21). This future state of affairs had already been set in motion in Christ. God was filling all things (Eph. 1:23) and would bring all things together as one in Christ (Eph. 1:9–10).

The Comprehensive Fatherhood of God

No other passage in Paul's letters approached these lofty thoughts about God's fatherly presence in all of creation. With this compact language about the Father, which kept in step with the condensed wording throughout this section of the passage, Paul presented God as Father to believers and even to all of creation. Paul affirmed believers' common access to God as Father (Eph. 2:18; 3:12; 4:6a) but knew that God's fatherhood extended beyond that. Nevertheless, Paul and other Jewish and Christian teachers did not promote God as Father of those who did not know the one true God. And not all people were considered children of God. An unqualified affirmation of the universal fatherhood of God has been identified as one of the hallmarks of a deficient Christianity that has lost its biblical moorings (Ladd, 1974, 55). As is true throughout Ephesians and the rest of Paul's letters, only those who had trusted in Christ had been adopted into God's family and enjoyed the right to call him "Abba, Father" (Rom. 8:15; Gal. 4:6). These same believers were being prepared for a future world in which God the Father would be directly present in all of his glory. Only those who knew God through faith in Christ did enjoy and would enjoy that intimate access to God as Father.

The Body of Christ, Equipped for Growth (4:7–16)

Christ was the triumphant and generous gift-giver who equipped believers for corporate spiritual growth in truth and love by supplying leaders for the church and ministry gifts for each believer.

4:7. After contemplating the oneness of believers' experience in the all-encompassing presence of God, Paul transitioned (δέ, "but") to examining each believer's contribution to corporate life in Christ. Paul began by noting Christ's ministry "to each one of us" (ἑνὶ ἑκάστῳ ἡμῶν) in the one body of Christ. Paul grouped himself with his readers and all other believers in this inclusive first-person pronoun. The unity of the church did not diminish the individual personhood of each member. Instead, individuals joined together as a united people who were built into God's dwelling place (Eph. 2:19–22) and displayed his glory to the world (Eph. 3:9–10). To each member of the body, "grace was given" (ἐδόθη ἡ χάρις) by Christ. "This grace" (ἡ χάρις) denoted the spiritual equipping for ministry that Paul discussed in the following verses. Paul similarly used grace to describe ministry giftedness in other places in his letters (Rom. 1:5; 12:3, 6; 15:15; 1 Cor. 3:10; 15:10; 2 Cor. 1:12; Gal. 2:9; Eph. 3:2, 7, 8). The wording "was given" (ἐδόθη, pass. voice) expressed that each believer was a recipient of Christ's generous overtures to them. Paul's readers had received this grace "according to the measure of Christ's gift" (κατὰ τὸ μέτρον τῆς δωρεᾶς τοῦ Χριστοῦ). The image of a "measure" (μέτρον) highlighted an intentionality that resulted in appropriate gifts for each believer. Christ gave generously but also strategically, knowing how to dispense gifts to his people in perfect measure.

4:8. Paul introduced a saying (διὸ λέγει, "that is why it says"), inspired by Psalm 68:18 (68:19 in the HB, 67:19 in the LXX), that affirmed that Jesus had ascended in victory over his enemies and had shared his kingly spoils of war with his people. Using Psalm 68:18, Paul connected Christ's victorious ascension (ἀναβὰς εἰς ὕψος, "he ascended on high") with his defeat of his enemies (ᾐχμαλώτευσεν αἰχμαλωσίαν, "he took captivity captive") and his generous equipping of his people (ἔδωκεν δόματα τοῖς ἀνθρώποις, "he gave gifts to people"). In the context of Ephesians the clause "he took captive captivity" (ᾐχμαλώτευσεν αἰχμαλωσίαν) likely referred to Christ's disarming of the powers of sin, death, and spiritual forces opposed to God (Eph. 1:20–22; Col. 2:13–15; Heb. 2:14–15). The exalted, triumphant Christ, who had conquered sin, death, and evil powers, now shared the victor's spoils with his redeemed people. Specifically, he provided divine empowerment in the form of spiritual gifts (4:7) and gifted leaders (4:11) so that the church could grow to maturity (4:12–16). Paul saw Christ as the exalted king who used his authority for the sake of the church by giving these good gifts to his people. The appearance of "he gave" (ἔδωκεν) tied Ephesians 4:8 to both 4:7 (ἐδόθη) and 4:11 (ἔδωκεν), but this also raises the question of the saying's relationship to Psalm 68 (see the sidebar).

Paul's Use of Psalm 68

In Ephesians 4:8, instead of a divine warrior receiving gifts among the people (ἔλαβες δόματα ἐν ἀνθρώπῳ, "he received gifts from people," Ps. 68:18 LXX), he distributed gifts to people (ἔδωκεν δόματα τοῖς ἀνθρώποις, "he gave gifts to people"). In Psalm 68, God ascended to his holy mountain to reign, took his enemies captive, and claimed the spoils of war to supply his kingdom with riches. In verse 18, the psalmist praised God as the rightful recipient of human tribute and service. The whole psalm, however, depicted God's triumphant support of his people in addition to his victory over his enemies. (Ps. 68:3–6, 9–10, 19–20, 32–35). In other words, God's triumphant glory aligned with his people's best interests. In Ephesians 4:8, Paul seemed to merge a main theme from the entire psalm with the focal verse, Psalm 68:18 (cf. Arnold, 2010, 251–52; Thielman, 2010, 267–68). When Christ ascended to heaven in victory (ἀναβὰς εἰς ὕψος, "ascended on high") he conquered his enemies (ᾐχμαλώτευσεν αἰχμαλωσίαν, "he took captivity captive") of sin, death, and all evil powers, and he gave gifts to his redeemed people (ἔδωκεν δόματα τοῖς ἀνθρώποις, "he gave gifts to people"). In keeping with the spirit of the original psalm as a whole, Paul viewed Christ sharing his victorious bounty with his people, who were now identified with him and connected to him as his body. This bounty came in the form of the gracious extension of his own glory and power to them (cf. Ps. 68:35). The juxtaposition in Psalm 68 of God's victory and his people's good came to fruition in Christ.

4:9. The quote from Psalm 68 prompted a detour in which Paul explored the significance of Christ's ascension into heaven. If Christ ascended to heaven, then that meant that he had (first) descended to this lowly earth. This conclusion was the most likely meaning of one of the most difficult to understand verses in all of the NT. Paul posed the question, "but what does 'he ascended' mean?" (τὸ δὲ ἀνέβη τί ἐστιν), since Psalm 68:18 began with the picture of God "ascending on high" (ἀναβὰς εἰς ὕψος). Paul drew the inference (εἰ μή, "if not," or "except") from Christ's ascension "that he also descended" (ὅτι καὶ κατέβη). With enigmatic language, Paul stated that Christ had descended "to the lower regions of the earth" (εἰς τὰ κατώτερα [μέρη] τῆς γῆς). The nature and destination of this descent rests at the heart of the debate over the meaning of this verse.

The descent most likely referred to Christ's incarnational ministry, which had consisted of his "descent" to the world in humble identification with humanity and had culminated in his sacrificial death for sinners (Barth, 1974, 433–34; Snodgrass, 1996, 202; Best, 1998, 386; Hoehner, 2002, 531–33; Talbert, 2007, 111–12; Witherington, 2007, 288–90; Bock, 2019, 124–25). According to this view Christ's ascent *to* heaven after his resurrection necessitated a prior descent *from* heaven to earth, and this descent encompassed his entire incarnational ministry but especially his death. This view accords with the centrality of the cross in God's plans (Eph. 2:13–17) and presents Jesus as an example of the humility and others-centeredness that Paul wanted his readers to display towards one another (Eph 4:2–3). Passages such as John 3:13, Philippians 2:6–11, and Ephesians also support this understanding of Christ's ascent and descent. In the end, both logical and thematic reasons support this option, and so it is the preferred option. It advanced Paul's secondary theme of the pairing of Christ's humble ministry and majestic exaltation without detracting from his primary focus in the broader section on Christ's gift-giving ministry.

Other Ways of Understanding Christ's Descent

Of the various interpretations there are two others that are also plausible. First, the descent could have portrayed Christ's activity through the Spirit in giving gifts to the church on earth (Abbott, 1897, 115–16; Lincoln, 1990, 246–47; Harris, 1994, 159–60; Klein, 2006, 113–14). According to this view, Paul drew upon a Jewish exegetical tradition, which may have been current as early as his generation, that Psalm 68:18 described the ascent of Moses to receive God's law and his descent to give that law to the people. In Ephesians 4:8, Paul spotlighted Christ, rather than Moses, as the heavenly ascender and giver of gifts. After Christ had ascended in glory to heaven, he fulfilled his promise to send his Spirit to equip and empower his people on earth (Acts 1:8). And, Paul's focus before and after the quote was on spiritual gifts. But the inference of a descent occurring *after* an ascent is not as natural of a reading as the logical necessity of a descent prior to an ascent. Moreover, verse 10 appears to insist on a tight correspondence between the one who had descended and the one who ascended. Though the Holy Spirit is indeed the Spirit of Christ, who mediates the presence of Christ when he fills God's people (Eph. 3:16–17; 5:18), it is unlikely that Paul would have pressed the equivalence of Christ and the Spirit in verse 10 to the degree that this view would require.

Second, the descent could have described Christ's visit to Hades and his triumphant proclamation of victory over evil spiritual powers, before he ascended to God's right hand in heaven (Arnold,

2010, 254; Thielman, 2010, 270–72). Though this descent is not as logically necessary as the incarnation, Ephesians 4:10 suggests that Paul was intrigued by the notion of Christ's triumphant presence filling any imaginable realm (cf. Eph. 1:23). This view does align with Paul's interest in hostile spiritual forces elsewhere in the letter, but in those other verses the spiritual opponents were located in "the heavenly places" rather than below the earth (Snodgrass, 1196, 202). Besides, verse 8 associated Christ's triumph over his enemies with his ascent rather than his descent. In the end, neither of these alternate views is quite as convincing as the idea that Christ's descent consisted of his incarnation.

Paul did specify further the destination for Christ's descent. Christ descended "to the lower regions of the earth" (κατέβη εἰς τὰ κατώτερα [μέρη] τῆς γῆς). The genitive modifier "of the earth" (τῆς γῆς) probably clarified Paul's understanding of the somewhat vague governing noun (τὰ κατώτερα, "the lower regions") as a genitive of apposition, meaning that when Paul spoke of "the lower regions" (τὰ κατώτερα) he had the earth, specifically, in mind. The comparative adjective ("lower than") probably compared the lower places with the "heights" of Christ's ascent (from 4:8). In other words, Paul likely meant that "[corresponding to the heights of his heavenly ascent] he also descended to the [universe's] lower regions—the earth," or more simply, "he also descended to this lower earth" (Wallace, 1996, 99–100; for the wording "lower earth," cf. Abbott, 1897, 115).

4:10. Paul wrapped up his exploration of Christ's descent and ascent by stressing the total expanse of Christ's authoritative presence. In a chiastic pattern, Paul started his portrayal of Christ with "the one who descended" (ὁ καταβάς) and emphasized that "he himself is also the one who ascended" (αὐτός ἐστιν καὶ ὁ ἀναβάς). The lowly sacrificial servant was now the victorious king. Paul traced Jesus's ascent to heights "high above all the heavens" (ὑπεράνω πάντων τῶν οὐρανῶν). In Ephesians 1:21, Paul had similarly portrayed Jesus's position "high above" (ὑπεράνω) all spiritual powers. These highest heights paralleled the lower depths of Jesus's descent, all for the purpose (ἵνα, "in order that") that Jesus "might fill everything" (πληρώσῃ τὰ πάντα). Paul ensured that the detour into the topic of the ascent and descent returned back to a central route concerning the all-encompassing presence and power of the rightful ruler of the universe.

4:11. With a mild transition (καί, "and"), Paul returned to his primary point about Christ's gift-giving. The added pronoun "he" (αὐτός) reinforced the continued focus on Christ as the main actor in the passage. As Paul had emphasized earlier (Eph. 4:7, 8), Christ "gave" (ἔδωκεν) good things to his people. In this case, he had furnished certain ministers with gifts and ministries for the church's benefit.

Paul identified five types of gifted ministers that contributed to the church's growth.[1] First, "he gave some as apostles" (ἔδωκεν τοὺς μὲν ἀποστόλους). Apostles were foundational ministers in the early church (Acts 2:42; 1 Cor. 12:28; Eph. 2:20) who testified about Christ's resurrection (Acts 1:21–22) and imparted knowledge that the Spirit had revealed to them about the implications of Christ's ministry (Eph. 3:5). Paul considered himself an apostle (Eph. 1:1), based on his encounter with the risen Christ (1 Cor. 9:1; 15:1–8; Gal. 1:16). Paul assumed that the apostles existed only during the era of the early church, since only the early Christians

1 The construction (μέν followed by multiple occurrences of δέ) "separates one thought from another in a series, so that they may be easily distinguished," with a resulting translation of "some . . . others . . . others" (BDAG, s.v. "μέν" 1βc, p. 630).

had witnessed Christ's resurrected state before his ascension. Paul, as the one exception to this rule, became the last person to receive a visit from the resurrected Christ (1 Cor. 15:8). Apostles served Christ and the church for a limited time, but their testimony about Christ rested at the center of church life and teaching (2 Peter 3:2; Jude 17; Rev. 21:14).

Next, "[Christ] supplied others as prophets" (ἔδωκεν . . . τοὺς δὲ προφήτας). Prophets followed on the heels of the apostles in several places (1 Cor. 12:28; Eph. 2:20; 3:5) as indispensable ministers in the church. The Holy Spirit was closely associated with the prophets' ministry (Joel 2:28; Acts 2:17–18; 1 Cor. 12:8–11). In the early church, prophets discerned the Spirit's guidance for important decisions in the church (Acts 13:1–3) and taught believers about the significance of Christ's ministry within God's greater plans (Eph. 3:5). Passages such as 1 Corinthians 12–14 can be understood to allow for an ongoing role for the prophets in local congregations, even beyond the early church period.

Third, "[Christ] gave others as evangelists" (ἔδωκεν . . . τοὺς δὲ εὐαγγελιστάς). The term for evangelist suggested its connection to "proclaiming the gospel" (εὐαγγελίζω), the good news about Jesus. This ministry often involved traveling to other locations in order to bring the message of good news to others (Matt. 24:14; Luke 9:6; Acts 8:40; 16:10; Rom. 15:20; 2 Cor. 10:16; cf. Thielman, 2010, 274). As an evangelist (Acts 21:8), Philip had preached the good news about Christ and the kingdom of God (Acts 8:12, 35, 40), and Paul instructed Timothy to do the work of an evangelist (2 Tim. 4:5) in the service of a gospel-focused ministry (2 Tim. 1:8; 2:8). The fact that Paul as an apostle proclaimed the good news (1 Cor. 15:1; 2 Cor. 11:7; Gal. 1:8; Eph. 3:8) suggested that the various ministries in this verse were interrelated and overlapping. Though evangelists typically engaged in ministry to those who had not heard of Christ (Acts 11:20; Rom. 10:14–15; 15:20), evangelists could also reach out to believers in Christ with the good news of Christ (Rom. 1:15). That service to believers seemed to be included in Ephesians 4:11–12, since the evangelists' ministry helped strengthen the church.

Fourth, "[Christ] equipped others as shepherds" (ἔδωκεν . . . τοὺς δὲ ποιμένας). The early church described spiritual leadership as "shepherding" God's people (Acts 20:28; 1 Peter 5:2). The responsibility of a shepherd (ποιμήν) carried with it connotations of providing wise and caring guidance and spiritual nourishment to other believers. Several NT passages also portrayed Christ as a shepherd (John 10:11, 14; Heb. 13:20; 1 Peter 2:25; 5:4). The OT referred to God as the Shepherd of his people (Ps. 23:1). God had also appointed human leaders among the Israelites to shepherd the flock on his behalf, but they had often failed in this task (Jer. 23:1–2; Ezek. 34:1–10; Zech. 11:15–17).

Fifth, Christ provided "others as teachers" ("and teachers," καὶ διδασκάλους) in the church. Christ placed teaching at the heart of the ministry of the Great Commission. Teachers in the early church taught sound doctrine about the message and ministry of Christ, seeing Christ's work as a fulfillment of the OT (Matt. 28:20; Acts 28:31; 1 Cor. 15:3–4; 1 Tim. 6:3; 2 Tim. 3:16). Though Paul encouraged all believers to teach one another (Col. 3:16), he expected some believers to give special attention to teaching (Rom. 12:7; 1 Tim. 3:2; 2 Tim. 2:24). Other passages grouped teachers with prophets (Acts 13:1) and apostles and prophets (1 Cor. 12:28). Paul described himself as a teacher in addition to a preacher and apostle (1 Tim. 2:7; 2 Tim. 1:11), and Luke mentioned that Paul and Barnabas were teaching and proclaiming the good news (from εὐαγγελίζω) of the word of the Lord (Acts 15:35).

4:12. Paul specified the purpose (πρός, "for") for Christ's provision of ministry gifts to people within the church. Christ's supply of these ministers contributed "to the equipping of the saints" (πρὸς τὸν καταρτισμὸν τῶν ἁγίων). The fact that the five groups of gifted ministers listed in Ephesians 4:11 focused primarily on delivering Christ-centered truth to congregations showed how vital gospel-oriented instruction was for the overall ministry effectiveness of the church. Regular exposure to gifted ministers who proclaimed and taught truth about Christ and the Christian life prepared believers for their own service in the name of Christ.

These believers were equipped "for the work of ministry" (εἰς ἔργον διακονίας). The general phrase "the work of ministry" encompassed a variety of Spirit-empowered contributions to the health and growth of the church (1 Cor. 12:5). Paul used the term "ministry" (διακομία) to describe his own Spirit-directed efforts at advancing God's work in the churches (Rom. 11:13; 2 Cor. 3:8; 4:1; 5:18; 6:3). At other times, a ministry was an assignment from God that ministers felt called to carry out (Acts 20:24; Col. 4:17; 2 Tim. 4:5). Paul did not limit the work of ministry to specific leaders in the church but explained that leaders equipped everyone else to engage in service to one another (Anizor and Voss, 2016, 139–40).

TRANSLATION ANALYSIS: The determination of the structure of this verse makes a big difference in translation and application. First, the phrases "for the equipping of the saints" (πρὸς τὸν καταρτισμὸν τῶν ἁγίων) and "for the work of ministry" (εἰς ἔργον διακονίας) could be parallel phrases that both described the direct ministry of the five types of gifted ministers (Lincoln, 1990, 253; Muddiman, 2001, 200). Second, "for the work of ministry" might have completed the thought begun with "for the equipping of the saints" (Snodgrass, 1996, 204; Klein, 2006, 116–17; Arnold, 2010, 262–63; Thielman, 2010, 277–79; Bock, 2019, 127). This second interpretation is superior. Though the prepositions governing both phrases are often translated the same in English ("for"), they are not the same in Greek. Also, the mobilization of all believers for service matches more the spirit of the passage as a whole. While leaders such as the apostles and prophets had important roles in the church, Christ had given grace to all believers (Eph. 4:7), and all believers contributed to the growth of the church (Eph. 4:16). All believers were careful stewards of the gifts Christ had given, and this stewardship was expressed in various forms of ministry.

Paul's readers had been equipped for the work of ministry "for the purpose of building up the body of Christ" (εἰς οἰκοδομὴν τοῦ σώματος τοῦ Χριστοῦ). In this context the term "building up" (οἰκοδομή; also in Eph. 4:16) described a corporate experience of spiritual advancement toward maturity. In other letters, Paul also enlisted this construction term figuratively to depict desired outcomes of interpersonal harmony and corporate edification (Rom. 14:19; 15:2; 1 Cor. 14:3, 5, 12, 26; 2 Cor. 10:8; 12:19; 13:10). The building term fit especially well in a letter that had already portrayed believers as a structure that was being built into a dwelling for God (Eph. 2:19–22). In this passage, though, Paul returned to the image of the body of Christ (Eph. 1:23; 3:6; 4:4) to highlight the church growing together, as a unit.

4:13. Paul further developed the picture of unified spiritual growth by describing the end result (μέχρι, "until") of that growth. Paul envisioned every single person in the church (οἱ πάντες, "we all") arriving at the destination (καταντήσωμεν, "attain") together. While the imperial cult supplied a form of unity for diverse people across the empire through a common vision of the glory of Rome and its leaders (Rives, 2007, 148–49), Christ Jesus had actually created a new humanity (Eph. 2:15) that could grow together under his loving authority.

Paul described three pictures of the church's ideal condition, each marked by the preposition "to" (εἰς). First, Paul's readers were designed to attain a twofold "unity" (ἡ ἑνότης) as the body of Christ. With "the unity of the faith" (εἰς τὴν ἑνότητα τῆς πίστεως), Paul revisited the shared life and common heritage that believers enjoyed (Eph. 4:3–6). God had provided this unity through Christ as a gift (Eph. 2:16), but the church needed to progressively grow into the fullness of that unity. Gifted ministers helped unleash the constructive potential within the body of Christ to reach that goal. Alongside the unity of the faith was the unity of "knowing the Son of God" (εἰς τὴν ἑνότητα . . . τῆς ἐπιγνώσεως τοῦ υἱοῦ τοῦ θεοῦ). Paul's readers shared the conviction that Jesus was the Messiah, the promised Son of God (2 Sam. 7:14; Ps. 2:7; 89:26–27; Rom. 1:3–4; cf. Bateman, 2012, 303–29). A unity in knowledge entailed both a common confession of belief that Jesus was the Christ and a relational communion with him. Paul had already prayed that his readers would cherish this intimate knowledge of Christ (Eph. 3:14–21; cf. 1 Cor. 1:9; Gal. 2:20). Here, he reaffirmed this shared relational knowledge, grounded in the truth of Christ, as the intended result for the body of Christ.

Second, echoing the first goal of unity, Paul's readers as a group were marching towards "becoming a mature adult" (εἰς ἄνδρα τέλειον). The term for "adult" (ἀνήρ) was often used generally for an adult man, but in this case it referred figuratively to the church as a united group of people. No doubt Paul still had in mind the "new humanity" that Christ had created for believing Jews and Gentiles (cf. the synonym ἄνθρωπος in Eph. 2:15). Christ had supplied this new, united entity with the means to become "mature," "perfect," or "complete" (τέλειος) in him (cf. 1 Cor. 2:6; 14:20; BDAG, s.v. "τέλειος" 2a, b, p. 995).

Third, Paul expressed the church's end goal of unity and maturity as progressing "to the highest stature, culminating in Christ's own fullness" (εἰς μέτρον ἡλικίας τοῦ πληρώματος τοῦ Χριστοῦ). Paul paired "measure" (μέτρον) with "stature" (ἡλικία) to communicate the image of bodily growth, in conjunction with the "mature adult" picture he had just introduced. Paul then used Christ's fullness as the comparison point for this growth. The body had been designed to reflect the perfection of the head. As the fullness of Christ dwelt within his people, they more completely bore his image. Paul's readers would reach their highest "stature" (ἡλικία) in their unity and maturity when they drew upon the full life found in Christ Jesus.

4:14. One purpose (ἵνα, "in order that") for this building up of the church was so that believers would no longer be "infants" (νήπιοι). Paul set this spiritual infancy in contrast to the mature adult he expected his readers to become. The use of first-person plural in "we may no longer be" (μηκέτι ὦμεν) softened Paul's stark portrayal of spiritual immaturity by making it less of a commentary on his readers' deficiencies and more of a sober assessment of the risks that all believers faced apart from a commitment to growth. Paul characterized this spiritual infancy in the rest of the verse, before once again returning to the rosier picture of the readers' march towards maturity.

Paul began his description of spiritual infancy by painting the picture of a vulnerable vessel on the rough seas. The spiritually immature were "tossed around by the waves" (κλυδωνιζόμενοι) and "blown around by every wind of teaching" (περιφερόμενοι παντὶ ἀνέμῳ τῆς διδασκαλίας). This effective imagery emphasized the helplessness of an immature church and its susceptibility to getting thrown off course by false teachings and other harmful ideologies.

Sea Travel in the Ancient World

Paul's own experiences in sea travel likely contributed to the vivid imagery that he used for a church that was storm-tossed and vulnerable without Christ's stabilizing work. Even before his famous shipwreck recounted in Acts 27, Paul had experienced three shipwrecks and being adrift at sea (2 Cor. 11:25–26). In Acts 27, Luke shared vivid descriptions of winds creating difficulties for navigation and putting cargo and lives at risk (27:7–10). Experienced sailors were able to use wind to their advantage but were still at the mercy of strong winds that could shift suddenly and violently (27:13–17). Luke mentioned that Paul and his fellow travelers had faced "a violent battering" from a storm that "continued raging" (27:18, 20; NIV), resulting in an eventual shipwreck (27:41). Especially in the winter months (November to March), shipwrecks were a real possibility (Schnabel, 2004, 635). Divers in recent years have continued to find sunken ships from the ancient times in the Aegean and Mediterranean seas.

Road to Ancient Harbor, Ephesus.
Courtesy of Greg MaGee.

In the rest of verse 14, Paul further described the harmful teaching that threatened to derail the church in its growth and mission. He used a collection of near synonyms to depict these teachings as pernicious and difficult for an immature church to deflect. Paul made a general connection (ἐν, instr. prep.) between the "wind of teaching" (ἄνεμος τῆς διδασκαλίας) and the motivation and strategies behind its propagation. The teaching was disseminated "through human craftiness" (ἐν τῇ κυβείᾳ τῶν ἀνθρώπων). These sly and deceptive human ideologies stood in contrast to God's perfect, eternal plans for the church (Eph. 1:3–10). Paul then restated this charge by characterizing the promotion of the subversive teaching as happening "through cunning" (ἐν πανουργίᾳ), which described an underhanded style of ministry that Paul disavowed elsewhere (2 Cor. 4:2). These cunning teachings were spread "with deceitful scheming" (πρὸς τὴν μεθοδείαν τῆς πλάνης), with "deceitful" (πλάνης, attributive gen.) functioning to modify "scheming" (μεθοδεία). Paul later noted that the devil also engaged in such scheming (Eph. 6:11). False teachers carried out crafty plans that sprung from error rather than the divine truth of the gospel (1 Thess. 2:3–4). Human agents, and perhaps demonic forces, with deliberate motives to lead the church astray, stood behind teachings that could work their way quite subtly into undiscerning congregations.

4:15. In contrast (δέ, "but") to being swayed by the false teachers' trickery and cunning, believers possessed a prescription for growth (αὐξήσωμεν, "that we may grow," governed by ἵνα from verse 14) that consisted of "speaking the truth in love" (ἀληθεύοντες . . . ἐν ἀγάπῃ). Speaking the truth most likely referred to teaching accurately about Christ, in conjunction with the ministries highlighted in verse 11. This shared commitment to sound teaching was carried out in a loving atmosphere that sought the ultimate good of believers in the church. This combination of benevolent motivation and Christ-centered instruction resulted in spiritual growth. Paul thus contrasted three things between this verse and the preceding verse: (1) truth-telling with false teaching, (2) loving motives with cunning schemes, and (3) spiritual growth with erratic drifting.

Recalling the picture of the "mature adult" (ἀνὴρ τέλειος) that resembled the fullness of Christ (Eph. 4:13), Paul envisioned the church growing up "to him" (εἰς αὐτόν), which referred to Christ. When believers in the church were mobilized and equipped for constructive ministry, the church grew toward greater conformity into the image of Christ. Paul commended this growth "in all ways" (τὰ πάντα) or all areas of the church's existence. The spiritual growth of the body occurred through its connection to Christ, the head (ὅς ἐστιν ἡ κεφαλή, Χριστός, "who is the head, Christ") of the body (Eph. 1:22; 5:23). Christ Jesus was the head of the body, just as he was the foundation of God's holy dwelling (Eph. 2:20). As the body grew it exhibited more and more the likeness of the head in all things.

4:16. Next, Paul looked at the inner workings of how the body grew into Christ, its head. The starting assumption was that corporate spiritual growth arose "from [Christ]" (ἐξ οὗ), through the body's union with Christ, the head. From Christ and drawing upon Christ's divine life, "the whole body engages in spiritual growth" (πᾶν τὸ σῶμα . . . τὴν αὔξησιν τοῦ σώματος ποιεῖται) through an extensive process involving each member. The body would grow "as it is joined and held together by every supporting attachment" (συναρμολογούμενον καὶ συμβιβαζόμενον διὰ πάσης ἀφῆς τῆς ἐπιχορηγίας). These two participles modified the main verb of the verse (ποιεῖται, "does," or "engages in") and showed the manner in which the body grew. The participles shared a familiar prefix (συν-, "co-") that expressed the idea of a shared experience (Eph. 2:5–6, 19–22; 3:6; 5:7, 11). Members of the body were "joined together" (as in the construction of a building or temple, συναρμολογούμενον) and were "held together" (by attaching joints or ligaments, as in a human body, συμβιβαζόμενον) so that they grew as a single entity. Paul painted the picture of a tightly knit group of people that had been created by God to operate as one unit as it grew toward maturity.

This process happened "according to the dynamic and appropriately arranged working of each part" (κατ' ἐνέργειαν ἐν μέτρῳ ἑνὸς ἑκάστου μέρους). Each believer received gracious gifts from Christ in proper measure (Eph. 4:7), so that each part could fulfill its role within the body. Believers drew on the enabling "work" (ἐνέργεια) of the one who always worked to accomplish his purposes for the world (Eph. 1:11, 19, 20; 3:7, 20). The end result (εἰς, "for"), once again, was "for the building up of the body in love" (εἰς οἰκοδομὴν ἀυτοῦ ἐν ἀγάπῃ). Believers could expect to see Christlike love permeate their congregations as they grew together in maturity. Their relationships within the body of Christ would be marked by genuine concern for one another's best long-term interests.

THEOLOGICAL FOCUS

The exegetical idea (when Paul's readers invested in their relationships with one another, embraced shared beliefs in Christ, and ministered according to the gracious gifts they received from the exalted Christ, they could experience spiritual growth and unity together, with each believer contributing to that growth) leads to this theological focus: Believers grow and experience unity together in Christ when they invest in their relationships with one another, celebrate shared beliefs, and draw upon Christ's gracious gifts for ministry.

This passage describes what investment in personal relationships within the body of Christ looks like with terms such as humility, meekness, patience, love, unity, and peace (vv. 2–3). These very qualities also marked Jesus's "walk" on earth. The passage acknowledges that these types of relationships take intentional effort, but believers are not starting from scratch. The love, peace, and unity they embrace are already secured for them in Christ and extended to them by the Spirit's work. When these mindsets and attitudes prevail in relationships, believers grow together in Christ.

This passage celebrates the shared beliefs that stand at the center of Christianity (vv. 4–6). With the Father, Son, and Spirit, Christians share a common object of worship. With faith, baptism, and hope, Christians share a common experience of a new life, new identity, and new destiny in Christ. Being the one body of Christ happens only in a context in which there is a shared confession of the triune God and a shared experience of being supernaturally integrated into his family by faith. These truths about God and believers' experience function as a focal point for Christian unity and growth.

The gracious gifts Christ provides for fruitful ministry flow from his authority and generosity (vv. 7–10). Christ has conquered sin, death, and Satan, and he shares his victory with believers by equipping them with divine enablement for ministry. The growth of the body of Christ is propelled by Christ's power and generosity, though growth still requires each believer's participation (v. 12). Believers contribute to the spiritual growth of the church when they use their spiritual gifts within the framework of a common faith forged by the earliest apostles and prophets and preserved by other church leaders across time (v. 11). The end result is a body of believers that matures over time and begins to resemble more and more the head, Jesus (v. 15–16).

PREACHING AND TEACHING STRATEGIES

Exegetical and Theological Synthesis

In light of the stirring depiction of God and his plan of salvation for the church (chapters 1–3), Paul exhorted the believers in Ephesus to live in accordance with their identity in Christ Jesus. The dominant exhortation in the passage is to "walk" (that is, "live") in a manner worthy of our calling (v. 1). In 4:1–16, the "worthy manner" relates to harmony among those who follow Christ. Through humility, gentleness, patience, bearing with one another in love, and speaking and receiving the truth, Paul's readers were to maintain the unity that God had created when he joined Jews and Gentiles into one body.

For Paul, relationships (vv. 2–3) and truth both mattered (vv. 4–6). Outside of Christ, believers tended to look out for their own interests rather than the interests of others, creating the potential for disunity. Thus Paul exhorted, "make every effort to keep the unity of the Spirit" (v. 3). He reminded the readers that the Spirit had made all members of the church one body. Believers *were* unified, so they needed to *preserve* that unity through humility and forbearance. The problem of false teachers who deceived immature believers, making a shipwreck of their faith, was also pervasive in the early church. In Paul's day (and ours), false teachers spouted heresies that separated people from God, so the Lord endowed the church with gifted leaders like apostles and pastors to help the body grow into the stature of Christ (vv. 7–11). Furthermore, God had also gifted what we call "laypeople" (v. 12). Like iron sharpening iron, all believers were to speak the truth in love to one another, and in that way grow up into Christ, who is the head (v. 15).

Preaching Idea

To live in unity, let's remove our pride, avoid the riptide, and not hide.

Contemporary Connections

What does it mean?

What does it mean to live in unity by removing our pride, avoiding the riptide, and not hiding? "Removing our pride" summarizes verses 2–6: be humble, gentle, patient, and forbearing, striving to maintain the unity of the Spirit. We might point out that God *has* unified his people, so the body of Christ simply actualizes what he has already done. The cause-effect reasoning can be compared to a gift card and a restaurant. The card is loaded with cash, but that cash is worthless until we put it into action. Only when we activate the card, pull it out, and swipe it can we access the cash. In the same way, God has "loaded" his body with unity, but we experience that unity only when we put it into practice with gentle, forbearing words and actions.

A review of context also helps clarify what it means to live in unity. Up to this point in Ephesians, a major theme had been how God has torn down the wall between Jews and Gentiles. That divide was wider than divisions we feel today with things like political parties. Divisions can be healed when we set aside our pride and communicate with gentleness and patience.

"Avoid the riptide" refers to verses 7–14 where Paul described how Jesus gave the church gifted leaders to protect it from false teaching. The image of "riptide" comes from verse 14 where Paul compared false teaching to the dangers of sea travel—tossed by waves and blown by winds. Gifted leaders are like lifeguards at the beach or the coast guard rescuing floundering ships. For resources on that theme, see the "Creativity in Presentation" section.

The last phrase, "do not hide," comes from verses 15–16, where we are enjoined to speak the truth in love. Rather than hiding behind a pseudo-unity created by silence, laypeople (not just ministers) are instructed to speak the truth openly and faithfully because that is how the body grows. Self-disclosure could demonstrate how someone spoke the truth in love to us with the result of deeper unity and more Christlikeness.

Is it true?

Is it true that removing pride, avoiding the riptide, and not hiding can help the church walk in unity? The preaching idea may raise the disquieting fact that the visible church is *not* unified. One legacy of Protestantism is the propensity to separate over minor doctrines. The legacy continues on the personal level when "church shoppers" join and leave congregations like hummingbirds flitting from flower to flower. One way to address these issues could be by making a modest claim, not a sweeping claim. While we cannot solve the problems of the universal church, unity within local churches—our own particular church—is the concern of this passage. We can hold out hope that by avoiding pride, the riptide, and hiding, the particular group of believers gathered to hear this sermon can experience unity.

Perhaps the preaching idea is best verified with concrete experience. An extended family with young people and old might share how they enjoyed a family reunion by setting aside their personal agendas. Unity between churches in the same geographical area can also provide concrete proof for the preaching idea. For example, churches might band together in a cooperative activity such as an evangelistic campaign, summer camp, vacation Bible school, or lay-seminary institute. Pastors might swap pulpits, demonstrating that they trust each other and that their unity is found in something deeper than church preferences or ethnic distinctives.

Now what?

How can we avoid pride, the riptide of false teaching, and the pseudo-unity that comes from hiding? One way found in this passage is by speaking the truth in love as when Paul rebuked Peter (Gal. 2:11–14). Likewise, Jesus rebuked the disciples for their pride when they argued who was top dog (Matt. 20:20–28).

A mnemonic device can help people apply the preaching idea, especially the last part about not hiding. When speaking the truth we should do so:

- privately (Matt. 18:15).
- purely (not being guilty of the same sin) (Matt. 7:3–5; Gal. 6:1).
- patiently (2 Tim. 4:2).
- placidly (2 Tim. 2:24–25).

In addition to biblical and personal examples, concrete action steps might also help listeners put the truth into action. For example, having a young person pray for an older person, and vice versa, could enhance unity. This could be done in the church service itself, or prayer partners could be arranged outside the service. In 2019, a video went viral that showed two high school football players kneeling in prayer after the game. The two young men had been opponents on the field. Wide receiver Gage Smith had just led Sherman High School to victory over Mesquite West, but afterward, he knelt to pray with Mesquite's Ty Jordan, whose mother was battling cancer. Smith said, "When you're playing the game, you're playing to win, and the other team is the enemy. But afterward, you still have respect for the other opponent. Football brings people together in so many different ways, and that was just one example of it that night."[2]

Creativity in Presentation

Pictures or stories of coast guard rescues might vivify how false teaching can destroy the church and how faithful teachers protect it. For great examples, search YouTube for top Coast Guard Rescues.

The metaphors in the preaching idea (remove pride, avoid the riptide, do not hide) could be pictured with visual aids or demonstrations. Two people could walk together (symbolizing unity). One outpaces the other (symbolizing disunity) because the slower walker is carrying a heavy backpack labeled "pride." He or she removes the backpack and the two are reunited and walk on at the same pace.

If your church or organization has gifted dramatists, a humorous sketch showing a business meeting could illustrate our need for truthful speech. In the sketch, perhaps the chairperson of the meeting suggests a ludicrous idea and groupthink takes over as the other members pick it up and run with it. One lone person might think the idea is crazy but won't speak the truth in love, and when the idea is put into action . . . disaster!

A story of people playing in the ocean where one is caught in a riptide can illustrate how false teaching separates companions and is potentially deadly.[3]

When teaching on verse 15 ("We will grow up into him who is the head"), we might show a picture of a toddler and point out one of the endearing qualities of young children: their head is large compared to the size of their body. When the child grows the body becomes proportionate to the head. You might even demonstrate this by bringing a young child to the platform and asking him or her to reach over their head to touch the opposite ear. Then show how an adult can easily do that. Explain that the body of the child will eventually grow just as we grow into the stature of Christ, our head. That happens when we speak the truth in love.

When the late actor Alec Guinness began pouring himself into a new character, the first thing he focused on was the legs. The goal was to discover how the character carried himself day after day. Once Guinness had the walk right, he could ask why the man walked that way. This would lead to the right posture, speech, and mannerisms. If he could get the feet, legs, and walk right, the rest would follow. Guinness's approach to character development works from the outside in, but Jesus's approach works from

---

2 Ashleigh Jackson, "High school football player goes viral after praying for opponent whose mom is battling cancer," KPTV.com, November 5, 2019, https://www.kptv.com/high-school-football-player-goes-viral-after-praying-for-opponent-whose-mom-is-battling-cancer/article_bb06f03f-2a20-580d-9873-3481688eda96.html.

3 Harvey Rice, "9 Isle lifeguards shaken after trying in vain to save man," *Houston Chronicle*, August 3, 2009, http://www.chron.com/disp/story.mpl/metropolitan/6558573.html.

the inside out. He changes the heart and that leads to the correct walk.[4]

A clip from the movie *Hoosiers* (directed by David Anspaugh, 1986) offers a simple but moving example of speaking the truth in love. Norman Dale (played by Gene Hackman), a basketball coach in small town Indiana, asks a middle-aged man with the nickname of "Shooter" (played by Dennis Hopper) to be his assistant coach. Shooter was a star athlete in high school and is now the father of one of the current players, but he has fallen on hard times. He lives in a shack in the woods, depends on handouts for money, and tries to forget his problems with alcohol. Shooter's son is embarrassed and disgusted by his father, but the coach takes pity on Shooter and extends grace by asking him to be assistant coach. But there is a catch: Shooter must give up drinking. He must be a role model for the team. Coach speaks kindly and gently, but also bluntly. Shooter is offended at first, but he eventually takes the offer and it turns his life around. (The scene occurs at 49:00. You may be able to find clips for it on the internet. Search for "*Hoosiers* clip, Shooter, assistant coach".)

However we choose to convey the primary teaching of this text, we will want to emphasize this: To live in unity let's remove our pride, avoid the riptide, and not hide.

A possible sermon outline:

- Introduction: How can we live in unity?
- Remove your pride (vv. 1–6).
- Avoid the riptide (vv. 7–14).
- Do not hide (vv. 15–16).

Because this passage is dense with theology, it could be turned into a miniseries.

DISCUSSION QUESTIONS

1. In what types of situations is it hard for you to bear with another person in love?
2. Is your church known for maintaining the unity of the Spirit? Why or why not?
3. Go through the list of unifying doctrines in Ephesians 4:4–6. Why is each one essential for maintaining unity within the church?
4. What are some concrete ways we can demonstrate the fact that God has made us one body?
5. How did the material on Christ descending and ascending (vv. 8–10) support Paul's emphasis on Christ's generosity and authority in the broader passage?
6. According to verse 12, why does God give churches pastors? How does that square with the job description of most pastors?
7. How do "deceitful schemers" spread false teaching today?
8. Has anyone ever spoken the truth in love to you? How did it help you grow spiritually?

4 Terry Mattingly, "What Your Stance Shows," PreachingToday.com, August 2000, https://www.preachingtoday.com/illustrations/2000/august/12591.html.

Ephesians 4:17–5:2

EXEGETICAL IDEA

Paul's readers needed to put off the spiritually resistant old person and its distorted thinking and behavior, be inwardly renewed in Christ, and put on the new person with Christlike treatment of other believers in areas such as constructive speech, conflict resolution, generosity, and forgiveness.

THEOLOGICAL FOCUS

Believers should embrace their new identity in Christ and express this new identity by their loving treatment of fellow believers.

PREACHING IDEA

New life in Christ sparks a new style of living.

PREACHING POINTERS

Many of Paul's Gentile readers lived in the shadow of their past, which was marked by separation from God, flawed perspectives, and self-centered behavior. OT texts such as Psalm 115:4–8 and Isaiah 44:9–20 recognized the absurdity of idolatry and the spiritual blindness that accompanied it. Now, Christ had saved Paul's readers and had incorporated them into his new family. These believers needed to make a clean break from their past. They inhabited two worlds—a broader world of idolatry and self-interest, and the new spiritual community that consisted of devoted but still flawed followers of Christ. Paul's readers needed reminders about how to detach themselves from worldly patterns and identify more strongly with Christ and his diverse people. Paul provided them with many practical examples about how to abandon old, misguided, and destructive habits and implement new, Christlike practices that built up the body of Christ and reflected God's love and forgiveness.

Followers of Christ today still feel pulled into mindsets and practices that are at odds with their new life in Christ. Some of the old practices are heard daily in blogs, talk radio, and political acrimony. A "tribalized" mindset can cause us to find people of like mind, preach our views to the choir, and demonize anyone who holds an opposite conviction. Another of the old practices is deceit, which can take the form of "spin" and propaganda and are common tools of persuasion. This passage is up to date on the issue of immorality too. Movies, television shows, and songs ranging from country to hip-hop make unchecked pursuits of sensual pleasures seem normal. For Christians, this is not how we learned Christ (v. 20). Foul talk, lying, outbursts of anger, and immorality belong to the distorted world of the old person, not the new, and the old ways must be put off (v. 22). Truthfulness, kindness, forgiveness, and love are our new virtues that help us imitate God as we allow new life in Christ to spark a new style of living.

A NEW IDENTITY BRINGS NEW PRACTICES (4:17–5:2)

LITERARY STRUCTURE AND THEMES (4:17–5:2)

In Ephesians 4:17–5:2, Paul continued to emphasize the individual and corporate implications of new life in Christ. The passage connects most directly to the preceding passage with the conjunction "therefore" (οὖν) and a return to using the word "walk" (περιπατέω) to describe the way people conducted their lives. The passage divides nicely into three main sections. In Ephesians 4:17–19, Paul challenged his readers to stand apart from the crowd by disassociating themselves from the mindset and lifestyle of the broader Gentile world. In verses 20–24, Paul then presented his vision of embracing a radical new identity in Christ in exchange for the old person. Finally, in 4:25–5:2, Paul applied this teaching about a transformed identity in a number of practical areas consisting of how to treat other members of the body of Christ and exhibit God's love.

Paul had established a distinct "before and after" contrast in Ephesians 2. Paul's readers had once been dead in their sins but had now been made alive in Christ (2:1–10). Formerly alienated Gentiles had been reconciled to God and included with Jewish believers in Christ to become a re-created humanity (2:11–22). In Ephesians 4:17–5:2, Paul expanded on this contrast and took it in a practical direction, driving home throughout the passage the sequence of putting off an old identity, internalizing a changed way of thinking, and putting on a new identity.

- ***Stand Apart from the Crowd (4:17–19)***
- ***Embrace a Radically New Identity in Christ (4:20–24)***
- ***Love One Another (4:25–5:2)***

EXPOSITION (4:17–5:2)

In the passage, Paul described a wholesale adoption of a new identity in exchange for the old. Paul knew that it would not be easy for his Gentile readers to embrace all of the practical implications of this change in loyalties. Their identity transfer needed to emerge from the renewed way of thinking that God brought about, and it would result in new motivations and actions in the way Paul's readers interacted with others in their churches. Paul offered a penetrating analysis of the old ways his Gentile readers had abandoned. The Gentile world was blinded to God and his truth because of rampant idolatry.[1] Paul described what it meant to live as spiritually transformed people in a community centered in Christ Jesus. Paul gave examples of how his readers' identity transfer should get worked out in concrete ways in the context of relationships with other believers. Along the way, Paul continued to intersperse brief reminders of the changed loyalties—to Christ and his people—that should motivate his readers' decisive shift from the old to the new.

Stand Apart from the Crowd (4:17–19)

Paul exhorted his readers to pursue a course that stood apart from the way of life of unbelieving Gentiles, whose spiritually resistant

1 In Ephesus alone there were temples connected to fifteen gods and goddesses during the first century (Wilson, 2012, 201).

hearts had led to distorted thinking and ungodly practices.

4:17. With "therefore" (οὖν), Paul built from his compelling vision of corporate Christian life in Ephesians 4:1–16 to an admonition to leave the old life behind. Paul solemnly charged his readers to not live like the unbelieving Gentiles did. Paul introduced his exhortation to the readers with two brief clauses (joined by καί, "and") that communicated the solemn and important nature of Paul's instructions. Paul led with "I say this" (λέγω τοῦτο), which prepared readers for the pronouncement that followed. He continued with "I insist [on this] in the Lord" (μαρτύρομαι ἐν κυρίῳ). The verb "insist" or "testify" (μαρτυρομαι) in this context indicated Paul's full insistence on the importance of the directive that followed (NET; BDAG, s.v. "μαρτυρέω" 2, p. 618). The inclusion of "in the Lord" (ἐν κυρίῳ) further solidified the unequivocal and serious tone of the instructions.

Paul gave a command about how to live by making a contrast with the conduct of unbelieving Gentiles. He wanted his readers to appreciate the dramatic difference between who they once had been and who they were now empowered to be. Paul used the verb "walk" (περιπατέω) throughout Ephesians to describe an established pattern of living (Eph. 2:1, 10; 4:1, 17; 5:2, 8, 15). Paul's readers needed to abandon a path of life that matched the course of "the Gentiles" (τὰ ἔθνη). In this context, Paul was speaking about Gentiles who did not believe in Christ. These Gentiles conducted their lives "in the futility of their thinking" (ἐν ματαιότητι τοῦ νοὸς αὐτῶν). The "futility" (ματαιότης) of the Gentiles' thinking (νοῦς) highlighted the fruitless or worthless outcome of that way of life (BDAG, s.v. "ματαιότης," p. 621).

The Futile Thinking of Idolatry

Jewish literature recognized the futile thinking of those who worshipped idols. Isaiah 44:10 contended that idols were "profitable for nothing" (ESV), and Psalm 115:8 suggested that people became like the idols that they worshipped. The Jewish work Wisdom of Solomon created a vivid description of the negative effects of idolatry on Gentile behavior, pointing to "theft and deceit, corruption, faithlessness, tumult, perjury, confusion over what is good, forgetfulness of favors, pollution of souls, sex perversion, disorder in marriage, adultery, and debauchery" (14:25–26 RSV). Paul targeted some of these behaviors in the verses that followed.

4:18. Paul delved deeper into a description of the spiritual condition of the Gentiles apart from Christ. Paul highlighted two reasons (ptc. of cause) why unbelieving Gentiles walked with futile thinking. First, "they have been darkened" (ἐσκοτωμένοι . . . ὄντες) in their understanding. Paul noted that their "understanding," or their "faculty of thinking, comprehending, and reasoning" (BDAG, s.v. "διάνοια" 1, p. 234) had been "darkened" (σκοτόω), or profoundly hindered from seeing the truth. This darkened understanding shaped the futile direction of their thinking and living.

The second reason these unbelieving Gentiles pursued a course of futile thinking was that they had been "excluded [or separated] from the life of God" (ἀπαλλοτριωμένοι τῆς ζωῆς τοῦ θεοῦ). They had no claim on the spiritual life that God had given. Previously, Paul had observed that his Gentile readers had once been "excluded" (ἀπαλλοτριόω) from citizenship in Israel (Eph. 2:12). The life that God gave was "transcendent life" (BDAG, s.v. "ζωή" 2, p. 430), which was a gift to those who were in Christ Jesus (Eph. 2:5). Apart from knowing Christ, Gentiles had no access to God's gift of life.

The reason for the Gentiles' separation from the life of God was "because of the ignorance that was in them" (διὰ τὴν ἄγνοιαν τὴν οὖσαν ἐν αὐτοῖς), which itself was "because of the hardness of their heart" (διὰ τὴν πώρωσιν τῆς καρδίας αὐτῶν). Paul's explanation moved logically from the heart to the mind to the spiritual standing of unbelieving Gentiles. Because their hearts were hardened, or stubbornly unresponsive to God, Gentiles were ignorant of God and his truth, which resulted in separation from the life God gave. The heart was "the center of human existence" (Ridderbos, 1975, 119), where Christ dwelt, by the Spirit, through faith (Eph. 3:17). The image of a hardened heart described a serious problem for people in both the Old and New Testaments (1 Sam. 6:6; 2 Chron. 36:13; Ps. 95:8; Heb. 3:13). People with hardened hearts were spiritually insensitive and did not yield to God's good work for them. Hardened hearts led to a persistent "ignorance" (ἄγνοια) of spiritual truth, keeping people separated from the life God gives.

4:19. Paul continued to describe the unbelieving Gentiles (rel. pron., οἵτινες, "who"), noting that since they had become spiritually callous, they had "given themselves over" (παραδίδωμι) to a whole spectrum of self-indulgent and immoral activities. Paul sometimes used this verb (παραδίδωμι) to describe handing people over to something unpleasant as a form of judgment or discipline. At times God handed them over (Rom. 1:24, 26, 28), at other times Paul did so (1 Cor. 5:5; 1 Tim. 1:20). Tragically, in this case, the unbelieving Gentiles themselves chose this fate. They handed themselves over to sin because (ptc. of cause, ἀπηλγηκότες) they had developed callous hearts, becoming uncaring about and unresponsive to spiritual and moral matters (BDAG, s.v. "ἀπαλγέω" 1, p. 96).

These Gentiles plunged themselves into inappropriate and licentious behavior, which was behavior that threw off all restraints and propriety (BDAG, s.v. "ἀσελγεία," p. 141). This behavior resulted in the practice of "every type of immoral behavior" (ἀκαθαρσίας πάσης). Paul used this sweeping and all-inclusive language to cover the range of sinful practices that characterized the lifestyle of unbelieving Gentiles. Paul added that immorality was often accompanied by greedy or self-indulgent living (ἐν πλεονεξίαι, "with an appetite for more"). The wording "appetite for more" (πλεονεξία) often denoted greed, but in this context it more likely described an appetite for vice that was insatiable (BDAG, s.v. "πλεονεξία," p. 824).

Paul's combination of multiple terms to describe vices captured the various dimensions of the Gentiles' behavior. Their actions were simultaneously self-centered, dismissive of community norms for behavior, and in violation of God's standards. The closing image of lust that was never satisfied (4:19) recalled Paul's picture from two verses earlier of "futile thinking" (ἐν ματαιότητι τοῦ νοὸς αὐτῶν) that led to nowhere. When Christ had saved Paul's readers, he had delivered them from this dark and seemingly hopeless condition.

Comparisons to Romans 1:18–32

Ephesians 4:17–19 bore striking resemblance to Paul's description of Gentile sins in Romans 1:18–32 (cf. Stott, 1979, 177–78; Lincoln, 1990, 273). In both passages, Paul connected outward sins to deeper spiritual rebellion that was rooted in the "mind" (νοῦς) and "heart" (καρδία). In both places, he depicted their mindset as "darkened" (σκοτόω/σκοτίζω) and "futile" (ματαιότης/ματαιόω), and he described their lifestyle as "immoral" (ἀκαθαρσία), oriented to "sinful desire" (ἐπιθυμία), and "greedy" or "self-indulgent" (πλεονεξία). In Ephesians, the unbelieving Gentiles "gave themselves over" (παραδίδωμι) to godless living, while in Romans 1, God "gave them over" (παραδίδωμι, repeated three times), allowing them to experience the bitter ends of their rejection of him. Taking these two perspectives together, people threw off restraints to pursue sin even as God released them to receive the destructive "freedom" they had asked for.

Embrace a Radically New Identity in Christ (4:20–24)

Paul reminded his readers that they had been instructed, with Christ-centered teaching, to put off the corrupted old person, to embrace ongoing, inward renewal in their thinking, and to put on the new person that had been created in God's likeness, in the righteousness and holiness that arose from the truth.

4:20. Paul decisively shifted the focus to the readers' new calling with the contrastive conjunction "but" (δέ). This section acted as a hinge section for Ephesians 4:17–5:2, providing the theological basis and spiritual mechanism for walking in a new way of life. Paul brought his encouraging words directly to his readers (ὑμεῖς, "you"), who were no longer trapped in their sinfulness. Christ was the difference-maker. Paul's readers had "not learned Christ this way" (οὐχ οὕτως ἐμάθετε τὸν Χριστόν), or in the way of spiritually blind, sinful living. Paul used the language of "learning Christ" as shorthand for being instructed in all of God's truth within the context of a relationship with Christ. Paul's readers had been instructed in a distinct way of walking with Christ that was incompatible with past ignorance and immorality.

4:21. It should have been obvious for Paul's readers that the way of the unbelieving world was completely incongruent with the way of Christ. Paul made this point by highlighting the distinctiveness of a Christ-shaped way of living. Beginning with "if indeed" (εἴ γε), Paul paused, with a rhetorical flourish, to verify that it was, in fact, Christ that they had heard and learned about. Paul noted that, if indeed *Christ* was the one they had heard (αὐτὸν ἠκούσατε, "it was him you heard") and "[it was] *in him* that they were taught" (ἐν αὐτῷ ἐδιδάχθητε), then Paul's ethical teaching necessarily applied to them. Paul's purposefully compact language further portrayed Christ as the sole focus of what they had heard. They had heard *him*, not just teachings about him. They had been spiritually formed *in him* when they were taught. Paul punctuated this thought with a reason (καθώς, "just as") that should have already been clear to his readers: "truth is found [only] in Jesus" (ἔστιν ἀλήθεια ἐν τῷ Ἰησοῦ). The mention of Jesus's name brought to mind the godly quality of life that Jesus had promoted and exhibited in his incarnational ministry. Paul's readers had begun to learn from and follow Jesus, in whom truth was found.

4:22. In verses 22 through 24, Paul unfolded a powerful summary of what ongoing identity formation in Christ looked like. All three steps were expressed with infinitive phrases that were grammatically dependent on "were taught" (ἐδιδάχθητε) from the previous verse.

TRANSLATION ANALYSIS: The infinitive phrases in verses 22–24 reflect either an underlying imperative force or an indicative force. In either case, Paul was reminding them of prior teaching (aorist tense of the head noun, ἐδιδάχθητε). The question is whether he recalled actions that they must still put into practice (impv. force) or whether he recalled their definitive life transformation when they had come to Christ by faith (indic. force). Grammatically, either meaning is possible (Wallace, 1996, 605). Both meanings fit Paul's theology, since he often portrayed both an initial move from the old self to the new self and the ongoing process of putting aside the old and putting on the new. Believers cultivated what Christ had already planted in their lives. This specific context favors an imperative force for three reasons. First, in this section of the letter Paul focused on how the readers were to live. Second, Ephesians 4:20–24 gives a general blueprint for living (with commands), and Ephesians 4:25–5:2 describes the specific areas of implementation. Third, "be renewed" (ἀνανεοῦσθαι, pres. inf.) makes more sense as part of a sequence of ongoing commands rather than as an ongoing process couched between two definitive actions of the past. For these reasons, it is more likely that Paul was reminding readers of their ongoing responsibility to put these teachings into practice.

Paul first reminded the readers (ὑμᾶς, "you") that they were to put off the old person. To "put off" (ἀποτίθημι) something was an image inspired by taking off clothing, and it meant to disassociate oneself from something (BDAG, s.v. "ἀποτίθημι" 1b, p. 123). In Romans 13:12 and Colossians 3:8, Paul exhorted readers to put off godless actions, but in Ephesians 4:22, the whole old person was to be cast aside. Paul used "the old person" (ὁ παλαιὸς ἄνθρωπος) to denote the readers' former lives that had been lived in darkness, apart from Christ. Paul further relegated the readers' old self to the past. The old person had been "according to the former way of life" (κατὰ τὴν προτέραν ἀναστροφὴν). The old person and its way of life needed to be rejected as an ongoing influence in the readers' lives.

Paul further cast the old person in a negative light. The old person "is being corrupted" (τὸν φθειρόμενον, pres. ptc.), or was undergoing an ongoing "deterioration of the inner life" (BDAG, s.v. "φθείρω" 2a, p. 1054). Paul continued to retain the tight connection from Ephesians 4:17–19 between outward sin and distorted inner thinking and affections. Specifically, this inward corruption occurred "because of deceitful desires" (κατὰ τὰς ἐπιθυμίας τῆς ἀπάτης) at work within a person. As sin took root in a person who did not know Christ, this sin moved aggressively and deceptively, creating corrosive effects in the person's life. Paul told his readers to want nothing to do with that sad state of affairs.

4:23. The second stage of the process (added with the conj. δέ, "and") that Paul's readers had been taught was that they should continually be renewed (pres. pass. inf., ἀνανεοῦσθαι) in their way of thinking. Significantly, Paul did not immediately charge readers to put on the new person after taking off the old person, lest the process seem routine or unthinking. Ongoing inward renewal had to accompany those actions. Paul spoke of a renewal that took place "in the spirit of your mind" (τῷ πνεύματι τοῦ νοὸς ὑμῶν). Paul described the renewal of the believer's own spirit (cf. most English translations; Rom. 8:16; 1 Cor. 2:11), rather than renewal of the mind by means of the Holy Spirit (though the Spirit was undoubtedly central in the process of renewing the believer—Eph. 3:16). Paul communicated a similar thought in Romans 12:2, where he spoke of transformation through the "renewal" (ἀνακαίνωσις) of the readers' minds. The inclusion of "spirit" (πνεῦμα) in Ephesians 4:23 may have captured the personal and active center of life that animated the readers' actions. Paul presented this vibrant and productive renewing of the "mind" (νοῦς) as a contrast to the dark and futile "thinking" (νοῦς) of unbelievers in 4:17–18.

4:24. Paul's readers had been instructed in a third way (linked to the other two with καί, "and"), which consisted of their responsibility "to put on the new person" (ἐνδύσασθαι τὸν καινὸν ἄνθροωπον). This third action stood as the necessary completion to putting off the old person. Paul enlisted the term "put on" (ἐνδύω), which described putting on clothing, to picture readers letting a new identity reconfigure everything about them, but from the inside out (v. 23). The readers' identity had changed from old to new (Eph. 2:1–10), so they needed to adopt the way of life of the new person instead of the old person (cf. Rom. 13:14; Gal. 3:27; Col. 3:10).

Just as Paul had further described the old person in Ephesians 4:22, he elaborated on the new person in this verse. The new person "has been created" (τὸν κτισθέντα), or fashioned, into something powerfully different. Paul had already occasionally sprinkled in theologically rich language of new creation in the letter. When God saved believers, he created them anew in Christ as individuals (2:10) and as part of his new humanity in Christ (2:15). This new creation was closely connected to God's gracious gift of new life in Christ (2:5). Here Paul said that believers were created "according to

God" (κατὰ θεόν), which meant that God himself epitomized what new creation in Christ looked like (cf. Rom. 8:29; Col. 3:10). Instead of becoming like the idols they had worshipped in their former lives (cf. Ps. 115:8), Paul's Gentile readers had been made new so that they could resemble God's character more and more. In Christ Jesus, believers were being restored into the original image and likeness of God, which had been God's original design for humanity (Gen. 1:26–27; cf. Irenaeus, *Haer*. 3.18.1; Marius Victorinus, *Epistle to the Ephesians* 2.4.23–24, ACCS, 164).

Paul specified what was to characterize his readers' new existence in the likeness of God. The new person was created "in [a state of] righteousness and holiness in the truth" (ἐν δικαιοσύνῃ καὶ ὁσιότητι τῆς ἀληθείας, with "in" [ἐν] conveying "a state or condition," cf. BDAG, s.v. "ἐν" 2, p. 327). This was the identity that Paul's readers were called to embrace and live out. The new person exhibited "righteousness" (δικαιοσύνη) and "holiness" (ὁσιότης). Used together, righteousness and holiness depicted excellent moral character and wholehearted devotion to God. These qualities were grounded in "the truth" (τῆς ἀληθείας, gen. of source, modifying both "righteousness" and "holiness"). This was appropriate, since truth was found only in Jesus (Eph. 4:21), and Jesus was the one in whom believers experienced a new existence (Eph. 2:5, 10, 15). The knowledge of the truth that eluded those with darkened understanding (Eph. 4:18) was the starting point for being restored into the image of God.

Love One Another (4:25–5:2)

Paul's readers needed to put off destructive behaviors and put on love for other believers, because they were all dearly loved members of Christ's one body.

4:25. After having set the stage with an overall vision of putting on a new identity in Christ (4:20–24), Paul made a strong shift (διό, "therefore") to applying this vision to specific areas of conduct. Paul continued to reflect the same general pattern of putting off the old and putting on the new. He also included crisp theological reasoning to support these changed actions in order to encourage the renewal of his readers' minds (Eph. 4:23). "Each" (ἕκαστος) individual reader was expected to work out this vision in cooperation with others, keeping other believers' spiritual health and growth in mind.

First, Paul instructed his readers to put off falsehood and speak truthfully to their neighbors, since they were united together in one body. Paul expected the readers to "put off falsehood" (ἀποθέμενοι τὸ ψεῦδος), returning to the verb "put off" (ἀποτίθημι) from Ephesians 4:22. This further highlighted the connection between the general command and the specific implementation. Specifically, Paul told the readers to put off "falsehood" (τὸ ψεῦδος), which in this context of interpersonal relationships meant telling lies to other people.

The flip side of putting off falsehood was that Paul's readers were to "speak truth" (λαλεῖτε . . . ἀλήθειαν). Falsehood and truth were natural opposites, so Paul logically forbade one and commended the other. The truth advocated for was not the spiritual truth of the gospel mentioned in Ephesians 4:21 and 4:24 but the more practical communication that corresponded to facts and helped build trust in relationships (BDAG, s.v. "ἀλήθεια" 2a, p. 42). Paul's specification that each reader speak truth "with his neighbor" (μετὰ τοῦ πλησίος αὐτοῦ) made this relational context clear. The wording of "neighbor" (πλησίον) rather than "brother" (ἀδελφός) may have arisen from Paul's dependence on Zechariah 8:16 (LXX), but in this context Paul had fellow believers in mind.

Paul directed readers to speak truth to one another, "since they are members of one another" (ὅτι ἐσμὲν ἀλλήλων μέλη). They were united together as one body of Christ. Paul provided this rationale to help spur on the renewed thinking that needed to undergird new actions (Eph. 4:22–24). Paul wanted his readers to reckon with their new corporate identity as one body in Christ and then treat each other accordingly. Paul had affirmed that believers from Jewish and Gentile backgrounds were part of the same body (Eph. 2:6), that there was just one body (Eph. 4:4), and that each part contributed to spiritual growth (Eph. 4:16). Later, he pointed out that believers were all members of Christ's body (Eph. 5:30; cf. Rom. 12:4–5; 1 Cor. 12:12–13, 27). The intimate relationships that bound believers to one another created the motivation to speak truthfully to one another.

4:26. Paul addressed anger next. Adopting exact wording from Psalm 4:5 (LXX; 4:4 in English versions), Paul warned his readers to avoid sinning against others in the midst of their anger. As had been the case with lying, lashing out in anger eroded trust and created divisions within the community of faith. Paul carried over the imperative mood of "be angry" (ὀργίζεσθε) from Psalm 4:5, though in the context of Ephesians 4:26, that first command just explained the circumstances in which the second command, "do not sin," was to be applied (as with the NIV). The accent was placed on the second command. Paul cautioned his readers that they must not sin (μὴ ἁμαρτάνετε, "do not sin"), against God or others, when they became angry.

TRANSLATION ANALYSIS: Scholars have debated the exact meaning and force of "be angry and do not sin" (ὀργίζεσθε καὶ μὴ ἁμαρτάνετε). Some argue for a dual emphasis on righteous anger and healthy responses to anger, arguing that this is the most straightforward reading of the sentence (Wallace, 1996, 491–92; Hoehner, 2002, 620–21; Arnold, 2010, 300–2). More likely, Paul stressed the second of these exhortations, without commenting on the potential benefits of righteous anger (BDF §387; Lincoln, 1990, 301–2; Schnackenburg, 1991, 207; Moritz, 1996, 90; Best, 1998, 449; Klein, 2006, 130; Thielman, 2010, 313–14). First, the remainder of verse 26 developed the topic of positive responses to anger, rather than the need to express outrage at sin or injustice. Second, the pattern throughout the passage is putting off godless practices, especially those that threaten the unity and health of the body of Christ, and replacing them with constructive habits. This would indicate that Paul was warning against the divisive effects of anger and promoting productive ways of dealing with anger instead.

As Paul's readers put off sinning in anger, they could instead put on an effective response to anger-inducing situations. Paul told them, "do not let the sun go down on your anger" (ὁ ἥλιος μὴ ἐπιδυέτω ἐπὶ παροργισμῷ ὑμῶν). Though the word for "anger" (παροργισμός) appeared just here in the NT, the cognate verb (παροργίζω) was used in Ephesians 6:4 for fathers provoking their children to anger (cf. a variant reading of Col. 3:21) and in Romans 10:19 for God using the Gentiles to provoke Israel to anger. In Ephesians 4:26, it may have been equivalent to the standard term for anger (ὀργή; Lincoln, 1990, 302; Arnold, 2010, 302), it may have signaled a stronger, festering anger (*EDNT* 2.529; Thielman, 2010, 314), or it may have pointed to what provoked people to anger (Wallace, 1996, 492). In any case, Paul recognized the dangers of not attending to anger and its underlying causes. Paul called for seeking a timely resolution to disputes that were causing anger, especially anger between fellow believers (cf. Jesus's similar directive in Matt. 5:23–24).

4:27. Paul instructed his readers that they should not, by neglecting conflict resolution, give the devil space to operate within the community of faith. Paul supplemented his direct commands about replacing harmful practices with restorative ones by providing this additional motivation (that would cultivate the renewing of his readers' minds—Eph. 4:23). Paul continued a string of prohibitions (μὴ . . . μὴ . . . μηδὲ . . .), with the last one carrying the force of "nor" and suggesting that this final action would result if the other prohibitions were neglected. Paul's readers ran the risk of opening a door to the devil's pernicious work in their midst. Paul told them that they must not "give an opportunity" (δίδοτε τόπον; BDAG, 1012 s.v. "τόπος" 4, p. 1012) to the "devil" (διάβολος), to create a chance for him to wreak havoc among believers. This metaphorical understanding of "giving place" as "giving opportunity" did not rule out the devil actually taking ground (cf. Arnold, 2010, 302–3) or gaining a "foothold" (NIV, NLT) in the lives of believers, individually or corporately. The devil engaged in schemes against God's people (Eph. 6:11), attempted to catch believers in his traps (1 Tim. 3:7; 2 Tim. 2:26), and otherwise sought to ruin believers (1 Peter 5:8). Paul did not want his readers to even entertain giving him an opportunity to sow further discord.

4:28. Paul pivoted next to the topic of stealing. Paul insisted that "those who steal" (κλέπτων) "must no longer steal" (μηκέτι κλεπτέτω). Those who committed theft needed to make a clean break from this practice as part of their shedding of the old person and its ways. Those who stole from others tried to gain something that they did not work for. This focus on a negative behavior also prepared the way for Paul to highlight its opposite, positive conduct.

Instead of stealing, Paul encouraged his readers to "rather" (μᾶλλον) work hard for productive purposes. Paul used the wording "he must labor" (κοπιάτω, impv.) to convey the main action that his readers needed to put on. With "labor" (κοπιάω), Paul described exerting oneself in hard work (BDAG, s.v. "κοπιάω" 2, p. 558). The immoral shortcut of stealing was to be replaced with diligently working to provide for needed material resources. Paul expressed the means by which readers must labor using the phrase "accomplishing productive work with his own hands" (ἐργαζόμενος ταῖς ἰδίαις χερσὶν τὸ ἀγαθόν, ptc. of cause). The term "working" (ἐργάζομαι) could mean "to work hard" or, in this context, "to accomplish something through hard work" (BDAG, s.v. "ἐργάζομαι" 2, p. 389). Paul challenged those who would otherwise steal to instead accomplish something "good," or "productive" (BDAG, s.v. "ἀγαθός" 2b, p. 3) with their labor. Paul's inclusion of "with his own hands" (ταῖς ἰδίαις χερσίν) reinforced the goal of personal investment in productive activities. Paul himself had labored by working with his own hands (1 Cor. 4:12), as a tentmaker.

Paul supported the new practice of productive work with a deeper purpose (ἵνα, "in order that"). He challenged his readers to aspire to work hard "in order to have [something] to share" (ἵνα ἔχῃ μεταδιδόναι). Those who worked diligently and accumulated material resources were to share "with those who have a material need" (τῷ χρείαν ἔχοντι). In Luke 3:11, John the Baptist used similar wording to challenge people to give items they did not really need to those who lacked them. Paul appealed to these principles of solidarity and generosity to encourage his readers to devote themselves to diligent labor.

Hard Work, Material Needs, and Generosity

Paul similarly promoted hard work in 1 and 2 Thessalonians. Some believers in Thessalonica had not directly stolen from others but were presuming upon the generosity of other believers to support them. Paul recognized a sense of laziness and entitlement in the believers there. Paul told the believers to work with their hands (1 Thess. 4:11), and he pointed to his own "hard work" (κόπος) as a model for them (2 Thess. 3:8; cf. 1 Cor. 4:12). In several other places (Rom. 12:8, 13; Gal. 6:9–10; 1 Tim. 6:18; Titus 3:14), Paul espoused being generous to the needy. Paul always insisted that those who were able to work should work hard, but he also acknowledged that legitimate material needs existed and that believers should be eager to help contribute to those needs. He wanted believers to be known for both hard work and generosity.

4:29. Paul continued to identify specific areas of life that needed to be shaped by his readers' new identity in Christ. His next target was his readers' speech. Paul claimed that "all foul talk" (πᾶς λόγος σαπρός) should be eliminated from his readers' speech. With "foul" (σαπρός) Paul envisioned remarks (not so much individual words; cf. BDAG, s.v. "λόγος" 1aγ, p. 600) that were "foul" (CSB), "unwholesome" (NET, NIV, NASB), "corrupt[ing]" (ESV, NKJV, KJV), or "evil" (NRSV). Any such talk "should not come out of their mouths" (ἐκ τοῦ στόματος ὑμῶν μὴ ἐκπορευέσθω). Paul spoke vividly about the potential harm any utterance could cause once it left his readers' mouths.

In contrast (ἀλλά, "but"), Paul encouraged readers to aim to speak words that built up others according to their needs. Far from needing to be silent altogether, "if there is something good" (εἴ τις ἀγαθός) to say, then Paul implied that his readers should say it. The word "good" (ἀγαθός) was a general term that stood in opposition to "foul" (σαπρός). This beneficial speech "prompted constructive growth in the area in which it was needed" (πρὸς οἰκοδομὴν τῆς χρείας). Paul returned to the term "edification" (οἰκοδομή; Eph. 4:12, 16) to portray the image of constructive growth within the body of Christ. His repetition of "need" (χρεία) from the previous verse reinforced the value of others-centeredness in these new actions the readers were to adopt. Paul indicated that readers should be on the lookout for fellow believers' needs. God wanted to use their new lives to bless others.

The final purpose (ἵνα, "so that") for readers sharing edifying speech to those around them was "so that they might give grace to those who hear" (ἵνα δῷ χάριν τοῖς ἀκούουσιν). The potential benefit of finding timely and constructive words to share became a reality in the actual provision of grace to the recipients of those words. At a basic level, "giving grace" to someone consisted of "benefitting" them (NIV), but Paul's understanding of grace may have run deeper than that. Paul believed that the Spirit worked through people to give grace to others, or facilitate spiritual growth in their lives (Eph. 3:2, 7; 4:7; cf. Rom. 12:6; 1 Cor. 15:10; cf. 1 Peter 2:10). The unity and spiritual growth of the body of Christ was emerging as one of Paul's chief concerns in Ephesians 4, and considerate, purposeful speech contributed to that.

4:30. Instead of moving to a new practical topic of life-change, Paul paused to exhort his readers, "and do not grieve the Holy Spirit of God" (καὶ μὴ λυπεῖτε τὸ πνεῦμα τὸ ἅγιον τοῦ θεοῦ). Paul probably intended for this admonition to strengthen all of the practical instruction he was giving in this section. Paul's use of "and" (καί) suggested a general correlation between the preceding instructions and the importance of honoring the Spirit's presence in their lives. "The Holy Spirit of God" (τὸ πρεῦμα τὸ ἅγιον τοῦ θεοῦ) mediated God's holy presence in the lives of Paul's readers (Eph. 2:22) and facilitated a relational intimacy between them and Jesus (Eph. 3:16–17). In this relational context, they ran the risk of "grieving" (λυπέω) the Spirit through sin and selfishness towards other believers. Jesus had been "grieved" (συλλυπέω) in similar circumstances (Mark 3:5), when he had observed religious leaders disregarding the wellbeing of a fellow Jew who was suffering.

Paul reinforced the gravity of grieving the Spirit by reminding his readers that the Spirit was the one "by whom you were sealed" (ἐν ᾧ ἐσφραγίσητε). This sealing by the Spirit (who was himself the seal; cf. Eph. 1:13) communicated that Paul's readers belonged to God, as evidenced by the Spirit's enduring presence in their lives (cf. the connection between grieving the Spirit and the Spirit being in the midst of God's people in Isa. 63:10–11; cf. Watts, 2009, 228). The image of a seal drew upon the practice in the ancient world of physically sealing items with wax seals as an indication of ownership (BDAG, s.v. "σφραγίζω"

3, p. 980). The Spirit's presence marked them as God's beloved children "until the day of redemption" (εἰς ἡμέραν ἀπολυτρώσεως), or the day when Christ would deliver them from sin, evil, and death, and put their status as God's victorious children on full display (Rom. 8:18–19). The redemption that was secured in Christ, through the shedding of his blood on the cross (Eph. 1:7), was accompanied by the gift of the Spirit. When Paul's readers thoughtlessly sinned against others in the ways mentioned in this passage, they grieved the Spirit who bound them together as God's adopted children. The logic was also similar to 1 Corinthians 8:11–12, where sin against fellow believers for whom Christ died constituted sin against Christ.

The Day of Redemption

Paul often spoke about a future "day" that consisted of the return of Christ in salvation and judgment (Rom. 2:5, 16; 1 Cor. 1:8; 3:13; 5:5; 2 Cor. 1:14; Phil. 1:6, 10; 2:16; 1 Thess. 5:2, 4; 2 Thess. 1:10; 2:2, 3; 2 Tim. 1:12, 18; 4:8). The return of Christ would launch the full establishment of the kingdom of God on earth. As God's anointed Messiah, Jesus would fulfill his kingly role of rewarding his loyal subjects and punishing his enemies on that day. The day had its origins in the day of the Lord, a day of God's decisive judgment that was promised in the OT (Isa. 13:9; Ezek. 30:2–3; Joel 2:11; Zeph. 1:14–16; Mal. 4:5). But recipients of God's grace and forgiveness would also experience the day of the Lord as the completion of their redemption, a redemption that had been inaugurated in Christ's first advent, through his sacrificial death (Eph. 1:7) and resurrection (1 Thess. 4:14). The Spirit's indwelling presence gave Paul's readers the assurance that their final redemption was coming.

4:31. Paul directed his readers to remove all bitterness, wrath, anger, heated arguments, and slander from their church community, along with all other kinds of evil. Paul used this verse to give brief examples of other harmful actions that he wanted his readers to eliminate from their lives. This fit with his overall theme of putting off the old self. A common thread in the list was unhealthy emotional reactions to feeling wronged by others, and so this verse tied together well with Paul's previous instructions on conflict resolution in Ephesians 4:26–27. Paul strung together these vices with the repetition of the conjunction "and" (καί), which had the effect of suggesting that the list could go on and on. Paul insisted that these behaviors "be removed" (pass. impv., ἀρθήτω) from their lives and interactions with one another (ἀφ' ὑμῶν, "from you").

Paul targeted "bitterness" (πικρία) first. Bitterness described relationships marred by entrenched distrust and harsh communication, perhaps in response to wrongs or perceived wrongs. When bitterness simmered in a person's life, it created a toxic effect in relationships. Paul told his readers to discard this demeanor as part of the old person (cf. Rom. 3:14).

The term "wrath" (θυμός) described deep-seated anger that resided in a person (BDAG, s.v. "θυμός" 2, p. 461). While God's holy wrath was rightly expressed against evil, sinfulness often corrupted human responses of wrath, and so Paul often grouped wrath with other sinful behaviors that had no place in the Christian life (2 Cor. 12:20; Gal. 5:20; Col. 3:8). This negative expression can rightly be translated as "rage" (NIV, NLT).

Relatedly, Paul said that "anger" (ὀργή) must be done away with. The term for anger often carried the connotation of heightened emotional disturbance (BDAG, s.v. "ὀργή" 1, p. 720). "Wrath" (θυμός) and "anger" (ὀργή) surfaced in poetic parallelism in many places in the Septuagint, especially when referring to God's wrath and anger against sin and injustice. Human wrath and anger were paired in Psalm 37:8 (36:8 LXX); Proverbs 15:1; 21:14; 27:4. As was the case with wrath, human anger in response to anger-inducing situations rarely reflected God's righteous anger and in fact often undermined righteousness (cf. James 1:20).

Continuing the chain of vices, Paul critiqued "heated arguments" (κραυγή), which can also be translated as "clamor" (NASB, ESV, NKJV, KJV), "quarreling" (NET), "brawling" (NIV), or "shouting" (CSB), from a word that typically described shouting or crying out (BDAG, s.v. "κραυγή" 1a, p. 565). Nestled in a list of harmful reactions to provocations, the word likely referred to loud words exchanged in the midst of a heated dispute.

Paul concluded his list by denouncing "slander" (βλασφημία). In this context, with its emphasis on interpersonal offenses, the term highlighted disrespectful and defaming speech towards others (BDAG, s.v. "βλασφημία" a, p. 178). The term contributed to the picture of malignant reactions to others that threatened to erode the unity and goodwill that ought to exist among believers.

4:32. Paul promoted a collection of Christ-like behaviors that stood in opposition to the harmful practices of the previous verse (δέ, "but"). As such, the actions represented the new-self qualities that the readers were to put on, especially in their responses to other imperfect people in their church community. Paul wanted his readers to be characterized by (γίνομαι, "become") specific virtues that reflected their identity as new people in Christ.

First, Paul directed his readers to be kind and tenderhearted toward one another. The adjective "kind" (χρηστός) communicated goodwill or benevolence toward others (BDAG, s.v. "χρηστός" 3b, p. 1090) and stemmed from God's own kindness to humanity (Luke 6:35; 1 Peter 2:3). Paul commended being "tenderhearted" (εὔσπλαγχνος) alongside being kind. The word conveyed the idea of warm and genuine affection flowing from the inner core of a person. Kindness and tenderheartedness formed striking contrasts with the boiling anger and caustic speech of the previous verse.

Paul presented "forgiving" (χαριζόμενοι, temp. adv. ptc.) as another practice that ought to accompany being kind and tenderhearted. He exhorted his readers to forgive "one another" (ἑαυτοῖς, with the sense of reciprocal action within the community of believers). When strained relationships developed within the church, Paul's readers needed to be ready to "forgive" (χαρίζομαι), which signified generously and charitably pardoning an offender rather than harboring resentment and anger (BDAG, s.v. "χαρίζομαι" 3, p. 1078).

Paul challenged his readers to forgive one another according to the pattern of how (καθὼς καί, "just as also") "God forgave you" (ὁ θεὸς . . . ἐχαρίσατο ὑμῖν). God's prior forgiveness of Paul's readers was to inspire their forgiveness of one another. God had forgiven believers "in Christ" (ἐν Χριστῷ). Earlier in the letter (Eph. 1:7; 2:16), Paul had accentuated the sacrificial death of Christ on the cross as the defining moment of God's saving plans. In this verse, "in Christ" returned to Jesus's sacrificial love on the cross once again (5:1–2). Paul celebrated God's amazing forgiveness through the love of Christ as the theological underpinning that fostered the renewal of his readers' minds, so that they could more wholeheartedly put on the new practice of forgiving one another.

5:1. With "therefore" (οὖν), Paul introduced a logical extension to letting God's forgiveness fuel the readers' forgiveness. Paul instructed readers to "be imitators of God" (γίνεσθε . . . μιμηταὶ τοῦ θεοῦ) in their actions toward one another. With the exhortation "be" or "become" (γίνομαι, pres. impv.), Paul stressed that imitating God was the norm for believers' lives. They were to take their cues from God in the way they lived.

Paul appealed to his readers' status "as dearly loved children" (ὡς τέκνα ἀγαπητά) to reinforce the need to imitate God and his love. This resembled Jesus's logic in Matthew 5:44–45, where he commanded his disciples to love their enemies "so that you may be [or become] sons of your Father" (ὅπως γένησθε υἱοὶ τοῦ πατρός). Children were expected to reflect the traits of the father. Paul's readers were "beloved" or "dearly loved" (ἀγαπητά) children, which was a relational gift bestowed as a result of adoption into God's family through faith in Jesus Christ (Eph. 1:5). This description of the readers as "dearly loved" children prepared Paul to zoom in on love as God's primary virtue the readers were to imitate in Ephesians 5:2.

5:2. Paul connected (καί, "and") his command to be imitators of God with the command to "walk in love" (περιπατεῖτε ἐν ἀγάπῃ). The resurfacing of the image of "walking" (περιπατέω) from Ephesians 4:17 signaled the conclusion of the entire section (Eph. 4:17–5:2) and bolstered the emphasis on practical behavior. The addition of "in love" (ἐν ἀγάπῃ) appropriately summarized the gist of Paul's instructions in Ephesians 4:25–5:2. Walking or living in love consisted of prioritizing the interests of others and supporting others in concrete ways such as truth-telling, generosity, conflict resolution, edifying speech, and forgiveness.

Paul pointed to Christ Jesus as the example who propelled Paul's readers forward in their walk of love (using καθὼς καί, "just as also"; cf. Eph. 4:32). In his earthly ministry, Christ (ὁ Χριστός) had done two things that served as examples for believers. First, "he loved us" (ἠγάπησεν ἡμᾶς). Christ's love was the standard for how Paul's readers strove to love. Paul grouped himself with his readers as a recipient of Christ's love. Paul had already featured God's love (Eph. 1:4, 6; 2:4; 3:17, 19) and believers' love for one another (Eph. 1:15; 4:2, 15, 16) elsewhere in the letter. Here he combined the two ideas in a powerful conclusion to the section.

Christ's love was an active love, as explained by the second clause, "he gave himself up for us" (παρέδωκεν ἑαυτὸν ὑπὲρ ἡμῶν; cf. Gal. 2:20 and Eph. 5:25). The expression "gave himself up" (παραδίδωμι ἑαυτόν) referred to willingly handing over oneself to an undesirable fate (BDAG, s.v. "παραδίδωμι" 1b, p. 762) and recalled Jesus's obedient march to the cross to suffer and die. Christ Jesus had given himself up "for us" (ὑπὲρ ἡμῶν), or on behalf of Paul and his readers. Christ had modeled a love that had the best interests of the recipients in mind. As a result of Christ's self-surrender, Paul and his readers had experienced deliverance from sin and reconciliation to God (Eph. 1:7; 2:16).

Paul applauded Christ's willing death as a sacrificial offering. Christ had given himself up "as an offering and sacrifice to God" (προσφορὰν καὶ θυσίαν τῷ θεῷ; the two acc. nouns modify ἑαυτόν as pred. acc.). The closely related terms "offering" (προσφορά) and "sacrifice" (θυσία) meant "something given or offered" (BDAG, s.v. "προσφορά" 2, p. 887) and "something sacrificed" (BDAG, s.v. "θυσία" 2, p. 462), respectively. Together, the terms portrayed Jesus's giving up of himself in death as a sacrificial offering presented "to God" (τῷ θεῷ). Christ had died for the sake of Paul and his readers, but his sacrificial offering had been made to God. Paul then indicated God's acceptance of Christ's sacrifice, saying that the offering "had resulted in a pleasing aroma" (εἰς ὀσμὴν εὐωδίας) to God. Christ's offering of himself on the cross had accomplished its intended purpose. Paul hoped that his readers would aspire to walk in this kind of active, productive love that truly benefited its recipients.

Christ's Sacrificial Offering to God

The people of Israel had obediently presented offerings and sacrifices to God within the context of a covenantal relationship with him. God had prescribed sacrifices for a variety of purposes, including to inaugurate covenants, to atone for the people's sins, and to allow the people to experience fellowship with God (Beckwith, *NDBT*, 756–58). The sacrifices had often required the death of an animal, whose shed blood represented the animal's life, which had been taken away in the sacrifice. Paul drew upon two familiar terms from the Septuagint (προσφορά and especially θυσία) to relate Jesus's death to sacrifices made to God under the old covenant, particularly as understood through the lens of the Passover (Exod. 12) and the suffering servant's sacrifice (Isa. 52:13–53:12; especially 53:10). In various places in the LXX, the acceptability of the sacrificial offering had been indicated with the description of the offering as a "pleasing aroma" (cf. Gen. 8:21; Exod. 29:18; Lev. 1:9; Num. 28:2; cf. Phil. 4:18). Christ's sacrifice on the cross was pleasing to God as the complete and final offering for sin.

THEOLOGICAL FOCUS

The exegetical idea (Paul's readers needed to put off the spiritually resistant old person and its distorted thinking and behavior, be inwardly renewed in Christ, and put on the new person with Christlike treatment of other believers in areas such as constructive speech, conflict resolution, generosity, and forgiveness) leads to this theological focus: Believers should embrace their new identity in Christ and express this new identity by their loving treatment of fellow believers.

The new identity that believers embrace must push aside an old identity shaped by their own sinful participation in a fallen world. Fallen humanity is described in stark terms throughout the passage. Unbelievers are spiritually resistant to God, ignorant of his glorious character, and unresponsive to his truth (4:17–18). Left to their own devices, they spiral downward into darkened thinking and an unquenchable thirst for sinful pleasures (4:19). In short, they are separated from a life-giving relationship with the God who makes all things new (4:18).

Believers experience a wholesale makeover when they encounter Christ (4:20). His ministry changes their spiritual status and gives them a new identity that is centered in Christ Jesus. God has forgiven them in Christ and has guaranteed their redemption when Christ returns. As the Spirit dwells in their lives, their thinking is renewed and they are refashioned into the likeness of the righteous and holy God they worship. Their present identity and future destiny is forever altered, and there is no looking back (4:22–24).

Believers are called to translate this radical new identity into new practices in all areas of life (4:25–5:2). They must especially value the body of Christ and be purposeful about building up rather than tearing down their fellow believers. Insensitivity or poor reactions to other believers can lead to divisions (4:25), vulnerability to the devil's schemes (4:27), and grieving the Holy Spirit (4:30). When a strong commitment to love prevails (5:1–2), believers experience the fullness of new life in Christ and participate in the strengthening of a unified body of Christ. Believers should follow in the footsteps of Christ, who lovingly laid down his life for their forgiveness and salvation (5:2).

PREACHING AND TEACHING STRATEGIES

Exegetical and Theological Synthesis

Continuing with the "practical" section of Ephesians, Paul exhorted the church how to live in light of their union with Christ. The Ephesians were to avoid the lifestyle of the Gentiles—idolatry, sensuality, selfish anger, and corrupt speech—and the apostle commanded them to put on the new lifestyle of love, sexual purity, putting aside anger, and cultivating truthful and edifying speech. The old ways grieved the Holy Spirit who had "sealed" them, marking them as authentic and owned by God.

Behind the old, self-indulgent lifestyle was a dark mind and hard heart (4:17–18), but Paul contended that in Christ, the mind was new and the heart was transformed. New identity in Christ needed to change the way the Ephesians thought and acted, especially within the local church. Paul described fellow believers as "neighbors" and "members of one another" (4:25). Thus they were to no longer sin against one another by lying (4:25), stealing (4:28), or slandering (4:31). Instead they were to speak the truth, deal with conflict constructively (4:26), work with their own hands so they could share with others (4:28), build up others with their words (4:29), and speak tender words of forgiveness (4:32). Above all, Paul reminded the Ephesian believers that they must love one another just as Christ had loved them (5:2).

Preaching Idea

New life in Christ sparks a new style of living.

Contemporary Connections

What does it mean?

What does it mean that new life in Christ sparks a new style of living? When a person has a heart transplant, he or she may be enabled to take on a new lifestyle—golf, tennis, and travel are now possible. That is what Christ does for us spiritually. He changes us from the inside by sharing his eternal life. This gives us a new set of motivations and new power for obedience. Ezekiel 36 prophesied how God would send his Spirit to give us hearts of flesh for hearts of stone. A medical condition might help illustrate the heart of stone, or as verses 18 and 19 put it: "hardness of heart" and a "calloused" heart. That condition is "familial dysautonomia," a genetic disease that affects sensory neurons. One of its many symptoms is insensitivity to pain. People with this condition do not know when they have hurt themselves. Just so, without the work of the Holy Spirit, we are deaf to God and insensate to his promptings. But now in Christ we can (and should) set aside the old ways of sensuality and greed and begin to act in accord with our new identity in Christ by speaking the truth, no longer stealing, and letting no corrupt talk escape our mouths.

Is it true?

Is it true that new life in Christ sparks a new style of living? Some listeners, discouraged in the battle against sins such as pornography or explosive anger, may doubt the preaching idea. In that case, a flesh-and-blood example of someone who has put off foul talk, stealing, or bitterness might demonstrate that the preaching idea is both true and attainable. For example, the testimony of superstar Kanye West shows someone who went from "I Am a God" (a track in the 2013 album *Yeezus*) to *Jesus Is King*, a 2019 album. One example of Kanye's repentance might be illustrated by his depiction of women. Formerly he objectified women in obscene sexual lyrics, but in his 2018 album, *Ye*, he asks God to forgive him because he is afraid of karma and now sees that women should be nurtured rather than something to conquer.[2]

In a day of relativism and tolerance, one of the ideas supporting the preaching idea may need backing—the strident depiction of unbelievers found in verses 17–19.

Now what?

If new life in Christ sparks a new style of living, how might we put that into practice? Perhaps by developing new habits that will result in a change of lifestyle. For example, to let no corrupting talk emanate from our mouths (4:29), we might curtail the amount of corrupt talk that enters our ears. As the computer adage says, "Garbage in, garbage out." To discover the

2 For a thoughtful analysis of West's radical shift, see Eugene Park, "Kanye West: From 'I Am a God' to 'Jesus Is King,'" The Gospel Coalition, October 28, 2019, https://www.thegospelcoalition.org/article/kanye-west-god-jesus-king.

amount of corrupt speech in a movie we are contemplating watching, we might adopt a new lifestyle of reading reviews from a trustworthy source like Kids-In-Mind. To forgive and love one another (4:32; 5:2), we might encourage listeners to regularly examine their consciences. In fact, we could place a moment of silence in the sermon itself to allow listeners to do this. The Spirit might prompt some listeners to apologize for their angry outburst last Tuesday, or to speak gently and kindly to their children.

The use of examples from actual cases can provide models of other people who are succeeding in developing a new lifestyle. The examples might come from a high school student who is learning to put off the old way of cheating on tests. Perhaps an executive who travels often is learning how to put off workaholism. Mike Breaux, former teaching pastor of Willow Creek Community Church, shared a simple trick he uses when going to the gym. To avoid looking lustfully at the lithe athletes, he takes out his contact lenses, making everyone a blur! The sidebar gives an illustration of verse 28, "Let the thief no longer steal, but rather let him labor . . . so that he may have something to share with anyone in need."

Labor with Your Own Hands to Share

Every year Tiny Tim's Toy Foundation in Utah gives away about 100,000 wooden toy cars to children's hospitals, charities around the world, and churches. To cut and shape the wood for the simple cars, owner Alton Thacker uses a volunteer workforce with an average age of eighty, and most of cars are painted by inmates at the Central Utah Correctional Facility. Retiree Wade Bender, who delivers the unfinished cars to the prison, has noticed tears in the eyes of the felons as he hands them boxes, especially before the holidays. Bender says, "They'll tell us, 'This is the first time I've done something for somebody else, thank you.' Many of them are fathers." (*Washington Post*, Dec. 11, 2018)

Creativity in Presentation

Adopting a new lifestyle is another way of saying "be imitators of God" (5:1). The idea of imitation could be illustrated with the old "telephone game." In that game, someone whispers a short paragraph into the ear of his or her neighbor, who whispers it to the next person, on down the line, until the last person says aloud the remnants of the paragraph. The original message is usually warped, often in humorous ways, because imitation failed little by little. If the preaching-teaching context for this message is children's church or youth group, the game *Dance, Dance Revolution* for PlayStation could illustrate the concept of imitation. The goal of the game is to follow an intricate series of instructions (dance steps) as long as you can while keeping up with a driving beat. The steps are indicated with arrows of where to place your feet, and when too many mistakes occur (failure to imitate well), the turn is over.

The command of Ephesians 5:1—be imitators of God as beloved children—can be illustrated with the story of Father Brennan Manning (sidebar).

Imitation Based on Love (Ephesians 5:1)

Brennan Manning's best friend growing up was Ray Brennan. They did everything together, including joining the army. When a grenade was thrown into their foxhole, Ray looked at his friend, smiled, and threw himself on the grenade. It exploded and killed him, but saved Manning. When Manning later became a priest he was instructed to take the name of a saint, so he took the name Brennan. Manning emulated his friend Brennan, chose to be called by the same name, and determined to find ways to lay down his own life for others. (Recounted in Smith, 2009, 142)

The contrast between the old lifestyle before receiving the life of Christ and the new lifestyle in Christ could be conveyed by speaking from two locations on the platform. "Before new life" could be expounded in one location, and then "New lifestyle" in another. Even if stationary behind the pulpit, the preacher might face one direction and then the other, or even use a simple gesture to show the contrast.

The metaphor of clothing ("put off," "put on") suggests a more elaborate visual component. Using pictures or demonstration, the preacher might show an individual dressed in ugly clothes and then re-dressed in clean and attractive clothes. The person could be a young person who volunteers to come to the stage, or could be yourself. As you describe the old, "Gentile" ways in the first half of the preaching idea, you could take off a discolored hat, a threadbare jacket, and an outdated necktie. The opposite process could take place for the second half of the preaching idea with clean and attractive clothes.

The long string of imperatives in this passage might overwhelm the ears of the listeners, so a visual aid that simply categorizes the commands might aid comprehension. The list can use colors, fonts, or spacing to indicate negative and positive commands:

Do Not:	Do:
Speak falsehood (4:25)	*Speak the truth* (4:25)
Sin when angry (4:26)	
Give the devil a foothold (4:27)	
Steal (4:28)	*Work hard so you can share* (4:28)
Use foul talk (4:29)	*Use speech that edifies* (4:29)
Grieve the Holy Spirit (4:30)	
React in bitterness, rage, anger, heated arguments, or slander (4:31)	*Be kind, tenderhearted, forgiving one another* (4:32)
	Imitate God (5:1)
	Walk in love (5:2)

The metaphor of being "sealed" with the Spirit could be taught with visual aids. When I (Jeffrey) taught this passage, I brought sealing wax and an impress to the stage and went through the process of melting wax and sealing a letter. I also brought other kinds of seals such as a name plate on a book to indicate ownership, and a notary's impress to indicate that a document is genuine. A cross-reference to Matthew 27:66, the seal that was placed on the tomb of Jesus, can help explain that a seal was a sign of authority, not an airtight stopper used when canning vegetables.

The sidebar provides an illustration of how people who are callous and stubborn (Eph. 4:19) may be deaf to the destruction they are headed toward.

Mount St. Helens and the Zone of Silence

On May 18, 1980, Mount St. Helens erupted in the state of Washington. Fifty-seven people died. The explosion could be heard six hundred miles away, but a number of people rescued within a few miles of the mountain testified to the most amazing thing: they didn't hear the explosion. How could that be? Scientists describe the "zone of silence" that occurs with the tremendous upward thrust of steam and debris. That force is so powerful that it actually carries sound with it. The sound bounces off of the atmosphere so that people at a distance hear it, but those nearest to the destruction hear nothing. It is possible that someone like stubborn, old Harry Truman—the man who, tragically, refused to leave his cabin even though warned repeatedly—didn't know he was about to die. He had ignored the warnings and placed himself so close to danger that he was deaf to it.

No matter what kind of outline we create and fill with creative illustrations, the point to emphasize is that those who trust Jesus have been made new, so now we should strive to behave according to our new identity. New life in Christ sparks a new style of living.

A possible outline:

- We're no longer who we were (4:17–19).
- Now we have new life in Christ (4:20–24).
- So let's adopt a new lifestyle (4:25–5:2).

DISCUSSION QUESTIONS

1. Does the Bible's depiction of the "Gentiles" in Ephesians 4:17–19 seem unfair to you? Why or why not?
2. Why is the life of the mind important—that is, how do beliefs lead to actions? Give an example.
3. What heart conditions lead to slander?
4. What heart conditions lead to forgiving one another?
5. What does speech that gives grace sound like? Give an example.
6. Has someone extended tenderness and kindness to you? Tell your story.
7. What can you learn about loving others by looking at Christ's sacrificial love for us?
8. What is one step of obedience from this passage that you can take immediately? Why do you think that the Holy Spirit is nudging you in this direction?

Ephesians 5:3–14

EXEGETICAL IDEA

Paul's readers needed to reject sexual immorality, greed, and other vices that clashed with their kingdom identity and live instead as Christ's light, being ready to shine Christ's powerful, transforming light in a dark world.

THEOLOGICAL FOCUS

Believers should reject conduct that clashes with their identity and live as Christ's light in a dark world.

PREACHING IDEA

Live as Christ's light in the midst of a dark culture.

PREACHING POINTERS

Paul had devoted much space to how his readers should live consistently with their new spiritual status. This suggested that some of Paul's readers were still vulnerable to falling back into the sinful patterns of their past. The Gentile world was known for its sexual immorality, wild parties, violent gladiator contests, and extravagant living. Other entanglements in sin were more subtle. Paul's readers ran the risk of treating sin too lightly and not understanding how out of place sin was in the Christian life. In this section, Paul wanted to draw distinct, unambiguous lines between two opposing cultures. The first was the rotten culture of unchecked sinful desires and disobedience. The second was the life-renewing culture of God's kingdom. For Paul, the choice was clear, and there was no middle ground. His readers needed to reject the sinful vestiges of their past and shine Christ's light into the darkness around them.

The Ephesians' story is a twenty-first-century story too. The sexual revolution of the 1960s has continued unabated, as seen when the popularity of the acronym YOLO, "You Only Live Once," is used to justify many self-indulgent activities. The surrounding culture may say "your body is your own" when it celebrates sexual immorality in movies, but God says something different. Then there is the sin of covetousness. It can saturate the church, not just the culture. The advertising industry tries to create discontent and desire for whatever is new, shiny, fast, and sexy. Credit cards make luxuries possible while they chain people with "easy" payments; and today even credit cards seem quaint as we pay with our phones—a fingerprint, pleasant ding, and the item is ours! This passage also addresses our speech. Imagine the manual laborer who wants to honor Christ yet finds himself slipping into crude speech. When break time comes his coworkers gather for coffee and off-color stories, and he finds it hard to swim against the tide. This passage helps believers live as light, and it gives hope that we can do so because of Christ. Thus, we can live as Christ's light in the midst of a dark culture.

SHINE CHRIST'S LIGHT IN A DARK WORLD (5:3–14)

LITERARY STRUCTURE AND THEMES (5:3–14)

Ephesians 5:3–14 relates closely to prior material, which prescribed community conduct that reflected the character of God. But the focus in this section moves from walking in the love of Christ to walking in the light of Christ. This section does not follow a linear path but instead revisits similar ideas from various angles and explores different aspects of choosing light over darkness.

The passage has two sections and a transitional verse (Eph. 5:7) in the middle. Though the conjunction "for" (γάρ) ties verse 8 to verse 7, the conjunction "therefore" (οὖν) in verse 7 also concludes the train of thought from previous verses and helps brings 5:3–7 together as a unit. The themes of darkness and light span across verses 8 to 14, creating a second unit from 5:8–14. In Ephesians 5:3–7, Paul urged his readers to reject conduct that clashed with God's kingdom and their identity as God's holy people. In 5:8–14, Paul provided instructions about walking in the light, which meant pursuing a fruitful and God-pleasing life while shining Christ's powerful, life-changing light into the darkness.

- ***Reject Conduct That Clashes with a Kingdom Identity (5:3–7)***
- ***Live as Christ's Light (5:8–14)***

EXPOSITION (5:3–14)

Paul gave more practical instruction for Christian living in this section, this time against the backdrop of two starkly contrasting realities. In Ephesians 5:3–7, Paul insisted that living to fulfill sinful desires did not match with God's holy reign and what he expected from his devoted people. In Ephesians 5:8–14, Paul brought attention to the goodness, righteousness, and truth of Christ's light, in contrast to the worthlessness and shamefulness of darkness, seen in practices such as prostitution, drunkenness, violent public entertainment, and exposure of infants to death. But light did not only stand against darkness, it exposed darkness. Believers shined Christ's light in the darkness with the assurance that the glory and power of Christ's presence could make all things new and could even bring life to the dead.

Reject Conduct That Clashes with a Kingdom Identity (5:3–7)

Paul directed his readers to reject sexual immorality, greed, and vulgar speech, since these were not fitting for God's holy people, they did not belong in God's kingdom, and they were sins that brought judgment on disobedient people.

5:3. With a mild transition (δέ, "but"), Paul moved to a new topic, telling his readers that there should be no mention of sexual immorality, any impurity, or greed among them, as was appropriate for God's people. This verse reflected a shift from a variety of sins that weakened the community of faith to two specific types of sins that arose from deep-rooted desires. Uncontrolled lust and uncontrolled greed posed significant threats to Paul's readers, since they were prevalent in the surrounding culture and could draw them away from their love for Christ and his kingdom. Paul said that these sins "must not even be named among you" (μηδὲ ὀνομαζέσθω ἐν ὑμῖν). The use of "not even" (μηδέ) communicated a zero-tolerance mindset for such behavior (1 Cor. 5:11; cf. Eph. 5:12). To rule out naming something suggested that it was beneath one's dignity to even mention the shameful behavior (BDAG, s.v. "ὀνομάζω" 2, p. 714). Paul used this artful rhetoric to promote a complete detachment from transgressions that were so obviously contrary to the way of Christ.

Sinful Practices in the Roman World

Though philosophers praised virtue and morality as signs of an honorable life, certain practices that were sometimes tolerated among the Gentiles were not fitting for God's people. Prostitution was practiced as both a business transaction and as part of fertility cults. Female slaves, and even children, were sometimes sold into prostitution, and prostitutes were available at some Roman inns (*DNTB*, 11–12). At dinner parties and pagan festivals, men drank excessively and engaged in sexual encounters with women and younger males (Keener, 2014, 695; cf. Eph. 5:18; 1 Peter 4:3–4). Festivals in honor of the gods such as Dionysus were known for drunken revelry and sexual obscenity (*OCD*, 481). Violent gladiatorial games were popular forms of entertainment in Ephesus, Pergamum, and Laodicea (Wilson, 223, 2012). Some people in the Roman world saw abandonment and the exposure of female infants and infants with serious physical problems as a necessary evil (*DNTB*, 359). The rich and powerful in the Roman world had a voracious appetite for wealth, even to the point that kidnapping was accepted as part of the slave trade (condemned in 1 Tim. 1:10; Rev. 18:11–13). Paul insisted that God's holy people should never be involved in things that clashed so drastically with God's kingdom (Eph. 5:5).

Paul began with "sexual immorality" (πορνεία), which was often a general term for sexual activity apart from marriage (BDAG, s.v. "πορνεία" 1, p. 854, 1; Wright, *DPL*, 871). It was associated with uncontrolled or misdirected sexual passion (1 Cor. 7:2) that was typical of the lifestyle of unredeemed Gentiles (1 Thess. 4:3–5). Jesus condemned sexual immorality as a vice that proceeded from the heart and defiled a person (Mark 7:21). Paul saw no place for sexual immorality in the lives of believers.

Paul also forbade "all impurity" (ἀκαθαρσία πᾶσα), meaning any kind of impurity. Paul connected this term closely with "sexual immorality" (πορνεία) elsewhere (2 Cor. 12:21; Gal. 5:19; Col. 3:5), and Paul linked the two together here (καί, "and"). Paul had already connected all kinds of impurity with the fallen practices of the Gentiles (Eph. 4:19). God's holy people were expected to live in stark contrast to the moral impurity of those who did not know Christ (Rom. 1:24; 6:19; 1 Thess. 4:7).

Next, with "or" (ἤ), Paul warned against a different vice—"greed" (πλεονεξία). When Paul had paired this term with impurity as part of his characterization of the Gentiles' corrupted desires in Ephesians 4:19, he had used it more generally to denote a longing that could never be satisfied. Here, though, in a general list of sins, it likely meant "greed" or "covetousness" (BDAG, s.v. "πλεονεξία," p. 824; Rom. 1:29; Col. 3:5). Paul recognized the dangers of the love of money on the affections and spiritual health of believers (1 Tim. 6:9, 10). He would soon equate greed with idolatry (Eph. 5:5, cf. Col. 3:5), suggesting that a quest for more and more wealth could become the central, illegitimate, goal of life. Greed worked to undermine spiritual strength and devotion to God and thus had to be eliminated from the Christian life.

Paul charged his readers to eradicate the sins of sexual immorality, impurity, and greed, "just as it is proper for God's holy people" (καθὼς πρέπει ἁγίοις). Paul thus communicated that vigilance against these sins was an expected and reasonable response from his readers. Paul appealed to conduct that "is appropriate" (πρέπω) to his readers' identity as "God's holy people" (NIV) or "saints" (ESV, NASB, NRSV, NKJV, NET, CSB, KJV). The term (ἅγιος) described those who were chosen and set apart by God to be his special people (Eph. 1:4). Their character was supposed to reflect the holy character of God, in direct contrast to the immorality, impurity, and greed forbidden earlier in the verse.

5:4. Paul had not finished denouncing behaviors that stood in contradiction to his readers' godly calling. Picking up an earlier concern (Eph. 4:29), Paul confronted indecent speech, using three related terms. First, Paul targeted "vulgarity," or "obscenity" (αἰσχρότης) which in this context probably had vulgar or obscene speech in mind. Such speech blatantly crossed moral lines (BDAG, s.v. "αἰσχρότης," p. 29). Second, Paul ruled out "foolish talk" (μωρολογία) that deviated from the wisdom his readers were called to aspire to and impart to others (Eph. 1:17; 3:10). Third, "crude joking" (ESV), "coarse joking" (NIV), or witty banter that ventured into morally lewd territory (BDAG, s.v. "εὐτραπελία," p. 414) needed to be abandoned.

Paul supported his injunctions against morally off-color speech with the relative clause "which does not belong" (ἃ οὐκ ἀνῆκεν). Needlessly crude speech did not belong (BDAG, s.v. "ἀνήκω" 2, p. 79) or was "out of place" (NIV, ESV, NRSV) within a community of believers set apart for a holy God.

Paul wanted thanksgiving rather than indecency to characterize believers' conversations. Paul signaled a strong contrast with "but rather" (ἀλλὰ μᾶλλον) to present thanksgiving as a much better fit for God's holy people. "Thanksgiving" (εὐχαριστία) appropriately acknowledged the blessings a good God had given in creation (1 Tim. 4:3–5; James 1:17) and redemption (Eph. 1:3; 2 Cor. 4:15). Paul himself regularly gave thanks for his readers' spiritual growth (Eph. 1:16). Whereas meaningless and profane speech aligned with a world that was alienated from God, purposeful and holy thanksgiving belonged among people whose lives had been forever changed by God.

5:5. Paul reinforced his admonitions from the previous verses (γάρ, "for") with a solemn warning. Paul ensured that his readers knew that no immoral, impure, or idolatrous greedy person had an inheritance in the kingdom of God. Paul signaled his serious tone with "know this for sure" (τοῦτο . . . ἴστε γινώσκοντες).

> *TRANSLATION ANALYSIS:* The verb "know" (ἴστε, *from* οἶδα) may be understood as either "you must know" (perf. impv.) or "you [do] know" (perf. indic.). In other words, Paul was either exhorting them to reckon with the truth he was sharing (NASB, NKJV, KJV) or affirming that they already knew the truth of his subsequent statement (NIV, ESV, CSB, NRSV, NET). Either way, Paul believed that the truth he introduced carried great weight.

Paul defined "this" (τοῦτο), or what they needed to know, with a clause governed by "that" (ὅτι), followed by the content of the warning. Paul declared that "no person" (πᾶς . . . οὐκ) who fit the categories of "sexually immoral" (πόρνος) or "impure" (ἀκάθαρτος) or "greedy" (πλεονέκτης) would have an inheritance in God's kingdom. These labels took the sinful activities of verse 3 and transferred them to people who were defined by these vices. Such people stood in contrast to God's holy people (Eph. 5:3). In fact, Paul viewed the greedy person as an idolater (ὅ ἐστιν εἰδωλολάτρης, "who is an idolater"). Greedy people treated wealth as an idol. As Jesus himself had said, no one can serve two masters, and money acted as a master that competed with God for human allegiance (Matt. 6:24; Luke 16:13).

No such person—immoral, impure, or greedy—"has an inheritance" (ἔχει κληρονομίαν) in God's kingdom. This was Paul's third mention of his readers' "inheritance" (κληρονομία) in this letter (Eph. 1:14, 18). The image of an inheritance emphasized believers' status as adopted children of God (Rom. 8:15–17; Gal. 4:6–7; Eph. 1:5) and spoke of a future reward awaiting them (Eph. 1:14; Col. 1:5, 12). That reward was likely the culmination of all of the divine blessings that were already rightfully theirs in Christ (Eph. 1:3). Paul understood that an inheritance in the kingdom of God was reserved for God's people alone. The immoral, impure, and greedy, who stood in contrast to God's holy people, were excluded from that inheritance. Similarly, Jesus had taught that when people chose a master they also chose a reward linked to that master (Matt. 6:19–24; 19:23, 24).

The inheritance withheld from the immoral, impure, and greedy was an inheritance "in the kingdom of Christ and of God" (ἐν τῇ βασιλείᾳ τοῦ Χριστοῦ καὶ θεοῦ). This inheritance would arrive when the fullness of the kingdom of God appeared (1 Cor. 15:50–52; 1 Peter 1:3–5). Paul's addition of "the Christ" (ὁ Χριστός) in the expression highlighted Jesus's mediatorial role in the kingdom, as Messiah. He was God's appointed and anointed king who would implement God's reign over all things in the future kingdom (Eph. 1:9–10; Dan. 7:13–14). The righteousness, peace, and joy that marked this kingdom (Rom. 14:17) left no place for immorality and idolatry. The reign of God in Christ and the reign of sin had no overlap. People cast their lot with one kingdom or the other.

The Ethical Requirements of the Kingdom of God

Jesus had announced the full arrival of the kingdom of God as good news ("gospel"). But he had also called on people to repent in preparation for its arrival (Mark 1:14–15). Jesus called kingdom citizens to embrace the values of the kingdom in the way they lived in the present (Matt. 5:1–7:29). In the final judgment when Jesus returned as triumphant king, he would remove "sons of the evil one" for judgment and then reign forever with the sons of the kingdom (Matt. 13:37–43). It was against this backdrop that Paul presented candid warnings about the ethical requirements for entering the kingdom of God. Ephesians 5:5 strongly resembled 1 Corinthians 6:9–11 and Galatians 5:19–21. All three passages warned that people with a fundamental allegiance to sin rather than to God would "not inherit the kingdom of God" (1 Cor. 6:10; Gal. 5:21) or "have no inheritance in the kingdom of Christ and of God" (Eph. 5:5). Paul expected his readers to embrace the ethical implications of their kingdom citizenship (Phil. 3:20) by spurning their former lives of sin.

5:6. Paul continued to alert his readers to the high stakes of this battle for their loyalties. He told his readers to "let no one deceive you" (μηδεὶς ὑμᾶς ἀπατάτω) with ideas that would contradict Paul's teachings about holy living. Readers were to guard against being "deceived" or "misled" (BDAG, s.v. "ἀπατάω" 1, p. 98) "with empty words" (κενοῖς λόγοις). These empty words existed in the form of false teaching. Empty words were words not backed by truth (BDAG, s.v. "κενός" 2a, p. 539). In this case, these empty words offered false promises that people, even though they were consumed by deep-seated patterns of sin, had nothing to worry about with God.

Deceptive Teachings

False teachings that minimized the seriousness of sin posed a threat to believers in the early church. Church leaders warned readers about how deceptive such teaching could be, especially to Gentile converts to Christ (Eph. 4:14; Rom. 16:17–19; 1 Cor. 6:9; Gal. 6:7–8; James 1:15–16, 22, 26; 2 Peter 2:13–20; 1 John 3:7–10; Jude 4; Rev. 2:20). Paul had even warned the Ephesian elders of this danger when he said goodbye to them on his way to Jerusalem (Acts 20:29–30). The human heart had always been prone to the deceitfulness of sin (Eph. 4:22; Rom. 7:11; Heb. 3:13). Satan himself was "the deceiver of the whole world" (Rev. 12:9). All people, believers included, were vulnerable to deception about the power and consequences of sin.

Paul explained (γάρ, "for") that "because of these things" (διὰ ταῦτα), referring back to sins of immorality, impurity, and greed, "the wrath of God is coming" (ἔρχεται ἡ ὀργὴ τοῦ θεοῦ). Paul contrasted God's certain judgment on sin with the false teachers' empty assurances that sin was tolerable. False teachers endorsed sins that merited God's judgment. Paul made it clear that his readers should want nothing to do with these sins.

God's "wrath" (ὀργή) was his righteous response to sin and evil (Eph. 2:3; Rom. 2:5; 5:9; 1 Thess. 1:10; 5:9). Unlike human wrath (Eph. 4:26, 31) God's wrath was governed by his perfect goodness and wisdom, and he discerned the true evil of sin and its connection to a fallen world system and its ruler (Eph. 2:2). Paul's claim that God's wrath "is coming" (pres. tense, ἔρχεται) conveyed a sense of certain judgment in the future (Col. 3:6; 1 Thess. 1:10; 5:2). Similar ideas surfaced sometimes in prophetic contexts (BDF §323, 1), though Paul was not speaking himself as a prophet but as one convinced of the prophetic teachings about judgment throughout Scripture. God would carry out his wrath "on the sons of disobedience" (ἐπὶ τοὺς υἱοὺς τῆς ἀπειθείας; cf. Eph. 2:2). Those characterized by disobedient lives were judged as enemies of God's kingdom. Paul presented a choice between two kingdoms, two ways, and two allegiances. One kingdom was destined for destruction when God visited the world in holy judgment.

5:7. Paul concluded this subsection (οὖν, "therefore") and launched a new one with this transitional verse. Paul admonished his readers to recognize the reality of God's wrath and shun any partnership with disobedient people through indulging in lives of sin. Paul told the readers to "not become partners with them" (μὴ . . . γίνεσθε συμμέτχοι αὐτῶν) in their sin-saturated lives. Far from being an inconsequential choice, pursuing sin would entangle Paul's readers in an unholy association with "the sons of disobedience." Forming such a partnership (συμμέτοχος, "partners") would be especially out of place, since believers who had been redeemed from the corrupt world of the godless Gentiles had already entered into a partnership with Jewish believers in Christ (Eph. 3:6) to receive the inheritance promised for God's children. This brief directive recalled Paul's more extensive teaching about misguided and objectionable partnerships with darkness in 2 Corinthians 6:14–7:1.

Live as Christ's Light (5:8–14)

Paul urged his readers to embrace their identity of being God-pleasing light rather than worthless darkness, shining light into dark places with the assurance that the glorious light of Christ saved and changed people so that they would be able to share in the life and light of Christ.

5:8. Paul unpacked the reason (γάρ, "since") for rejecting unholy partnerships with sinners by initiating an extended exploration of the themes of darkness and light. Paul's readers were no longer who they once were. He reminded them that "you were formerly darkness" (ἦτε . . . ποτε σκότος). Darkness and Christ's kingdom were in opposition to one another (Col. 1:13). Paul's blunt and direct description (they *were* darkness, as opposed simply to being *in* darkness) highlighted the centrality of darkness to the readers' past identity. Their lives had consisted of spiritual blindness to the truth and a corresponding appetite for sin.

In contrast (δέ, "but") to their past darkness, Paul's readers were "now light in the Lord" (νῦν . . . φῶς ἐν κυρίῳ). Paul returned to the "then" (ποτέ) and "now" (νῦν) contrast that believers experienced through encountering Christ by faith (Eph. 2:11–13; cf. 2:1–5). Believers' spiritual condition of darkness became replaced with the polar opposite—light. This new identity became a reality "in the Lord" (ἐν κυρίῳ). Jesus was the light of the world and freely gave "the light of life" to those who followed him (John 8:12). Believers who became united with Christ by faith partook in his divine life and righteousness.

Because of their dramatic change in status, Paul's readers "must walk as children of light" (ὡς τέκνα φωτὸς περιπατεῖτε). Paul again used the verb "walk" (περιπατέω) to indicate a purposeful pattern of living. Paul instructed his readers to walk, or live, differently than the unbelieving Gentiles did (Eph. 2:2; 4:17). He wanted them to live consistently with their calling (Eph. 4:1) and the good works accompanying their calling (Eph. 2:10), reflecting the love of Christ (Eph. 5:2). According to this verse (Eph. 5:8), the way that believers lived needed to correspond to (ὡς, "as") their identity as children of light. The phrase "children of light" (τέκνα φωτός; cf. "sons" of light in 1 Thess. 5:5; John 12:36) designated Paul's readers as possessing and exhibiting the characteristics of light (BDAG, s.v. "τέκνον" 6, p. 994). The language of "sons" of disobedience and "children" of light reinforced opposite categories of people, rather than just antithetical behaviors, suggesting that Paul was contrasting entrenched characteristics (flowing from identities) rather than simply individual choices or actions.

Light and Darkness

The metaphorical contrast between light and darkness is featured prominently throughout the Bible to describe the stark difference between God's life-giving truth and moral depravity and blindness. Isaiah 9:2 promised that God would shine light into a dark land, and the arrival of Jesus's ministry fulfilled this (Matt. 4:15–16). Jesus's presence in his first advent continued to confront darkness with light (John 1:5; 3:19) and offered people the hope of being rescued from darkness (John 8:12; 12:35, 46). In Paul's earlier letters, he challenged readers to cast aside works of darkness and put on light-filled living (Rom. 13:12), to reject partnership with darkness (2 Cor. 6:14), and to embrace the moral implications of their identity as children ("sons") of light (1 Thess. 5:4–5). Paul advanced very similar ideas in Ephesians 5:8. Related ideas were found earlier in the Dead Sea Scrolls (1QM 1:1, 8–15; 13:10–16; 1Q28 1:9–10). Decades after Paul wrote Ephesians, John appealed to a similar, fundamental incompatibility between light and darkness to motivate his readers to live godly lives (1 John 1:5–11).

5:9. Paul paused to explain (γάρ, "for") what specific moral and spiritual qualities emerged from a life of light. Paul pointed to "the fruit of light" (ὁ . . . καρπὸς τοῦ φωτός) that indicated the underlying presence of light. "Fruit" (καρπός) was a metaphor that denoted observable characteristics reflecting a deeper spiritual reality (Matt. 3:8; 7:15–20; Rom. 6:22; Gal. 5:22; Phil. 1:11). Paul observed that the fruit of life consisted (verb implied) "in all goodness, righteousness, and truth" (ἐν πάσῃ ἀγαθωσύνῃ καὶ δικαιοσύνῃ καὶ ἀληθείᾳ). The modifier "all" (πᾶς) suggested that light manifested itself in any authentic expression of goodness, righteousness, and truth. The first characteristic, "goodness" (ἀγαθωσύνη), described wholesome and beneficial conduct. The final two terms, "righteousness" (δικαιοσύνη) and "truth" (ἀλήθεια) were particularly appropriate indicators of life—earlier in this extended section on moral transformation Paul had used these to define the new identity in Christ that his readers should put on (Eph. 4:24). "Righteousness" (δικαιοσύνη) envisioned a lifestyle that revealed the upright and excellent character of God. "Truth" (ἀλήθεια) that was anchored in Jesus (Eph. 4:21) represented reality, especially spiritual reality, accurately and dependably. Light made its presence known in expressions of goodness, righteousness, and truth.

5:10. Paul resumed his train of thought from verse 8 by presenting the means by which his readers should walk, or live, as children of light (adv. ptc., δοκιμάζοντες, modifying the main verb περιπατεῖτε). Their approach to life was to be characterized by "determining what is pleasing to the Lord" (δοκιμάζοντες τί ἐστιν εὐάρεστον τῷ κυρίῳ). The term "to determine" suggested ascertaining through careful examination (BDAG, s.v. "δοκιμάζω" 1, p. 255). To live as children of light, Paul's readers needed to diligently pursue a high standard—what was pleasing to the Lord (cf. Rom. 12:1–2; 2 Cor. 5:9). Pleasing the Lord consisted of thankful obedience to Christ, in step with the values of God's kingdom (Eph. 5:4–5). In Romans 12:1–2, Paul similarly offered his readers an ongoing vision for new life in Christ through showing wholehearted devotion to God and "thoughtfully determining" (δοκιμάζω) what was "pleasing" (εὐάρεστος) to him.

5:11. Paul continued to develop his overall train of thought (καί, "and") by returning to the topic of avoiding complicity with the corrupt practices of this world. In seeking to please the Lord, Paul's readers "should not take part in" (μὴ συγκοινωνεῖτε) or immerse themselves in activities that reflected the values of a fallen world rather than the kingdom of God. Paul often used the idea of taking part, or partnering with others in a deep and meaningful sense among believers in Christ (cf. Rom. 11:17; 1 Cor. 9:23; Phil. 1:7; 4:14). In Ephesians, Paul had used similar words with "co-" (συν-) prefixes to convey shared life and blessings with Christ and with other believers (Eph. 2:5, 6, 19–22; 3:6; 4:16), but in Ephesians 5:7 and 5:11 these words cautioned against destructive participation in ungodly practices.

Specifically, Paul denounced taking part "in the fruitless works of darkness" (τοῖς ἔργοις τοῖς ἀκάρποις τοῦ σκότους). Paul used "works" (ἔργα) generally to describe a range of activities one might take part in (BDAG, s.v. "ἔργον" 1c, p. 390). The common thread was that these activities were "fruitless" (ἄκαρπος). The metaphor "fruitless" indicates worthlessness. These works stood in contrast to the "fruit" (καρπός) that resulted from living in the light of Christ (Eph. 5:9). These were fruitless or worthless "works of darkness" (ἔργα σκότους) that arose from a state of separation from God and consisted of the rampant gratification of sinful desires (cf. Rom. 13:12–14).

Paul suggested a much superior alternative to partnering with evil. "Instead" (μᾶλλον δέ), his readers "must even expose" (καὶ ἐλέγχετε) those fruitless works of darkness. Paul advocated exposing these deeds to reveal their dark and worthless quality. John 3:20, the most instructive parallel passage for this verse, described people fearing that the light of Christ would expose their evil deeds of darkness. Sinful practices looked all the more morally repugnant in the light of goodness, righteousness, and truth. Paul believed that his readers could expose evil by shining Christ's light into dark places. Paul likely had in mind the totality of the domain or realm of darkness (Col. 1:13), under the governance of evil powers (Eph. 6:12), as the dark place that needed exposure to light (with Stott, 1979, 200; Lincoln, 1990, 329–30). Paul encouraged his readers to recognize that sins such as sexual immorality, impurity, and greed were dark and morally worthless rather than harmless and acceptable.

5:12. Paul reasoned (γάρ, "since") that things done in secret were shameful even to mention. This observation strengthened his admonition to avoid taking part in evil (5:11a) and gave additional rationale for the need to expose such conduct for censure. Paul described works of darkness as "that which is done in secret" (τὰ . . . κρυφῇ γινόμενα). Darkness allowed for secrecy, and people took advantage of darkness to engage in vile and destructive behaviors. These sins were done "by them" (ὑπ᾽ αὐτῶν), likely referring to unbelieving Gentiles, whose wicked and detrimental lifestyle had been under investigation ever since Ephesians 4:17.

The activities characteristic of unbelieving Gentiles "are shameful even to mention" (αἰσχρόν ἐστιν καὶ λέγειν). The term "shameful" (αἰσχρός) referred to morally aberrant behavior. By observing that this behavior was shameful to even mention, Paul did not intend to dilute his exhortation to expose these works for what they really were. Instead, Paul used heightened rhetoric to communicate the appalling nature of godless activities done in secret and his desire to spare his readers the details of these wayward pursuits, which could include sexual immorality (Eph. 5:3; Rom. 13:13) and drunkenness (Eph. 5:18; 1 Thess. 5:7), among other vices.

5:13. Paul transitioned (δέ, "but") from the scandal of darkness to the benefits of exposing the works of darkness (5:11b; Thielman, 2010, 344). Paul shared the readily observable insight that "everything exposed by the light is disclosed" (τὰ πάντα ἐλεγχόμενα ὑπὸ τοῦ φωτὸς φανεροῦται). This general truth about light's capability applied metaphorically to the spiritual light that believers shone into darkness. Paul's readers carried out the command to expose works of darkness (Eph. 5:11), with the added understanding that they did so by bringing Christ's light into those dark places ("by the light" more likely modified "expose" than "is disclosed"). They were "light in the Lord" (Eph. 5:8) and thus were mediators of Christ and his light (cf. the same image with different wording in Phil. 2:15).

The passive voice form "are disclosed" (φανεροῦται) stressed that things in dark places were acted upon and potentially even transformed by the light. Paul viewed this disclosure of secret things to be a positive outcome (cf. Matt. 10:26; Mark 4:22–23; Luke 8:17). Jesus had promised that the Spirit would "convict" (ἐλέγχω) the world of sin, righteousness, and judgment (John 16:8–10). Conviction of sin could have positive effects in the lives of those whose secrets (1 Cor. 14:24–25) and general heart condition (Rom. 7:13) were exposed, leading to repentance. Paul turned his attention to the transforming potential of light in the next verse.

5:14. Paul elaborated (γάρ, "for") on the significance of being illuminated by light with a compact and somewhat enigmatic comment, followed by a quotation that is intriguing and difficult to interpret. Paul affirmed that "everything disclosed *is* light" (πᾶν . . . τὸ φανερούμενον φῶς ἐστιν).

> *TRANSLATION ANALYSIS:* The form "disclosed" (φανερούμενον) was most likely passive voice rather than middle voice. In other words, the clause should be translated "everything [being] disclosed is light" (ESV, NASB, NRSV, NET; Stott, 1979, 200–201; Lincoln, 1990, 331; Moritz, 1996, 113; Snodgrass, 1996, 273; Best, 1998, 496; Muddiman, 2001, 241–42; Hoehner, 2002, 684–85; Thielman, 2010, 347) rather than "that which discloses everything is light" (NIV, CSB, NKJV, KJV, NLT; Abbott, 1897, 156; Arnold, 2010, 333). The occurrence of the same verb in passive form in the previous verse, along with Paul's standard usage of the passive form of the verb, suggests a passive use in this verse. Paul was advancing his argument with an expanded thought about the powerful effects of light.

Unlike the previous verse, the observation that whatever was disclosed (by light) is light did not reflect reality in the physical world, but Paul still contended that it held true spiritually. The statement acted as a bridge from the overall discussion of light and darkness to the Christ-centered quote that followed, but what did it mean? Paul likely had a fuller, eschatological understanding of "disclosed" (φανερόω) in mind. For Paul the idea of being disclosed or revealed by Christ's light was brimming with possibilities. Once things were in the light, they were no longer part of the kingdom of darkness, since light and darkness were mutually exclusive (Eph. 5:5–8; Acts 26:18; Col. 1:12–14; 1 John 2:8). Anything that was fully and definitively disclosed by the light was no longer in darkness. When Christ returned, believers' full glory would be "disclosed" (φανερόω) because of their union with the glorified Christ (Col. 3:4; 1 John 3:2; cf. Rom. 8:19). That which was truly illuminated through an initial and ongoing exposure to Christ's glorious light was transformed to embody and reflect that light (2 Cor. 3:18; 4:4–6), so that instead of *being* darkness, Paul's readers and other believers could *be* the light of Christ (Eph. 5:8). Paul's brief comment can be understood as the marvelous thought that "everything fully disclosed in Christ light's actually becomes light."

Next, Paul concluded the section with a striking quotation, introduced by "this is why it is said" (διὸ λέγει; NIV; NLT; cf. Eph. 4:8). The quotation, likely familiar from worship settings in early Christian circles, proclaimed, "Wake up, sleeper, and rise from the dead, and Christ will shine on you." Though Paul himself did not write the quote, he found it relevant to the topic at hand, and he may have even purposefully laid the groundwork for the quote in the discussion leading up to it. The quote supported Paul's contention that anything truly illuminated by Christ was now considered to actually be light. The quote also made explicit the unstated assumption from the last several verses—that Christ was the ultimate light source that shone in and through Paul's readers.

An Early Christian Hymn

Scholars believe that Ephesians 5:14b reflected an early Christian hymn. The introductory formula signaled that these words were not Paul's own, and no single OT verse stands out as an obvious source. In addition, the wording had a poetic quality, with crisp sentences, vivid imagery, and an exultant tone. Early believers may have used the hymn as part of a baptismal service (Lincoln, 1990, 319; cf. Rom. 6:4; Col. 2:12), though more generally the hymn magnified the power of the gospel—the good news of Christ's saving and transforming work. The hymn was likely inspired by several passages in Isaiah (Moritz, 1996, 100–105; Lunde and Dunne, 2012, 87–110). Isaiah 60:1–2 (especially in the Hebrew) supplied the celebratory tone, the sense of invitation, and the imagery of the light of God's glory rising (cf. Isa. 60:19). Similar imagery was seen in Isaiah 9:2 (9:1 LXX), along with a mention of death. Isaiah 26:19 (or Dan. 12:2) could have provided the language of resurrection and rising from the dead. Overall, the hymn proclaimed the triumph of light over darkness and life over death in Christ.

First, Paul said "wake up, sleeper" (ἔγειρε, ὁ καθεύδων). The tone of this line and the lines that followed in the hymn was joyful and hopeful, in keeping with the passages from Isaiah (such as 60:1–2) that had likely shaped the hymn. Much of the language in the hymn hinted at a double meaning in keeping with the seamless connection between the "already" and "not yet" of Christ's saving work. This first line thus functioned as a summons to "be awakened" (BDAG, s.v "ἐγείρω" 13, p. 272) to God's truth and goodness as well as a vivid preview of resurrection victory (ἐγείρω was also used to describe being raised from the dead; BDAG, s.v. "ἐγείρω" 7, p. 272; 1 Cor. 15:35, 52). "The one sleeping" (ὁ καθεύδων) may have represented both those who were in a state of spiritual slumber (BDAG, s.v. "καθεύδω" 2, p. 490; cf. 1 Thess. 5:4–7) and those who slept in death (1 Thess. 4:13–17; 5:10; 1 Cor. 15:50–52; Dan. 12:2). Both types of sleepers were impacted by the ministry of Christ.

The second line of the hymn called for a corresponding rising from the dead (καὶ ἀνάστα ἐκ τῶν νεκρῶν, "and rise from the dead"). Those who encountered Christ's saving work and turned from sin and darkness experienced new life in Christ (Rom. 6:3–4; Col. 2:12; Eph. 2:4–6). The language of resurrection also anticipated the final resurrection of the dead (ἀνίστημι, 1 Thess. 4:16), in keeping with the seamless connection between Christ both giving new spiritual life and raising believers to everlasting life.

The final line announced the promise "and the Christ will shine on you" (καὶ ἐπιφαύσει σοι ὁ Χριστός). The verb "shine" (ἐπιφαύσκω) occurred just this once in the NT but was used of the shining of the sun and moon in other places (cf. Job 25:5; 31:26 LXX). Christ shone a brilliant light on the sleeping and the dead. This light that shone was the light of his glorious presence (2 Cor. 4:4–6; Luke 2:32; Rev. 21:23–24; Isa. 60:1–2, 19). Perhaps in this instance the article ("the") before Christ (ὁ Χριστός) recalled Jesus's arrival as the Messiah who would fulfill the promises made in the passages (such as Isa. 60:1–2) that had inspired this hymn.

The hymn's third line tied most directly to the statement preceding the hymn—that everything disclosed *is* light. The light displaced darkness (cf. John 1:5). Through Christ's radiating, glorious presence, he rescued those who were united with him from death and darkness and shared his light with them. Their transformation had begun through their current union with him and would culminate when Christ and believers were together revealed in glory (Col. 3:3–4; cf. 2 Cor. 3:18; Phil. 3:20–21). Christ Jesus had previewed this majestic display of his light in the transfiguration (Matt. 17:2), and Paul had experienced the life-changing effects of Christ's radiant self-disclosure on the road to Damascus (Acts 9:3; 22:6; 26:13). Paul drew upon this image of Christ's shining and life-giving presence to lift the readers' eyes to the greatness and power of Christ so that they might find renewed motivation to live as Christ's light in a dark world.

THEOLOGICAL FOCUS

The exegetical idea (Paul's readers needed to reject sexual immorality, greed, and other vices that clashed with their kingdom identity and live instead as Christ's light, being ready to shine Christ's powerful, transforming light in a dark world) leads to this theological focus: Believers should reject conduct that clashes with their identity and live as Christ's light in a dark world.

This passage appeals to believers' identity and association with God's kingdom as motivation to separate from immoral practices (v. 5). Certain conduct is simply not fitting or appropriate for those who belong to God (vv. 3–4). Believers are God's holy people, so they should reject sexual immorality, impurity, and greed. They are recipients of God's amazing grace and mercy in Christ, so their speech should be marked by thanksgiving rather than vulgarity (v. 4). The kingdom of God is at hand, and when Christ consummates the kingdom at his return, he will judge enemies of the kingdom and reward loyal citizens (vv. 5–6). Believers should think twice about casting their lot with enemies of the kingdom through immoral living.

Believers should live their lives with discernment and moral clarity, but they should also be eager to participate in God's mission of bringing light into the darkness. Light consists of goodness, righteousness, truth, and anything that pleases the Lord (vv. 9–10). Darkness is characterized by all sorts of evil practices that people try to hide from exposure (v. 12). Believers should not be deceived into thinking that darkness and light can coexist in their lives.

Though light and darkness are two mutually exclusive categories, they are not equally powerful in the spiritual realm. Light can encroach into dark places, exposing evil and even transforming the dark environment with its radiating influence (v. 14a). Jesus himself is the light of the world, and he came into the world to deliver people from darkness and bring them into his life-giving light (v. 14b, cf. John 8:12; Acts 26:18; Col. 1:12–14; 1 Peter 2:9). Believers, since they are united with Christ, live in the light and are children of light (v. 8). They participate in the mission of shining Christ's light in the dark world (cf. Matt. 5:14–16; Phil. 2:15). Christ's brilliant light awakens those asleep in the darkness and brings resurrected life to the dead (Eph. 5:14).

PREACHING AND TEACHING STRATEGIES

Exegetical and Theological Synthesis

In this passage, Paul continued to exhort readers to live in accordance with the theology presented in the early chapters of the book, particularly the lordship of Christ, believers' union with him, and the incompatibility of the world with Christ's kingdom. The exhortation was needed because although the Ephesian believers had become "light in the Lord" (v. 8), they continued to act in ways that Paul called "darkness." The dark ways mentioned in this passage were sexual immorality, impure speech, and greed (vv. 3–4). The readers were in danger of being deceived with empty words from false teachers (v. 6) who tried to convince them that God did not care what believers do with their bodies and words.

To address the Ephesians' susceptibility to stumble in the darkness, God supplied all that was necessary—full acceptance and love (v. 1), warning about judgment (v. 6), a summons to awake and receive the transformative grace of Christ (v. 14), and most importantly, a new nature (v. 8). And Paul commanded the followers of Christ to not only do deeds of righteousness such as giving thanks and practicing sexual purity, they were also to expose unrighteousness in society (v. 11) and bring the light of Christ into dark places (vv. 13–14).

Preaching Idea

Live as Christ's light in the midst of a dark culture.

Contemporary Connections

What does it mean?

What does it mean to live as Christ's light in the midst of a dark culture? The metaphor of light and darkness appears throughout the Bible. "Darkness" is a shorthand term for life outside of Christ: spiritual blindness and calloused hearts. "Light" means the opposite: spiritual understanding and hearts responsive to the will of God. Darkness expresses itself in sexual immorality, crude speech, and greed. Sexual immorality (*porneia*) was pervasive in the first century. Adultery, the use of slaves for homosexual and heterosexual sex, prostitution, and "sacred" sex in temples were common.

Contemporary culture provides its own examples such as the trend in North America for "serial monogamy." This is the idea that we should be sexually "faithful" to our current significant other. It is okay to have sex with that person but not okay to "cheat" by having sex with others. Once the relationship is broken, sex with the next significant other is permissible and even expected. Another trend is "polyamory." From the Greek for "many" and the Latin for "love" this refers to the desire for or practice of having more than one intimate partner with the consent of all partners. A 2019 study estimates that about 5 percent of Americans were involved in such relationships, and another study found that 70 percent of nonreligious Americans between ages 24 and 35 believe it is okay. In *Cheap Sex* (2017), Mark Regnerus says that 24 percent of churchgoing people believe that consensual polyamorous relationships are morally permissible.[1]

It may also be helpful to contextualize the three "dark" terms related to speech in verse 4: "vulgarity," "foolish talk," and "crude joking." Standards evaluating ungodly speech vary from culture to culture, but across cultures impure

1 Cited in Preston Sprinkle and Branson Parler, "Polyamory: Pastors' Next Sexual Frontier," *Christianity Today*, September 25, 2019, https://www.christianitytoday.com/pastors/2019/fall/polyamory-next-sexual-frontier.html.

speech often deals with sex and scatology. Cornelius Plantinga (1995) puts it this way:

> Late-afternoon and late-night TV talk shows present hours of lightweight nihilism carried along by a chatter that is sometimes rancorous and sometimes mildly amusing, but that is mostly what the Bible calls "unwholesome talk"—a kind of talk that is foolish, coarse, dismissive, incessant, and vain. ("So he goes, 'You're sexy.'" And I'm like—'Whoa! This guy's sleeping with my mom!' But he's, like, kinda cute, so I go. . . ."). ("Background Noise," *Christianity Today* [July 17, 1995]: 42)

Concerning greed, we might encourage the congregation that members of religions give more to charity than do nonreligious people.[2] Still, even religious people need regular challenges to see if their spending on luxuries could be reduced in order to help people less fortunate.

Is it true?

Is it true that we are to live as Christ's light in the midst of a dark culture? Jesus came as the light of the world (John 1:9; 3:19; 8:12), and he commissioned his followers as the light of the world (Matt. 5:14). Just as light dispels darkness, whether it is a flashlight, headlights on a car, or a miner's head lamp, so are followers of Jesus to do what he did—present a stark contrast to the immoral and greedy culture. When we do this, Peter says that we "proclaim the excellencies of him who called you out of darkness into his marvelous light" (1 Peter 2:9).

When we love, trust, and sacrifice for money, it replaces God. Examples of greed can be found in advertisements. Communications professor Richard F. Taflinger (1996) gives dozens of examples and states, "Greed, no matter what anybody says, is a part of the human psychological make-up. Everybody wants more. Thus, as an advertising tool, greed (or acquisition of property, to make it sound better) works well."[3]

In the movie *Wall Street* (directed by Oliver Stone, 1987), Gordon Gekko (played by Michael Douglas) gives a memorable speech that praises covetousness: "Greed, for lack of a better word, is good. . . . Greed in all of its forms—greed for life, for money, for love, knowledge—has marked the upward surge of mankind."[4]

Greed exists in the church, not just society, in the form of the "health and wealth gospel" where people are taught that God wants all Christians to be rich and healthy in this life. A radio advertisement for an investment seminar tried to lure listeners to attend with these words: "Are you tired of just getting by? Learn how to get what you want out of life. Learn how to earn wealth that lasts and prosperity without regrets. Come prepared to role play, and bring your Bible."

The need for believers to be distinctive in terms of sexual immorality might focus on society's voracious consumption of pornography. It is not a "victimless crime" because it harms the one who views it, not to mention the actors and models who pose for it, and the children who are warped by it. Matthew Lee Anderson (2019) writes about how pornography makes us less human and less humane. He compares it to murder: while porn "may represent a less vicious deviance than that which murder depends on, [it] trades on the same destructive, dehumanizing impulses. And comparing the

---

2 Bradford Richardson, "Religious People More Likely to Give to Charity, Study Shows," *Washington Times*, October 30, 2017, https://www.washingtontimes.com/news/2017/oct/30/religious-people-more-likely-give-charity-study.

3 For more examples of this, search for lectures and transcripts by Richard F. Taflinger, specifically, "I Want It, I Want It Now: Greed and Advertising," chapter 7 in *Taking ADvantage: The Psychology of Consumer Behavior*.

4 For an example of this clip, search YouTube for "Greed Is Good," *Wall Street*.

two disturbs our complacent, lazy acceptance of pornography as a benign and harmless form of amusement."[5]

Perhaps the most controversial idea undergirding the preaching idea is that God's wrath comes upon those who conform to sinful practices of society (v. 6)

Now what?

How can we live as Christ's light in the midst of a dark culture? The text points to three practices. First, replace crude speech with pure words like thanksgiving. This is modeled in the Song of Songs—refreshingly frank about sex without descending to crudeness. Children can be taught that sex is a beautiful gift from God intended for husband and wife. Parents can model how to talk about it. They might read Randy Alcorn's *The Purity Principle* (Sisters, OR: Multnomah Books, 2003) with their children.

"How to Talk to Your Kids about Sex"

- If you don't know the facts, don't be embarrassed. Just find out.
- Always teach about sex in the context of values and marriage.
- Answer your child's questions honestly.
- Don't procrastinate.
- Don't come on too strong.

When verse 4 contrasts vulgar speech with thankful speech, an analogy may show the relationship: one method of ridding a lawn of weeds is to fertilize the grass so much that it dominates the weeds and they die off. Proper use of the tongue such as giving thanks crowds out sinful speech patterns. Instead of telling off-color jokes, we can use appropriate humor. Instead of talking about sex with double entendre and titillation, a husband or wife can write a poem or letter to one's spouse complimenting the other's beauty and attractive qualities. Instead of tearing down someone behind their back, we can speak kindly. Robertson McQuilkin, former president of Columbia International University, had a plaque above the fireplace in his home that said, "Absent friends are safe here."

The second practice is found in verses 7 and 11: Do not partner with the "sons of disobedience," and "take no part in the unfruitful works of darkness." This metaphorical language describes partnerships that include, but are not limited to, personal choices of how we spend money and time. For example, when believers pay money to watch sexually impure movies, they are partnering with the studio and allowing the darkness to establish a beachhead in their hearts. They subtly approve of and aid the darkness.

The third practice is also found in verse 11: expose the world's system of darkness. This practice can be done simply by living as the light of Christ in the world. At work, places of entertainment, local government, and other venues of daily life, Christians can display the righteousness, holiness, love, and mercy of God by the way they talk and act. Acts of kindness, encouraging words, truthfulness, and integrity expose the darkness by way of contrast. As Paul says in Philippians 2:14–15, simply refusing to complain and argue is a powerful way to shine. Exposing darkness can also be done when we humbly and lovingly admonish a friend, exposing their sin. As a previous chapter in this commentary suggested, admonition should be carried out

- *privately.* (See the four-stage process in Matthew 18 where verse 15 uses the same verb as Ephesians 5:11 for "pointing out" or "exposing" a fellow believer's sin.)

5 Matthew Lee Anderson, "How Pornography Makes Us Less Human and Less Humane," The Gospel Coalition, August 26, 2019, https://www.thegospelcoalition.org/article/pornography-human-humane.

- *purely.* (The one who admonishes must not be guilty of the same sin; Gal. 6:1; Matt. 7:3–5.)
- *patiently* (2 Tim. 4:2).
- *placidly* (2 Tim. 2:24–25).

Exposing the darkness raises the possibility of public actions such as protesting and boycotting. Such actions should not be entered into lightly, yet we feel that in certain cases when they are done legally and in the Spirit of Jesus Christ for the glory of God, they can be tools for shining in this dark world. As when the church fueled the civil rights movement, Christians today can overcome darkness.

Some churches are combatting the power of greed (v. 5) by implementing the "Advent Conspiracy." This is a multiweek emphasis prior to Christmas in which followers of Jesus use Advent to bless the poor, not accumulate more gadgets and trinkets. This passage from Ephesians could lay the groundwork for your own Advent Conspiracy—a countercultural way to shine in the darkness.[6]

Creativity in Presentation

The preaching idea might be conveyed visually with the use of light and darkness. For example, the illumination on the platform could be arranged so that one side is relatively dark and the other bright. As the sermon proceeds, the preacher could walk from the darkness to the light. Similarly, a lamp turned off and on can make the idea memorable.

A movie illustration of darkness and light can be found in *The Lord of the Rings: The Two Towers* (directed by Peter Jackson, 2002). At night, wave after wave of bloodthirsty orcs attack Helm's Deep, a fortress in the land of Rohan. As the darkness continues, things go from bad to worse and all seems lost. The defenders are close to despair because they have forgotten the words of Gandalf: "Look to my coming, at first light, on the fifth day. At dawn, look to the East." True to his word, as the dawn breaks Gandalf and the riders of Rohan sweep down upon the orcs and light vanquishes the darkness.

Another movie clip illustrates that we should behave according to our true identity. In "Windsor," season 1, episode 3, of *The Crown* (created by Peter Morgan, 2016–), young Queen Elizabeth is nervous before her first appointment with the legendary prime minister Winston Churchill. Elizabeth's husband, Prince Philip, encourages her: "Don't be nervous. . . . I know it's Winston Churchill and all that, but remember who you are." Elizabeth interrupts, "I'm nobody," but Philip carries on without pausing, "*The Queen of England*." Christ-followers can shine because God has made us light. That is our identity.

Just as the passage concludes with a hymn that magnifies the power of Christ's light, so might the sermon. The congregation could sing Chris Tomlin's "Awakening."

As a reminder that followers of Christ are "light in the Lord" (v. 8), perhaps your church or organization could hand out key chains with small flashlights. When we fumble in the darkness and then shine the light, we might remember our identity.

Throughout the sermon, we will want to focus on this: Christ followers are now "light in the Lord," so they should behave accordingly in their speech, sexuality, and attitudes toward money. We should not return to the "dark" behaviors we used to endorse before being spiritually rescued. Those behaviors arouse God's anger. We should live as Christ's light in the midst of a dark culture.

A possible outline:

- Walk in Christ's light by living sexually pure lives (vv. 3, 5–6).

6 For more information on the concept of Advent Conspiracy, search YouTube for "Advent Conspiracy."

- Walk in Christ's light by speaking pure words (vv. 4, 12).
- Walk in Christ's light by rejecting greed (vv. 3, 5).
- Walk in Christ's light by exposing evil practices (vv. 7–11, 13).
- Remember the saving and transforming power of Christ's light (v. 14).

DISCUSSION QUESTIONS

1. What are the three sins this passage mentions as examples of "darkness"?
2. Why do you think that God calls greed "idolatry"?
3. What motivates a person to tell crude jokes? What is in the heart that produces those words?
4. What are some things that you are thankful for? Express your thanks to God.
5. What makes the common biblical imagery of darkness and light so effective? What does it capture about God's work in the world?
6. How do you feel about exposing the unfruitful works of darkness? Have you ever done this? What was the outcome?
7. Does verse 14, an early Christian hymn or creedal statement, bring to mind any modern songs? If you're with a discussion group, remind them of the words.

FOR FURTHER READING

Bonhoeffer, Dietrich. 1954. *Life Together*. New York: Harper and Row.

Colson, Charles, and Ellen Santilli Vaughn. 1992. *The Body: Being Light in Darkness*. Dallas: Word.

Getz, Gene. 1976. *Building Up One Another*. Colorado Springs: David C. Cook.

Kruger, Melissa, ed. 2018. *Identity Theft: Reclaiming the Truth of Who We Are in Christ*. Deerfield, IL: Gospel Coalition.

Moore, Russell. 2015. *Onward: Engaging the Culture without Losing the Gospel*. Nashville: B&H Publishing.

Packer, J. I., and Thomas C. Oden. 2004. *One Faith: The Evangelical Consensus*. Downers Grove, IL: InterVarsity.

SPIRIT-FILLED RELATIONSHIPS AND DIVINE RESOURCES FOR SPIRITUAL BATTLE (5:15–6:24)

Paul concluded the letter with another practical section that was grounded in the theological reality of new life in Christ. Paul directed believers to walk wisely in the world and be filled with the Spirit in their worship and relationships with one another (5:15–21). Paul then placed a special focus on the relationships between husbands and wives, promoting relationships that reflected the union, order, and love between Christ and his church (5:22–33). Paul explained that Christ should also govern and shape the way children and parents, and slaves and masters, interacted with one another (6:1–9). Finally, Paul's readers needed to stand firm against evil, using the divine armor God supplied, and prioritize prayer for fellow believers and Paul's ministry (6:10–24).

The fifth major section for the letter has the title Spirit-filled Relationships and Divine Resources for Spiritual Battle (5:15–6:24). Four preaching units make up this final section: "Strategic and Spirit-filled Living" (5:15–21), "Marriages That Reflect the Union of Christ and the Church" (5:22–5:33), "Honoring the Lord in Household Relationships" (6:1–9), and "Equipped in Christ for Spiritual Battle" (6:10–24).

Ephesians 5:15–21

EXEGETICAL IDEA

Paul's readers were called to live wisely and strategically in the broader, evil world, to seek to understand and follow God's will, and to be filled with the Spirit's presence and influence in their corporate worship, outlook, and relationships.

THEOLOGICAL FOCUS

Believers should live strategically in their interactions with those who do not know Christ and keep in tune with the Spirit in corporate worship and relationships.

PREACHING IDEA

To live strategically, sync with the Spirit.

PREACHING POINTERS

As their identity as followers of Christ became more firmly established, Paul's readers needed to grapple with the implications of their identity. First, how should they represent Christ and his kingdom to those people who worshipped idols and glorified power and pleasure? They needed to disengage from their old practices in that environment but remain as a force for light in dark settings. Paul's readers likely saw this as a daunting task and recognized their need for Paul's input and God's wisdom. Second, how should they strengthen themselves internally in their churches to facilitate vibrant worship, spiritual growth, and harmony in relationships? They knew that God had provided his Spirit to dwell among them, but how could they make the most of the Spirit's presence? Paul gave them guidance for living strategically with people outside the church while shoring up their spiritual strength as a community of believers.

We too live in a pluralistic world. Urbanization as well as the ubiquity of social media mean that we live in a global village like never before, so guidance is needed. Today, we increasingly rub shoulders with people of many cultures and religions. A United Nations report indicates that by 2050, two-thirds of humanity will live in cities, up from 55 percent in 2018 (Lardiei, 2018) Most people in Western culture have floated down the stream into post-Christendom as seen in the rising group of "nones" who do not identify with any religion. Perhaps your congregation has a public school teacher who swims in a lake of humanism, or public school students who face a blitzkrieg of relativism. How can they represent Christ in a school where anything goes if it is deemed "authentic" to who you define yourself to be? How can they live missionally and present a striking contrast to the current milieu? We can live strategically by syncing with the Spirit.

STRATEGIC AND SPIRIT-FILLED LIVING (5:15–21)

LITERARY STRUCTURE AND THEMES (5:15–21)

In Ephesians 5:15–21, Paul continued to develop material about carrying Christ's light in a world of darkness (5:8–14) while preparing the way for practical instructions on fostering constructive and harmonious relationships within households (5:22–6:9). Paul paused to communicate the importance of being properly oriented in both mission and corporate spiritual life. The key was dependence upon God, through seeking his will and relying on his Spirit.

Structurally, Paul began with a collection of three negative actions to avoid, followed by the corresponding positive exhortation, at times with explanatory comments that reinforced the positive step (5:15–18). Then, he expanded on the final positive command to be filled with the Spirit (v. 18), with a series of four participial phrases that showed the readers how to put the main command into practice (vv. 19–21). Thematically, the passage consisted of two sections, moving from an emphasis on readers' interactions with the wider world (vv. 15–17) to readers' internal practices and relationships as a body of believers (vv. 18–21). This chapter follows these thematic divisions (vv. 15–17 and 18–21) in its organization.

- ***Live Strategically in the Broader World (5:15–17)***
- ***Keep in Tune with the Spirit, Together (5:18–21)***

EXPOSITION (5:15–21)

To help his readers navigate life in their multicultural environment, Paul promoted being wise over being unwise (Eph. 5:15), understanding the Lord's will rather than being foolish (5:17), and being filled with the Spirit rather than being drunk with wine (5:18). Paul supplemented these instructions with a reminder that his readers lived in a fallen world system whose days were numbered, so they needed to take advantage of their window of opportunity by living strategically for Christ (5:16). Finally, Paul gave specific examples of how to keep in tune with the Spirit's activity by edifying one another with spiritual songs, directing songs and praises to God, cultivating a thankful attitude, and humbly submitting to one another in the church.

Live Strategically in the Broader World (5:15–17)

Paul advised his readers to be careful to live wisely and strategically among nonbelievers during the evil times they lived in, rejecting foolishness and seeking to understand and follow God's will.

5:15. Paul presented an exhortation that built off of (οὖν, "therefore") the preceding discussion about light and darkness. Paul advised his readers to "consider carefully how they walk" (βλέπετε . . . ἀκριβῶς πῶς περιπατεῖτε). Paul recognized that the stakes were high for how his readers lived in their broader environment. The light of God's kingdom was advancing against the forces of darkness, and there was no room for compromise. Similar constructions of "consider" (βλέπω) followed by "how" (πώς) instructed hearers to give careful attention to what they would do (Luke 8:18; 1 Cor. 3:10; BDAG, s.v. "βλέπω" 6c, p. 179). Paul directed his readers to make choices "carefully" (ἀκριβῶς) about how they should "walk" (περιπατέω) or conduct their lives within a pluralistic culture in which many different gods and goddesses were worshipped.

An Ephesian Describes a Multitude of Deities

A passage from a practitioner in divination named Artemidorus of Ephesus gives a glimpse into the many divine powers venerated (second century A.D.). Artemidorus grouped the deities according to their regions of authority, whether the aether (the upper heavens), heavens, the earth, the sea, or the underworld: "Zeus, Hera, Aphrodite Ourania (of the Heavens), Artemis, Apollo, Aetherial Fire, and Athena are reasonably said to belong to the aether. Helios (Sun), Selene (Moon), the Stars, the Clouds, the Winds . . . and Iris (Rainbow) belong to the heavens . . . . Of the gods who belong to the earth . . . Hekate, Pan, Ephialtes, and Asklepios . . . the Dioskouroi, Herakles, Dionysos, Hermes, Nemesis, Aphrodite Pandemos (of the People), Tyche (Fortune), Peitho (Persuasion), the Graces, the Hours, the Nymphs, and Hestia. The sea gods . . . are Poseiden, Amphitrite, Nereus, the Nereids, Leukothea, and Phorkys . . . Thalassa (the Sea) itself, the Waves, the Seashores, the Rivers, the Marshes, the Nymphs, and Acheloös (the longest river in Greece). The underworld gods are Pluto, Persephone, Demeter, Kore, Iakkhos, Sarapis, Isis, Anubis, Harpokrates, underworld Hekate, the Furies, the *daimones* who attend them, and Phobos (Fear) and Deimos (Panic), whom some call the sons of Ares."[1]

Paul had already guided his readers to walk in love (Eph. 5:2) and walk as children of light by living ethically (5:8). Now, he urged them to walk, or live, wisely. Paul highlighted this point by first admonishing them to *not* live as unwise people did (μὴ ὡς ἄσοφοι, "not as unwise"). In contrast (ἀλλά, "but"), they were to live as wise people did (ὡς σοφοί, "as wise"). The two terms for "unwise" and "wise" people are lexical opposites (the α-prefix negates the noun). These two antithetical categories reflected the stark difference between light and darkness. Living wisely rather than foolishly meant navigating a world filled with sin and error by keeping God's calling and the values of his kingdom in mind. Earlier in the letter Paul had prayed that his readers would grow in the wisdom that the Spirit cultivated in their lives (Eph. 1:17). God exhibited perfect wisdom in everything he did (Eph. 1:8; Rom. 16:27), and he had revealed his wisdom definitively in Christ Jesus and his saving work (1 Cor. 1:24, 30; 2:6–7; Col. 2:3).

Walking Wisely and the Book of Daniel

Paul's emphasis in this verse on being "wise" (σοφοί) is intriguing when compared to Daniel 12:1–3. Though the wording was somewhat different, the passages (Dan. 12:1–3 and Eph. 5:13–17) had striking conceptual similarities. Daniel 12 (LXX) spoke about God delivering his people during a time of distress (Dan. 12:1). Those who "sleep" (καθεύδω) would awake, or be resurrected, some to eternal life and some to eternal judgment (Dan. 12:2). Those resurrected to eternal life were those who showed wisdom during troubled times (Dan. 11:33), and they would shine brightly forever (Dan. 12:3). Paul similarly associated wise living in dark times (Eph. 5:15–17) with the glorious, life-giving light of Christ shining on (and through) believers (Eph. 5:14).

5:16. The means by which Paul's readers were to forge their path in life was by "capitalizing on this window of opportunity" (ἐξαγοραζόμενοι τὸν καιρόν, adv. ptc. phrase). The term "capitalize" (ἐξαγοράζω) was often used in financial contexts ("redeem" or "buy back," BDAG, s.v. "ἐξαγοράζω," p. 343; Snodgrass, 1996, 288), so the translation "capitalizing" captures some of that connotation. The middle form (ἐξαγοραζόμενοι) conveyed the idea of doing

1 Excerpts from translation found in Rives, 2007, 16.

something about one's own situation (Wallace, 1996, 419–21). Paul challenged his readers to seize the day, living intentionally and strategically rather than passively. Paul spoke of "this window of opportunity" (καιρός) with a term that sometimes designated a critical period of time or season leading up to the return of Christ (ἐξαγοράζω, *EDNT*, vol. 2, 1), at the "fullness of time" (also with καιρός, Eph. 1:9–10). Elsewhere, Paul talked about this "time" (καιρός) as a relatively short window of time (1 Cor. 7:29) and related it to the return of Christ, which was drawing nearer and nearer (Rom. 13:11).

The reason (ὅτι, "since") the readers needed to live such focused lives was because "the days are evil" (αἱ ἡμέραι πονηραί εἰσιν). Paul's use of "the days" (αἱ ἡμέραι) aligned with the ripe "time of opportunity" (καιρός) that he had mentioned in the first half of the verse. The days that made up the present world were "evil" (πονηρός), since the world was marred by sin and was under Satan's governance (Eph. 2:1–3). In the darkness of the world, evil festered. In major cities of Asia Minor such as Ephesus, Laodicea, and Pergamum, there were structures devoted to idolatry, power, and pleasure. Along with temples to many gods and statues and inscriptions venerating human rulers, there were venues for bloody gladiatorial games, and taverns and inns in which heavy drinking and prostitution were common. In such an environment, readers' lives had strategic importance. Their lives testified to the coming kingdom of God (Eph. 1:9–10; 3:10; 6:19–20) in the midst of a current, evil age (Gal. 1:4; cf. Matt. 13:43; Phil. 2:15) that was passing away (1 Cor. 7:31). As bearers of Christ's light, Paul's readers illuminated a better way.

Moral Vigilance and Mission

This verse calls for both moral clarity and commitment to mission in view of the return of Christ. The first piece, moral vigilance, is more obvious in the immediate context, since Paul's readers had to be wary of evil that was in their surroundings. But the preceding passage had talked about exposing darkness with the light of Christ and expecting powerful results when the light penetrated the darkness (Eph. 5:13–14). Additionally, the idea of "capitalizing on this window of opportunity" (τὸν καιρὸν ἐξαγοραζόμενοι) implied a proactive approach (Ridderbos, 1975, 494–95). When Paul used similar language in Colossians 4:5–6, he prescribed a posture of outreach to "outsiders" that paralleled his own ministry of declaring the mystery of Christ (Col. 4:3–4). In Ephesians 5:15–16, Paul promoted wise and intentional living not simply for abstaining from evil but also for representing God's kingdom by shining the light of Christ.

5:17. Paul referred back to at least Ephesians 5:16b as the reason (διὰ τοῦτο, "for this reason") for his next exhortation to his readers. Because the days were evil, Paul instructed his readers, "Do not become foolish" (μὴ γίνεσθε ἄφρονες). Foolishness denoted a deficiency of good sense (BDAG, s.v. "ἄφρων," p. 159). In the NT, the term was sometimes used pejoratively to label someone who stubbornly resisted God's truth or God's ways (Luke 11:40; 12:20; 1 Cor. 15:36; 1 Peter 2:15). Likewise, in the Septuagint the term sometimes described those who spurned God and his truth (Ps. 14:1; 53:1; 74:18; Prov. 1:22; Jer. 4:22)

Instead (ἀλλά, "but"), Paul's readers were to aspire to the opposite of foolishness. They needed to "understand what the Lord's will is" (συνίετε τί τὸ θέλημα τοῦ κυρίου). This resembled Paul's earlier admonition to determine what pleases the Lord (Eph. 5:10). The verb "understand" (συνίημι) often suggested gaining an understanding of something challenging but important (Matt. 16:12; 17:13; Luke 2:50; 18:34; 24:45; Acts 13:27; Rom. 15:21; BDAG, s.v. "συνίημι," p. 972). This understanding of spiritual truth was assumed to be accompanied by obedience (Matt. 13:15,

23; Rom. 3:11; 2 Cor. 10:12). Paul wanted his readers to be committed to the Lord's will in both understanding and action.

To understand the will of the Lord in this context meant to discern the appropriate way to live morally excellent and missionally purposeful lives in a world of darkness. God's "will" (θέλημα) was God's own sovereign purpose that he fulfilled when he accomplished his grand plans to save sinners and establish Christ's reign over the world (Eph. 1:5, 9–11). Paul typically used "Lord" (κύριος) to refer to Christ in Ephesians, and this title did justice to Christ's exalted authority as head of his body. Christ now carried out God's governance over the world and the church (Eph. 1:20–23). The church thus looked to follow Christ's lead and discern his will, which was perfectly aligned with God's eternal plans of redemption.

Keep in Tune with the Spirit, Together (5:18–21)

Paul instructed his readers to be filled with the Spirit's presence and influence in their corporate lives as believers, by building up each other with songs of spiritual truth, expressing heartfelt worship to God, giving thanks in all circumstances, and deferring to one another in their interpersonal relationships.

5:18. Paul made a slight transition (καί, "and") to a new focus on the command to be filled with the Spirit, along with the ways in which the Spirit would fill them as group of believers. Paul first prohibited getting drunk with wine (μὴ μεθύσκεσθε οἴνῳ, "do not get drunk with wine"). Paul had in mind excessive drinking of wine that led to intoxication. Paul criticized drunkenness in several places in his letters as a vice that conflicted with his readers' identity and calling (Rom. 13:13; Gal. 5:21; 1 Thess. 5:7; 1 Tim. 3:8). Paul further explained that getting drunk with wine involved or consisted of (ἐν ᾧ ἐστιν, "in which is") "debauchery" (NIV, ESV, NRSV, NET), or "dissipation" (NASB, NKJV), which was a state of being out of control in "reckless living" (CSB). This unrestrained living was often associated with wild parties in the Roman world (BDAG, s.v. "ἀσωτία," p. 148). Paul may have singled out drunkenness here because immoderate drinking brought people under the influence of alcohol, and Paul wanted his readers to be controlled by God's Spirit instead.

In sharp contrast (ἀλλά, "but") to getting drunk, Paul urged his readers to "be filled with the Spirit" (πληροῦσθε ἐν πνεύματι). The form of the verb (pres. pass. impv.) presented the readers as being acted upon by another but taking responsibility to allow this to happen as an ongoing pursuit. Paul spoke frequently in Ephesians of God's "filling" (πληρόω) and "fullness" (πλήρωμα) as a desired goal for his readers. In this case, his readers would open themselves to the Spirit's full influence and keep in tune, or in sync, with the Spirit in their lives together. Paul envisioned God working mightily by his Spirit in the readers' corporate worship, outlook, and interpersonal relationships. Paul expected that the Spirit should permeate and influence everything that his readers did as a community of believers.

> *TRANSLATION ANALYSIS:* A translation of being filled "with" (ἐν) the Spirit (NIV, ESV, NASB, NRSV, NKJV, KJV, NLT; Arnold, 2010, 351) is preferable to "by" the Spirit (CSB, NET; Wallace, 1996, 375; Hoehner, 2002, 703–4) or "in" the Spirit (Heil, 2007, 506–516; Thielman, 2010, 359–360). The option of "with" the Spirit is a plausible rendering of the prepositional phrase in this context (cf. Arnold, 2010, 350). The contrast between wine and the Spirit filling the reader supports an understanding of "with the Spirit" as well. Though in Ephesians Paul often associated filling, fullness, and God's indwelling presence with Christ (Eph. 1:23; 3:17 4:10, 13) and God (Eph. 2:22; 3:19), Paul was known to speak quite flexibly about the presence and activity of God the Father, the Son, and

the Spirit within or among believers (Eph. 2:18–22; 3:16–17; Rom. 8:9–11; 1 Cor. 3:16–17; 12:4–6, 12–13; 2 Cor. 3:16–18; Gal. 4:6; Titus 3:5–6 cf. 1 Cor. 12:13). Even the Spirit's sealing (Eph. 1:13; 4:30) implied the presence of the Spirit in believers (cf. Eph. 1:17; 4:3–4). In this case, "be filled *with* the Spirit" better captures Paul's choice to put the spotlight on the Spirit's dynamic activity among believers.

5:19. In the next three verses, Paul rolled out four parallel explanations (adv. ptc.) that described what being filled with the Spirit looked like within his readers' congregations. These were not separate commands (as in the NIV) but accompanying descriptions of how Paul's readers could experience the Spirit's presence and work in their midst, as a congregation of believers.

TRANSLATION ANALYSIS: The four adverbial participial phrases likely identified the means by which believers lived out their Spirit-filled lives (though not in a strict sense of providing the necessary steps for making possible the Spirit's filling). The phrases provided greater clarity about what being filled with the Spirit consisted of in his readers' corporate worship and interactions. Others have understood the phrases as identifying the result of being filled with the Spirit, emphasizing that the Spirit's filling precedes and empowers the believers' own obedient steps. In this corporate context, however, the participles explained the actual ways that believers together experienced the Spirit's work in their midst (Gombis, 2002, 268–71). In other words, they answered the question of how to operate as a Spirit-led community of faith. This emphasis on the practical outworking of the Spirit's empowering presence fit well with the force of "be filled with the Spirit" (πληροῦσθε ἐν πνεύματι, pass. impv.), with its dual emphasis on seeking the Spirit's empowering help while taking responsibility to be empowered (cf. Phil. 2:12–13).

The first way that Paul expected the readers to draw upon the Spirit's work in their midst was by "speaking to one another" (λαλοῦντες ἑαυτοῖς) with various spiritually edifying messages. Right away the "one another" language confirms that Paul had in mind a corporate outworking of the Spirit's filling. Paul painted the picture of a community of believers who were directing spiritually purposeful communication to one another. Unlike the specific communication of ministers such as apostles, prophets, evangelists, shepherds, and teachers (Eph. 4:11), every believer contributed to corporate spiritual growth through sharing spiritually edifying content to one another.

Paul told the readers to speak to one another "in psalms and hymns and spiritual songs" (ἐν ψαλμοῖς καὶ ὕμνοις καὶ ᾠδαῖς πνευματικαῖς). All three forms of speech that Paul mentioned were musical expressions. Fifty years after this letter was written, even the Roman governor Pliny the Younger knew that Christians incorporated singing in their weekly worship (Pliny, *Ep.* 10.96; cf. Talbert, 2007, 129). Believers kept in tune with the Spirit by singing tunes of spiritual truth to another. Paul's inclusion of the three terms in rapid succession suggested various forms of worship in which spiritual messages were sung and perhaps accompanied by music (psalms in particular were linked to stringed instruments in Israel's practice; Hoehner, 2002, 708).

The first, "psalms" (ψαλμοί), were songs patterned after the book of Psalms of the OT and may have included some of those actual psalms. Paul expected believers to share these psalms in worship settings in order to build up the body of Christ (1 Cor. 14:26). Second, believers were to sing "hymns" (ὕμνοι), which were songs of praise, such as the ones that Paul and Silas had sung to God while they were in prison in Philippi (Acts 16:25). Third, with "spiritual songs" (ᾠδαί πνευματικαί) Paul connected back to the Spirit's filling with the adjective "spiritual" (πνευματικός), referring to songs that were prompted by the Spirit's presence in their midst. All three types of songs contained substantive spiritual instruction that would help Paul's readers grow spiritually (1 Cor. 14:26; Col. 3:16; cf. Eph. 4:15–16).

The second way of being filled with the Spirit (with two actions paired together) reinforced the thought of speaking to one another in psalms, hymns, and spiritual songs. Paul's readers engaged with the Spirit by "singing songs and singing praises in your hearts to the Lord" (ᾄδοντες καὶ ψάλλοντες τῇ καρδίᾳ ὑμῶν τῷ κυρίῳ). Both actions of "singing songs" (ᾄδοντες) and "singing praises" (ψάλλοντες) built upon the corresponding noun forms from the first participial phrase in the list. In addition to building up one another with singing (Eph. 5:19a), Paul's readers were to address their heartfelt singing to the Lord, as an act of worship. The Spirit worked in the heart (Eph. 1:17–18; 3:16–17), or at the center of believers' existence, to impart a knowledge of God's glorious truth and Christ's boundless love. In response, believers drew from the heart to direct genuine praise to the Lord. Paul identified the Lord (κύριος) Jesus as the recipient of believers' praises (see Eph. 5:30).

5:20. Paul added a third way of experiencing the Spirit's directive presence by prescribing "giving thanks" (εὐχαριστοῦντες). This expression of the Spirit's filling flowed naturally from songs of praise. Paul himself practiced giving thanks (Eph. 1:16) and saw it as especially fitting for his readers' new lives in Christ (Eph. 5:4). Paul directed the readers to give thanks "always" (πάντοτε) and "for everything" (ὑπὲρ πάντων). Recipients of God's grace and abiding presence had reason to recognize God's hand in every situation and thus needed to always acknowledge God's goodness by giving thanks to him (cf. Pao, 2002, 104–5). They declared this thanksgiving "in the name of our Lord, Jesus Christ" (ἐν ὀνόματι τοῦ κυρίου ἡμῶν Ἰησοῦ) and directed this thanksgiving "to [our] God and Father" (τῷ θεῷ καὶ πατρί). The name of Christ was often invoked in the worship settings of the early church (1 Cor. 5:4; Col. 3:17; BDAG, s.v. "ὄνομα" 1dɔ, p. 713). Speaking Christ's name while thanking God reiterated Christ's central place in giving believers access to God (Eph. 2:18; 3:12). God the Father was worthy of believers' thanks because he was the giver of all spiritual blessings (Eph. 1:3), and he shared his love and presence as a gift to his children (Eph. 3:14–19). Assuming that this thanksgiving was expressed in a corporate setting, the words that were addressed to God nonetheless also strengthened the faith of others in the congregation (see 1 Cor. 14:16–17).

5:21. The fourth and final way of living in step with the Spirit's work was in "submitting to one another out of reverence for Christ" (ὑποτασσόμενοι ἀλλήλοις ἐν φόβῳ Χριστοῦ). This directive simultaneously wrapped up Paul's list on Spirit-filled living and prepared the way for his discussion about how wives and husbands should treat each other in marriage. Once again, believers participated in the Spirit's movements corporately, this time in the actions of mutual submission. The middle voice form of "submit" (ὑποτασσόμενοι) meant to place oneself under the authority of someone else "in recognition of an ordered structure" of relationships (BDAG, s.v. "ὑποτάσσω" bβ, p. 1042). Paul used the term in this passage to describe deferring to other believers and recognizing their interests above one's own interests, as part of fostering harmonious relationships within the body of Christ (cf. Rom. 12:10; Phil. 2:3–4; Eph. 4:2–3).

Paul identified reverence for Christ Jesus as the ultimate motivating force behind his readers' submission to one another. Paul insisted that his readers' common "fear of Christ" (φόβος Χριστοῦ) should shape the way that they all treated each other. This fear of Christ was a reverence that acknowledged Christ's exalted position (see Eph. 1:9–10, 20–22; 4:9–10) and recognized his authority over one's life

(Acts 9:31; cf. 2 Cor. 7:1; Phil. 2:12; 1 Peter 1:17). The readers' reverent submission to Christ's authority compelled them to honor one another and submit to one another.

THEOLOGICAL FOCUS

The exegetical idea (Paul's readers were called to live wisely and strategically in the broader, evil world, to seek to understand and follow God's will, and to be filled with the Spirit's presence and influence in their corporate worship, outlook, and relationships) leads to this theological focus: Believers should live strategically in their interactions with those who do not know Christ and keep in tune with the Spirit in corporate worship and relationships.

The passage introduces theological concepts relevant to both Christian mission and the church's worship and fellowship. First, the text presents a vision of Christian mission marked by discernment and strategic focus. Believers must think carefully about how they fit within the surrounding culture and how they are called to represent Christ in their setting (vv. 15–16). This requires great wisdom, which God supplies graciously through his Spirit (Eph. 1:17). Living wisely consists of discerning the Lord's will for each situation and being ready to act in step with Christ's priorities (5:17). This can feel challenging when living in a complex world that operates by different assumptions and values than those of God's kingdom. But the world system that is characteristic of this present evil age is marked for judgment (v. 16a), which means that believers must engage in strategic mission while they have the chance. They are not content to simply isolate themselves from sinful environments and bury their talents while they await the coming kingdom of God. They capitalize on their window of opportunity (v. 16b) and shine the light of Christ in each circumstance.

Second, believers who want to advance Christ's mission effectively must tend to their own spiritual growth and strengthening as a church. All of Ephesians imparts this vision of believers drawing together as the one, unified body of Christ. God supplies his Spirit to dwell within the body of Christ and empower his people for corporate worship and shared life together (v. 18). Believers should be filled with the Spirit, or be in sync with the Spirit's ministry among them, by sharing songs of spiritual truth to each other, singing praises to God with sincere hearts, giving thanks to God at all times for all that he does, and loving other believers enough to put their interests and perspectives ahead of their own (vv. 18–21). These Spirit-filled attitudes and practices towards God, circumstances, and fellow believers allow the body of Christ to be a healthy and dynamic representative of God's kingdom to the surrounding world.

PREACHING AND TEACHING STRATEGIES

Exegetical and Theological Synthesis

Paul stated the main idea of this passage up front like a headline: "consider carefully how you walk [live]" (v. 15). The rest of the passage develops how and why he commanded the Ephesians to do so. In verses 15 and 16, Paul described the days as "evil." By this he implied that judgment was coming, so believers were challenged to capitalize on the current window of opportunity to live for Christ and represent him to the people they related to outside the church. Rather than being controlled by alcohol or other longings, believers were to be controlled by the Spirit (v. 18). With four phrases (vv. 19–21) Paul expanded on how to be filled—by speaking to one another in songs, by singing and making melody to the Lord, by giving thanks to the Father at all times and for everything, and by submitting to one another. All was to be done in the name of the Lord Jesus, out of reverence for Christ, by being filled with the Holy Spirit. This would help the followers of Christ nurture their own spiritual lives and corporate identity, and thus to be equipped to live strategically for Christ with discernment and a focus on mission.

Preaching Idea

To live strategically, sync with the Spirit.

Contemporary Connections

What does it mean?

What does it mean that to live strategically, we should sync with the Spirit? "Strategy" refers to a deliberate, planned approach to accomplishing a goal. Sometimes the term is used in business, as with a "sales strategy," and sometimes in the military as in "the strategy to defend London from the Blitz." In the preaching idea, the term captures the emphasis in the passage on living missionally and purposefully in society. As Greg says, we should take advantage or be "capitalizing on this window of opportunity." The word "sync" (also spelled "synch") comes from "synchronization." It means a harmonious, coordinated relationship, as in: "The dancers were in perfect sync"; or "The picture and the soundtrack were out of sync." So, to "sync with the Spirit" means that the believer's words, actions, and attitudes mesh with the character of God. Paul's letter to the Ephesians has described God's character as gracious, loving, merciful, holy, truthful, and wise. So when we sync with the Spirit, we will extend grace, speak the truth, and so forth. In these ways, we will be effective witnesses for Christ in these evil days. Examples from church history, recent history, and the congregation's immediate context can flesh out what it looks like to sync with the Spirit. For example, in the 1800s the Quakers helped enslaved people escape to Canada, thus displaying the compassion and justice of God. Those same qualities were present in Rwanda during the 1994 genocide when some brave Tutsi men and women sheltered their Hutu neighbors. Perhaps your church or organization has a ministry to unwed mothers, walking with them rather than condemning them. Highlighting that ministry shows how being in sync with the Spirit leads us to display the character of God in tangible ways.

A case study of Daniel could help explain the preaching idea. As Greg pointed out in the exposition, Paul may have had the book of Daniel in mind as he wrote this passage. The OT sage was a foreigner in a Gentile and pagan land. His peers opposed him, yet he embodied courage, wisdom, and steadfastness. Thus Daniel made the most of his opportunities and shined in the midst of the pagan culture. The sermon could even be expanded into two sermons by spending an extra week on Daniel; or a discussion session following the sermon could focus on Daniel.

Is it true?

Is it true that followers of Christ should live strategically by syncing with the Spirit? Self-disclosure could answer that—a self-effacing example of when you were conformed to the culture more than the character of God. Perhaps you were cut off in traffic and responded poorly, or there was a time when your children got under your skin and you lashed out. Biblical examples can also show the need to sync with the Spirit. In Galatians, Paul described how Peter feared the Jews and refused to eat with Gentiles. That was not Spirit-led! The disciples fled when Jesus was arrested in the Garden of Gethsemane, but in contrast, the women around the cross were in sync with the Spirit. They bravely stayed with their Savior.

One way to live strategically by syncing with the Spirit is by speaking to one another in spiritual songs, but the connection may not be self-evident to listeners. A reminder of the power of words (Prov. 18:21) can show that the words we say to each other help or hinder how we live godly lives. Similarly, a reminder of the power of music can support the preaching idea. When words are conveyed with melody and rhythm, they penetrate the heart. As Plato said, poets and singers have more influence in a state than the lawmakers because "rhythm and melody above all penetrate to the innermost part of the soul." (Plato, *Resp*. III, 401d [trans. Emlyn-Jones, Preddy, LCL]).

Two phrases that support the preaching idea may need development. Those phrases are "give thanks always and for everything," and the other is "submitting to one another."

Now what?

How can we live strategically by syncing with the Spirit? The four participial phrases of verses 19–21 give practical advice:

- addressing one another by singing psalms, hymns, and spiritual songs
- singing and making melody in your heart to the Lord
- giving thanks always and for everything
- submitting to one another

The first phrase, "address one another by singing" could be applied by having the congregation face each other as they sing. Perhaps the chairs could be arranged in a circle, or part of the congregation (such as people seated in the balcony) could sing a portion of a song, and then another part of the congregation could sing the next portion. Similarly, antiphonal singing as in Psalm 136 might give the worshippers an opportunity to sing not only to God but to each other. Perhaps a gifted musician in your group could write a song designed for that group. It might deal with an incident that happened in the community or might tie together the themes the church learned in a previous sermon series. I have a friend who did this when her husband finished preaching through the book of Revelation. She wrote a song about persecution, martyrdom, the Lamb that was slain, and the hope of the second coming of Christ, thus reminding (speaking to) the congregation.

The second phrase, "singing in one's heart," can be made concrete with self-disclosure. Some people sing as part of their daily devotions. Others may journal and write their own psalms. Others sing when they drive or listen to praise music as they exercise. Through rhythm and harmony, the theology of the songs finds its way into the soul.

The third phrase, "giving thanks always," can be put into daily life with the use of check points throughout the day. We might pause at mealtimes to say thank you for more than just the food. Some people set an alarm on their watch to remind themselves to pause, clear their minds, and express thanks.

The fourth phrase, "submitting to each other," can take place in a variety of ways. We might practice the discipline of "not having the last word" when disagreement flares. Or we could volunteer for an unpleasant task that no one enjoys. On a mission trip if we are staying at a facility with limited amenities, we might let our teammates use the shower before we do, or let them sleep near the window in the stuffy room.

Creativity in Presentation

Consider the following suggestions to illustrate "being in sync."

- Show an example of lip-syncing done poorly, such as Lin Miaoke, the adorable child who sang the Chinese national anthem at the Beijing Olympics. It was discovered later that she was not the actual singer, but was a stand-in for Yang Peiyi.[2]

- Show a clip from the classic movie *Singing in the Rain* (directed by Stanley Donen and Gene Kelly, 1952) staring Gene Kelly, Donald O'Connor, and Debbie Reynolds. The film is set in the

2 For an example of this, search for Beijing Olympics 2009 Lin Miaoke Ode to the Motherland on YouTube. Specifically look for the subsection "Girl lip-synching to recording by another singer" in "2008 Summer Olympics opening ceremony."

early days of "talkies" in Hollywood, and a hilarious fiasco occurs at the premier showing of a movie when the audio goes out of sync with the visual.[3]

- We might warn about living in sync with the values of sinful culture rather than with the Spirit with an analogy of the Millennium Bridge in London, a steel suspension bridge for pedestrians crossing the River Thames. When it opened in June of 2000, thousands of pedestrians began to walk unintentionally in the same rhythm. They were too much in sync with one another. This caused the bridge to sway alarmingly, and it had to be shut down for extensive study and modification, reopening in February of 2002. Morally speaking, Christians must watch carefully how they walk (v. 15) so as not to be conformed to (or in sync with) the evil in society.[4]

- Children in the congregation could volunteer for the following exercise: Have them follow your movements such as patting your head, swaying left, and marching in place. As the movements increase one after the other and the pace quickens, they may have trouble staying in sync with you.

Verse 21, "submitting to one another," might be actualized with a foot-washing ceremony. I (Jeffrey) did not grow up in a tradition that practices foot washing, and in the handful of times I have experienced it, I have found it to be a moving, symbolic act of what we should be doing day in and day out—serving one another. Older people washing young people's feet, or the pastoral staff washing the "laity," picture how the members of the body submit to each other.

Using a timer or alarm clock could illustrate the idea of living strategically by "redeeming the time" ("capitalizing on this window of opportunity"). Listeners might be instructed to learn as many new names of people in the congregation as they can in sixty seconds. After the buzzer sounds, the preacher or worship leader could "interview" the winner, asking what techniques helped him or her make the most of the opportunity.

The sidebars contain other illustrations that could be used to illustrate "living strategically."

Dying Man Redeems the Time

In 2015, Owen Williams and his wife moved into a new home in Wales and befriended their eighty-year-old neighbor, Ken Watson. When the Owens' daughter, Cadi, was born in 2017, Watson became a grandfather figure for her, but his days were limited and he seems to have known it. He wanted to have a continuing role in Cadi's life even after his death, so he made the most of his time. He collected fourteen Christmas gifts for Cadi to be opened, one per year until she was sixteen.[5]

Actor Plays Real-Life Superhero

Mark Ruffalo plays Dr. Bruce Banner / The Hulk in Marvel superhero films, but he also produced and starred in *Dark Waters* (directed by Todd Haynes, 2019), which tells the true story of a man whom Ruffalo considers to be a real-life superhero. Ruffalo produced the film after being challenged by a fan to make more films that depict Christians honorably. The film is set in

3 For an example, search "Singin' in the Rain" on YouTube.

4 For an example, search "London Millenium Bridge Opening," on YouTube.

5 Allison Klein, "A Dying Man Bought 14 Years Worth of Christmas Gifts for His 2-year-old Neighbor," December 18, 2018, *Washington Post*, https://www.washingtonpost.com/lifestyle/2018/12/18/twitter-weighs-after-neighbors-death-give-all-presents-now-or-one-year/?wpisrc=nl_optimist&wpmm=1.

a West Virginia town and traces its legal battle against a major chemical corporation for polluting the local water. The protagonist is a corporate defense attorney who is a devout Christian living missionally, finding ways to reflect the light of Christ by taking action against injustice. Ruffalo plays this attorney named Robert Bilott, who initiated the lawsuit after a local rancher convinced him that toxic waste was killing his cattle. Ruffalo said, "I believe our heroes, real heroes in the world, are the ones who are like Rob Bilott. . . . [I]t was a story that we needed to see and hear at this particular moment in time."[6]

Be sure to emphasize this point: Believers should conduct themselves according to wisdom, not foolishness. That is strategic living that helps us "redeem" the time. In this passage wisdom looks like not getting drunk, but rather being filled with the Spirit. To live strategically, sync with the Spirit.

A possible sermon outline:

- Our External Relationships: Live Strategically by Syncing with the Spirt (vv. 15–18a).
- Our Internal Relationship: Live Harmoniously by Syncing with the Spirit (vv. 18b–21).
    - Speak to one another in worship music.
    - Sing and make music in your heart to the Lord.
    - Give thanks always for everything.
    - Submit to one another.

DISCUSSION QUESTIONS

1. In what sense are the days evil in this present world? Give some examples.
2. How does living strategically in the world include both moral vigilance and intentional mission?
3. Name an OT character who made the most of his or her opportunities in dark days. Name some of that person's actions and attitudes.
4. Why does the passage contrast getting drunk with being filled with the Spirit?
5. Of the four ways that help us stay in sync with the Spirit, which do you find easiest? Hardest?
6. What does it look like to give thanks always for everything, whether in good or bad circumstances?
7. In what ways have you seen the presence or absence of mutual submission shape the relational culture of a church or organization in good or bad ways?

6 Emily McFarlan Miller, "Actor Mark Ruffalo Blends Film and Faith-fueled Activism in 'Dark Waters,'" *Religious News Service*, December 10, 2019, https://religionnews.com/2019/12/10/actor-mark-ruffalo-blends-film-and-faith-fueled-activism-in-dark-waters.

Ephesians 5:22–33

EXEGETICAL IDEA

Paul's readers cultivated strong marriages when wives respectfully submitted themselves to their husbands and husbands selflessly loved and tenderly cared for their wives, since marriages reflected the intimate bond and ordered structure of Christ's union with his body, the church, and Christ had sacrificially loved and purposefully led the church.

THEOLOGICAL FOCUS

Wives and husbands are to treat one another in marriage according to the model of the ordered, loving, and united relationship between Christ and the church.

PREACHING IDEA

A good marriage is a great mirror of Christ and the church.

PREACHING POINTERS

Paul's vision of a new humanity in Christ needed to make a meaningful difference in his readers' household relationships. Like other people in Greco-Roman society, Paul's readers lived in households that often included husbands and wives, children, other relatives, and slaves. Paul's readers' new life in Christ gave them an opportunity to experience relationships that were uniquely different from their old way of life. Marriage relationships were fundamental in Paul's time, and they could be undermined through disrespect, abuse, and adultery. The presence of God's Spirit in their midst meant that Paul's readers needed to commit to a better way. How was Paul's readers' new status as adopted children of God in Christ supposed to influence their relationships with their spouses? Paul found a potent answer in the ordered, loving, and intimate bond between Christ and the church.

From domestic abuse, to passive aggressive behavior, to no-fault divorce, the institution of marriage needs a shot in the arm today. The divorce statistics in the United States may seem encouraging because divorce is declining, but take a closer look. The likely reason why divorce is declining is because fewer people are marrying. Living together outside the covenant of marriage is on the rise. Using the magnificent theology of Christ and the church, this passage shows us how wives submit to and respect their husbands and how husbands love and sacrifice for their wives. Christian devotion rises no higher than our home lives. The passive husband who escapes to the TV room can grow in Christlikeness when he hears how the Lord Jesus loved the church and gave himself for her. Christ's love is selfless, tender, and attentive. The frustrated wife who derides her husband can grow in Christlikeness too when she hears how the church submits to Christ. In the same way, she should submit to and respect her husband.

MARRIAGES THAT REFLECT THE UNION OF CHRIST AND THE CHURCH (5:22–33)

LITERARY STRUCTURE AND THEMES (5:22–33)

Ephesians 5:22–33 is one part of the household instructions in Ephesians 5:22–6:9, and in four sections the passage examines how husbands and wives should relate to one another. In the first section (5:22–24), Paul directed wives to submit to their husbands as a way of honoring the Lord and acknowledging the ordered structure of the household. In the second section (5:25–28a), Paul urged husbands to love their wives, imitating Christ's sacrificial love for the church. In the third section (5:28b–32), Paul persuaded husbands to show attentive and tender care for their wives, since marriages brought husbands and wives into intimate union with each other, and this union pointed to an even more profound union between Christ and the church. In the fourth section (5:33), Paul summarized the passages by instructing husbands to love their wives and wives to respect their husbands.

The passage springboards directly off of Ephesians 5:21 and its admonition to Paul's readers to voluntarily yield their rights to one another in interpersonal relationships. More generally, the section builds upon all of Ephesians 5:15–21, which was punctuated by the command to "be filled with the Spirit" (Eph. 5:18; Fee, 1994, 719). Paul thus gave instructions about what being filled with the Spirit and fostering an attitude of others-centeredness should look like within the context of marriage relationships. Analogies abound in this passage—primarily through a comparison of husbands and wives to Christ and the church. Paul the theologian was obviously energized by his comprehension of Christ's amazing bond with his body, the church. Paul revealed significant truth about both the husband-wife relationship and the nature of Christ's authority, love, and unity with respect to the church.

- ***Wives, Submit to Your Husbands, Honoring the Lord (5:22–24)***
- ***Husbands, Love Your Wives, Imitating Christ's Love (5:25–28a)***
- ***Tender Marital Unity Points to Christ and the Church (5:28b–32)***
- ***Husbands Should Love and Wives Should Show Respect (5:33)***

EXPOSITION (5:22–33)

Paul's primary purpose in this passage was to strengthen marriages, since he began and ended on that note, as part of the broader household teachings of Ephesians 5:22–6:9, The teachings continued to reflect the basic equality among all believers that was assumed in Ephesians 5:21 (cf. Gal. 3:28). Paul spoke to wives and husbands directly and in turn, communicating their agency to carry out the instructions rather than any need to be compelled by others to obey. He imparted wisdom that raised a high bar for both wives and husbands, in a way that stood apart from a broader culture in which even gods and goddesses were known for acts of seduction and adultery (*DNTB*, 8). Paul emphasized acts that valued the personhood and calling of the other person and that built harmony, trust, and intimacy in the marriage.

Paul's important secondary purpose, however, was to display a rich theology of Christ's loving bond with his body, the church. Human marriages were to be patterned after Christ's connection with his church, and marriages were even meant to further display the beauty of Christ's covenantal union with his church. At times, Paul even moved beyond the direct comparison between human marriages and Christ's relationship with the church to explore more fully Christ's work as Savior and purifier of the church. Far from simply prescribing conventional lives for his readers, Paul wanted to inspire them with a majestic picture of where they fit within the sweeping plans of a mighty and loving God.

Wives, Submit to Your Husbands, Honoring the Lord (5:22–24)

Paul directed the wives among his readers to be willing to submit themselves to their own husbands out of devotion to Christ and in recognition of the husband's position of leadership that mirrored Christ's leadership of the church.

5:22. Paul began a new section by directing wives to submit to their husbands (αἱ γυναῖκες τοῖς ἰδίοις ἀνδράσιν, "wives . . . to your own husbands"). These were part of Paul's integration of life in Christ into the fabric of household relationships (Eph. 5:22–6:9). Households in Paul's world included husbands and wives, children, other relatives, and even slaves. Paul talked about households as family units in various places in his letters (1 Cor. 1:16; 16:5; 1 Tim. 3:4–5, 12; 5:4, 8; 2 Tim. 1:16; 3:6; Titus 1:11).

Paul made a shift to the new topic of relationships within the household, though grammatically and thematically verse 22 is tied to verse 21. In verse 21, Paul had endorsed "submitting to one another" (ὑποτασσόμενοι ἀλλήλοις), or fostering mutual humility and deference to others in interpersonal relationships within the body of Christ. In verse 22, Paul linked to the prior participle "submitting" (ὑποτασσόμενοι), without restating it, and applied it to exhortations given to "wives" (αἱ γυναῖκες).

Paul explained that in their marriages, wives should submit to their husbands. The term "submit" (ὑποτάσσω) suggested voluntarily and respectfully deferring to another's leadership, within an acknowledged, legitimate ordering of relationships (BDAG, s.v. "ὑποτάσσω" 1bβ, p. 1042). In various passages of Scripture, wives submitted themselves to husbands (Col. 3:18), believers submitted themselves to spiritual leaders (1 Peter 2:18), household slaves submitted themselves to their masters (Titus 2:9), people submitted themselves to governing authorities (Rom. 13:1–5), and Jesus even submitted himself to his parents (Luke 2:51). Indeed, the world of Paul and his readers was structured in such a way that people were aware of contours of authority and submission in all areas of their lives (Cohick, 2010, 135).

The idea of everyone yielding to one another (Eph. 5:21) did not negate the validity of ordered relationships of authority and submission, though it did lend credence to the view that voluntary rather than enforced submission was in mind. It also suggested that Paul did not consider Christlike submission to be demeaning for anyone. He believed that a culture of willing submission and regard for others should permeate the early church in all relationships, even beyond the typical ordered spheres recognized by society. Within those ordered spheres, though, further instruction about submission was needed. God himself had arranged a design for marriage (note Paul's quotation of Gen. 2:24 later in the passage), as part of his broader creation of an orderly world (Gen. 1:1–2:3). In Ephesians 5:22, then, Paul advocated voluntary submission of wives to husbands within the ordered structure of marriage.

Household Codes

Paul and other Jewish and Greek thinkers discussed proper structuring of relationships within households. Scholars call these similar writings "household codes" (*Haustafeln* in German). Aristotle was interested in effectively managed households, organized around relationships between husbands and wives, fathers and children, and masters and slaves, because he believed that strong households were crucial for strong societies (Aristotle, *Pol.* 1.2.1–3; 1.5.1–2). Jewish teachers (Josephus, *Ag. Ap.* 2.199–201; Philo, *Hypoth.* 7.3, as reported by Eusebius in *Praep. ev.* 8.7.3) similarly saw the importance of maintaining relationships that preserved order and hierarchy within households. These Jewish examples may have looked back to the household-focused teachings found within the Ten Commandments (cf. Exod. 20; Moritz, 1996, 158–59). Both Greco-Roman and Jewish household codes specified how the male head of the family should exercise his authority, and they sometimes also explained how the wife, children, and slaves should defer to the head of the family. Paul delivered a similar framework of teachings in Ephesians 5:22–6:9 (cf. Col. 3:18–4:1), though without any indication that he was using these other writings directly as a source. In fact, Paul organized all of his instructions around the readers' new life in Christ, drawing upon guidance from the authority and love Christ exercises towards the church.

Since the structure and subject matter of Paul's ideas resembles the teaching from the Jewish and Greco-Roman worlds, it prompts the question of Paul's purpose for covering this similar ground. Did Paul have primarily an instructive goal, hoping to reinforce these familiar expectations for relationships within the household, while orienting the relationships around Christ (Dudrey, 1999, 40–41; Hoehner, 2002, 725–26; Witherington, 2007, 321–323; Thielman, 2010, 368–69; Bock, 2019, 170–71)? Or, did Paul have a missionary goal, hoping to help Christian households be faithful to Christ while avoiding unnecessary clashes with their surrounding culture (Keener, 1992, 145–47; Lincoln, 1990, 357–58; Towner, *DPL*, 419; cf. Titus 2:1–10)? Or is it possible that Paul's Christ-centered instructions were meant to expose the inadequacies of popular notions of household relationships by presenting a vision for family life that greatly exceeded the common formula (Gombis, 2005, 317–20; Arnold, 2010, 369–79)? Most likely, Paul had the first two purposes in mind as complementary goals for his churches. Paul wanted to ensure that his readers made the most of their window of opportunity as lights in the world (Eph. 5:16), so they needed to think intentionally about how their own ordered households could testify meaningfully to the loving and powerful presence of Christ in their midst.

Paul addressed "the wives" (αἱ γυναῖκες) directly (nom. of address). Though the term Paul used (γυνή) could refer to women, wives, or even newly married women (BDAG, s.v. "γυνή," p. 208–9), in this context wives in general were certainly in view. The adjective "own" (ἴδίος), modifying "husbands" (ἀνήρ), specified that wives were to submit specifically to their own husbands (not to all men in general).

The compact clause "as to the Lord" (ὡς τῷ κυρίῳ) encouraged the wives to submit to their husbands with a focus on the Lord as the ultimate recipient of their actions. The subordinating conjunction "as" (ὡς) introduced the mindset with which something is undertaken (BDAG, s.v. "ὡς" 3aα, p. 1104–5). In Ephesians 6:7, Paul used the same phrase (ὡς τῷ κυρίῳ) in contrast to "not to people" (οὐκ ἀνθρώποις) to indicate the proper motivation for slaves' work (cf. Col. 3:23). Paul directed wives to support husbands with an attitude of wanting to please Christ in doing so (cf. Col. 3:18; Eph. 5:21). The addition of "to the Lord" specified the wives' ultimate loyalty, ensuring that any submission was shaped by obedience to Christ and thus would not involve violating the will of God.

5:23. Paul identified that a reason (ὅτι, "since") for wives' submission to their husbands was found in an analogous relationship the church had with Christ. Paul began the first half of the comparison with the statement that "a husband is the head of the wife" (ἀνήρ ἐστιν κεφαλὴ τῆς γυναικός). The term "head" (κεφαλή) likely implied a role of authority in this context. The husband was entrusted with a role of oversight in relation to the wife that was part of the ordered arrangement of the household (cf. 1 Tim. 3:4).

TRANSLATION ANALYSIS: The word "head" (κεφαλή) often described a literal head of a body but typically communicated a meaning of "superior rank" (BDAG, s.v. "κεφαλή" 2a, p. 542), or "preeminence" (Hoehner, 2002, 739) when used metaphorically. All major English versions of the Bible translate the two occurrences of the term (κεφαλή) as "head" in Ephesians 5:23. When Paul introduced "head" as a metaphor for Christ's relationship to the church in Ephesians 1:22–23, the term pointed to Christ's authority over the church, as a sign of his rule over all things. Ephesians 4:15–16 depicted the church body's dependency upon Christ, the head, for its growth. In Ephesians 5:22–24, the association of submission (within an ordered relationship that involved recognition of authority) with headship in Ephesians 5:22–24 supports a sense of leadership for "head" in this context. Other related passages also suggest a notion of authority in Paul's use of "head" in Ephesians 5:23 (1 Cor. 11:3; Col. 1:18; 2:10). When Paul used the term "head" in Ephesians 5:23, he recognized a leadership role for husbands in marriage that paralleled Christ's relationship to the church.

Paul made the comparison (ὡς καί, "as also") that the husband was the head of his wife as "Christ [was] head of the church" (ὁ Χριστὸς κεφαλὴ τῆς ἐκκλησίας). Paul's choice of "head" (κεφαλή) to describe the husband's role in a marriage was inspired by Christ's position as head of the church, his body (Eph. 1:22–23; cf. 2:16; 4:4, 12, 15–16). In both instances, the head exercised a role of leadership in the context of an intimate, unified relationship (cf. Eph. 5:28–32). This correlation between the husband's relationship with his wife and Christ's relationship with the church provided a basis for wives' submission of themselves to their husbands.

Paul further characterized Christ's relationship to the church by identifying him as "Savior of the body" (αὐτὸς σωτὴρ τοῦ σώματος). Paul's emphatic use of "he himself" (αὐτός) confirmed an application of the title "Savior" (σωτήρ) to Christ alone. "Savior" no longer functioned as part of the direct analogy describing husbands' role with their wives. The title "Savior" (σωτήρ) described one who rescued or delivered, and when applied to God or Christ spoke of deliverance from sin, death, and judgment, as an expression of God's love for the world (Eph. 1:13; 2:5, 8; 6:17). Jesus had secured salvation from sin and its penalty through his death on the cross (Titus 3:4–6; cf. 1 Cor. 15:1–4), and he promised to return to bring final victory over death for his people (Phil. 3:20; Titus 2:13; cf. Rom. 13:11; 1 Thess. 5:9). He saved "the body" (τὸ σῶμα), the church, which was composed of redeemed Jews and Gentiles who were in unbreakable, intimate union with him (Eph. 2:5–6; 13–22; 3:16–17; 4:15–16). By mentioning Christ's role as Savior in conjunction with his headship, Paul painted the picture of Christ's strong, caring leadership that had the best interests of the body in mind (cf. Eph. 5:25–27).

5:24. Paul further developed the correspondence between husbands and wives and Christ and the church by relating wives' submission to their husbands to the church's submission to Christ. The conjunction "but" (ἀλλά) contains a contrastive force that shifted the focus back to the main point at hand. Paul used the common comparative construction "as . . . so also" (ὡς . . . οὕτως καί) to show how the church's submission to Christ should shape wives' submission to their husbands.

The starting point for the comparison was that "the church submits to Christ" (ἡ ἐκκλησία ὑποτάσσεται τῷ Χριστῷ). This time the term "submit" (ὑποτάσσω) showed up overtly in the verse, unlike the implied imperative in verse 22. The indicative form of "submit" stated the way that the church interacted with Christ. The church followed the lead of its head, recognizing the ordered nature of the relationship between Christ and the church.

Paul expected wives to adopt this same posture toward their husbands. Paul did not repeat the verb "submit" but carried it over to the second part of the comparison. Wives' submission to their husbands was grounded in and aspired after the model of the church's submission to Christ. Paul specified that wives should submit to their husbands "in everything" (ἐν παντί). This was also the implied scope of the church's submission to Christ. This comprehensive picture of wives' submission anticipated Paul's discussion of the complete unity of the husband and wife in marriage (Eph. 5:31). Paul's purpose was to establish a general norm for the marital relationship rather than to delve into what this would look like in all possible scenarios. Unlike in 1 Corinthians 7, where he offered more practical guidance for married people, Paul was not responding to his readers' specific questions. His argument rested on his understanding of God's design for marriage. God intended for marriages to reflect the order, love, and unity of Christ's relationship with his church.

Husbands, Love Your Wives, Imitating Christ's Love (5:25–28a)

Paul informed the husbands that their love for their wives should imitate Christ's love for the church, which Christ expressed through offering himself on the cross, for the purpose of setting apart the church through a spiritual cleansing, in anticipation of a final presentation of his glorious bride, the church, in a state of beautiful moral perfection.

5:25. Next, Paul addressed husbands' responsibilities toward their wives (nom. of address, cf. v. 22). Paul called for affectionate and self-giving love modeled after Christ's love for the church. Paul declared, "Husbands, love your wives" (οἱ ἄνδρες, ἀγαπᾶτε τὰς γυναῖκας). The verb "love" (ἀγαπάω) in this context was unusual, appearing only rarely in broader literature related to marriage, and would not have been the natural inverse of "submit" (Best, 1998, 540). Loving others entailed expressing care for them and seeking their best interests (BDAG, s.v. "ἀγαπάω" 1, p. 5). Paul defined Christlike love in great detail in 1 Corinthians 13:4–7, commending qualities such as patience and not seeking one's own interests. Paul's readers were already expected to walk in love toward one another, by treating one another with genuine kindness and forgiveness (Eph. 4:32–5:2), but in this passage Paul zoomed in on the more particular love a husband should have for his wife.

A husband's love for his wife was compared to (καθὼς καί, "just as also"), and thus motivated by, two powerful, interrelated actions by Christ (in two parallel clauses). First, Paul said that husbands should love their wives just as "Christ loved the church" (ὁ Χριστὸς ἠγάπησεν τὴν ἐκκλησίαν). The church consisted of people, such as Paul's readers, who had been given new life in Christ, through faith. This love involved Christ's heartfelt concern for all people in the church, whether male or female, young or old, slave or free, but Paul also viewed Christ's love as an active love, not a mere sentiment (Eph. 2:4–6; 5:2; Rom. 5:8; 2 Cor. 5:14–15). In fact, in the second supporting clause, Paul immediately associated Christ's love with his sacrificial offering of himself for the church. Christ "gave himself up for her" (ἑαυτὸν παρέδωκεν ὑπὲρ αὐτῆς), referring to his willing offering of himself on the cross for believers' sins (Eph. 1:7; 2:13–16). Paul had used the same pairing of Christ loving and giving himself up for believers in Ephesians 5:2 (cf. Gal. 2:20). Christ's sacrificial love set a high bar for the love that husbands were expected to aspire to. Christ had set aside his own interests and had accepted a painful and humiliating death on the cross (Phil. 2:6–8) for the sake of his church. This was how he had demonstrated his love. Paul challenged husbands to treat this remarkable display of Christ's love as a pattern for their own love for their wives.

5:26. Paul identified Christ's purpose (ἵνα, "in order that") for loving and giving himself up for his people, the church. At this point in the discourse, the focus on husbands and wives faded temporarily into the background. For the time being, Paul sought to further develop the way in which Christ fulfilled his role as husband to the church.

Christ offered himself "in order that he might sanctify her [the church]" (ἵνα αὐτὴν ἁγιάσῃ). To "sanctify" (ἁγιάζω) meant to consecrate or set apart someone, in order to provide access to a relationship with a holy God (BDAG, s.v. "ἁγιάζω" 2, p. 10). Paul had set the stage for this truth of Christ's sanctifying work earlier in the letter. Paul had proclaimed that God chose believers in Christ for a purpose—that they would be "holy" (ἅγιος) and blameless before him, in love (Eph. 1:4; cf. 1 Cor. 1:2). Christ's reconciling ministry consisted of providing access to the Father for both Jews and Gentiles (Eph. 2:18; 3:12). Now, in Ephesians 5:26, Paul reiterated that Christ's sacrificial offering of himself for the church was what made this sanctification possible. Christ sanctified the church to set apart the church for a special relationship with himself.

Next, Paul indicated the means (adv. ptc. of means, καθαρίσας) by which Christ sanctified the church. He accomplished this "by cleansing [her]" (καθαρίσας). This action of cleansing was more likely contemporaneous with the sanctifying (NIV, NRSV, NET, CSB), rather than prior to it (ESV, NASB). The implied recipient of the cleansing was the church. In this context, the term "to cleanse" (καθαρίζω) meant "to purify through ritual cleansing" (BDAG, s.v. "καθαρίζω" 3, p. 488), or to remove sins that prevented a relationship with God. Cleansing thus supported Christ's purpose of sanctifying his church, so that both Jews and Gentiles could enter into a permanent relationship with him and represent him as a new humanity (Eph. 2:14–18; Titus 2:14).

Cleansing

Christ's act of cleansing carried particular significance in the religious environment of Paul's readers. A major theological debate in the early church was about whether Gentiles who believed in Christ could be considered clean without taking on all of the requirements of the Jewish law. Through two successive experiences, God communicated to the apostle Peter that Gentiles were now clean in Christ, without needing to become Jews (Acts 10:9–48). First, he gave Peter a heavenly vision that all foods were now considered clean, since God had made them clean (καθαρίζω; cf. Mark 7:19). Immediately after that, Peter preached the gospel to Cornelius and other Gentiles with him. When they believed in Christ, God poured out his Spirit on them (cf. Eph. 1:13). Taken together, these two episodes drove home the point that as part of the new covenant, God was cleansing people through Christ's sacrifice and the gift of his Spirit. Disputes about this issue persisted, however, so the church leaders all gathered for what is now known as the Jerusalem Council (Acts 15:1–35). There, the apostles and other leaders determined once for all that God no longer distinguished between Jews and Gentiles who were in Christ (Eph. 2:15), since God had given believers from both groups his Holy Spirit and had "cleansed" their hearts by faith (Acts 15:9).

Christ accomplished his cleansing "with the washing of water" (τῷ λουτρῷ τοῦ ὕδατος). The language of washing with water could have referred to baptism (Abbott, 1897, 168; Stott, 1979, 227; Lincoln, 1990, 375; Best, 1998, 542–43; Muddiman, 2001, 265), but Paul more likely described an inward cleansing or purification from sins (Barth, 1974, 699; Hoehner, 2002, 752–54; Witherington, 2007, 330; Thielman, 2010, 383–84; Arnold, 2010, 387–89; Bock, 2019, 178). OT imagery about God's covenantal marriage to his people had likely inspired Paul's wording. In particular, Ezekiel 16:8–14 portrayed the dedicated and unmerited love God showed to Israel when he bathed her with water (16:9), to help prepare her for a covenantal marriage ceremony. Jewish brides took part in an actual ceremonial bath (Ferguson, 2003, 74; Keener, 2014, 552–53) that resembled the preparations described in the passage. Ezekiel 36:25–28 also correlated God's cleansing of Israel with the gift of the Spirit, as part of his radical renewal of his covenant with his people. Paul likely reflected this association between cleansing and inward renewal by the Spirit in Ephesians 5:27 (cf. John 3:5; Titus 3:5).

Paul's final inclusion of "by the word" (ἐν ῥήματι), which probably modified "cleansing" (καθαρίσας), anchored this cleansing in the preached message of salvation in Christ. The singular use of "word" (ῥῆμα) likely carried a collective force to refer to the spoken words of the gospel (BDAG, s.v. "ῥῆμα" 1, p. 905). The use of one term for "word" (ῥῆμα) rather than another term Paul had already used (λόγος; cf. Eph. 1:13) to denote the word of the gospel may have put an extra accent on the power of the verbally proclaimed message (cf. Rom. 10:8, 17; 1 Peter 1:25; Heb. 1:3). In fact, earlier Paul had celebrated Christ's proclamation of good news to the near and the far in Ephesians 2:17. Christ fulfilled his powerful word of good news so that his bride, the church, could be cleansed and set apart for a covenantal bond of marriage with her Savior.

5:27. The next purpose clause (ἵνα, "in order that") modified verse 26 as a whole, providing the purpose for Christ's loving cleansing of his bride, the church. Christ wanted "to present the church to himself in a glorious state" (ἵνα παραστήσῃ αὐτὸς ἑαυτῷ ἔνδοξον τὴν ἐκκλησίαν), as the morally excellent bride that was ready for an everlasting marital union. The term "present" (παρίστημι) pictured Christ, having carefully prepared the church as his bride, now presenting her to himself. Paul highlighted the striking point that the same one who had cleansed and set apart the church (Christ) was both the presenter (αὐτός, "he") and the recipient (ἑαυτῶι, "to himself") of the prepared bride (cf. Titus 2:14).

Because of Christ's cleansing and sanctifying work, the church was made to be "glorious" (ἔνδοξος). The translation "glorious" (NET, NKJV, KJV), rather than "radiant" (NIV) or "splendid" (ESV, NRSV, CSB), envisioned the likely eschatological horizon of the presentation and captured the sense of the church sharing in Christ's glory (since they were united with Christ—Eph. 1:4; cf. Col. 3:3–4). The presentation of the bride would become final at the return of Christ, at the end of the church's preparation and cleansing (cf. 1 Thess. 5:23, where sanctification was shown to continue until the return of Christ; cf. 1 Thess. 3:13; Col. 1:22; 2 Cor. 4:14; 11:2; Dunn, 1998, 467). Christ's return promised to bring the church into eternal communion with Christ, who rejoiced in his fully prepared bride. Christ had forged an eternal, intimate relationship with all who had received his saving work.

The Presentation of the Bride

In Genesis 2:22, God brought Eve to Adam as a response to Adam's need for companionship and help (Gen. 2:18). After forming Eve from a rib taken from Adam's own body, God presented Eve to Adam. Adam gratefully acknowledged God's provision of this bride that God had so thoughtfully prepared. In Ephesians 5:26–27, Christ lovingly prepared his own bride and presented her to himself in a glorious state. In keeping with the comparisons between human marriage and Christ's union with the church in Ephesians 5:22–33, it was not surprising that Paul quoted from Genesis 2:24 later in this passage.

Paul continued the metaphor of the church as Christ's bride by further depicting the glory of the purified people of God. Paul specified that the church's glory consisted of "not having spot or wrinkle, or any such thing" (μὴ ἔχουσαν σπίλον ἢ ῥυτίδα ἤ τι τῶν τοιούτων). The terms "spot" (σπίλος) and "wrinkle" (ῥυτίς) could denote physical imperfections that might stand out on a person, but as part of the metaphor here they represented spiritual or moral blemishes that Christ had cleansed from the church. Christ had removed moral defects of any kind from the church through his cleansing power.

Far from leaving the church marred by spiritual or moral blemishes, Christ instead (ἀλλά, "but") advanced the goal (ἵνα, "in order that") that the church "would be holy and blameless" (ᾖ ἁγία καὶ ἄμωμος). A "holy" (ἅγια) church was set apart in single-minded devotion to Christ and shared in Christ's holiness. Being "blameless" (ἄμωμος) indicated "being without fault" in moral and spiritual character (BDAG, s.v. "ἄμωμος" 2, p. 56). The characterization of the church as holy and blameless hearkened back to God's purpose for choosing the church (Eph. 1:4). What God had arranged for his chosen church—to be holy and blameless—became a reality at Christ's return. Paul highlighted believers' moral purity and excellence as an intended eschatological outcome in several passages (1 Cor. 1:8; Col. 1:22; 1 Thess. 3:13; 5:23). The church would be in this state because Christ himself had loved and given himself for the church (Eph. 5:25). What had started as the standard for husbands' love for wives had become a brief but deep exploration into Christ's purposeful and effective love for the church, resulting in her readiness to live forever in Christ's presence as his glorious bride.

5:28a. Paul returned to holding up Christ's highest, self-sacrificing love for the church (Eph. 5:25) as a model for the way that husbands strove to love their wives. Paul contended that "in the same way" (οὕτως), or the way that Christ sacrificially loved his bride, "husbands also ought to love their own wives" (ὀφείλουσιν καὶ οἱ ἄνδρες ἀγαπᾶν τὰς ἑαυτῶν γυναῖκας). The tender and intentional care Christ showed for his church ought to inspire husbands' love for their wives. Paul insisted that husbands "ought to love" (ὀφείλουσιν . . . ἀγαπᾶν), or have a spiritual obligation (BDAG, s.v. "ὀφείλω" 2β, p. 743) to love their wives, according to this high standard. This love entailed practical expression of concern and commitment to his wife's best interests. Just as Christ had extended his love to his own bride, husbands were to love "their own wives" (τὰς ἑαυτῶν γυναῖκας). This emphasis on a husband's own wife hinted at an intimate connection between a husband and wife that mirrored Christ's affectionate bond with his bride, the church. Paul built upon this connection in the next clause.

Paul urged husbands to love their own wives "as their own bodies" (ὡς τὰ ἑαυτῶν σώματα). The word "as" (ὡς) introduced a second comparison in this verse, but one that was tightly related to the previous comparison (between Christ's love for the church and husbands' love for their wives). This additional comparison challenged husbands to aspire to love their wives in the way that they loved their own bodies. Paul appealed to the husbands' natural inclination for self-care. Husbands took care of their "bodies" (σώματα). This self-care consisted of tending to their entire well-being. Husbands' devotion to their wives' well-being needed to be this deeply ingrained in their mindset and habits. With this introduction of the idea of husbands loving their wives as their own bodies, Paul had set the stage for the next subsection.

Tender Marital Unity Points to Christ and the Church (5:28b–32)

The nourishment and tender care that husbands showed themselves was meant to be extended to their wives, through an imitation of Christ's spiritual nurture of his body, the church, since husbands and wives were part of an intimate union of lives and bodies that reflected Christ's marvelous union with the church.

5:28b. The next subsection moved from the motivating example of Christ's love to a recognition of the unity of husband and wife, a unity that reflected a deeper oneness between Christ and the church. With Paul's previous exhortation for husbands to love their own wives as their own bodies, Paul had initiated a transition to this related topic. Paul reinforced this point with the observation that "the one who loves his own wife loves himself" (ὁ ἀγαπῶν τὴν ἑαυτοῦ γυναῖκα ἑαυτὸν ἀγαπᾷ). Paul established an equivalency between husbands loving their wives and husbands loving themselves. He wanted this equation to take root in the husbands' thinking. The repetition of "his own" (ἑαυτοῦ) wife and "his own self" (ἑαυτόν) further underscored what Paul wanted the husbands to grasp—that they should enlarge the way they measured their own well-being to include their wives' well-being. Paul affirmed this point based on an underlying assumption that he would reveal in several verses—that husbands and wives actually became one body when they were united in marriage (Eph. 5:31).

5:29. Paul continued his exploration (γάρ, "for") of how a husband's love for his wife was related to his dedication to his own needs by noting that "no one ever hated his own flesh" (οὐδεὶς ... ποτε τὴν ἑαυτοῦ σάρκα ἐμίσησεν). Paul shared this as a general rule that would be readily acknowledged by his readers. People did not typically hate their own bodies. In this context, the term "hate" (μισέω) meant the opposite of "love" (ἀγαπάω) and encompassed both feelings of "aversion" (BDAG, s.v. "μισέω" 1b, p. 652) toward the body and actions such as mistreating or neglecting the body. Paul used "flesh" (σάρξ) as a synonym for "body" (σῶμα), foreshadowing the appearance of "one flesh" in the quote from Genesis 2:24 in verse 31. The term "flesh" (σάρξ) may have also acknowledged the physical vulnerability of the body (2 Cor. 12:7; Gal. 4:13; Col. 1:24) and its need to be nurtured, which Paul described in the contrasting idea that followed.

In contrast (ἀλλά, "but") to despising or abusing their bodies, people responded to the legitimate needs of their bodies. A person typically "nourishes and cares for [the body]" (ἐκτρέφει καὶ θάλπει αὐτήν). The term "nourishes" (ESV, NASB, NRSV, NKJV, KJV), "provides for" (CSB), or "feeds" (NIV, NET, NLT) denoted providing food for health and growth (BDAG, s.v. "ἐκτρέφω" 1, p. 311; Eph. 6:4). The accompanying verb "cares for" (NIV, CSB, NLT), "tenderly cares for" (NRSV), or "cherishes" (ESV, NASB, NKJV, KJV) conveyed a broader sense of giving caring attention to the overall well-being of the body (BDAG, s.v. "θάλπω," p. 442; 1 Thess. 2:7). People readily gave this type of devoted attention to their own bodies. Paul provided all of this description of generous self-care to support the command that husbands must love their wives in a similar way. This thoughtful love involved attention to wives' physical and relational needs, including needs for security, provision, gentle understanding, and support. If the wife indeed was considered to be united with the husband's body, then the care the husband demonstrated to his own body was to characterize his love for his wife.

Paul then shifted his focus back to his examination of Christ's love for his people, the church. The way people nourished and cared for their own bodies resembled (καθὼς καί, "just as also") Christ's ongoing affectionate commitment to the church. Paul highlighted the same dynamic of nourishing and caring but inserted "Christ" (ὁ Χριστός) as the supplier and "the church" (ἡ ἐκκλησία) as the recipient. Christ Jesus abundantly provided for the church's spiritual growth (Eph. 4:7–16) and communicated a tender love for the church that surpassed knowledge (Eph. 3:16–19). Christ had demonstrated his love initially and definitively at the cross (Eph. 5:25–26), but this verse showed that he continued to lovingly minister to his church, by his Spirit, through ongoing spiritual nourishment and support.

5:30. The reason (ὅτι, "since") that Christ gave such attentive care to the church was because "we are members of his body" (μέλη ἐσμὲν τοῦ σώματος αὐτοῦ). This followed logically from the teaching that Christ was the head and believers were the body (Eph. 1:22–23; 4:15–16; 5:23) that was united to Christ. The head and body had been joined together in an eternal, unbreakable union, so Christ was understandably concerned about the welfare of the body. Paul once again used the term "members" (μέλη; Eph. 4:25) as an appropriate word to describe believers who were parts of Christ's body. Christ valued believers, since they were members of his body.

> *TRANSLATION ANALYSIS: Two notable English translations (*KJV, NKJV*) include additional wording at the end of verse 30.* This is because some significant manuscripts attest to the presence of "from his flesh and from his bones" (ἐκ τῆς σαρκὸς αὐτοῦ καὶ ἐκ τῶν ὀστέων αὐτοῦ) at the end of this verse (D, F, G, Ψ, 0278, 0285). Most other English translations follow the shorter reading that omits these phrases, as found in 𝔓[46], א*, A, B, 048, 33, 1739*, 1881. Though there is a possibility that a later scribe accidentally skipped from one "his" (αὐτοῦ) to the other, the manuscript evidence is slightly stronger for the shorter reading, and a later scribe may have inserted wording inspired by Genesis 2:23 to pave the way for Paul's quote of Genesis 2:24 (cf. Metzger, 1994, 541). If the additional phrases did originate with Paul, he probably hoped to reinforce a transition from the unity of Christ (the head) and the church (his body) to Adam and Eve's bone-and-flesh unity from Genesis 2:23–24.

5:31. The truth that Paul and his readers belonged to Christ's body prompted Paul to examine the original one-flesh marriage of Adam and Eve in Genesis 2. Paul began the quote from Genesis 2:24 with "for this reason" (ἀντὶ τούτου). The logical connection between Ephesians 5:31 and previous verses was fairly loose. Though the overall passage examined both human marriages and Christ's union with the church, both the immediately preceding verses in this subsection (5:28b–30) and the verse that followed (5:32) indicated that the quote's application was not limited to human marriages alone. In fact, the verses in the immediate context suggested that Paul was placing his primary focus on Christ and the church. Still, he undoubtedly assumed the relevance of the quotation to human marriages as well. Therefore, when he revisited God's original design for marriage Paul reinforced what he wanted to say about his readers' marriages while pointing to the greater significance of their marriages as signs of Christ's loving union with the church.

Paul repeated the three main clauses from Genesis 2:24 that described the process of a man leaving his family of birth, becoming joined to his wife, and experiencing full intimacy and oneness with her. In Genesis 2, Adam's union with Eve provided a template for all future marriages (note the fut. tense in the LXX). Paul followed the OT (Gen. 1:27; 2:18, 24) and Jesus (Matt. 19:3–9) in anchoring union and permanence in marriage to God's design in creation. God did not intend for marriages to end in divorce, but divorces were still a reality in the ancient world.

Excerpt from an Ancient Divorce Agreement (13 B.C.)

"Zois and Antipater agree that they have separated from each other, severing the union which they had formed . . . . The agreement of marriage shall henceforth be null, and neither Zois nor other person acting for her shall take proceedings against Antipater for restitution of the dowry, nor shall either party take proceedings against the other about cohabitation or any other matter whatsoever up to the present day, and hereafter it shall be lawful both for Zois to marry another man and for Antipater to marry another woman without either of them being answerable" (*BGU* 1103 [trans. Hunt and Edgar, LCL]).

First, "a man will leave [his] father and mother" (καταλείψει ἄνθρωπος πατέρα καὶ μητέρα). All future marriages would require a separation from parents to allow for the full union that God had ordained for husbands and wives. This step to "leave behind" (καταλείπω) parents did not sever those relationships altogether (at times, married couples in Paul's day even continued to live in their parents' household—Ferguson, 2003, 72). Instead, leaving parents consisted of untying the tight bonds of loyalty to one family unit to prepare for the formation of a new family unit.

The second step, linked with "and" (καί), was that a husband "will be joined to his wife" (προσκολληθήσεται πρὸς τὴν γυναῖκα αὐτοῦ). The verb "to adhere to" or "to join" (προσκολλάω) was a compound verb from a term that described attaching things using a binding agent (BDAG, s.v. "κολλάω" 1, p. 555). In this context, it referred to a permanent relational coupling that replaced the attachments that husbands (and wives) had possessed with their parents. The husband was joined "to his wife" (πρὸς τὴν γυναῖκα αὐτοῦ), which emphasized the exclusive nature of the union. One man came together with one woman to establish a new family together.

Third, the final outcome (the final item in the series, introduced by καί, "and") of a husband leaving parents and being joined to a wife was that "the two will become one flesh" (ἔσονται οἱ δύο εἰς σάρκα μίαν). Eve had been taken from Adam's body, and in their marriage they had become united as one flesh once again, as complementary partners. This one-flesh union had established a pattern for all marriages that would follow. In the context of Ephesians 5:22–33, becoming one flesh encompassed an intimate union of lives, including bodies, in marriage. Paul drew upon this same excerpt from Genesis 2:24 in a discussion of illicit sexual union outside of marriage (1 Cor. 6:16). God had designed sexual intimacy to take place within the context of a lifelong covenant between a husband and wife in marriage, as part of becoming one flesh. In Ephesians, the complete union of the husband and wife also assumed a uniting of interests and goals, supporting the original point of the subsection that husbands who loved their wives loved themselves (Eph. 5:28a).

5:32. Paul paused to reflect on Genesis 2:24 by commenting that "this mystery is profound" (τὸ μυστήριον τοῦτο μέγα ἐστιν). Paul's reference to "this mystery" (τὸ μυστήριον τοῦτο) pointed to something he had been discussing in the passage; namely, the one-flesh union between Christ and the church that was vividly portrayed in marriage. The predicate adjective μέγας, translated as "great" (NASB, NRSV, NET, NKJV, KJV), or "profound" (NIV, ESV, CSB), was often used outside the NT in combination with "mystery" to indicate a "great, sublime, important" mystery (BDAG, s.v. "μέγας" 4b, p. 624). Paul understood "mystery" (μυστήριον) as a divine secret about God's redemptive plans that had once been hidden from understanding but had now been made clear in Christ (Eph. 1:9; 3:3–4, 9; 6:19). This typical usage suggested that Paul was delving into topics even deeper than the wonder of human marriage. He was marveling at something that was newly disclosed in the incarnational ministry of Christ.

Indeed, Paul interjected the comment "but I am saying this in reference to Christ and the church" (ἐγὼ δὲ λέγω εἰς Χριστὸν καὶ εἰς τὴν ἐκκλησίαν) to clarify what exactly he was labeling a profound mystery from Genesis 2:24. Paul used the personal pronoun "I" (ἐγώ) to narrow in on his own interest in the mystery of Genesis 2:24 (cf. BDF §277.1). Paul said "I speak with reference to" (λέγω εἰς; cf. BDAG, s.v. "λέγω" 2e, p. 590; cf. ESV, NASB, NRSV, NET, CSB) to specify what he was referring to when he spoke about this mystery, and by extension, how he was applying Genesis 2:24 to a more specific topic. That topic was the nature of the relationship between Christ and the church. Paul revealed that the relational union between Christ and the church was the mystery that fascinated him. He understood human marriage as a signpost to this greater spiritual reality.

The Mystery Revealed

Paul had diverted his attention to Christ's love for the church in Ephesians 5:29b. He had anchored this love in the fact that the church belonged to Christ, as members of his body. So, when he recalled Genesis 2:24 and its depiction of intimate union between a husband and wife, Paul saw this as a manifestation of a deeper, eternal union between Christ and his church. This deeper significance of human marriage became fully known only in the light of Christ's first advent. Christ fulfilled the hope, presented with vivid marital imagery, that God would restore a permanent covenantal relationship with his people (Isa. 54:1–10; 62:1–5; Jer. 2:2; Ezek. 16:8–14; Hos. 2:19–23). God's creational design for human marriage (Gen. 2:24) was displayed spiritually in God's redemptive plans when Christ died for, set apart for himself, and cleansed his own bride (Eph. 5:25–26). A state of perfect union will come to fruition when Christ presents his glorious bride the church to himself when he returns (Eph. 5:27; cf. Rev. 19:7–9).

Husbands Should Love and Wives Should Show Respect (5:33)

Paul summarized the whole section by addressing each husband and wife, challenging husbands to love their own wives as they love themselves within a unified marriage, and advising wives to respect their husbands within an ordered marriage.

5:33. Having completed his extended discussion of the husband's Christlike love for his wife, Paul was ready to give summary exhortations to both husbands and wives. The conjunction "in any case" (πλὴν) functioned to "conclude a discussion and emphasize what was essential" (BDF §449.2). Paul used the conjunction to return to his primary point of instructing wives and husbands in godly marriages.

Paul's use of the plural "you" (ὑμεῖς) reinforced his return to instructing his readers in their marriages. The particle "also" (καί) modified "you" and suggested that Paul was giving husbands an action point that corresponded to Christ's ministry to the church. Paul then personalized the teaching by adding "individually" (οἱ καθ' ἕνα; cf. Rom. 12:5; 1 Cor. 14:31; Moule, 1960, 60) and "each" (ἕκαστος) to emphasize the personal responsibility each husband had in his marriage to carry out these directives. Each husband was to be purposeful and committed to Paul's teachings in his interactions with his wife, and by extension, each wife needed to take the initiative to implement Paul's teachings in her relationship with her husband.

Paul summarized his message to husbands as, "each [husband] must love his own wife as himself" (ἕκαστος τὴν ἑαυτοῦ γυναῖκα οὕτως ἀγαπάτω ὡς ἑαυτόν). This summary fittingly captured Paul's emphasis on love in Ephesians 5:25–28a and his description of the unity of husbands and wives in marriage in 5:28b–32. Paul wanted each husband to appreciate his overarching sense of responsibility to love his wife well. Paul wanted the powerful picture of

Christ's love for the church to continue to be imprinted in each husband's mind and heart. The comparative construction "in this way . . . as" (οὕτως . . . ὡς) encouraged the husband to love his wife as he loved himself. Paul taught that each husband's love for his wife should be motivated by a deep recognition of the unity he shared with his wife in marriage. They were one flesh together, as designed and ordained by God from the beginning.

Paul saw a corresponding obligation for each wife (ἡ δὲ γυνή, "and the wife"). He instructed the wife using a less direct style (shifting from an impv. verb to a subjunc. construction): "she is to respect [her] husband" (ἵνα φοβῆται τὸν ἄνδρα; cf. CSB). Instead of repeating the injunction for wives to submit themselves to their husbands, Paul enlisted the term "respect" (φοβέω). This showed that Paul saw voluntary submission and respect as complementary ideas. Respecting someone involved showing sincere honor to that person (BDAG, s.v. "φοβέω" 2b, p. 1061), and in this case wives' respect demonstrated their acknowledgement of the husband's role within the purposeful structure of a marriage.

THEOLOGICAL FOCUS

The exegetical idea (Paul's readers cultivated strong marriages when wives respectfully submitted themselves to their husbands and husbands selflessly loved and tenderly cared for their wives, since marriages reflected the intimate bond and ordered structure of Christ's union with his body, the church, and Christ had sacrificially loved and purposefully led the church) leads to this theological focus: Wives and husbands are to treat one another in marriage according to the model of the ordered, loving, and united relationship between Christ and the church.

Husbands and wives both bore a responsibility in marriage to help the marriage accomplish the purpose for which it was designed by God. In their actions and attitudes they must implement Spirit-filled living (Eph. 5:18) and appreciate the general call for all believers to honor one another and prioritize one another's interests (5:21). Their marriages must reflect the beautiful centrality of Christ to their new identity and existence. The specific focus of this passage is that interactions between husbands and wives are inspired by the nature of the relationship between Christ and the church.

The relationship between Christ and the church is an ordered relationship. Christ functions as head of the church, which is his body (v. 23). The body submits to the head and lives in dependence upon the head (v. 24). Christ is also Savior of the church and has sanctified and cleansed the church as his bride, in preparation for a final wedding celebration (vv. 25–27). Though some aspects of Christ's relationship to the church have no direct parallel to the husband's responsibility for his wife, they still describe a relationship in which Christ is differentiated from the church, in a structured and harmonious relationship that results in great blessing for the church. In view of this ordered relationship between Christ and the church, wives are to willingly and respectfully submit themselves to their husbands.

The relationship between Christ and the church is also a loving relationship. Christ definitively and consistently shows his love for the church, with a commitment to the church's ultimate needs and interests. He selflessly gave himself up for the church as a sacrificial offering for believers (v. 25). He set the church apart by cleansing believers' sins through his fulfillment of the promises of the new covenant and the gift of the Spirit (v. 26). He continues to prepare his bride for when he presents her to himself in full and perfect glory when he returns (v. 27). Christ sets the standard for husbands' love for their wives. Husbands are to love their wives selflessly and purposefully, imitating the way that Christ does this for the church.

Finally, the passage describes a perfectly united relationship between Christ and the church. The church is not a distant recipient of

Christ's loving support. The church is the very body of Christ, belonging to Christ in inseparable union (v. 30). Christ thus ministers to his body through his loving provision and tender care for the church's spiritual needs. Christ's ministry to the church reflects the wondrous one-flesh union that defines all marriages, including the covenantal marriage between Christ and his bride (vv. 31–32). Husbands are to treat their wives accordingly, with thoughtfulness and attentive care, being aware of their wives' needs for physical and relational support. They must remember that their marriages to their wives reflect the marvelous covenantal union and intimacy between Christ and the church.

PREACHING AND TEACHING STRATEGIES

Exegetical and Theological Synthesis

Reflecting the form of the household code from Greco-Roman culture, the apostle Paul affirmed elements of the code even while he subverted other elements. In Christ, wives were to submit to their husbands. That was standard fare in the household codes of the day, but Paul also undercut the codes with theology when he assumed that wives have dignity and choice. All bore the *imago Dei.* For Paul, the husband was the "head of the wife"—standard fare in the codes of the day—but in Christ this meant that the husband served, honored, nourished, and loved his wife—revolutionary in Paul's day (vv. 25, 28, 33). In Christ, husbands were to lay down their lives and love their wives as they loved their own bodies (v. 28). Paul described the husband-wife relationship in overtly theological categories and called marriage a "profound mystery" (v. 32). This passage is about Christ and the church as much as it is about the one-flesh relationship of husband and wife.

Preaching Idea

A good marriage is a great mirror of Christ and the church.

Contemporary Connections

What does it mean?

What does it mean that a good marriage is a great mirror of Christ and the church? A mirror reflects an object. Without the object there is no reflection, and the better the mirror, the more accurate is the reflection. In this passage, mirroring means that wives submit to and respect their husbands, just as the church submits to Jesus; and husbands love, sacrifice for, nurture, and cherish their wives, just as Jesus does this for the church. The one-flesh relationship of marriage is like Christ's relationship with the church; but as Paul candidly admits, this teaching is a "mystery." It can be pictured with examples of good marriages such as the relationship of Tim and Kathy Keller, who have written about marriage (*The Meaning of Marriage*, rev. ed, 2013). See Creativity for more resources featuring the Kellers.

Is it true?

Does God really expect husbands and wives to mirror Christ and the church? Images of spousal abuse may cause listeners justifiably to raise their shields. When preaching this passage, we will want to acknowledge and condemn this tragedy, contrasting it with the beautiful picture of the church and Christ, wives and husbands.

A marriage that mirrors Christ and the church is seen when the husband turns off the television when his wife wants to talk. It is seen when the wife sends notes expressing her love and respect. The differences in the ways men and women often speak create many opportunities for spouses to alter their preferred communication style as a way of submitting to and honoring the other person, thus mirroring the relationship between Christ and the church. Deborah Tannen (2009) coined the term "genderlects" to describe those differences (*You Just Don't Understand: Men and Women in Conversation*, Ballantine, 2009). Though these observed patterns do not hold true for the way that all men and women communicate, some husbands and wives may be able to relate to them. If the husband uses communication as a way to solve problems, typical of the male genderlect, he may want to alter that when speaking to his wife, who uses communication as a way to build rapport, typical of the female genderlect. Likewise, the wife will want to be on guard against interrupting her husband. In the female genderlect, interrupting is way of expressing support and agreement with what is being said, but in the male genderlect, interrupting is a way to dominate the conversation. By humbly curbing their natural inclinations husband and wife can mirror Christ's selfless love and the church's readiness to submit.

Now what?

If a good marriage is a great mirror of Christ and the church, how can we exhibit positive examples of sacrificial love and submission? Areas of application could include household chores (both husbands and wives should do their share), childrearing (same), use of joint income, sex, listening, and verbal affirmation. Tim and Kathy Keller pray together every night before drifting off to sleep. Even when Tim is traveling the world, he calls and they pray. One of my friends has adopted the practice of holding hands with his wife when they argue. It reminds them that even while disagreeing, they are one. Another friend has instituted "talk time." Every night from 9:00 to 9:30, husband and wife simply talk. Even though single people are not addressed in this passage, you may want to add something to the sermon to which they could relate.

Creativity in Communication

Tim and Kathy Keller enjoy, listen to, and celebrate each other. For a playful and informative two-minute overview of their book on marriage, search YouTube for Tim and Kathy Keller. You will also find several videos illustrating a longer interaction (more than an hour) when they were interviewed at Gordon-Conwell Theological Seminary in 2017.

Paul's brief analogy of loving our own bodies might afford an opportunity for humor as the preacher describes men's exercise routines, youth-enhancing procedures, and preening in front of the mirror. Just as husbands love their own bodies, so should they nourish and cherish their wives. As Greg says in the exposition, this love is "tender and affectionate and selfless."

To model an Ephesians 5 marriage, perhaps there is a couple in the church who has been married for decades. Through thick and thin they have served and honored each other. An interview could bring out the secrets of their relationship with humor, pathos, and wisdom. When visiting Saddleback Church in California on the Sunday closest to Valentine's Day, I (Jeffrey) saw such an interview with an old woman whose husband had died less than a year before. It was charming, delightful, inspiring, funny, and moving.

Teaching on submission and love may need time to sink in and thus might be conveyed most effectively if joined with a question and answer session, small group discussion, or counseling. When teaching on marriage, Jeffrey separated men and women so that each had their own session. A woman taught the females the portions of the text that relate to them, and a man did the same for the males. Conversely, it might be interesting to have a woman share her perspective on the passage with the men, and a man do the same for the women.

Visual aids: To convey the preaching idea in an engaging way, you might remove the pulpit and have a bride and groom dressed in their finery stand on stage while you walk around the couple as you teach. Symbols could be used the same way. Place on pedestals a wedding veil and bow tie, or rolling pin and hammer (but we will want to be careful of stereotypes). When referring to the wife or husband, stand near the appropriate pedestal.

The one-flesh relationship of a good marriage is not the joining of two similar things like tying together two sticks (tie two sticks with string or a rubber band). It is the joining of two dissimilar things to make a third thing, like combining hydrogen and oxygen to make water. Conversely, marriage cannot be broken simply and cleanly like breaking a stick in two (break a stick). It is more like separating hydrogen and oxygen, a difficult process that requires much energy.

Skit: Many conflicts in marriage occur because husband and wife see things differently. The skit, "A Problem of Perspective," demonstrates this humorously. A tired husband comes home to an equally tired wife and the fireworks fly. The skit goes through the same scene three times: once neutrally, once from the husband's perspective, and once from the wife's as they recount their experience to a counselor. To find this skit, search the internet for "A Problem with Perspective."

Story: For an inspiring example of faithfulness, the story of the former president of Columbia International University, Robertson McQuilkin, may serve. He cared for his wife for twenty-five years as she progressed through Alzheimer's disease.[1]

Story: For a contrasting story, but with its own encouragement, we might summarize Sarah Edwards's marriage to the Jonathan Edwards, the famous theologian who was a "difficult man." That story is the subject of Elisabeth D. Dodd's biography titled *Marriage to a Difficult Man: The Uncommon Union of Jonathan and Sarah Edwards* (Audubon, 2005).

Quotations: The following quotations could be woven into the outline below (or an outline of your own creation) to support the points being made.

> This might be placed in the introduction or conclusion:
>
> *"Where thou art, that is home." —Emily Dickinson*
>
> This could be used to speak about the oneness husband and wife share:
>
> *[When her husband, John Adams, was criticized]*
> *"When he is wounded, I bleed." —Abigail Adams*
>
> Use in a lighthearted introduction or when talking about either wives or husbands:
>
> *"Marriage is the bond between a person who never remembers anniversaries and another who never forgets." —Ogden Nash*

Statistics: Patterns of marriage and divorce in the United States:

> 1860s–2010 (this study shows a steady decline in both marriages and divorces from 1980 to 2010)[2]
>
> 1990–2018 (this study shows that the decline in the divorce rate has continued to fall from 2010 to 2018)[3]

---

1 For an example of this story, search the internet for Stan Guthrie, "The Gradual Grief of Alzheimer's," in *Christianity Today*.

2 Ana Swanson, "144 Years of Marriage and Divorce in the United States, in One Chart," *Washington Post*, June 23, 2015, https://www.washingtonpost.com/news/wonk/wp/2015/06/23/144-years-of-marriage-and-divorce-in-the-united-states-in-one-chart/?noredirect=on.

3 Eric Duffin, "Divorce Rate in the United States from 1990 to 2018 (per 1,000 of population)," Statistica.com, January 3, 2020, https://www.statista.com/statistics/195955/divorce-rate-in-the-united-states-since-1990.

The main point is this: God designed marriage to be an earthly picture of Christ's relationship with the church. That involves submission on the part of the church and sacrificial love on the part of Jesus. So, a good marriage is a great mirror of Christ and the church.

A possible sermon outline:

- In a great marriage, wives submit to their husbands as the church submits to Christ (vv. 22–24, 33).
- In a great marriage, husbands love their wives as Christ loves the church (vv. 25–28, 33).
- This type of marriage mirrors Christ and the church (vv. 29–32).

DISCUSSION QUESTIONS

1. In what ways is the prior command, "be filled with the Spirit" (Eph. 5:18), relevant to how we understand this passage?
2. Do the commands to "submit" and "respect" seem achievable for wives? Why or why not?
3. Does the command to "love his wife as himself" seem achievable for husbands? Why or why not?
4. In your own words, how is Christ's sacrificial and caring love for the church described in this passage?
5. Did you have positive role models of husband-wife relations when you grew up? Describe.
6. What does "one flesh" mean in this passage?
7. How is the marital relationship like Christ's relationship with the church?

Ephesians 6:1–9

EXEGETICAL IDEA

As the authority and promises of Christ the Lord shaped harmonious relationships between children and parents and then slaves and masters within the structure of Paul's readers' households, children would obey their parents, fathers would patiently train their children spiritually, slaves would obey their masters, and masters would acknowledge slaves' equal dignity through fair treatment.

THEOLOGICAL FOCUS

Believers should remember the authority and promises of Christ the Lord as they live spiritually purposeful and constructive lives within their household and in other important relationships.

PREACHING IDEA

Under the same roof, Christians are under the same Lord.

PREACHING POINTERS

Paul hoped that his readers would buy into his vision that the whole created order would one day be renewed under Christ's leadership (Eph. 1:9–10). They had begun to experience the first effects of that through their shared experiences of Christ's presence. But Greco-Roman society still operated by flawed systems and norms that fell far short of God's perfect kingdom standards. It was not easy for them to consistently put into practice kingdom values in a setting in which those values clashed with societal patterns. Some of Paul's readers were witnessing a breakdown in relationships between children and parents. Paul's readers lived in a broader society that they could not change structurally right away, but with a focus on the Lord and an eternal perspective they could still make changes so that their households might reflect the light of Christ more powerfully through values of equality and relationships of harmony.

We live in a vastly different culture today, but points of relevance are still abundant. Slavery is condemned, but this passage about slaves and masters is still relevant to other relational arrangements. In Christ, all are equal in value and dignity, even if they have differing roles that call for submission and obedience. Our culture today also differs from the first century in terms of parents and children. Children are sometimes pampered, or perhaps children are neglected by absentee fathers. This passage has plenty of relevance for both children and parents. The middle schooler who thinks disobedience is clever can grow in Christlikeness with this passage. Parents who are given to habits that exasperate sons and daughters must put away those habits. Everyone who wields authority or is under authority is addressed, as we learn that Christians under the same roof are under the same Lord.

HONORING THE LORD IN HOUSEHOLD RELATIONSHIPS (6:1–9)

LITERARY STRUCTURE AND THEMES (6:1–9)

Ephesians 6:1–9 is comprised of two clearly defined sections, one on the relationship between children and parents (6:1–4) and another on the relationship between household slaves and masters (6:5–9). The passage is the completion of the household code instructions that began in Ephesians 5:22–33. These instructions were still meant to reveal the way that Paul's readers should express being filled with the Spirit together (5:18).

As was the case with husbands and wives (Eph. 5:22–33), Paul addressed both parties in the two sets of relationships. This reflected Paul's conviction that all of his readers were equal in Christ and possessed abilities to discern and implement Christ-honoring habits. These habits would help them grow spiritually and help them contribute to the growth of those around them. Paul devoted more space to children's and slaves' responsibilities than fathers' and masters' obligations. This could have been because Paul saw fathers' and masters' duties as being clear-cut and definitive but wanted to give additional theological reasoning to help children and slaves live out their spiritual freedom within a structure that likely felt constraining and even frustrating to them on a practical level.

Like other passages in the back half of the letter, Ephesians 6:1–9 integrates theological reasoning and practical instruction. Paul's teachings on children's and slaves' obedience, fathers' careful spiritual instruction, and masters' just and enlightened leadership were clear commands. But Paul made reference to "the Lord" (or "Christ") in nearly every verse. Paul wanted to ensure that every decision that was made in this crucial arena of household relationships was governed by the presence and authority of Christ in their midst. Paul affirmed that a believer's every action should be done intentionally, guided by the heart of Christ and the reality of the new life experienced in him.

- ***Purposeful Relational Harmony between Children and Parents (6:1–4)***
- ***Recognizing the Lord in Slaves' Obedience and Masters' Fair Treatment (6:5–9)***

EXPOSITION (6:1–9)

Paul's instructions to his readers in this passage stood out against a broader background in which the absolute authority of a father (*patria potestas*) as the head of the household (*paterfamilias*) was ingrained in culture. These ancient households often included slaves. In his teachings for parents and children, Paul wanted his readers to value children's opportunity to experience God's blessing and be strengthened in the faith. In the slave and master portion, Paul insisted that the equality among diverse believers that characterized the body of Christ must reshape the relationships between household slaves and masters. He also sought to focus the attention of both parties on the future rewards and judgments that their all-seeing Master in heaven would administer to both slaves and masters when he returned.

Purposeful Relational Harmony between Children and Parents (6:1–4)

Paul believed that Christ should govern the relationships between children and parents, so that children obeyed and honored their parents, and fathers patiently and purposefully trained and admonished their children, with the end result that children would grow spiritually as part of a Christ-centered and harmonious household.

6:1. Paul began his next section on household relationships by addressing "children" (τὰ τέκνα, nom. of address). Ancient Roman household codes typically covered the relationship between fathers and children (cf. Aristotle, *Pol.* 1.3, 12–13). Paul used the word "child" to refer to "an offspring of human parents" (BDAG, s.v. "τέκνον" 1, p. 994) who still lived with his parents as part of the household (1 Cor. 7:14; Col. 3:20–21; 1 Tim. 3:4, 12; 5:4; Titus 1:6). A similar term for child (παιδίον) often stressed the young age of a child, while the term for "child" (τέκνον) in this verse more often denoted the relationship of the child to the parents, without a comment on the age of the child (Moritz, 1996, 168–71). Paul appealed to children here as responsible and capable followers of Christ.

Paul told children to "obey your parents" (ὑπακούετε τοῖς γονεῦσιν ὑμῶν). To "obey" (ὑπακούω) meant to "follow instructions" or "be subject to" one who held authority (BDAG, s.v. "ὑπακούω" 1, p. 1028). In this context, children obeyed by recognizing their parents' authority and living according to their guidelines and instructions. Paul denounced disobedience to parents elsewhere (Rom. 1:30; 2 Tim. 3:2). Children's obedience varied in expression depending on the age of the child (some adult children continued to live in their parents' household in that era). Even though "submit" (ὑποτάσσω) and "obey" (ὑπακούω) sometimes functioned as synonyms in the NT (cf. ὑποτάσσω in Luke 2:51; Titus 2:9), in this context it is notable that Paul chose one word, "obey" (ὑπακούω, act. voice) for children's response to their parents (and slaves' response to masters) and the other word, "submit" (ὑποτάσσω, mid. voice, and applied to them only indirectly) for wives' approach toward their husbands. This differentiation likely placed a stronger and more direct accent on children's duties than on those of the wives to their husbands (cf. Thielman, 2010, 396). The term for "parents" (γονεῖς) was inclusive of both fathers and mothers. Paul added the possessive pronoun "your" (ὑμῶν) to clarify that he wanted children to obey their own parents.

Paul then identified a mindset that should accompany children's obedience to their parents. He told them to obey them "in the Lord" (ἐν κυρίῳ). Paul used references to "the Lord" Jesus throughout this section to give repeated reminders that Jesus's lordship should be the defining influence on how Paul's readers carried out their responsibilities. In this case, the compact phrase "in the Lord" (ἐν κυρίῳ) resembled Paul's use of "in Christ" and its equivalents in Ephesians. Thus, the phrase was probably a shorthand way of saying that children's new existence of being united with Christ their Lord should motivate them to carry out their obedience to their parents. Additionally, the phrase may have indicated the opportunity for children to draw upon the Lord's spiritual resources as they strove to obey their parents (cf. Eph. 6:10; Arnold, 2010, 416).

Next, Paul supplied a first reason (γάρ, "since") for children to carry out this command, stating simply that "this is right" (τοῦτο . . . ἐστιν δίκαιον). Something that was "right" measured up to standards that were appropriate to the setting at hand (BDAG, s.v. "δίκαιος" 2, p. 247; Matt. 20:4; Acts 4:19; Phil. 1:7; 2 Thess. 1:6). Paul likely meant that children's obedience was the right thing to do for God's people in particular. Earlier, Paul had used similar appeals to fittingness to promote holy living that was consistent with believers' identity as holy people (Eph. 5:3–5).

6:2. Paul supplemented his reasoning for children obeying their parents with a quote from the Ten Commandments (Exod. 20:12 LXX) that applied directly to his instructions. Paul repeated the direct command given to children in the verse: "Honor your father and mother" (τίμα τὸν πατέρα σου καὶ τὴν μητέρα). In Hebrew, to show honor meant to express respect for someone by recognizing their status or upholding their dignity (כבד; *HALOT*, 1:455–456; Judg. 13:17; 1 Sam. 15:30; Ps. 15:4; Mal. 1:6). The meaning in Greek was the same (BDAG, s.v. "τιμάω," p. 1004, 2; Acts 28:10; 1 Peter 2:17). Oftentimes the opposite of honoring parents was cursing them, which betrayed children's contempt and dismissal of their parents' authority and worth (Exod. 21:17; Lev. 20:9; Matt. 15:4; Mark. 7:10). Showing honor to whom it was due was especially important in an honor-shame culture like the one that Paul and his readers lived in. Paul contended that honor ought to characterize the general posture of children towards their parents and set the tone for children's obedience to their parents. They were called to uphold God's established order for the household by rendering proper honor and respect to their parents.

Paul interjected the observation that the command to honor one's parents (the command referred to with the rel. pron. ἥτις, "which") was "the first commandment with a promise" (ἐντολὴ πρώτη ἐν ἐπαγγελίᾳ). In both the Ten Commandments and the Mosaic Law as a whole, the commandment to honor one's parents was the first one with an explicit promise attached to it (Lincoln, 1990, 404; Moritz, 1996, 156; Hoehner, 2002, 790; Arnold, 2010, 417). Paul intended to recognize the benefits of following the command by highlighting the promise accompanying it. Paul similarly emphasized a reward later in his instructions to slaves (Eph. 6:8). Promises of rewards directed the readers' focus to the future and encouraged them to live with the future in mind (cf. the promise of an inheritance in Eph. 1:14, 18; 5:5). The challenges that children faced in carrying out the command to obey and honor their parents were eclipsed by the reward awaiting them.

6:3. As Paul continued his quote of Exodus 20:12, he put the spotlight on the promise mentioned there. Paul explained that a child should feel motivated to honor his or her father and mother with a two-part promise in view (ἵνα, "in order that"). First, they needed to honor their parents "in order that it may go well for you" (ἵνα εὖ σοι γένηται). The first part of the promise conveyed the broad benefit of honoring parents. The verb translated "go" (γίνομαι) meant "turn out" or "occur as a process or result" (BDAG, s.v. "γίνομαι" 4, p. 197), and the combination of the verb with the adverb "well" (εὖ) communicated that a positive outcome would result "for you" (σοι), or the child who honored his or her parents. For Paul, the general promise of benefit became more specific in the second part of the promise.

The second part of the respectful child's promised benefit, joined to the first part by "and" (καί), was "that you will live long on the earth" (ἵνα . . . ἔσῃ μακροχρόνιος ἐπὶ τῆς γῆς). Paul implied that this second promise was still applicable to his readers by drawing attention to the presence of the promise and including the promise in the quotation. In other words, he wanted to suggest the enduring relevance of the promise that transcended time and cultures.

In Israel's context the promise of long life "in the land" (ἐπὶ τῆς γῆς) had offered hope of long life in "the good land that the Lord their God had given them" (Exod. 20:12), which had gone along with the broader blessings and curses associated with the Mosaic covenant. Paul bypassed the wording that linked the land to God's good gift, which suggested that he wanted to generalize the promise ("on the earth") in a way that was more applicable to Jews and Gentiles in the new covenant era. Paul saw a wider application to the promise in the wake of Christ's redemptive ministry. The promise expanded to include Gentiles who were in Christ (Eph. 2:11–22; 3:6; cf. Rom. 4:13–16; Gal. 3:7–9, 14, 26–29). Therefore, Paul did not intend to limit the meaning of the phrase (ἐπὶ τῆς γῆς) to "in the [promised] land" (ESV, CSB) but assumed a meaning of "on the earth" instead (NIV, NASB, NRSV, NET, NKJV, KJV). Paul likely understood this promise of long life on the earth as being enjoyed in both this life and in the life to come.

Long Life on the Earth

Paul likely envisioned long life for children as a blessing for both this world and the world to come. As elsewhere in the letter, Paul likely assumed a tight connection between the already and the not yet of Christ's blessings for his people. The final inheritance of God's new family in Christ would be experienced as part of a comprehensive new creation (Eph. 1:9–10; 2 Peter 3:13; Rev. 21:1–4; Isa. 65:17–25). But believers could begin to enjoy these blessings even now (Eph. 1:3), and those blessings included a life that benefitted from being in greater harmony with God's will (Eph. 1:11; 5:17), greater alignment with what was good (Eph. 2:10; 4:22–24; 5:8–10) and peace with the people he had placed in their lives (Eph. 2:14–16; 4:2–3; 5:21). Children who honored their parents' Christ-centered teaching would likewise reap the harvest that arose from a life well lived, and they were assured of their reward (cf. Eph. 6:8) in the world to come (cf. 1 Tim. 4:8).

6:4. Paul next moved from addressing the children to speaking to their fathers (καὶ οἱ πατέρες, "and fathers"). Paul directed his comments to fathers in particular, reflecting fathers' status as heads of the family in Paul's time (cf. 1 Tim. 3:4–5, 12). The corresponding piece to children's obeying and honoring their parents was for fathers to avoid provoking their children to anger and to bring them up in the training and admonition of the Lord. Paul began with the negative command: "Do not provoke your children to anger" (μὴ παροργίζετε τὰ τέκνα ὑμῶν). Paul cautioned against the common problem of an overbearing and harsh demeanor toward children and placed limits on the exercise of fathers' authority. An overly stern approach that set unrealistic or arbitrary expectations for children's progress or doled out excessive discipline tended to "provoke anger" in them (παροργίζω; ESV, NASB, NRSV, NET), "stir up anger" in them (CSB), or "exasperate" them (NIV). Paul wanted fathers to guard against being insensitive to their children's needs and perspectives, even as they sought their children's ultimate good by implementing the positive instructions that followed.

This warning against provoking anger set up a positive prescription in contrast (ἀλλά, "but"). Paul urged fathers to "raise them [children] in the training and admonition of the Lord" (ἐκτρέφετε αὐτὰ ἐν παιδείᾳ καὶ νουθεσίᾳ κυρίου). Paul directed fathers to oversee a process that would have featured the mother's significant input as well (cf. 1 Tim. 5:14; 2 Tim. 1:5; 3:14–15; Ferguson, 2003, 77–78). Paul began with the general term "bring up" (ἐκτρέφω; NIV, ESV, NASB, NRSV, CSB, NKJV, KJV), or "raise" (NET), to describe the process of helping a child grow to adulthood (cf. 1 Kings 11:20; Job 31:18; Hos. 9:12).

The first way fathers were to raise their children was by giving attention to their "training" (παιδεία). The term sometimes indicated "discipline" (ESV, NASB, NRSV, NET), as in Hebrews 12:5–11 (cf. 1 Cor. 11:32; Rev. 3:19), but in this verse it more likely held the nuance of "training" (NIV, CSB, NKJV), as in 2 Timothy 3:16 (cf. Acts 7:22; 22:3; Titus 2:12). The second component of bringing up children consisted in "admonition" (νουθεσία). The translation "admonition" (NKJV, KJV) was probably preferable to "instruction" (NIV, ESV, NASB, NRSV, CSB, NET). The noun and its related verb form (νουθετέω) at times referred to "instruction" in general (Rom. 15:14; Col. 3:16; 1 Thess. 5:12), though the instruction was often delivered with a strong or urgent tone (Acts 20:31; 1 Cor. 4:14; Col. 1:28) or as a warning (1 Thess. 5:14; 2 Thess. 3:15; Titus 3:10). Together, "training and admonition" conveyed the sense of fathers' purposeful, wise, and heartfelt investment in their children's growth. This stood in contrast to a haphazard, reckless, or insensitive style that provoked children to anger.

The notion of training and admonition entailed a comprehensive plan for children's growth into maturity. The genitive modifier "of the Lord" (κυρίου) specified that Paul had spiritual maturity in mind as the end goal. As he did throughout this section (Eph. 6:1, 5, 6, 7, 8, 9), Paul oriented his teachings around the Lord (Christ Jesus). In this case, Paul wanted the fathers to align the training and admonition of their children with Christ's goals for children's growth. The Lord Jesus worked through fathers' caring and determined leadership to instill an understanding of the Lord and his ways in their children's lives. This emphasis on the Lord stood in contrast to the more general training and instruction that the writers and thinkers of the Greco-Roman world prescribed for children within the household (cf. Plutarch, *Mor.* 1.1–10).

Training Children in the Lord

Paul's description of intentional, Christ-centered instruction was reminiscent of the emphasis in Deuteronomy (6:1–9; 11:18–21) on constantly teaching children about Yahweh and his good laws, passing down the knowledge of God from one generation to another. This vision for instilling a lasting knowledge of the Lord was an essential component of Israel's preparation to enter the good land that God was giving them. Paul wanted his readers who were fathers to take similar responsibility for the spiritual formation of their children, to help prepare them to live a new life in Christ, as part of the body of Christ. Fathers did this by imparting beliefs and habits in thoughtful ways that would help them be well-received and would result in spiritual blessing for their children.

Recognizing the Lord in Slaves' Obedience and Masters' Fair Treatment (6:5–9)

Paul instructed the household slaves among his readers to provide obedient service to masters that was inspired by faithfulness to Christ, sincere goodwill to their masters, and expectation of the Lord's future reward, while he commanded masters to treat slaves fairly, in recognition of a Master in heaven who viewed slaves and masters equally and judged accordingly.

6:5. Paul supplied a Christ-shaped treatment of the master-slave relationship next, continuing to reflect a pattern familiar from the ancient household code genre, while providing distinctly different instructions for how believers in Christ should engage in these relationships. As he had already done with wives and children, Paul first spoke to a group (in this case, the household slaves) that was under the authority of another party, before turning his attention to the other party in the relationship. Paul addressed his guidelines directly to "slaves" (οἱ δοῦλοι, nom. of address) who were in the churches in Asia Minor. Most English translations rightly render this word as "slaves" (NIV, ESV, NASB, NRSV, CSB, NET, NLT) instead of "servants" (KJV) or "bondservants" (NKJV). The term "slave" (δοῦλος) recognized the legal obligation of the slave to the master in that context (as opposed to a voluntary work agreement that was entered into). Paul communicated respect for the slaves' personhood, despite their disadvantaged status in Roman society, by giving them instructions alongside the counsel he gave to masters (Lincoln, 1990, 420). Paul helped slaves take responsibility for their own spiritual lives and service within the household structure.

Slavery in Greco-Roman Society

A multitude of ancient sources help scholars construct a clear picture of the nature of slavery in Greco-Roman society (Ferguson, 2003, 59–61; *DPL*, 881–83). Slavery was interwoven into the socioeconomic system of the Greco-Roman world. The empire owed much of its economic growth to the participation of slaves. Condemned criminals, people conquered by Rome in war, and other people seized by force became slaves against their will. Others entered into slavery when they or family members owed debts that they could not pay. While convicted criminals or prisoners of war were often assigned the most grueling tasks such as labor in the mines, many debt-slaves carried out a variety of tasks that advanced the business interests of the household or tended to needs within the household. From a legal perspective, household slaves belonged to their masters and were even considered property, but they were also protected with legal rights from gross mistreatment. These household slaves often lived in the same house as the master and the master's family (Harrill, 2016, 312). Household slaves could also often gain release from slavery (manumission) after gradually accumulating enough savings from serving their masters (cf. 1 Cor. 7:21; Philem. 18). Others were granted some measure of freedom according to instructions in their masters' wills. Paul advocated a radical equality between slaves and masters (1 Cor. 12:13; Gal. 3:28; Col. 3:11) without striking directly at the institution of slavery (though note his condemnation of slave traders in 1 Tim. 1:10). Instead, he guided his readers, as politically powerless participants in a vulnerable religious movement, to reflect Christ as much as they could within the master-slave relationships that were the legal and societal norm in the Roman Empire.

Paul told the household slaves who were receiving his letter to "obey" (ὑπακούω) their earthly masters, using the same word as he did to describe children's obedience to their parents (Eph. 6:1). Paul's readers who were slaves were to obey their "earthly masters" (οἱ κατὰ σάρκα κύριοι; NIV, ESV, NRSV), or "human masters" (CSB, NET), translations that are clearer than the literal rendering of "masters according to the flesh" (NASB, NKJV, KJV). According to Roman law, a "master" (κύριος) had legal authority over his slave (cf. Gaius, *Inst.* 1.52). Nevertheless, these earthly masters were insignificant in comparison to Jesus, the true master (the same word κύριος was his title), who according to Ephesians 6:9 was "in heaven" (ἐν οὐρανοῖς). The brief addition Paul made with the wording "human" (κατὰ σάρκα) recognized the limited reality of earthly status that was nothing in comparison to the spiritual reality of Christ's authority (cf. the similar use of the phrase in Rom. 1:3; 9:3, 5; 1 Cor. 10:18). Though Paul and other early Christians were in no position to overturn the Roman system of slavery, Paul could remind his readers that human masters' authority was greatly limited.

Multiple phrases modified the way in which Paul thought that slaves who were followers of Christ in the first century ought to express obedience to their earthly masters. Paul began with two prepositional phrases. First, slaves were to obey "with fear and trembling" (μετὰ φόβου καὶ τρόμου). The term "fear" (φόβος) depicted a posture of fear or reverence, while "trembling" (τρόμος) envisioned a physical response accompanying fear. When Paul combined "fear" and "trembling" he conveyed the metaphorical sense of an attitude of respect and seriousness, often with an awareness of God's authority lingering in the background of a relationship or situation (1 Cor. 2:3; 2 Cor. 7:15; Phil. 2:12). As was confirmed in the verses that followed, Paul wanted a reverent acknowledgement of God to guide slaves' respectful service towards their masters.

Second, Paul advised the slaves in Asia Minor to obey "in the sincerity of your heart" (ἐν ἁπλότητι τῆς καρδίας ὑμῶν). The phrase pictured sincere, honest service that came from the heart (BDAG, s.v. "ἁπλότης" 1, p. 104; cf. 2 Cor. 1:12; 11:3; Col. 3:22). For Paul's readers who were slaves, obedience was to reflect transparently the good intentions that they harbored toward their masters in their hearts. Paul instructed slaves to avoid superficial obedience that masked devious schemes.

Christ motivated this sincere service. Paul's readers who were slaves needed to obey sincerely, from their hearts, "as to Christ" (ὡς τῷ Χριστῷ). Using this comparative construction Paul presented obedience to Christ as the standard for service that slaves in Paul's churches should aspire to. Household slaves strived to serve their masters as part of their greater service to Christ. Christ was the constant point of reference for how to interact with others in all household relationships. Paul wanted the slaves receiving his letter to think about Christ as the ultimate recipient of their obedient and loyal service.

6:6. This verse supplemented the meaning of the previous verse to further describe what slaves' obedience to their masters should look like in the original readers' setting. Paul noted a contrast to the prior idea of sincere service by emphasizing that slaves should obey, "not just when being watched, as those who are performing to an audience" (μὴ κατ᾽ ὀφθαλμοδουλίαν, ὡς ἀνθρωπάρεσκοι). Translations that capture the overall sense of these phrases (NIV, NRSV, CSB, NET) are more helpful than the more literal translations (ESV, NASB, NKJV, KJV). The first term was literally "eye-service," and it described a superficial obedience that was only on display when someone was watching (BDAG, s.v. "ὀφθαλμοδουλία," pp. 743–744). The second description was translated literally as "people-pleasers," but the idea was less about genuinely wanting to please people than about creating an artificially inflated impression of excellent work (BDAG, s.v. "ἀνθρωπαρεσκέω," p. 80). Together, the two terms portrayed doing just enough to keep the master satisfied. Paul hoped that the slaves receiving his letter would not be content to serve just to be viewed favorably by their masters.

Instead (ἀλλά, "but"), household slaves were to obey "as slaves of Christ" (ὡς δοῦλοι Χριστοῦ). Having this mindset would help slaves sustain a more genuine and excellent level of service that reflected the difference that Christ made in any situation. Early Christians such as Paul spoke of themselves as "slaves of Christ" (Rom. 1:1; 1 Cor. 7:22; Gal. 1:10; Phil. 1:1; Col. 4:12; 2 Tim. 2:24; Titus 1:1; James 1:1; 1 Peter 2:16; 2 Peter 1:1; Jude 1; Rev. 1:1). This label acknowledged their ultimate allegiance to Christ as their master. Paul believed that this recognition should influence the way that slaves in the early church carried out their duties to their masters, since any action took on greater significance when undertaken as a service to Christ.

Paul explained that for Roman household slaves, being a slave of Christ involved "doing the will of God from the heart" (ποιοῦντες τὸ θέλημα τοῦ θεοῦ ἐκ ψυχῆς, ptc. of means). The inclusion of "doing God's will" showed that in their current circumstances, these household slaves were faithful to God's greater purposes when they offered high-quality service to their earthly masters. Earlier, Paul had promoted seeking the Lord's will in all areas of life (Eph. 5:17). He provided slaves of his era with a clear path for fulfilling the will of God in their daily activities within the household. The "heart" or "soul" (ψυχή) in this context represented the place of a person's deepest motivations and emotions (BDAG, s.v. "ψυχή" 2c, p. 1099; Matt. 26:38; Mark. 12:30; Luke. 1:46; Col. 3:23; 1 Thess. 2:8). To do the will of God from the heart meant that Paul's readers who were household slaves would exceed just going through the motions and would tap into their central convictions about how to please God when they served their earthly masters.

6:7. Paul added more description about the desired manner for how the slaves in his setting should obey their masters. Household slaves obeyed "by serving with a good attitude" (μετ᾽ εὐνοίας δουλεύοντες). Household slaves obeyed their masters through offering good-hearted service to them. The phrase "with a good attitude" (μετ᾽ εὐνοίας; CSB) can also be translated as "with enthusiasm" (NRSV, NET), "wholeheartedly" (NIV), or "with [a] good will" (ESV, NASB, NKJV, KJV). Paul directed household slaves to let their supportive and benevolent intentions shine through in their service. Paul expected that this was possible when slaves were serving "as to the Lord and not to men" (ὡς τῷ κυρίῳ καὶ οὐκ ἀνθρώποις). Paul returned to the fundamental contrast he had developed in these few verses: slaves were to see their obedience to masters primarily as a service to Christ rather than to their masters. Every difficult or mundane task took on greater significance when they served with a view toward their ultimate master, Jesus.

6:8. Paul strengthened the force of the last thought by providing a reason (adv. ptc. of cause, εἰδότες, "knowing") for having a mindset of serving the Lord. He affirmed that household slaves should serve knowing that the Lord would reward them. Paul identified a powerful spiritual truth that should motivate household slaves' service. This truth held for "each person" (ἕκαστος). At the end of the verse, Paul emphasized that this was true for anyone, "whether slave or free" (εἴτε δοῦλος εἴτε ἐλεύθερος). In other words, Paul was taking a broader truth and applying it to the situation of those readers who were slaves. A slave enjoyed the same access to God's fairness and generosity as a free person did.

Paul introduced the promise with an "if . . . then" statement (in third-class conditional form). Paul claimed that "for each person, if that person does something good" (ἕκαστος ἐάν τι ποιήσῃ ἀγαθόν), then there would be a good outcome that resulted. Paul often used "good" (ἀγαθός) as a noun or adjective to depict beneficial actions that emerged from hearts of faith and were in line with God's will (Rom. 12:2, 9; 13:3; 2 Cor. 5:10; 9:8; Gal. 6:10; Eph. 2:10; Col. 1:10; 1 Thess. 5:15; 2 Thess. 2:17; 1 Tim. 2:10; 5:10; 2 Tim. 2:21; 3:17; Titus 3:1). For any such good work, "this [good thing] would be compensated for with a reward" (τοῦτο κομίσεται) that came "from the Lord" (παρὰ κυρίου). The Lord himself would acknowledge the good things that a person had done with a corresponding and abundant provision for that person. Paul pictured an eternal reward that awaited people after their lifetime (2 Cor. 5:10; Col. 3:25; Heb. 10:36; 11:39; 1 Peter 5:4). No good service evaded the gaze of Christ, who was a just and caring Master. This principle was something that was true across the board, no matter how limiting one's circumstances might be. Paul promised that any person, including the household slaves he addressed, could expect to receive compensation from the Lord when they served the Lord and did good in whatever situation they found themselves in.

Eternal Rewards

Paul's teachings on appropriate recompense for good deeds built upon Jesus's teachings in the Gospels. Jesus appealed to eternal rewards as a motivation for righteous living in the current world (Matt. 5:10–12; 6:1–21; 10:41–42; Luke 6:35). He even acknowledged that every selfless act done for his sake would be noticed and compensated for in the world to come (Matt. 19:27–30). Paul likewise saw a future reward for the good that believers had done (1 Cor. 3:14; 2 Cor. 5:10) and even looked to eternal rewards to spur himself on in his service to Christ (1 Cor. 9:24–27; Phil. 3:14; 2 Tim. 4:8). Through Christ, God opened up his kingdom to sinners, which was good news and an act of grace that created profound gratitude in the lives of believers. But kingdom citizens still fixed their eyes on a future reward as a complementary motivation to live faithfully for God (cf. Mohrlang, 2013, 114–17). Paul gave this encouraging reminder to household slaves to help inspire them to serve Christ well while they carried out their duties as slaves.

6:9. After his extensive directions to household slaves, Paul gave corresponding (καί, "and") instructions to "the masters" (οἱ κύριοι). Within a household context in the Roman world, masters had legal authority and ownership over their slaves (BDAG, s.v. "κύριος" 1b, p. 577). This legal standing sometimes gave cover for poor and inhumane treatment of slaves, including harsh physical punishment and sexual abuse, both of which were rationalized as being within the master's rights (Hubbard, 2010, 193–94; Harrill, 2016, 310–11). Paul insisted on a radically different way of leadership. The commands he gave limited the exercise of masters' authority and reshaped them around the lordship of Christ.

First, Paul insisted that masters "must do the same things towards them [the slaves]" (τὰ αὐτὰ ποιεῖτε πρὸς αὐτούς). With "the same things" (τὰ αὐτά) Paul envisioned masters adopting the Christ-centered behavior that he had directed the slaves to display to their masters, even though the masters occupied a drastically different position within the household structure.

Second, Paul clarified what this similar behavior should look like with the participial phrase "ceasing with threat-making" (ἀνιέντες τὴν ἀπειλήν). The verb "to cease" or "to stop" (ESV, NRSV), or "give up" (NASB, NET, NKJV) doing something (ἀνίημι) did not necessarily mean that Paul had heard reports that the household masters among his readers had been making threats. Instead, Paul counseled masters to abandon what was a common societal approach for trying to control their slaves (cf. Seneca, *Ep.* 47.5; Philo, *Virt.* 124). "Threat-making" (ἀπειλή) referred to using words to promise harm to someone (Acts 4:29; 9:1; cf. 1 Peter 2:23). Paul forbade the Christian masters receiving his letter from threatening to harm their household slaves as a ploy to influence their behavior.

Paul supported these instructions with a theological reason, using the same term (εἰδότες, "knowing," ptc. of cause) that he had enlisted to inspire household slaves' mindset in Ephesians 6:8. The masters needed to know two related truths about Christ. First, Paul told them to know "that both their [the slaves'] master and your [the masters'] master is in heaven" (ὅτι καὶ αὐτῶν καὶ ὑμῶν ὁ κύριός ἐστιν ἐν οὐρανοῖς). Paul celebrated a great leveling principle in this reason for masters' fair treatment of their household slaves. The masters and slaves in the churches of Asia Minor served a common Master who was in heaven. Paul called Jesus the Master of both the human masters and slaves among Paul's readers. The term "Master" (κύριος), usually translated as "Lord," echoed the title for human masters in this context. Some of Paul's readers were earthly masters (Eph. 6:5), but both masters and slaves answered to their same heavenly Master. Their Master Jesus was "in heaven" (ἐν οὐρανοῖς) and exercised his all-encompassing authority from there (Eph. 1:20–23). Masters and slaves thus shared equal standing in their heavenly Master's sight.

Paul added the second point, with "and" (καί), that "there is no partiality with him" (προσωπολημψία οὐκ ἔστιν παρ' αὐτῷ). Paul affirmed that the masters' Lord in heaven was characterized by his absence of "partiality" (ESV, NASB, NRSV, NKJV), or "favoritism" (NIV, CSB, NET), which meant that he valued household slaves and masters equally (1 Cor. 12:13; Gal. 3:28; Col. 3:11) and held them equally accountable for their actions. Christ was ready to reward (Eph. 6:8) or judge (Eph. 6:9; cf. Col. 3:25) every person with full knowledge and fairness. Christ's reign reflected the character of God, who showed no partiality in his estimation of humans who stood before him in judgment (Deut. 10:17; 2 Chron. 19:7; Job 34:19; Acts 10:34; Rom. 2:11; Gal. 2:6; 1 Peter 1:17; cf. Lincoln, 1990, 423–24). By extension, Paul's readers were to repudiate and avoid partiality in their midst (Lev. 19:15; Prov. 18:5; Col. 3:25; James 2:9), which meant that human masters should affirm the equal dignity that slaves shared as fellow believers. Paul expected that the masters receiving his letter should to strive for Christlike interactions with their household slaves and disavow threatening words, since they were equals with their slaves in Christ's sight. Paul reminded human masters that their actions were weighed by a Master who applied equal standards of justice, regardless of the human status of the one being judged.

Slavery in Colossians and Philemon

After affirming the spiritual reality that in Christ there was no Gentile or Jew, nor slave or free (Col. 3:11), Paul supplied teaching to household slaves and masters (Col. 3:22–25) that strongly resembled what was found in Ephesians 6:5–9. He stressed the household slaves' sincere and heartfelt service, driven by reverence for Christ, and masters' sense of accountability to their heavenly Master. Paul's letter to Philemon likely accompanied the letter of Colossians, but the letter to Philemon provided a glimpse into a different side of Paul's overall perspective on slavery. Paul challenged Philemon to radically reconfigure his relationship with his slave Onesimus around Christ, and many scholars even think that Paul was seeking to persuade Philemon to release Onesimus from his legal obligation to continue in slavery (cf. hints of this especially in Philem. 8–9, 13, 14, 18–21; Bruce, 1984, 199, 217; Thielman, 2005, 388–89; Moo, 2008, 373). The letter of Philemon represented a more direct and forceful application of Paul's belief in complete equality in Christ (Gal. 3:28; Col. 3:11) and the reality that all believers were a new creation in Christ (2 Cor. 5:16–17) to a specific master-slave relationship.

THEOLOGICAL FOCUS

The exegetical idea (as the authority and promises of Christ the Lord shaped harmonious relationships between children and parents and then slaves and masters within the structure of Paul's readers' households, children would obey their parents, fathers would patiently train their children spiritually, slaves would obey their masters, and masters would acknowledge slaves' equal dignity through fair treatment) leads to this theological focus: Believers should remember the authority and promises of Christ the Lord as they live spiritually purposeful and constructive lives within their household and in other important relationships.

Followers of Christ in any setting must learn to navigate structured relationships that involve exercising authority and living under authority. These Christ followers must honor Christ's presence and let his authority and promises renew and reshape their relationships. It is clear from the frequent mentions of "Christ" (vv. 5, 6) and "the Lord" (vv. 1, 4, 7, 8, 9) throughout this passage that the truth of Christ's presence should be ringing in believers' ears. For those under human authority, this means tapping into a deeper motivation for responding well to the authority figures in their lives (vv. 1, 5–7). Their respectful service takes on eternal significance when offered as a service to Christ. For those in authority, it means leading reasonably, thoughtfully, and rejecting abusive or demeaning forms of persuasion and leadership, knowing that Christ has called them to a higher way that honors each person they oversee (vv. 4, 9).

A recognition of Christ's authority and presence should propel believers towards purposeful and constructive spiritual growth in the context of familial and other relationships. This pathway to constructive growth is opened up to children who trust the Lord enough to honor their parents' leadership, even when the children cannot see the logic or greater purpose behind that leadership (vv. 2–3). Parents can adopt an intentional and long-term approach to cultivating spiritual growth in their children (v. 4). Outside the immediate family, those with relatively less clout in a relationship can reflect Christ through displaying the difference Christ makes for motivating excellent service (vv. 6–8). Those in authority can mirror Christ's affirmation of the equal dignity of all people (v. 9). This passage creates the hope that both parties can directly and indirectly remind the people around them that the eternal time frame matters most (vv. 3, 8), and the good and just Lord who will be in charge forever sees and remembers what each person does in this life (v. 9).

PREACHING AND TEACHING STRATEGIES

Exegetical and Theological Synthesis

Throughout the letter to the Ephesians, Paul stressed the benefits and moral implications of being "in Christ," and that theology is front and center in this intensely practical section addressed to children, parents, slaves, and masters. Adopting the form of the Roman "household code," Paul showed how being in Christ made a profound difference in the home. Submission and love (showcased in the previous passage), and obedience and respect (showcased in this passage) were to be the Christian's watchwords. Paul stated that all four groups—children, parents, slaves, and masters—were to conduct themselves "in the Lord" (v. 1), a phrase that appears in various forms five times. Children were to obey in the Lord and remain motivated by the promise of reward that Paul cited from the Ten Commandments (vv. 2–3). Parents' (lit., "fathers'") duty was to not provoke their children but to bring them up in the discipline and admonition of the Lord (v. 4). Slaves were to obey their masters as they would Christ, sincerely and with fear (vv. 5–6). Finally, masters were to stop threatening their slaves and to treat them with respect because in the Christian household, all had the same Master in heaven (v. 9).

Preaching Idea

Under the same roof, Christians are under the same Lord.

Contemporary Connections

What does it mean?

What does it mean that under the same roof, Christians are under the same Lord? The first phrase "under the same roof" refers to all members of a family, especially when the family is still living together. In many ways Christian homes look similar to other homes, but the second phrase "under the same Lord" makes the Christian home remarkably countercultural. The passage subtly turns the household code on its ear. Children are to obey "in the Lord." Fathers must rear their children "in the training and admonition of the Lord." Slaves should obey "as servants of Christ." Masters must remember that they too have a master in heaven.

Paul's Emphasis on Being "in the Lord" in the Home

Phrase	Addressed to	Verse
Obey your parents in the Lord	Children	1
In the training and admonition of the Lord	Parents	4
Obey . . . as to Christ	Slaves	5
As slaves of Christ	Slaves	6
With a good attitude, as to the Lord	Slaves	7
Will be compensated with a reward from the Lord	Everyone	8
Both their Master and yours is in heaven	Masters	9

The use of cultural background such as attitudes toward slavery and the Roman law of "power of a father" (*patria potestas*) might be helpful in explaining the subversive power of the preaching idea, and then modern examples could bridge to the current context. Parents can provoke their children when they are inconsistent with discipline, stinting with praise, or hypocritical. "Do as I say, not as I do" is a recipe for producing discouraged or rebellious children. Conversely, children should not spin the truth to their parents or cut corners when following household rules. The command for children to obey (v. 1) raises the question of age. That is, are adult children obligated to obey, and when does one pass from being a child to an adult? The preaching idea provides guidance, but we will want to offer it as a principle, not a law: as long as a child is "under the same roof," verse 1 can apply. Wise parents will, of course, modify household rules as the child grows, and once the child moves out his or her duty shifts to "honoring" the parents (Exod. 20:12) rather than "obeying."

Slavery is illegal today, but it seems valid to contextualize the verses addressed to slaves and masters to employees and bosses by reasoning from the lesser to the greater. That is, if slaves were commanded to obey not with eye-service, *how much more* should Christian employees work with integrity? If masters were commanded to treat their household slaves justly and fairly, *how much more* should Christian employers do so? All of us have a Master in heaven. Of course, those who teach this text will want to acknowledge differences between the first century and the twenty-first century. Unlike slavery, employment is voluntary, remunerated, and governed by a contract. Some employees may feel enslaved because of their lack of opportunities and dependence on medical insurance, so employers must treat them fairly and with dignity.

To describe relationships between employers and employees, the concept of "power distance" might be enlightening (the term was coined by Geert Hofstede). It is a way to categorize cultures by the degree to which they expect and accept power to be distributed unevenly.

Is it true?

Is it true that all members of the Christian household are under the same Lord? Yes. Each member of the household has his or her duties to carry out in Christ. The preaching idea might be clarified by contrasting it with negative examples. Today absentee fathers are common. Television shows sometimes make fathers look foolish in the eyes of their sharp and conniving children. A scene from *The Chosen* (1967) by Chaim Potok depicts a father who is simultaneously tender, playful, and attentive to his young children, but also silent, distant, frowning, and cold to his oldest son. The father is a Hasidic rabbi and brings up his son "in silence" as a way to teach him humility and compassion. The film version of *The Chosen* (directed by Jeremy Paul Kagan, 1981) starring Robby Benson has a poignant scene about halfway through the movie where the son watches his father singing nursery songs with the younger children as Benson looks on wistfully.

After presenting negative examples, positive examples might include families that worship together—all are "under the same Lord." Parents can show that they are under the same Lord by confessing to their children when they have made mistakes. If an employee's position is cut during difficult economic times, he or she can show what it looks like to be under the Lord by not complaining and railing against their employer. Episode 3 from another film with the same name—*The Chosen*—presents a beautiful picture of a parent figure, Jesus, as he spends time teaching, playing with and listening to the children of Capernaum.[1]

1 For an example, search "The Chosen Global Livestream: Episode Three," on YouTube.

One of the subordinate ideas that supports the preaching idea may need to be addressed: slavery.

Now what?

What difference does it make to live under the same roof *and* under the same Lord? All the difference in the world. As Greg states in the exposition, fathers' discipline must not be "haphazard, reckless, or insensitive." Examples, self-disclosure, and stories can show both negative and positive modes of child-rearing. I (Jeffrey) remember well my own father reading aloud to my brother and me on Saturday mornings when we were young. We would position ourselves on either side of him on the couch, snuggling close, while he opened vistas of imagination—science fiction, historical fiction, poetry, and tall tales. On the other hand, I also remember a boss yelling at me in front of other employees. I had taken a temp job in a factory where we used all sorts of power saws (not my forte). The boss was unable to control his temper and regularly showed disgust when employees made mistakes, as I did often. Perhaps members of the church could share their stories as well. A small business owner might share how she or he remembers his Master in heaven. A teenager might share about his or first summer job and what was learned not only about the skills of the job but about serving Christ through the job.

Creativity in Presentation

In addition to the suggestions above, the following options might be adopted. These could be coordinated with the sermon outline below.

Visual aids: pictures or objects might represent each of the four groups addressed—children, parents, slaves, and masters. For example, a tricycle and soccer ball could represent children; a necktie and earrings could represent parents; a to-do list could represent employees; and a contract or corner office could represent the employer. As you address each of these groups, you might stand near the visual or pick it up and handle it.

Quotation: Concerning child-rearing, John Wesley, the father of Methodism, said:

> Self-will is the root of all sin and misery, so whatever cherishes this in children insures their after-wretchedness and irreligion; whatever checks and mortifies it promotes their future happiness and piety. . . . Religion is nothing else than the doing the will of God and not our own. The one grand impediment to our temporal and eternal happiness being this self-will, no indulgencies of it can be trivial, no denial unprofitable. Heaven or hell depends on this alone. So that the parent who studies to subdue it [self-will] in his child works together with God in the renewing and saving a soul. The parent who indulges it does the devil's work, makes religion impracticable, salvation unattainable; and does all that in him lies to damn his child, soul and body forever.[2]

Film: To show a demanding and belittling boss, the film *The Proposal* (directed by Anne Fletcher, 2009) shows how the whole office fears Margaret Tate (played by Sandra Bullock) and talks behind her back.[3]

Skits: For a humorous scene of leadership at the workplace, with all the clichés and tired formulas of management, you might like to consider "Leader Challenged."[4]

For an ironic look at parents who set new ground rules for their technology-addicted

2 *The Journal of John Wesley*, https://www.ccel.org/ccel/wesley/journal.

3 For an example, search YouTube for video clips of *The Proposal*.

4 For an example, search the internet for transcripts of the skit, "Leader Challenged."

kids, see "The Family Meeting," (parts 1 and 2).[5] After a week of the rules everyone is too exhausted to continue and the parents give in to the children.

Illustration: To illustrate how being watched alters behavior (the Master in heaven is watching us work), the following story may serve. People who live in seaside towns know how aggressive seagulls can be in snatching food, but in Great Britain researchers have suggested a new, simple way to deter the flying scavengers—stare at them. In a research project, when a human stared at herring gulls, the birds took, on average, twenty-one seconds longer to approach a bag of potato chips. Most gulls would not approach at all. Being watched, including being watched by the omniscient eye of God, alters our behavior! Christians work not just when their masters' eyes are on them (v. 6), because they remember that God sees all and will reward us (v. 9).[6]

This passage teaches that all members of the family who have placed their faith in Jesus follow him as Lord. In the Christian household, all members have their roles to play, but we also have a common role: honoring Christ the Lord. Under the same roof, Christians are under the same Lord.

A possible sermon outline:

- Instructions to children (vv. 1–3)
  - The theology behind the instructions (union with Christ and promise of reward).
  - Application—obey your parents.
- Instructions to fathers (v. 4)
  - The theology behind the instructions (union with Christ and delegated authority from the Lord).
  - Application—do not exasperate your children, but bring them up in the nurture of the Lord.
- Instructions to slaves (vv. 5–8)
  - The theology behind the instructions (union with Christ and the promise of reward).
  - Application—do not serve insincerely but wholeheartedly.
- Instructions to masters (v. 9).
  - The theology behind the instructions (equality before God who will judge all).
  - Application—treat slaves with respect and do not threaten.

5 For an example, search then internet for transcripts of the skit, "The Family Meeting."

6 Reuters Staff, "Staring at Seagulls Can Stop Them Stealing Food, Research Shows," Reuters.com, August 7, 2019, https://www.reuters.com/article/us-britain-seagulls/staring-at-seagulls-can-stop-them-stealing-food-research-shows-idUSKCN1UX1I2.

DISCUSSION QUESTIONS

1. In what ways are the instructions in Ephesians 6:1–9 to children, parents, slaves, and masters unsurprising? How were they part of the sociology of the Greco-Roman world?

2. In what ways are the instructions surprising and countercultural? How did they overturn the values of Greco-Roman society?

3. How did the New Testament plant the seeds of abolition?

4. Which is harder—being a child or a parent? Why?

5. This passage mentions parents (vv. 1–2), but it also singles out fathers (v. 4). Why do you think this is so?

6. Are you motivated by God's promise of rewards? Why or why not?

7. Are the instructions to slaves and masters applicable to our culture? Give examples.

Ephesians 6:10–24

EXEGETICAL IDEA

Paul's readers could stand strong in their identity and mission in Christ, against the Devil and other hostile spiritual powers, by taking full advantage of God's spiritual armor and praying for all believers and for Paul's ministry as an imprisoned ambassador for Christ.

THEOLOGICAL FOCUS

Believers should stand strong against spiritual opposition by taking advantage of Christ's divine resources and praying for the church's effective mission.

PREACHING IDEA

For protection against spiritual forces, put on the armor of God.

PREACHING POINTERS

Though Paul's readers had experienced the challenges of living as a marginalized group that was out of step with the world around it, they may have wrongly assumed two things. First, they may have identified humans or earthly authorities as their true enemies. Second, they may have felt that they were not up to the task of standing their ground within this hostile spiritual environment. Paul turned his readers' attention to the spiritual forces behind their troubles and encouraged them that God had given them everything they needed to not only survive but also thrive within their adverse settings. Gentiles throughout Asia Minor sought protection from hostile spiritual forces by summoning their own spiritual power through magic and incantations, and the Jewish people of that day also recognized the need for protection against spiritual darkness. Paul identified Christ as his readers' ultimate hope for standing strong against spiritual evil. By reminding his readers of the divine power found in Christ, Paul emboldened them with the hope that echoed Jesus's promise that "I will build my church, and the gates of Hades will not prevail against it" (Matt. 16:18).

Believers today can also be confused about our true enemy, thinking it is the grouchy boss, the government, or Hollywood. But behind people and institutions are the spiritual forces of evil in the heavenly places (Eph. 6:12). Some are interested in spiritism, and palm readers and psychic advisers are common. James Emery White summarizes: "Most Americans mix traditional faith with beliefs in psychics, reincarnation, and spiritual energy that they say can be found in physical objects such as mountains, trees and crystals." This passage helps us see the reality of spiritual forces and how to resist them. God offers all that is necessary. For protection against spiritual forces, we put on the armor of God.

EQUIPPED IN CHRIST FOR SPIRITUAL BATTLE (6:10–24)

LITERARY STRUCTURE AND THEMES (6:10–24)

In this final section of Ephesians, Paul moved from household instructions to broader guidance about negotiating the challenges of living in a dark world. The passage contains three sections about standing strong in Christ in the face of spiritual opposition, followed by brief concluding remarks and a benediction. Paul began by identifying hostile spiritual forces as believers' true enemy but assuring his readers that Christ had equipped them to stand strong against the Devil and his accomplices (Eph. 6:10–13). Second, he exhorted his readers to take full advantage of different pieces of armor that represented divine resources accessible to the believer (6:14–17). Third, Paul advocated vigilant prayer for other believers and for his own boldness while representing Christ in prison (6:18–20). Finally, Paul promised that his colleague Tychicus would give them a full update on Paul's situation, and he offered a benediction that directed his readers back to fundamental blessings in the Christian life (6:21–24).

Paul introduced new images such as standing strong and the whole armor of God in this final passage. He also integrated familiar ideas from earlier in the letter such as the authority of Christ over all spiritual powers, operating in the Lord and in the Spirit, receiving and appropriating the benefits of God's gracious salvation, and Paul's priorities of prayer and advancing the gospel.

- ***Stand Firm in Christ's Strength against Evil Powers (6:10–13)***
- ***Each Piece of Divine Armor Helps Believers Stand (6:14–17)***
- ***Prioritize Prayer for Fellow Believers and Paul's Ministry (6:18–20)***
- ***A Promised Update and a Benediction (6:21–24)***

EXPOSITION (6:10–24)

Paul did not mince words when describing the sober reality of the spiritual forces opposing his readers. Paul's readers lived in a spiritually minded world. Across Asia Minor both Gentiles and Jews who did not know Christ Jesus pursued a variety of rituals that promised them guidance and protection within a dizzying spiritual environment (19:13–16, 19; cf. Acts 13:6–11; 16:16–18; Col 2:8, 18). Gentiles practiced divination to avoid spiritual harm and seek spiritual favor, and they sought to keep the gods pleased through proper rituals. Jews were familiar with the cosmic struggle between spiritual light and darkness from literature such as Tobit, 1 Enoch, and Jubilees. Paul agreed that spiritual forces operated in intimidating ways behind the scenes but proclaimed that finding strength in Jesus's resources was the only hope for his readers. After naming the Devil as his readers' primary enemy, Paul described various other malevolent spiritual powers in rapid-fire succession. But in response to the existence of these imposing adversaries Paul emphasized standing strong and having the God-given ability to do so. To stand strong in Christ meant to unswervingly pursue corporate growth and mission. Paul drew upon the imagery of armor, inspired by several passages in Isaiah, to paint a vivid picture of the powerful spiritual resources his readers had at their disposal because of their union with Christ. He wanted his readers to make full use of this equipment and commit to frequent and steadfast prayer for others' growth and ministry as well. Paul prayed that the blessings of peace, love, faith, and grace would continue to accompany them as they stayed devoted to Christ in their struggle against evil.

Stand Firm in Christ's Strength against Evil Powers (6:10–13)

Paul's readers had the ability to stand strong against the schemes of the devil and any onslaught of attacks initiated by spiritual powers, and not humans, because Christ had equipped readers with his mighty strength and divine resources.

6:10. Paul signaled his intent to bring the letter to a close with "finally" (τοῦ λοιποῦ). Similar wording appeared toward the end of some of Paul's other letters (2 Cor. 13:11; Phil. 4:8; 2 Thess. 3:1), though Paul sometimes initiated his closing well before he actually finished the letter (Phil. 3:1; 1 Thess. 4:1).

First, Paul exhorted his readers, "be strong" (ἐνδυναμοῦσθε). This wording (pres. pass. impv. of ἐνδυναμόω) conveyed the idea of finding sustained strength to meet a challenge (cf. Rom. 4:20, where Abraham was strengthened in his faith while waiting for God to fulfill the promise of giving him and Sarah a child). Paul indicated that his readers should find this strength in two related sources (joined by καί, "and"). First, they should be strong "in the Lord" (ἐν κυρίῳ). Throughout the letter Paul had celebrated the Christian journey as being "in Christ" or "in the Lord." Believers received a claim to all spiritual blessings and resources because of their participation in Christ's divine life, through faith in him. Now, the strength they needed for confronting the forces of evil was found in the Lord, via their union with him.

Next, Paul said that his readers should be strong "in his mighty strength" (ἐν τῷ κράτει τῆς ἰσχύος αὐτοῦ). Paul stacked together words related to power and strength to emphasize the impressive access readers had to a strength that was more than sufficient for their needs. The terms "strength" (κράτος) and "might" (ἰσχύς) both referred to inner strength and capability, and when they were combined (cf. Eph. 1:19) they further intensified the strength that Christ offers believers. Paul's readers could draw upon the Lord's unlimited power (Eph. 1:19) to live out their calling in a hostile environment. They derived their strength from the strength of the one who had included them in his body and generously shared his divine resources with them.

6:11. Paul wanted his readers to enlist God's strength for resisting the devil's devious activity. Paul proceeded to vividly portray what being strengthened in the Lord's mighty power looked like by turning to the image of a soldier's gear, with description of armor that was similar to what was found in literature from the Greco-Roman world (cf. Dionysius of Halicarnassus, *Ant. rom.* 14.9). Paul gave the exhortation "put on the whole armor of God" (ἐνδύσασθε τὴν πανοπλίαν τοῦ θεοῦ). Paul had earlier adopted the clothing metaphor of "putting on" (ἐνδύω) something when he described putting on the new self in Christ, in replacement of the old self that had been corrupted by sin (Eph. 4:24). Jerome was likely correct, then, that putting on spiritual armor amounted to believers drawing fully upon their identity in Christ and the spiritual resources they possessed in union with him (Jerome, Comm. Eph. 3.6.11, ACCS 197).

This current verse also resembled the idea found in 1 Thessalonians 5:8 of putting on spiritual armor in terms of making full use of God-given spiritual equipment needed for a battle against evil. While 1 Thessalonians 5:8 talked about putting on several individual pieces of a soldier's armor, in this passage Paul introduced putting on a whole set of military armor (BDAG, s.v. "πανοπλία," p. 754; Luke

11:22), before moving on to the individual parts. A passage from Wisdom of Solomon (Wis 5:17–20a), itself likely inspired by Isaiah 59:17, also talked about "the whole armor" of the Lord before describing specific pieces of armor (deSilva, 158, 2018; cf. Witherington, 2017, 300–301). The modifier "of God" (τοῦ θεοῦ, gen. of source) specified that God supplied this supernatural equipment to Paul's readers. Resources suitable and appropriate for spiritual battle must come from God (2 Cor. 10:3–5).

to clothe themselves in God's armor "so that you will be able to stand" (πρὸς τὸ δύνασθαι ὑμᾶς στῆναι). This was Paul's first of three uses of the term "stand" (ἵστημι) in this passage (in addition to the closely related term ἀνθίστημι in Eph. 6:13). With the term "stand" (ἵστημι), Paul meant "hold one's ground" (BDAG, s.v. "ἵστημι" B4, p. 482), which depicted a determined persistence in faith in the midst of uncertain or unfavorable spiritual conditions (Rom. 11:20; 1 Cor. 15:1; 2 Cor. 1:24; Col. 4:12).

Equipment for a Roman Soldier (photograph taken in Ephesus). Courtesy of Greg MaGee.

Gear of a Roman Gladiator (photograph taken in Izmir [Smyrna]). Courtesy of Greg MaGee.

The metaphorical armor from God that Paul described equipped believers to stand against the Devil's schemes. Paul noted the purpose for putting on God's full armor (πρὸς τό, "so that"). Paul exhorted his readers

Paul assured his readers that they could be equipped to stand firm "against the schemes of the devil" (πρὸς τὰς μεθοδείας τοῦ διαβόλου). The preposition "against" (πρός) conveyed the sense of an adversarial relationship (BDAG, s.v. "πρός" 3dα, p. 874). Paul earlier had spoken of the scheming involved in false teaching that afflicted churches (Eph. 4:14). Paul portrayed the "devil" (διάβολος) as being crafty, involved in schemes that could harm the church (cf. Eph. 4:27). The one who had tempted Jesus in the wilderness (Matt. 4:1–11), had enticed Judas to betray Jesus (John 13:2), and who was known for his deception (Rev. 20:7–10), posed a threat to the church. But just as Jesus had promised that the church would overcome the forces of evil (Matt. 16:18), Paul knew that God could equip his readers for victory over the Devil's schemes as well.

6:12. Paul explained (ὅτι, "for") that his readers' actual struggle was indeed against spiritual rather than earthly powers. The mention of the Devil sparked an important reminder to Paul's readers about the nature of the battle that they endured as representatives of God's kingdom in a world of evil. Paul specified that "our struggle is not against flesh and blood" (οὐκ ἔστιν ἡμῖν ἡ πάλη πρὸς αἷμα καὶ σάρκα). Paul mentioned "our" (ἡμῖν) struggle in recognition of the scope of the battle, which extended well beyond just the readers' churches. This struggle (NIV, NASB, NRSV, CSB, NET), or "wrestling" (ESV, NKJV, KJV), depicted a grueling struggle (BDAG, s.v. "πάλη," p. 752) that kept the church occupied against an opponent. But Paul insisted that the struggle was not "against flesh and blood" (πρὸς αἷμα καὶ σάρκα; the NRSV keeps the original order "blood and flesh"), where "flesh and blood" referred to people. Humans, even powerful humans who were leaders of antagonistic governments or institutions, were not the ultimate adversaries of the church.

Instead (ἀλλά, "but"), those who followed Christ struggled against a host of spiritual forces that were aligned with a fallen world system. Paul repeated "against" (πρός) four times to emphasize the true targets of believers' resistance, and he attached a string of terms that portrayed a wide array of spiritual forces (cf. Eph. 1:21). Paul described a spiritual realm that was "congested with demons, cluttered with angels, and permeated by diabolical powers" (Hubbard, 2010, 51).

The Supernatural Environment of Asia Minor

Jews and Gentiles in Asia Minor took for granted that there were unseen spiritual forces at work in their world. Ephesus and other cities in the areas exhibited a particularly heightened interest in magic, astrology, mystery religions, and supernatural powers (Arnold, 1992, 39–40; 123). Gentiles and even some Jews in the region were known to practice magic with spells and charms, amulets, and tablets on which curses against others were written (Ferguson, 2003, 232–233; Acts 19:13–14). Such practices promised people a means of exercising spiritual power but also kept people in bondage to fear. Other Jews looked to God and his angels for support against adverse spiritual powers. Jewish literature described God's angelic forces protecting God's people against demons (Tob 3:7–17; 6:1–17; 8:1–3) and warring against fallen angels (1 En. 8–10; Jub. 5:1–6). Fascination with and fear of spiritual powers ruled the day. Within this climate, Paul wanted to redirect his readers' focus to God's all-sufficient power in Christ Jesus that helped believers withstand of any force of evil.

Paul started with "rulers" (ἀρχαί) and "authorities" (ἐξουσίαι), which appeared in tandem in other places in Paul's writings to refer to adversarial cosmic powers that were nonetheless subject to Christ's authority (Eph. 1:21; 3:10; 1 Cor. 15:24; Col. 1:16; 2:10, 15). Next, Paul mentioned believers' conflict "against the cosmic rulers of this darkness" (πρὸς τοὺς κοσμοκράτορας τοῦ σκότους τούτου). The wording formed a key link to the darkness introduced earlier in the letter (Eph. 4:18; 5:8, 11), a darkness that kept people entrapped by sin, evil, and spiritual blindness (cf. 2 Cor. 4:4). Some English translations seek to clarify the meaning of "this darkness" with "this present darkness" (ESV, NRSV), or "this dark world" (NIV). The cosmic powers reigned within the dark state of this present age. The term "cosmic powers" (κοσμοκράτορες) appeared in certain magical texts written shortly after Ephesians, and the word described evil spiritual forces that could be summoned by name (Arnold, 1992, 65–66). Paul's readers struggled against these cosmic powers and against "the spiritual forces of evil" (τὰ πνευματικὰ τῆς πονηρίας). With this wording Paul covered all possible spiritual activity affiliated with evil. Paul would soon speak of "the day of evil" (Eph. 6:13) and the "evil one" (Eph. 6:16). These evil spiritual forces were "in the heavenly places" (ἐν τοῖς ἐπουρανίοις), which meant they originated in the world beyond what people saw (Eph. 1:3, 20; 2:6; 3:10).

What Do the Powers Control?

In Ephesians 6:12, Paul described the church's intense struggle against forces of evil. This was a battle that the church was assured and equipped to win, since Christ had struck a fatal blow against these spiritual entities (Eph. 1:21–22; cf. Col. 2:15). But what aspects of human existence were in league with these spiritual powers? In the broadest sense, the whole evil age was governed by the Devil and the spiritual forces aligned with him (Eph. 2:1–3; cf. John 12:31; Acts 26:8; 2 Cor. 4:4; Gal. 1:4; Col. 1:13). The combination of various general terms for powers and authorities in Ephesians 6:12 fit well with the entire world system being held in the grip of spiritual forces of evil (Paul similarly grouped all sorts of human hardships and spiritual opponents in Romans 8:31–39). It was quite possible, though, that Paul also perceived the operation of evil forces behind human governments and institutions that opposed God's plans and people (cf. Wink, 1984, 85–86; Wright, 2013, 1287). The prophet Daniel established the groundwork for such thinking (Dan. 10:13, 20–21), and this perspective was reflected in the Qumran War Scroll (1QM 1:1–14) as well (*DPL*, 748). Even if human authorities were entangled with transcendent powers, in Ephesians 6:12 Paul wanted his readers to focus their opposition on the spiritual enemy rather than the human collaborators.

6:13. Because of the nature of the struggle (διὰ τοῦτο, "for this reason"), Paul's readers were to be ready to implement the instructions Paul was giving them. Paul resumed his line of thinking from Ephesians 6:11. He directed his readers to "take up the whole armor of God" (ἀναλάβετε τὴν πανοπλίαν τοῦ θεοῦ). With "take up" (ἀναλαμβάνω; ESV, NASB, NRSV, CSB, NKJV, KJV) Paul varied the wording slightly from verse 11, but the meaning was still to take up the armor so that they could put it on (cf. NIV). They needed to undergo this resolute preparation "in order that you might be able to stand your ground" (ἵνα δυνηθῆτε ἀντιστῆναι). The idea of "standing" was still present in this compound form of ἵστημι, and in this oppositional context the translation of "stand your ground" is appropriate (NIV, NET).

Paul's readers were able to stand strong "in the evil day" (ἐν τῇ ἡμέρᾳ τῇ πονερᾷ). They lived in a world of spiritual darkness (Eph. 5:13–14), a world that was under the control of Satan and other spiritual powers (Eph. 2:2; 6:12). God's armor was more than sufficient for the readers' protection and strengthening even within the dark and evil context of their world.

What Is "the Evil Day"?

A singular day often denoted Christ's return and the salvation and judgment that would accompany his return (Rom. 2:5, 16; 1 Cor. 1:8; 3:13; 5:5; 2 Cor. 1:14; Eph. 4:30; Phil. 1:6; 1:10; 2:16; 1 Thess. 5:2, 4; 2 Thess. 1:10; 2:2; 2 Tim. 1:12). In Ephesians 6:13, however, "the evil day" did not match with the victorious tone that often accompanied a description of the day of the Lord. Though the NT noted that an intense period of tribulation for believers would precede Christ's return (Mark 13:1–23; 2 Thess. 2:3–7), Paul did not seem to limit the need for spiritual vigilance to that time in particular. It was more likely that the phrase "the evil day" referred to the current evil age, though with a sense of eschatological expectation (cf. Lincoln, 1990, 446; Moritz, 1996, 196–97; Hoehner, 2002, 834; Arnold, 2010, 449–50; Thielman, 2010, 423), which resembled Paul's comment that "the days are evil" earlier (Eph. 5:16). The idea of standing firm "in the evil day" (ESV, NASB, CSB, NET, NKJV, KJV) is thus better understood as "in the time of evil" (NLT) than as "when the day of evil comes" (NIV).

In the end, Paul's readers were also able, "having done everything, to stand" (ἅπαντα κατεργασάμενοι στῆναι). This wording was grammatically dependent on "in order that you might be able" (ἵνα δυνηθῆτε) from earlier in the verse. The "and" (καί) connected this as an additional point. Paul assured his readers that once they had made all of their necessary preparations through becoming equipped with God's spiritual resources, they would know that they were ready for the fight. Paul restated their ability "to stand" (στῆναι), or face any spiritual challenge or opponent, in God's armor (cf. Eph. 6:11). Paul thus summarized his overall point before moving on to individual pieces of the armor.

Each Piece of Divine Armor Helps Believers Stand (6:14–17)

Paul encouraged his readers to take full advantage of the different pieces of God's armor, which represented divine blessings and characteristics God provided to believers in Christ, so that the readers could stand firm in their identity and mission within an antagonistic spiritual environment.

6:14. Paul transitioned (οὖν, "therefore") to an examination of different pieces of spiritual armor, connecting them to specific spiritual resources. For a final time in the passage, Paul enlisted the verb "stand" (ἵστημι), this time as a command. He began to present the specific ways to stand with four phrases (ptc. of means). First, Paul's readers were to stand "by fastening truth as a belt around your waist" (περιζωσάμενοι τὴν ὀσφὺν ὑμῶν ἐν ἀληθείᾳ). The literal wording of "girding your loins" (περιζωσάμενοι τὴν ὀσφὺν ὑμῶν; NASB; cf. NKJV, KJV), without a specific mention of the type of belt or fastener used, pictured the first step of readiness, whether for a journey (BDAG, s.v. "ὀσφῦς" 1, p. 730), for service (Luke 12:35), or for battle (Eph. 6:14). The gathering of inner garments around the midsection of a soldier allowed for both basic protection of the midsection and ease of movement (Hoehner, 2002, 839). Paul said that this preparatory belt-fastening was done "with truth" (ἐν ἀληθείᾳ). Paul had given truth a place of prominence in this letter. He credited the gospel message of truth with bringing salvation to his readers (Eph. 1:13), being central to the unity and growth of the church (Eph. 4:4–6, 15), and being a fundamental characteristic of new life in Christ (Eph. 4:21, 24, 25). In Ephesians 6:14, Paul appropriately valued the place of gospel truth in his readers' readiness for spiritual battle.

Characteristics of the Spiritual Armor

Paul's description of the individual pieces of armor functioned primarily to support the overall picture of spiritual readiness he conveyed in the passage. The different parts of armor were not even always mentioned (Paul mentioned only the preparatory function of the belt and footwear), and the imagery as a whole was inspired by passages from Isaiah (and the Wisdom of Solomon) that did not describe the pieces with precision. A look at the pieces of armor suggested that God supplied the armor for both "defensive" purposes of protecting and sustaining the church for corporate growth (Eph 4:14–16) and "offensive" purposes of empowering the church to carry the light of Christ's kingdom in careful but strategic ways to the surrounding world (Eph 5:15–17; cf.

Wink, 1984, 86). Finally, the spiritual resources God provided were a mix of positional spiritual blessings secured for those who have new life in Christ and believers' corresponding new way of walking in Christ. Either way, believers had access to these resources because God had provided them through Christ. In short, Paul used armor imagery to emphasize standing firm spiritually by using the divine resources God had provided for spiritual life and ministry.

The second way Paul wanted his readers to stand firm was "by putting on the breastplate of righteousness" (ἐνδυσάμενοι τὸν θώρακα τῆς δικαιοσύνης). A soldier's breastplate was made out of metal that was attached to leather (Keener, 2014, 554), and it guarded the entire area around his chest and back (BDAG, s.v. "θώραξ" 1, p. 463; *DBIm*, 46). The breastplate imagery surfaced in 1 Thessalonians 5:8 as well, but there it was connected to faith and love instead, suggesting Paul's flexibility in applying the image. Here, though, Paul linked the breastplate to righteousness because of its inclusion in Isaiah 11:5 and 59:17. Paul talked about carrying his own "weapons of righteousness" (τὰ ὅπλα τῆς δικαιοσύνης) for accomplishing God-honoring and fruitful ministry in oppressive contexts (2 Cor. 6:7). The term "righteousness" (δικαιοσύνη) likely referred to reflecting God's morally outstanding character and interactions with the world (BDAG, s.v. "δικαιοσύνη" 3, p. 248; Isa. 11:5; 59:16–17), which was the designed outcome of new life in Christ (Eph. 4:24; 5:9; cf. Rom. 6:13–19; 14:17; Phil. 1:11). Paul highlighted the "righteousness" shared by Christ with the believer (cf. Phil. 3:9) and lived out by the believer as essential for Paul's readers' effectiveness in spiritual battle.

The Influence of Isaiah 11:5, 59:17, and 52:7

Paul drew upon three passages from Isaiah as inspiration for his description of believers' armor. All three passages portrayed God, or his anointed Messiah, achieving victory in battle. First, Isaiah 11:5 (LXX) displayed the Spirit-empowered messianic heir of David (Isa. 11:1–10) "having his loins girded" (ἐζωσμένος τὴν ὀσφὺν αὐτοῦ) with righteousness. A parallel expression highlighted "truth" (ἀλήθεια) as well. Second, Isaiah 59:17 (LXX) proclaimed that God "put on righteousness as a breastplate and placed the helmet of salvation on his head" (ἐνεδύσατο δικαιοσύνην ὡς θώρακα καὶ περιέθετο περικεφαλαίαν σωτηρίου ἐπὶ τῆς κεφαλῆς) when he delivered the salvation and judgment that only he could supply for Israel. Finally, Isaiah 52:7 (cf. Eph. 2:17) celebrated "feet proclaiming the good-news message of peace" (πόδες εὐαγγελιζομένου ἀκοὴν εἰρήνης) that was characteristic of God's coming kingdom. Paul rounded out the list with some of his own additions and claimed that his readers were able to share in these divine resources as gifts extended to them via their union with Christ.

6:15. The third way that Paul counseled his readers to stand strong in hostile environments was "by strapping in your feet [in footwear]" (ὑποδησάμενοι τοὺς πόδας). Ancient footwear had straps that helped hold the feet in the sole (BDAG, s.v. "ὑπόδημα," p. 1037). Paul incorporated this image of strapped footwear to further stress being ready for battle. He did not specify a specific type of shoe, sandal, or boot with this wording, choosing to put the focus on readiness instead.

Paul said that the footwear should be put in place "in the readiness of the gospel of peace" (ἐν ἑτοιμασίᾳ τοῦ εὐαγγελίου τῆς εἰρήνης), meaning the readiness appropriate for announcing the good news of peace that God promised to bring. The equipment recalled the feet in Isaiah 52:7 that announced the good news of the peace resulting from the arrival of God's saving reign. The gospel of peace promised the arrival of the restoring work of God, and God called his people to live in joyful readiness of his coming through being faithful to his covenant and representing him to the nations. Christ announced that the kingdom was at hand (Mark 1:14–15) and began to fulfill the gospel of peace through his ministry of reconciling sinners to God, and Jews and Gentiles to one another (Eph. 2:13–17; cf. Rom. 10:15). Paul challenged his readers to express the readiness of the gospel of peace through shining the light of Christ in the dark world (Eph. 5:8–14) and joining Paul in being ambassadors for Christ's kingdom (Eph. 6:19–20). This was a strategic response to spiritual opposition, and God had equipped believers for success in the task.

6:16. Fourth, Paul's readers can stand faithfully for Christ "by taking up the shield of faith in all circumstances" (ἐν πᾶσιν ἀναλαβόντες τὸν θυρεὸν τῆς πίστεως). Paul sees this spiritual resource as beneficial for any given situation ("in all circumstances," ἐν πᾶσιν), no matter how difficult. Paul repeated the verb "take up" (ἀναλαμβάνω) from verse 13 to describe putting the equipment to use. "The shield of faith" (ὁ θυρεὸς τῆς πίστεως) viewed the believer's faith as a long, protective shield (BDAG, s.v. "θυρεός," p. 462). Such shields were typically constructed with thick leather placed upon a wooden or metal frame (*DBIm*, 45). The term "faith" (πίστις) involved an exercise of trust or confidence in an object of faith. In this case, Paul wanted his readers to exercise faith in Christ in an ongoing sense. Paul's readers were able to stand against spiritual opposition and represent Christ well by relying upon his completed work on the cross and his ongoing provision of spiritual strength and protection.

With a relative clause (ἐν ᾧ; instr. use) that further elaborated on the use of the shield of faith, Paul introduced vivid imagery to show the effectiveness of the shield in the face of fiery attacks. Paul assured readers that with the shield of faith "you will be able to extinguish all the flaming arrows of the evil one" (δυνήσεσθε πάντα τὰ βέλη τοῦ πονηροῦ πεπυρωμένα σβέσαι). Paul once again stressed the enabling power (δυνήσεσθε, "you will be able") that God provided for his readers. In this case the shield of faith available to believers allowed them to "extinguish" (σβέννυμι) "arrows" (βέλη) that were "flaming" (πυρόω; NIV, ESV, NASB, CSB, NRSV, NET) or "fiery" (NKJV, KJV). These flaming arrows were directed at them by "the evil one" (ὁ πονηρός). New Testament writers often ascribed the title "the evil one" to the Devil (Matt. 13:19, 38; John 17:15; 2 Thess. 3:3; 1 John 2:13, 14; 3:12; 5:18, 19). The Devil adopted a number of destructive tactics such as deception (John 8:44; Acts 5:3; 13:10; 2 Cor. 11:14; Rev. 12:9; 20:10), temptation (Matt. 4:1–11; 1 Cor. 7:5), and subversive plots against God's kingdom (Matt. 13:38; 16:23; Mark 4:15; John 8:44; 13:2; Acts 13:10; 26:18; 2 Cor. 2:11; Eph. 4:27; 1 Thess. 2:18; 2 Thess. 2:9; 1 Tim. 3:6–7; 2 Tim. 2:26; 1 Peter 5:8; 1 John 3:8; Rev. 2:10). The shield of faith neutralized the intimidating attacks of the Devil against God's people.

6:17. Paul shifted the structure (from ptc. to impv.) with the next two items of spiritual armor. He told his readers that "you must take" (δέξασθε) two pieces of equipment. The idea of "taking" (δέχομαι) the pieces of armor was similar to "putting them on" (Eph. 6:11) or "taking them up" (Eph. 6:13, 16), with the additional nuance of receiving what was given by God.

First, readers were encouraged to take "the helmet of salvation" (ἡ περικεφαλαία τοῦ σωτηρίου). Helmets were typically made of metal or leather and provided vital protection for a crucial part of the soldier's body (*DBIm*, 45). The image was inspired by Isaiah 59:16–17, where God himself put on the helmet in order to achieve salvation for his people. Isaiah 59 emphasized that God would provide what only he could deliver. God accomplished this salvation in the sacrificial work of Christ, as a gift (Eph. 1:13; 2:4–9; 5:23). Paul's readers stood complete in the saving work of Christ and were thus assured of God's unending spiritual support. Nothing that opposed them should frighten them, because Christ had already secured a permanent place in God's family for them (cf. Rom. 8:31–39).

The next piece of spiritual armor for Paul's readers was "the sword of the Spirit" (ἡ μάχαιρα τοῦ πνεύματος). The word for "sword" (μάχαιρα) was a commonly used word in the NT for a short sword or dagger (BDAG, s.v. "μάχαιρα" 1, p. 622). Though each piece of armor had the same overall purpose of helping readers stand firm in their identity and calling, the sword did stand out as a more aggressive instrument. It was especially potent spiritually since it was the sword of the Spirit, which meant that believers had access to the very sword the Spirit used (gen. of possession or source) to accomplish God's purpose in the world.

The qualifier "which is the word of God" (ὅ ἐστιν ῥῆμα θεοῦ) equated the sword of the Spirit with the word of God. The "spoken word of God" (ῥῆμα θεοῦ) in the singular form was equivalent to the message of the gospel and was God's means for enlightening hearers with the knowledge of Christ for salvation (Eph. 5:26; Rom. 10:17; Heb. 6:5; 1 Peter 1:25). The Spirit used God's word as a sword when he delivered God's convicting truth (John 16:7–11; cf. Heb. 4:12) and testified about Christ (John 3:34; 14:17; 15:26; 1 John 5:6). Paul's readers had encountered Christ through the preached message of the gospel (Eph. 1:13), which the Spirit had delivered through chosen ministers (Eph. 3:5). As believers now proclaimed God's truth amidst a dark world they could expect the Spirit to use the message of the gospel in people's lives (Acts 1:8; 1 Cor. 2:12–13). This piece of armor correlated well with the readiness of the gospel of peace (Eph. 6:15), since they both envisioned a church that was actively representing Christ by witnessing to the sacrificial work of Christ and the hope of God's kingdom.

Prioritize Prayer for Fellow Believers and Paul's Ministry (6:18–20)

Paul's readers were able to stand firm within a dark world by praying constantly with the Spirit's help, being diligent in prayers for all of God's people, and prayerfully seeking God's help for Paul's bold and effective preaching ministry, in which he continued to represent Christ even while he was imprisoned.

6:18. With a pivot away from the imagery of spiritual armor, Paul endorsed two additional actions: praying and keeping prayerfully alert. These two participles depended loosely on the original command to stand strong in the Lord in the midst of adverse environments (Eph. 6:14). First, Paul instructed his readers to stand strong "by praying" (προσευχόμενοι). With the surrounding words, Paul emphasized frequent prayer for all sorts of occasions. He persuaded his readers to pray "with all [possible] prayer and petition" (διὰ πάσης προσευχῆς καὶ δεήσεως; Moule, 1960, 57, 94). Paul linked prayers and "petitions" (NASB, NET) or "supplications" (ESV, NRSV, NKJV, KJV) elsewhere (Phil. 4:6; 1 Tim. 2:1; 5:5), and they had similar meanings, except that petitions sometimes reflected more of a sense of urgency (BDAG, s.v. "δέησις," p. 213; Rom. 10:1; 2 Cor. 1:11; Phil. 1:19). Prayer "at all times" (ἐν παντὶ καιρῷ) further called for a serious commitment to prayer to be a top priority.

Paul also advocated praying "in the Spirit" (ἐν πνεύματι), which likely meant praying with an awareness of the Spirit's guiding and empowering presence in readers' midst. The relationship believers enjoyed with God was "in the Spirit" (Eph. 2:18, 22), who dwelt in them through their union with Christ. From this intimate vantage point the Spirit assisted believers in their prayers (Rom. 8:26). Knowledge of this truth reminded Paul's readers that when they prayed they were engaged in a deeply spiritual exercise that involved communion with a relational God who cared about them. Altogether,

Paul painted a picture of continual, urgent, and spiritually dependent prayer that took God's listening ear seriously. Paul himself prayed for his readers in this way (Eph. 1:16).

With "and to this end" (καὶ εἰς αὐτό), Paul indicated that the second action (being alert) supported the fulfillment of the first (praying), as part of the overall command to stand (Eph. 6:14). Paul encouraged readers to stand firm by praying, and they were to pursue that "by keeping alert" (ἀγρυπνοῦντες). An attitude of alertness needed to characterize prayer (Luke 21:36; cf. Mark 14:38), so that opportunities to seek God's help were not missed. Paul's readers needed alertness especially within an environment of spiritual warfare, in which Satan and his forces of evil were at work (Pao, 2002, 142–43).

Paul indicated that alertness should be accompanied "with all perseverance and every [possible] petition" (ἐν πάσῃ προσκαρτερήσει καὶ δεήσει). Though the term for "perseverance" (προσκαρτέρησις) showed up only in this verse in the NT, the related verb "to persevere" (προσκαρτερέω) described being devoted to an activity (BDAG, s.v. "προσκαρτερέω," p. 881). Paul wanted his readers to have stamina in their watchful prayers and to sustain their energy for every "petition" (δέησις). Paul described petitions offered "for all the saints" (περὶ πάντων τῶν ἁγίων), which referred to all fellow believers whom his readers were in contact with and were informed about. Paul expected church participants to pray for each other within their churches and pray for believers in other cities who were part of a growing network of congregations in the early church era (cf. Eph. 1:15; 1 Cor. 1:2). These churches were praying for each other (2 Cor. 9:14) and contributing to one another's needs (Rom. 15:25–27; 1 Cor. 16:1–4; 2 Cor. 8:1–7) as part of an extended family.

6:19. By adding "and for me" (καὶ ὑπὲρ ἐμοῦ), Paul asked that they include his needs in their prayerful petitions. He targeted his prayer request for ministry in particular (cf. Col. 4:3; 2 Thess. 3:1), asking that they would pray "that the right words may be given to me each time I open my mouth" (ἵνα μοι δοθῇ λόγος ἐν ἀνοίξει τοῦ στόματός μου). With this expression Paul acknowledged his dependence upon God (pass. voice construction, with God as the implied provider). He needed for God to supply him with just the right words for communicating with the people he encountered. As a servant who was called to please his Master, Paul simply sought God's wisdom for articulating truth accurately and effectively.

The purpose of this prayer for the right words was "to boldly make known the mystery of the gospel" (ἐν παρρησίᾳ γνωρίσαι τὸ μυστήριον τοῦ εὐαγγελίου). Paul wanted his every conversation to be geared toward making known the gospel. Paul understood that this disclosure of knowledge was perfectly in line with God's desire to "make known" (γνωρίζω) his eternal plans to the church and even to the spiritual powers in the heavenly places (Eph. 1:9; 3:3, 5, 10; cf. Col. 1:27). The "mystery of the gospel" (τὸ μυστήριον τοῦ εὐαγγελίου) consisted of the good news about God's saving plans in Christ, news that had been a mystery because it had not been fully known before Christ had come but had now been revealed in him (cf. Eph. 1:9; 3:3, 4, 9; 5:32). Christ's ministry brought to fruition everything God had foreordained from before the creation of the world (Eph. 1:4, 11). Paul sought God's help in proclaiming this revealed truth "boldly" (ESV, NASB, NRSV, CSB, NKJV, KJV), "confidently" (NET), or "fearlessly" (NIV), using a phrase (ἐν παρρησίᾳ) that captured Paul's courageous approach of proclaiming Christ no matter what the risks to his personal safety and well-being (Phil. 1:20). Paul requested prayers to be able to continue to proclaim the gospel message effectively and boldly.

6:20. Paul continued to expound upon the reasons for his prayer needs in ministry. He expressed his own sense of calling to "be an ambassador" (πρεσβεύω) for the gospel. Paul explained this role of being an ambassador more thoroughly in 2 Corinthians 5:20. When Paul communicated the gospel of reconciliation to his audience, he understood that God was communicating through him. God had completed his reconciling work in Christ, so Paul just had to make known the opportunity for reconciliation. In the case of Ephesians, Paul served as a special type of ambassador, one who was "in chains" (ἐν ἁλύσει). This referred in general to Paul's imprisonment, but with the striking image of a painful chain limiting the prisoner's freedom. The honored role of an ambassador clashed ironically with the lowly status of a prisoner (cf. Cassidy, 2001, 101–3; Arnold, 2010, 468). Paul did not see his imprisonment as a limitation to his role of representing Christ and the good news of his ministry (cf. Acts 28:20). In fact, his unusual circumstances potentially created special opportunities to explain the gospel to governing or judicial authorities (cf. Acts 24:24–26; 26:1–29; Phil. 1:12–18).

Paul reiterated what type of prayer he sought (ἵνα, "that"). "When making known the gospel" (ἐν αὐτῷ, "in it") in these circumstances, Paul desired to "speak boldly" (παρρησιάσωμαι). Paul had previous experience with showing boldness when speaking the gospel in adverse conditions (1 Thess. 2:2). He wanted to demonstrate that same boldness in his current situation. Paul desired to speak boldly, "as I ought to speak" (ὡς δεῖ με λαλῆσαι). Paul's motivation to speak boldly about the gospel arose primarily from a sense of obligation to fulfill the calling God had given him (cf. Col. 4:4). As a recipient of God's gift of revelation and the stewardship of ministry (Eph. 3:2–8), Paul longed to carry out his commission with fidelity and excellence (cf. 1 Cor. 4:1–2).

A Promised Update and a Benediction (6:21–24)

In a spirit of goodwill and mutual awareness, Paul had sent Tychicus to give his readers updates on his situation, and he prayerfully expressed best wishes for their growth in the peace, love, faith, and grace that came from God the Father and the Lord Jesus Christ.

6:21. Paul refrained from saying more about his imprisonment and ongoing ministry, knowing that Tychicus would bring his readers up to speed. Paul identified his goal (ἵνα, "in order that") that just as he had enjoyed hearing about his readers' spiritual progress (Eph. 1:15), he wanted his readers also ("you also," καὶ ὑμεῖς) to know about "his circumstances" (τὰ κατ᾽ ἐμέ). In other words, he wanted them to know "how I am doing" (τί πράσσω). Paul assured them that "Tychicus will make known to you everything" (πάντα γνωρίσει ὑμῖν Τύχικος) about his situation. Tychicus had the responsibility of carrying the letter of Ephesians to the various churches in the province of Asia. He also delivered the letters of Colossians and perhaps Philemon as well (Col. 4:7–9). Tychicus and Paul's readers were both from the Roman province of Asia (Acts 20:4).

Paul described his associate Tychicus in two ways. First, he was "the beloved brother" (ὁ ἀγαπητὸς ἀδελφός). Paul began with an affectionate term that acknowledged the close familial bond that believers shared in Christ. Tychicus was the spiritual brother of Paul and the readers. Paul labeled him as a "beloved" (ἀγαπητός) brother, enlisting a description that applied to all believers in Christ (Eph. 5:1) but also designated the person as an especially valued colleague (Rom. 16:5, 8, 9, 12; 1 Cor. 4:17; Col. 1:7; 4:9, 14; Philem. 1). Tychicus was also a "faithful minister" (πιστὸς διάκονος), which more directly recognized Tychicus as Paul's coworker (cf. Col. 4:7; 2 Tim. 4:12; Titus 3:12). Paul extended a title to Tychicus that he also used for himself (Eph. 3:7). A "minister"

(ESV, NASB, NRSV, NKJV, KJV) or "servant" (NIV, CSB, NET) was an agent who carried out God's plans (BDAG, s.v. "διάκονος" 1, p. 230). Tychicus had been "faithful" in his duties, which Paul saw as an essential requirement for those who had been entrusted with the gospel (1 Cor. 4:2). The status of Tychicus as both beloved brother and faithful servant was governed by the phrase "in the Lord" (ἐν κυρίῳ). In this context, the phrase affirmed relational bonds that were strengthened because of believers' shared life in the Lord Jesus. Tychicus was a brother and minister in the spiritual sense, which Paul saw as all the more significant.

6:22. Paul explained that Tychicus was the one "whom I sent to you" (ὃν ἔπεμψα πρὸς ὑμᾶς). Paul spoke in the past tense (epist. aor.) in the realization that Tychicus would have already arrived once the readers actually heard the letter being read (cf. Moule, 1960, 12). Paul then noted two specific purposes (εἰς αὐτὸ τοῦτο, ἵνα; "for this very reason, that") for sending Tychicus. First, he sent him in order that "you might know of our circumstances" (γνῶτε τὰ περὶ ἡμῶν), which restated what Paul mentioned in the previous verse, with the inclusion of unspecified associates around him in the plural "our" (ἡμῶν). Second, he hoped that Tychicus "might encourage your hearts" (παρακαλέσῃ τὰς καρδίας ὑμῶν). Tychicus was ready to act on Paul's behalf to further strengthen (Eph. 4:1) the readers in their faith and encourage them to embrace all of the truths Paul highlighted in the letter. Paul hoped that the encouragement would affect his readers' hearts, renewing them in the depths of their inner life (cf. Eph. 1:8; 3:17).

6:23. Paul concluded the letter with a benediction (the prayerful sharing of "good words"). It consisted of a series of brief but carefully chosen expressions of goodwill. First, Paul wished "peace" (εἰρήνη) "to the brothers" (τοῖς ἀδελφοῖς), which included all believers who heard the letter read, whether male or female. This peace recalled Christ's reconciling work of bringing Jews and Gentiles into right relationship with God and one another (Eph. 2:13–17). Paul hoped that his readers would savor and guard this peace in their relationships (Eph. 4:3). Next, Paul prayerfully extended "love with faith" (ἀγάπη μετὰ πίστεως), which introduced two more parallel blessings rather than some mixture of the two. Paul had already commended his readers' love and faith (Eph. 1:15) and had prayed that his readers would deeply experience God's love through faith (Eph. 3:14–19). Paul acknowledged that this peace, love, and faith came "from God the Father and the Lord Jesus Christ" (ἀπὸ θεοῦ πατρὸς καὶ κυρίου Ἰησοῦ Χριστοῦ). Peace, love, and faith were not simply virtues to cultivate but were blessings to let sink in and permeate believers' lives. These blessings flowed from God the Father and the Lord Jesus Christ.

6:24. Finally, Paul prayed for his readers' appropriation of "grace" (χάρις). The grace of God first received in the sacrificial work of Christ that had brought forgiveness to Paul's readers (Eph. 1:7; 4:32) could still be experienced in the gift of God's ongoing presence and blessings in their lives (Eph. 1:3, 6). Paul affirmed his hope that this grace would be "with all those who love our Lord Jesus Christ" (μετὰ πάντων τῶν ἀγαπώντων τὸν κύριον ἡμῶν Ἰησοῦν Χριστὸν). Though God bestowed all blessings on his children as an act of his grace, believers were expected to respond in loving devotion to Christ. This was an aspirational description of Paul's readers' lives (cf. Rom. 8:28). He wanted them to be inspired to love Christ in this way as they grew in God's grace.

Paul urged readers to love their Lord Jesus Christ "with an undying" love (ἐν ἀφθαρσίᾳ).

Paul used a term (ἀφθαρσία) that in the NT often referred to incorruptibility or immortality as a gift from God to believers (1 Cor. 15:42, 50–54; 2 Tim. 1:10; cf. 1 Cor. 9:25; 1 Peter 1:4, 23). In this context, it probably denoted a believer's loving devotion to God that did not wane (NIV, ESV, NASB, NRSV, CSB, NET; Hoehner, 2002, 875–77), rather than loving with sincerity (NKJV, KJV; Thielman, 2010, 448) or the association of God's grace with the gift of incorruptible or immortal life (Lincoln, 1990, 467–68; Arnold, 2010, 482–83). God had given Paul's readers a great and boundless love through Christ (Eph, 2:4; 3:19; 5:2), and they were to offer this same love to him in return. Paul added this one final qualifier with the aim of lifting up readers' eyes to a noble goal and ending the letter with a flourish.

THEOLOGICAL FOCUS

The exegetical idea (Paul's readers could stand strong in their identity and mission in Christ, against the Devil and other hostile spiritual powers, by taking full advantage of God's spiritual armor and praying for all believers and for Paul's ministry as an imprisoned ambassador for Christ) leads to this theological focus: Believers should stand strong against spiritual opposition by taking advantage of Christ's divine resources and praying for the church's effective mission.

Believers must stand strong, or act decisively, to be faithful to their calling in a world of spiritual obstacles and resistance. This opposition refers to the Devil and other spiritual authorities who are in cahoots with him, not to individual unbelievers or human adversaries (v. 12). This call to arms is for prayer and spiritual and moral vigilance rather than for becoming a cultural warrior against human ideological opponents. The passage's repetition of "stand" or "stand your ground" (vv. 11, 13, 14) highlights the importance of the responsibility to be faithful. Believers undertake this action in Christ's strength, taking advantage of the complete and empowering armor that God supplies (vv. 10–13).

God has supplied, in Christ, everything believers need to stand firm as well as participate in God's kingdom as witnesses and ambassadors. The passage describes pieces of armor that were first wielded by God, through Christ, in bringing his salvation, peace, truth, and righteousness to the world. Now since believers are united with Christ, they too have access to each of these pieces of spiritual equipment (vv. 14–17). They draw upon these spiritual resources through faith and reliance on the word of God as they interface with the world.

Paul's every step forward in ministry was interwoven with prayer. He expected his readers to integrate prayer into every aspect of their individual and corporate lives as well. Through spiritual alertness believers are to pray continually for the needs of other believers around them (v. 18). Believers and churches should pray especially for mission effectiveness in their communities and in other places around the world (vv. 19–20). Believers are all part of a broad network of family members who share the same goal of seeing Christ proclaimed and represented in all settings.

PREACHING AND TEACHING STRATEGIES

Exegetical and Theological Synthesis

In previous chapters, the apostle Paul had taught the Ephesians how they were seated with Christ in the heavenly places and how they were to live in this world in a way that was consistent with their spiritual state. In this passage, he taught them how to stand against evil powers. In one of the most detailed metaphors in the NT, Paul described how six pieces of spiritual armor and vigilant prayer equipped believers to battle the Devil and his forces. Drawing on Isaiah, Paul described

God's provision: put on (or take up) the belt, breastplate, shoes, shield, helmet, and sword. These pieces of armor equipped Christ followers to resist the Devil and his forces (v. 12), and alert prayer would help Paul boldly proclaim the mystery of the gospel (v. 19).

Preaching Idea

For protection against spiritual forces, put on the armor of God.

Contemporary Connections

What does it mean?

What does it mean that for protection against spiritual forces we should put on the armor of God? Believers can resist evil forces by donning the six pieces armor of God and by utilizing prayer. Listeners may benefit by first understanding the ancient culture. Pictures of the armor that Paul probably had in mind can be found earlier in this chapter or at Google Images, "armor of God." Modern analogies can also help clarify. The breastplate might be a Kevlar vest, the shoes might be hiking boots or crampons for walking on ice, and the flaming arrows of the devil might be napalm dropped from above.

The activities of Satan can be paranormal spectacles, culturally accepted practices such as the use of crystals, or subtle temptations. Cross-references can help clarify Satan's tactics. For example, Deuteronomy 18:1–12 warns about necromancy: "Let no one be found among you who . . . practices . . . sorcery, engages in witchcraft or casts spells. . . . Anyone who does these things is detestable to the Lord" (NIV). Important background for Ephesians 6:10–20 can be found in Acts 19, which depicts the worship of Artemis, the seven sons of Sceva who tried to exorcise demons, and the prevalence of books of magical arts. On the other hand, the Devil, or Satan, also uses subtle schemes that do not seem to partake of the paranormal.

- Satan may exploit tendencies toward natural impulses like anger (Eph. 4:27), sexual desire, and covetousness (Eph. 5:3).
- Satan may inspire false teachers with plausible but deadly ideas (Eph. 4:14; 5:6).
- Satan may use physical affliction (2 Cor. 12:7).
- Satan may entice people to lie (Acts 5:3).
- The temptations of Christ and of Eve are paradigmatic of how Satan works: misquoting Scripture (Matt. 4:6; Gen. 3:1) and promising that good can come from doing evil (Luke 4:6–7; Gen. 3:4).

Is it true?

Is it true that the armor of God protects us from spiritual forces? From my own experience, I (Jeffrey) answer affirmatively. After college I went through a season of doubt that could have doused my faith and crippled my spiritual state. But through the counsel of friends, I learned that I needed to pick up the shield of faith and buckle on the belt of truth. Specifically, by expressing my doubts transparently to God and others, and asking for help (from God and others), the Lord strengthened my faith. I was also helped by reading and discussion.

Christians who have not come from a worldview that believes easily in invisible spirits may have trouble believing in spiritual forces, but Paul was addressing people from a shamanistic culture, as revealed in Acts 19. Skepticism about evil spirits is evident today. But the preaching idea nevertheless is true. Belief in the unseen world of spirits persists in much of the earth's population, perhaps the *majority* of the population. Perhaps this should cause Westerners to approach the topic with humility, not assuming that their view is normative. And the Bible's clear and repeated message is that spiritual forces are real, present, and powerful. Minimization can be part of Devil's strategy. Hiding his malevolent presence is a strategy to make us less watchful, less inclined to pray, and less dependent on God. C. S. Lewis (1942, ix) says the following in the introduction to *The Screwtape Letters*:

> There are two equal and opposite errors into which our race can fall about the devils. One is to disbelieve in their existence. The other is to believe, and to feel an excessive and unhealthy interest in them. They themselves are equally pleased by both errors and hail a materialist or a magician with the same delight. . . . Readers are advised to remember that the devil is a liar.

Now what?

How can we find protection by putting on the armor of God? For most people this begins by acknowledging that spiritual forces exist. Once that truth is accepted, then the context of Ephesians suggests how to put on the armor:

- Understand the word, will, and power of God. That is what Paul prayed for twice in the first half of the book—1:15 and 3:14. To know the will of God, Bible study and giving full attention to the public reading and teaching of Scripture are crucial, so any aid to concentration is to be commended. For example, some people take notes during the sermon that can be reviewed later.
- Participate deeply in church life. Each member is a supporting ligament so that the body will build itself up to attain the stature of Christ (4:11ff.). Spiritual friendships can help us resist the Devil. Some churches include a discussion forum on their website to encourage the body to share wisdom, experience, and prayer.
- Pray for oneself and others (6:18–20). To put the preaching idea into practice, we might join the pulpit ministry with the prayer ministry of the church or organization. From the pulpit we can model how to pray following Paul's lead in Ephesians by praying not just for daily bread, but also for spiritual illumination, unity, and boldness in proclamation. From outside the pulpit we might create opportunities for the congregation to pray. Perhaps we could hold an extended prayer meeting or form a team of people whose primary ministry is prayer.

Five Signs You Might Not Be Waging Spiritual Warfare

1. Your friends, family, or coworkers are surprised to learn you are a churchgoing Christian.
2. You never think about or even remember the Sunday sermon on Monday.
3. There is absolutely no conflict between your Christianity and your political party.
4. You've never had a "truth-in-love" conversation with a fellow Christian.
5. No one in your church could identify any area of growth they have seen in you in the past two years.[1]

Creativity in Presentation

Testimonies of answered prayer can demonstrate the efficacy of spiritual armor. These testimonies might also be placed in the church newsletter or website. If a missionary is on

1 Adapted from Brent McCracken, "8 Signs Your Christianity Is Too Comfortable," The Gospel Coalition, October 21, 2017, https://www.thegospelcoalition.org/article/8-signs-your-christianity-is-too-comfortable.

home assignment, he or she might have a story of overt spiritual warfare.

As stated above, the image of armor is one of the longest figures of speech in the NT. Paul's extended metaphor can be brought home with pictures, diagrams, or other forms of visual communication. A quick search on Google Images gives many options for slides. For a children's sermon, I once saw a man put on each piece of armor as he taught. Elaborate visuals like that may be hard to employ week in and week out, but if your church has a creative arts team, they might like the challenge.

In *Mere Christianity*, C. S. Lewis (1952, 51) uses this analogy to describe spiritual warfare: Christians live behind the lines in enemy-occupied territory. We are the resistance and receive our instructions through the wireless:

> Christianity is the story of how the rightful king has landed . . . and is calling us all to take part in a great campaign of sabotage. When you go to church, you are really listening in to the secret-wireless from our friends: that is why the enemy is so anxious to prevent us from going.

To see how someone with an anti-supernatural worldview discusses the worldwide phenomenon of demon possession and exorcism, you might find Benjamin Radford's article helpful: "Exorcism: Facts and Fiction about Demonic Possession."[2]

A reading from *Pilgrim's Progress* (1678) could be presented by a gifted reader or group of readers. The youth group might enjoy creating a short drama out of the reading, dividing it into various voices and staging it with some movement and scenery. The same could be done with Lewis's *Screwtape Letters,* which has been made into an audio drama, available on Amazon, as well as a theatrical production with Max McLean.

In whatever way we choose to creatively express the teaching of this passage, we will want to remember the main idea: For protection against spiritual forces, put on the armor of God.

A possible sermon outline:

- Why put on the armor of God (vv. 10–12)?
- What is the armor (vv. 13–18)?
- Why stand strong on our knees (vv. 19–20)?

2 Benjamin Radford, "Exorcism: Facts and Fiction about Demonic Possession," LiveScience, March 7, 2013, https://www.livescience.com/27727-exorcism-facts-and-fiction.html. Here are some other websites that speak of possession: The Lineup Staff, "9 Disturbing Cases of Real-Life Exorcism and Possession," The Lineup, January 10, 2018, https://the-line-up.com/demonic-possession-cases; WND Staff, "Real-life Case of Demon Possession Documented," WND (WorldNetDaily.com), March 13, 2008, https://www.wnd.com/2008/03/58835.

DISCUSSION QUESTIONS

1. What did the apostle Paul mean in Ephesians 6:14 when he said that we should "stand"?
2. Why do you think it is so important to identify the true enemy as evil spiritual forces, rather than as human or governmental opponents?
3. Do you believe in Satan and demons? Explain your view.
4. Which piece of armor is most meaningful for you right now, and why?
5. Why did Paul ask for prayer (vv. 19–20)? How does that request compare with most of our requests?
6. Who are some "ambassadors for the gospel" today that you want to pray for more faithfully, and what could help remind you to pray for them?
7. Why was it so appropriate for Paul to end this letter by highlighting peace, love, faith, and grace?

FOR FURTHER READING

Duguid, Ian. 2019. *The Whole Armor of God: How Christ's Victory Strengthens Us for Spiritual Warfare.* Wheaton, IL: Crossway.

Fee, Gordon D. 1994. *God's Empowering Presence: The Holy Spirit in the Letters of Paul.* Peabody, MA: Hendrickson.

Hofstede, Geert H. 1980. *Culture's Consequences: International Differences in Work-Related Values.* Beverly Hills, CA: Sage.

Keller, Timothy. 2016. *Preaching: Communicating Faith in an Age of Skepticism.* New York: Penguin.

Keller, Tim, with Kathy Keller. 2013. *The Meaning of Marriage: Facing the Complexities of Commitment with the Wisdom of God.* New York: Riverhead Books.

Miller, Paul E. 2017. *A Praying Life: Connecting with God in a Distracting World.* Colorado Springs: NavPress.

Packer, J. I. 2005. *Keep in Step with the Spirit: Finding Fullness in Our Walk with God.* Rev. ed. Grand Rapids: Baker.

REFERENCES

Abbott, T. K. 1897. *A Critical and Exegetical Commentary on the Epistles to the Ephesians and to the Colossians.* International Critical Commentary. Edinburgh: T&T Clark.

Alexander, T. D., B. S. Rosner, D. A. Carson, and G. Goldsworthy, eds. 2000. *New Dictionary of Biblical Theology*. Leicester: InterVarsity.

Ando, C., ed. 2003. *Roman Religion*. Edinburgh Readings on the Ancient World. Edinburgh: Edinburgh University Press.

Anizor, U., and H. Voss. 2016. *Representing Christ: A Vision for the Priesthood of All Believers*. Downers Grove, IL: InterVarsity.

Arnold, C. E. 1992. *Power and Magic: The Concept of Power in Ephesians*. Grand Rapids: Eerdmans.

______. 1996. *The Colossian Syncretism: The Interface between Christianity and Folk Belief at Colossae*. Grand Rapids: Baker.

______. 2010. *Ephesians*. Wissenschaftliche Untersuchungen zum Neuen Testament. Grand Rapids: Zondervan.

______. 2012. "Sceva, Solomon, and Shamanism: The Jewish Roots of the Problem at Colossae." *Journal of the Evangelical Theological Society* 55(1):7–26.

Assayas, M. 2006. *Bono: In Conversation with Michka Assayas*. New York: Riverhead.

Balz, H., and G. Schneider, eds. 1990–1993. *Exegetical Dictionary of the New Testament*. 3 vols. Grand Rapids: Eerdmans.

Barclay, J. M. G. 1996. *Jews in the Mediterranean Diaspora: From Alexandria to Trajan (323 BCE–117 CE)*. Edinburgh: T&T Clark.

______. 2011. *Pauline Churches and Diaspora Jews*. Grand Rapids: Eerdmans.

Barr, G. K. 2002. "The Impact of Scalometry on New Testament Letters." *Expository Time* 114:3–9.

Barrett, C. K. 1973–74. "Pauline Controversies in the Post-Pauline Period," *New Testament Studies* 20(3):229–45.

______. 1987. *The New Testament Background: Writings from Ancient Greece and the Roman Empire That Illuminate Christian Origins*. Rev. ed. San Francisco: HarperCollins San Francisco.

Barth, M. 1974. *Ephesians: Introduction, Translation, and Commentary*. 2 vols. Anchor Bible 34. Garden City, NY: Doubleday.

Bateman IV, H. W., D. L. Bock, and G. H. Johnston. 2012. *Jesus the Messiah: Tracing the Promises, Expectations, and Coming of Israel's King*. Grand Rapids: Kregel.

Bauer, Walter, Frederick W. Danker, William F. Arndt, and F. Wilbur Gingrich, and. 2000. *A Greek-English Lexicon of the New Testament and Other Early Christian Literature*. 3rd ed. Chicago: University of Chicago Press.

Beale, G. K., and D. A. Carson, eds. 2007. *Commentary on the New Testament Use of the Old Testament*. Grand Rapids: Baker; Nottingham: Apollos.

Berger, Peter J. 1970. *A Rumor of Angels: Modern Society and the Rediscovery of the Supernatural*. Garden City, NY: Anchor Books.

Best, Ernst. 1998. *A Critical and Exegetical Commentary on Ephesians*. International Critical Commentary. Edinburgh: T. & T. Clark.

Blass, F., and A. Debrunner. 1961. *A Greek Grammar of the New Testament and Other Early Christian Literature*.

Translated and revised by R. W. Funk. Chicago: University of Chicago Press.

Bock, Darrell L. 2019. *Ephesians.* Tyndale New Testament Commentaries 10. Downers Grove, IL: InterVarsity.

Bockmuehl, Markus. 1990. *Revelation and Mystery in Ancient Judaism and Pauline Christianity.* Grand Rapids: Eerdmans.

Boer, Martinus C. de. 1980. "Images of Paul in the Post-Apostolic Period," *Catholic Biblical Quarterly* 42: 359–80.

Boers, Hendrikus. 1975. "The Form Critical Study of Paul's Letters. 1 Thessalonians as a Case Study." *New Testament Studies* 22: 140–58.

Bonhoeffer, Dietrich. 1954. *Life Together.* New York: Harper and Row.

Bruce, F. F. 1977. *Paul: Apostle of the Heart Set Free.* Grand Rapids: Eerdmans.

______. 1984. *The Epistles to the Colossians, to Philemon, and to the Ephesians.* New Covenant Commentary Series. Grand Rapids: Eerdmans.

Bunyan, John. 1991. *The Pilgrim's Progress.* Translated by Cheryl V. Ford. Wheaton, IL: Tyndale.

Calvin, John. 1965. *The Epistles of Paul the Apostle to the Galatians, Ephesians, Philippians, and Colossians.* Translated by T. H. L. Parker. Edited by David W. Torrance and Thomas F. Torrance. Calvin's Commentaries (Repr., 1548). Grand Rapids: Eerdmans.

Campbell, Constantine. 2012. *Paul and Union with Christ: An Exegetical and Theological Study.* Grand Rapids: Eerdmans.

Carson, D. A. 2004. "Mystery and Fulfillment: Toward a More Comprehensive Paradigm of Paul's Understanding of the Old and the New." Pages 393–436 in *Justification and Variegated Nomism.* Vol. 2. Edited by D. A. Carson et al. Grand Rapids: Baker.

______. 2014. *Praying with Paul: A Call to Spiritual Reformation.* 2nd ed. Grand Rapids, Baker.

Carson, D. A., and Douglas Moo. 2005. *An Introduction to the New Testament.* 2nd ed. Grand Rapids: Zondervan.

Cassidy, Richard J. 2001. *Paul in Chains: Roman Imprisonment and the Letters of St. Paul.* New York: Herder & Herder.

Chapell, Bryan. 2005. *Christ-Centered Preaching.* 2nd ed. Grand Rapids: Baker.

Chapell, Bryan, with Kathy Chapell. 2006. *Each for the Other.* Grand Rapids: Baker.

Charles, R. H. 1913. *The Apocrypha and Pseudepigrapha of the Old Testament in English: With Introductions and Critical and Explanatory Notes to the Several Books.* Vol. 2. Oxford: Clarendon Press.

Cohick, Lynn H. 2010. *Ephesians.* New Covenant Commentary Series. Eugene, OR: Cascade.

Collins, Raymond F. 1988. L*etters That Paul Did Not Write: The Epistle to the Hebrews and the Pauline Pseudepigapha. Good News Studies* 28. Wilmington: Glazier.

Colson, Charles W. 1977. *Born Again.* Old Tappan, NJ: Spire Books.

Colson, Charles, and Ellen Santilli Vaughn. 1992. *The Body: Being Light in Darkness.* Dallas: Word.

Cooper, J. M. and J. F. Procopé, eds. 2005. *Seneca, Moral and Political Essays.* Cambridge: Cambridge University Press.

Cotton, Hannah M., et. al., eds. 2010. *Corpus Inscriptionum Iudaeae/Palaestinae: A Multi-lingual corpus of the Inscriptions from Alexander to Muhammed.* Vol. I, part 1. Berlin: De Gruyter.

Dalton, W. J. 1983. "Pseudepigraphy in the New Testament." *Criswell Theological Review* 5: 29–35.

Demarest, Bruce. 1997. *The Cross and Salvation: The Doctrine of Salvation.* Foundations of Evangelical Theology. Wheaton, IL: Crossway.

Dempster, Stephen G. 2003. *Dominion and Dynasty: A Theology of the Hebrew Bible.* New Studies in Biblical Theology 15.

Leicester: Apollos; Downers Grove, IL: InterVarsity.

deSilva, David A. 2016. "Paul, Honor, and Shame." In *Paul in the Greco-Roman World: A Handbook*. Edited by J. Paul Sampley. Vol. 2, 26–47. London: Bloomsbury.

______. 2018. *Introducing the Apocrypha: Message, Context, and Significance*. 2nd ed. Grand Rapids: Baker.

Dodds, Elisabeth D. 2004. *Marriage to a Difficult Man: The Uncommon Union of Jonathan & Sarah Edwards*. Laurel, MS: Audubon.

Dudrey, Russ. 1999. "'Submit Yourselves to One Another': A Socio-Historical Look at the Household Code of Ephesians 5:15–6:9." *Restoration Quarterly* 41: 27–44.

Duguid, Ian. 2019. *The Whole Armor of God: How Christ's Victory Strengthens Us for Spiritual Warfare*. Wheaton, IL: Crossway.

Dunn, James D. G. 1998. *The Theology of Paul the Apostle*. Grand Rapids: Eerdmans.

Edwards, Mark J., and Thomas C. Oden, eds. 1999. *Galatians, Ephesians, Philippians*. Ancient Christian Commentary on Scripture, New Testament VIII. Downers Grove, IL: InterVarsity.

Ehrman, Bart D. 2013. *Forgery and Counterforgery: The Use of Literary Deceit in Early Christian Polemics*. Oxford: Oxford University Press.

Eswine, Zack. 2006. *Kindled Fire: How the Methods of C. H. Spurgeon Can Help Your Preaching*. Fearn, Scotland: Mentor.

Evans, Craig A., and Stanley E. Porter, eds. 2000. *Dictionary of New Testament Background*. Downers Grove, IL: InterVarsity.

Fee, Gordon D. 1994. *God's Empowering Presence: The Holy Spirit in the Letters of Paul*. Peabody, MA: Hendrickson.

Ferguson, Everett, 2003. *Backgrounds of Early Christianity*. 3rd ed. Grand Rapids: Eerdmans.

Finegan, Jack. 1992. *The Archeology of the New Testament: The Life of Jesus and the Beginning of the Early Church*. Rev. Ed. Princeton, NJ: Princeton University Press.

Foster, Paul. 2002. "The First Contribution to the πίστις Χριστοῦ Debate: A Study of Ephesians 3.12." *Journal for the Study of the New Testament* 85: 75–96.

Fuchs, Rüdiger. 2014. "I Kneel Before the Father and Pray for You (Ephesians 3:14): Date and Significance of Ephesians, Part 2." *European Journal of Theology* 23.2: 116–22.

______. 2015. "I Kneel Before the Father and Pray for You (Ephesians 3:14): Date and Significance of Ephesians, Part 3." *European Journal of Theology* 24.1: 33–41.

Furman, Gloria. 2017. *Alive in Him: How Being Embraced by the Love of Christ Changes Everything*. Wheaton, IL: Crossway.

Getz, Gene. 1976. *Building Up One Another*. Colorado Springs: David C. Cook.

Goldingay, John. 2014. *Isaiah 56–66: A Critical and Exegetical Commentary*. International Critical Commentary. London: Bloomsbury T & T Clark.

Gombis, Timothy G. 2004. "Ephesians 3:2-13: Pointless Digression, or Epitome of the Triumph of God in Christ?" *Westminster Theological Journal* 66: 313–23

______. 2005. "A Radically New Humanity: The Function of the Haustafel in Ephesians." *Journal of the Evangelical Theological Society* 48: 317–30.

Gray, Patrick. 2012. *Opening Paul's Letters: A Reader's Guide to Genre and Interpretation*. Grand Rapids: Baker.

Grindheim, Sigurd. 2003. "What the OT Prophets Did Not Know: The Mystery of the Church in Eph 3,2–13," *Biblica* 84: 531–53.

Gurevich, Andrew, and Jeffrey Arthurs. 2000. "Theological and Rhetorical Perspectives on Self-Disclosure in Preaching." *Bibliotheca Sacra* 157: 215–26.

Harrill, J. Albert. 2016. "Paul and Slavery." Pages 301–346 in *Paul in the Greco-Roman World: A Handbook*. Vol. 2. Edited by J. Paul Sampley. London: Bloomsbury T & T Clark.

Harris, W. Hall, III. 1994. "The Ascent and Descent of Christ in Ephesians 4:9-10." *Bibliotheca Sacra* 151: 198–214.

Hawthorne, Gerald F., Ralph P. Martin, and Daniel G. Reid, eds. 1993. *Dictionary of Paul and His Letters*. Downers Grove, IL: InterVarsity.

Heil, John Paul. 2007. *Empowerment to walk in Love for the Unity of All in Christ*. Society of Biblical Literature Studies in Biblical Literature 13. Atlanta: SBL.

Hengel, Martin. 1977. *Crucifixion*. Philadelphia: Fortress.

Hoehner, Harold W. 2002. *Ephesians: An Exegetical Commentary*. Grand Rapids: Baker.

Hofstede, Geert H. 1980. *Culture's Consequences: International Differences in Work-Related Values*. Beverly Hills, CA: Sage.

Holmes, Michael W. ed. 1999. *The Apostolic Fathers: Greek Texts and English Translations*. Grand Rapids: Baker.

Hornblower, Simon, and Antony Spawforth, eds. 1996. *The Oxford Classical Dictionary*. 3rd ed. Oxford: Oxford University Press.

Horsley, Richard A. 1997. "Introduction: The Gospel of Imperial Salvation." In *Paul and Empire: Religion and Power in Roman Imperial Society*. Ed. Richard A. Horsley. Harrisburg, PA: Trinity Press International.

Hubbard, Moyer V. 2010. *Christianity in the Greco-Roman World: A Narrative Introduction*. Grand Rapids: Baker.

Keener, Craig. 2014. *The IVP Bible Background Commentary: New Testament*. 2nd ed. Downers Grove, IL: InterVarsity.

Keller, Timothy. 2016. *Preaching: Communicating Faith in an Age of Skepticism*. New York: Penguin.

Keller, Tim, with Kathy Keller. 2013. *The Meaning of Marriage: Facing the Complexities of Commitment with the Wisdom of God*. New York: Riverhead Books.

Kirby, John C. 1968. *Ephesians, Baptism and Pentecost: An Inquiry into the Structure and Purpose of the Epistle to the Ephesians*. Montreal: McGill.

Kittel, G., and G. Friedrich, eds. 1964–1976. *Theological Dictionary of the New Testament*. 10 vols. Grand Rapids: Eerdmans.

Klein, William W. 2006. "Ephesians." Pages 19–173 in *The Expositor's Bible Commentary*. Rev. ed. Vol. 12. Grand Rapids: Zondervan.

Koehler, Ludwig, and Walter Baumgartner. 2001. *Hebrew and Aramaic Lexicon of the Old Testament*. 2 vols. Leiden: Brill.

Kruger, Melissa, ed. 2018. *Identity Theft: Reclaiming the Truth of Who We Are in Christ*. Deerfield, IL: Gospel Coalition.

Kümmel, Werner Georg. 1975. *Introduction to the New Testament*. Translated by Howard Clark Kee. Rev. ed. Nashville: Abingdon.

Ladd, George Eldon. 1974. *A Theology of the New Testament*. Grand Rapids: Eerdmans.

Larsen, David L. 2019. "Can the Center Hold?" *Preaching* (Fall issue).

Lewis, C. S. 1942. *The Screwtape Letters*. New York: Harper Collins.

______. 1945. *The Problem of Pain*. New York: Harper Collins.

______. 1949. *The Weight of Glory and Other Addresses*. New York: Harper Collins.

______. 1952. *Mere Christianity*. New York: Macmillian.

______. 2009. *The Last Battle*. Repr., 1956. New York: Harper Collins.

Lincoln, Andrew T. 1990. *Ephesians*. Word Biblical Commentary 42. Nashville: Thomas Nelson.

Lunde, Jonathan M. and John Anthony Dunne. 2012. "Paul's Creative and Contextual Use of Isaiah in Ephesians 5:14." *Journal of the Evangelical Theological Society* 55: 87–110.

Lyall, Francis. 1969. "Roman Law in the Writings of Paul—Adoption." *Journal of Biblical Literature* 88: 458–66

MaGee, Gregory S. 2013. *Portrait of an Apostle: A Case for Paul's Authorship of Colossians and Ephesians*. Eugene, OR: Pickwick.

Martin, Ralph P., and Peter H. Davids, eds. 1997. *Dictionary of the Later New Testament and Its Developments*. Downers Grove, IL: InterVarsity.

Matera, Frank, 2012. *God's Saving Grace: A Pauline Theology*. Grand Rapids: Eerdmans.

McKim, Donald K., ed. 2007. *Dictionary of Major Biblical Interpreters.* Downers Grove, IL: IVP Academic.

McQuilkin, Robertson. Feb. 2004. "The Gradual Grief of Alzheimer's." *Christianity Today*: 64–5.

Meade, David G. 1986. *Pseudonymity and Canon: An Investigation into the Relationship of Authorship and Authority in Jewish and Earliest Christian Tradition.* Wissenschaftliche Untersuchungen zum Neuen Testament 39. Tübingen: Mohr.

Mealand, D. L. 1995. "The Extent of the Pauline Corpus: A Multivariate Approach." *Journal for the Study of the New Testament* 59: 61–92.

Meeks, Wayne A. 1983. *The First Urban Christians: The Social World of the Apostle Paul*. New Haven, CT: Yale University Press.

Metzger, Bruce M. 1994. *A Textual Commentary on the Greek New Testament*. 2nd ed. Stuttgart: Deutsche Bibelgesellschaft.

Miller, Colin. 2010. "The Imperial Cult in the Pauline Cities of Asia Minor and Greece" *Catholic Biblical Quarterly* 72: 314–32.

Miller, Paul E. 2017. *A Praying Life: Connecting with God in a Distracting World.* Colorado Springs: NavPress.

Mitchell, Henry H. 2010. *Celebration and Experience in Black Preaching*. Rev. ed. Nashville: Abingdon.

Mitton, C. L. 1951. *Ephesians: Its Authorship, Origin, and Purpose*. Oxford: Clarendon.

Mohrlang, Roger. 2013. *Paul and His Life-Transforming Theology: A Concise Introduction*. Eugene, OR: Wipf & Stock.

Mommsen, Theodor, and Paul Krueger, eds. 1985. *The Digest of Justinian*. Translated by Alan Watson. Vol. 4. Philadelphia: University of Pennsylvania Press.

Moo, Douglas J. 2008. *The Letters to the Colossians and to Philemon*. PNTC. Grand Rapids: Eerdmans.

Moore, Russell. 2015. *Onward: Engaging the Culture without Losing the Gospel*. Nashville: B&H Publishing.

Moritz, Thorsten. 1996. *A Profound Mystery: The Use of the Old Testament in Ephesians*. NovTSup 85. Leiden: Brill.

Moule, C. F. D. 1960. *An Idiom Book of New Testament Greek*. Cambridge: Cambridge University Press.

Muddiman, John. 2001. *A Commentary on the Epistle to the Ephesians*. Black's New Testament Commentaries. London: Continuum.

Neumann, Kenneth J. 1990. *The Authenticity of the Pauline Epistles in Light of Stylostatistical Analysis*. Society of Biblical Literature Dissertation Series 120. Atlanta: Scholars Press.

Packer, J. I. 1993. *Knowing God*. Downers Grove, IL: InterVarsity.

______. 2005. *Keep in Step with the Spirit: Finding Fullness in Our Walk with God.* Rev. ed. Grand Rapids: Baker.

Packer, J. I., and Thomas C. Oden. 2004. *One Faith: The Evangelical Consensus*. Downers Grove, IL: InterVarsity.

Pao, David W. 2002. *Thanksgiving: An Investigation of a Pauline Theme*. New Studies in Biblical Theology 13. Leicester: Apollos; Downers Grove, IL: InterVarsity.

Paul, Shalom M. 2012. *Isaiah 40–66: Translation and Commentary*. Eerdmans Critical Commentary. Grand Rapids: Eerdmans.

Polhill, John B. 1999. *Paul and His Letters*. Nashville: Broadman & Holman.

Rapske, Brian. 1994. *The Book of Acts and Paul in Roman Custody*. The Book of Acts in Its First Century Setting, Vol. 3. Edited by Bruce W. Winter. Grand Rapids: Eerdmans.

Reeves, Michael. 2012. *Delighting in the Trinity: An Introduction to the Christian Faith*. Downers Grove, IL: InterVarsity.

Richards, E. Randolph. 2004. *Paul and First-Century Letter Writing: Secretaries, Composition and Collection*. Downers Grove, IL: InterVarsity.

Ridderbos, Herman. 1975. *Paul: An Outline of His Theology*. Translated by John R. DeWitt. Grand Rapids: Eerdmans.

Rives, James B. 2007. *Religion in the Roman Empire*. Malden, MA: Blackwell.

Roberts, Alexander, and James Donaldson, eds. *Ante-Nicene Fathers: The Writings of the Fathers down to A.D. 325*. Revised by A. Cleveland Coxe. 10 vols. Peabody, MA: Hendrickson.

Roberts, Mark D. 2016. *Ephesians*. Story of God Bible Commentary. Grand Rapids: Zondervan.

Robertson, A. T. 1934. *A Grammar of the Greek New Testament in Light of Historical Research*. 4th ed. Nashville: Broadman.

Ryken, Leland, James C. Wilhoit, and Tremper Longman III, eds. 1998. *Dictionary of Biblical Imagery*. Downers Grove, IL: InterVarsity.

Sanders, Fred. 2017. *The Deep Things of God: How the Trinity Changes Everything*. 2nd ed. Wheaton, IL: Crossway.

Schnabel, Eckhard J. 2004. *Jesus and the Twelve. Vol. 1 of Early Christian Mission*. Downers Grove, IL: InterVarsity; Leicester: Apollos.

______. 2004. *Paul and the Early Church. Vol. 2 of Early Christian Mission*. Downers Grove, IL: InterVarsity; Leicester: Apollos.

Schnackenburg, Rudolf. 1991. *The Epistle to the Ephesians: A Commentary*. Translated by Helen Heron. Edinburgh: T & T Clark.

Schnelle, Udo. 2003. *Apostle Paul: His Life and Theology*. Translated by M. Eugene Boring. Grand Rapids: Baker.

Schreiner, Thomas R. 2001. *Paul, Apostle of God's Glory in Christ*. Downers Grove, IL: InterVarsity.

Shelton, Jo-Ann. 1998. *As the Romans Did: A Sourcebook in Roman Social History*. 2nd ed. New York: Oxford University Press.

Sherwood, Aaron. 2012. "Paul's Imprisonment as the Glory of the Ethnē: A Discourse Analysis of Ephesians 3:1–13." *Bulletin for Biblical Research* 22.1: 97–112.

Simpson, E. K., and F. F. Bruce. 1957. *The Epistles to the Ephesians and Colossians*. New Covenant Commentary Series. Grand Rapids: Eerdmans.

Smith, Christian, and Melinda Lunquist Denton. 2005. *Soul Searching: The Religious and Spiritual Lives of American Teenagers*. Oxford: Oxford University Press.

Smith, Gary V. 2009. *Isaiah 40-66: An Exegetical and Theological Exposition of Scripture*. New American Commentary 15B. Nashville: B&H Publishing.

Smith, James Bryan. 2009. *The Good and Beautiful God: Falling in Love with the God Jesus Knows*. Downers Grove, IL: InterVarsity.

Snodgrass, Klyne. 1996. *Ephesians*. NIV Application Commentary. Grand Rapids: Zondervan.

Stott, John R. W. 1979. *The Message of Ephesians*. Leicester: Inter-Varsity.

______. 2006. *The Cross of Christ*. 20th Anniversary ed. Downers Grove, IL: InterVarsity.

Stowers, Stanley K. 1986. *Letter Writing in Greco-Roman Antiquity*. LEC. Philadelphia: The Westminster Press.

Stuhlmacher, Peter. 1986. "'He is Our Peace' (Eph. 2:14). On the Exegesis and Significance of Ephesians 2:14–18." Pages 182–200 in *Reconciliation, Law, and Righteousness*. Translated by Everett R. Kalin. Philadelphia: Fortress.

Talbert, Charles H. 2007. *Ephesians and Colossians*. ΠΑΙΔΕΙΑ Commentaries on the New Testament. Grand Rapids: Baker.

Thielman, Frank. 2005. *Theology of the New Testament: A Canonical and Synthetic Approach*. Grand Rapids: Zondervan.

______. 2010. *Ephesians*. Baker Exegetical Commentary on the New Testament. Grand Rapids: Baker.

Trebilco, Paul. 2004. *The Early Christians in Ephesus from Paul to Ignatius*. Grand Rapids: Eerdmans.

______. 2012. *Self-designations and Group Identity in the New Testament*. Cambridge: Cambridge University Press.

van Roon, A. 1974. *The Authenticity of Ephesians*. NovTSup 39. Leiden: Brill.

Wallace, Daniel B. 1996. *Greek Grammar beyond the Basics: An Exegetical Syntax of the New Testament*. Grand Rapids: Zondervan.

Watts, Rikk E. 2009. "Isaiah in the New Testament." Pages 213–233 in *Interpreting Isaiah: Issues and Approaches*. Edited by David G. Firth and H. G. M. Williamson. Nottingham: Apollos; Downers Grove, IL: InterVarsity.

Weir, Kirsten. 2012. "Alone, in 'the Hole': Psychologists Prove the Mental Health Effects of Solitary Confinement." *Monitor on Psychology* 43.5.

Westerholm, Stephen. 2013. "Righteousness, Cosmic and Microcosmic." Pages 21–38 in *Apocalyptic Paul: Cosmos and Anthropos in Romans 5–8*. Edited by Beverly Roberts Gaventa. Waco, TX: Baylor University Press.

Whybray, R. N. 1981. *Isaiah 40–66*. New Century Bible Commentary. Grand Rapids: Eerdmans.

Wilson, Mark. 2012. *Biblical Turkey: A Guide to the Jewish and Christian Sites of Asia Minor*. Istanbul: Ege Yayinlari.

Wilson, Paul Scott. 2008. *Setting Words on Fire*. Nashville: Abingdon.

Wink, Walter. 1984. *Naming the Powers: The Language of Power in the New Testament*. Philadelphia: Fortress.

Witherington III, Ben. 2007. *The Letters to Philemon, the Colossians, and the Ephesians: A Socio-Rhetorical Commentary on the Captivity Epistles*. Grand Rapids: Eerdmans.

Wright, Christopher J. H. 2019. *The Old Testament in Seven Sentences: A Small Introduction to a Vast Topic*. Downers Grove, IL: InterVarsity.

______. 2017. *Isaiah Old and New: Exegesis, Intertexuality, and Hermeneutics*. Minneapolis: Fortress.

Wright, N. T. 2013. *Paul and the Faithfulness of God*. 2 vols. Minneapolis: Fortress.